T0392141

How to Make a New Spain

How to Make a New Spain

The Material Worlds of Colonial Mexico City

ENRIQUE RODRÍGUEZ-ALEGRÍA

OXFORD
UNIVERSITY PRESS

OXFORD
UNIVERSITY PRESS

Oxford University Press is a department of the University of Oxford. It furthers
the University's objective of excellence in research, scholarship, and education
by publishing worldwide. Oxford is a registered trade mark of Oxford University
Press in the UK and certain other countries.

Published in the United States of America by Oxford University Press
198 Madison Avenue, New York, NY 10016, United States of America.

Library of Congress Cataloging-in-Publication Data
Names: Rodríguez-Alegría, Enrique, author.
Title: How to make a new Spain : the material worlds of colonial
Mexico City / Enrique Rodríguez-Alegría.
Description: 1 Edition. | New York : Oxford University Press, [2023] |
Includes bibliographical references and index.
Identifiers: LCCN 2022040670 (print) | LCCN 2022040671 (ebook) |
ISBN 9780197682296 (hardback) | ISBN 9780197682302 (epub) |
ISBN 9780197682326 (ebook) | ISBN 9780197682319
Subjects: LCSH: Wealth—Mexico—Mexico City—History. |
Taxation—Mexico—Mexico City—History. | Mexico—Colonization—History.
Classification: LCC HC140.W4 R63 2023 (print) | LCC HC140.W4 (ebook) |
DDC 338.72/53—dc23/eng/20230104
LC record available at https://lccn.loc.gov/2022040670
LC ebook record available at https://lccn.loc.gov/2022040671

DOI: 10.1093/oso/9780197682296.001.0001

1 3 5 7 9 8 6 4 2

Printed by Integrated Books International, United States of America

Contents

Preface

As I finish writing this book, the people and the government of Mexico City are celebrating 500 years of resistance to the Spanish conquest. People in Mexico City, a few with painted faces and clothing in Mexica styles, participated in the celebration. The government decorated the buildings around the Zócalo, the main plaza in the city, with lighted images based on pre-Columbian monuments and artifacts. They include giant plumed serpents, geometric motifs, and even a reinterpretation of the great Coyolxauhqui monument whose discovery led to the excavations at the Templo Mayor (Matos Moctezuma 1988). The image portrayed in the Mexica monument is dismembered. All four limbs are torn from the torso, and the head is severed. The image used in the celebration of resistance is intact; the body is unharmed. Instead of communicating death and defeat, as did the Mexica monument, the lights and modern imagery communicate life and action. The image looks as if it were about to dance. The contrast between the permanence of the stone monument, which survived 500 years buried under the city, and the ephemerality of the lights display is striking. But the lighted display was transmitted immediately over the internet, potentially reaching people all over the world faster than the monument did. The lights may survive on the internet, as long as people are interested in watching them, but they will probably not survive for 500 years.

The ceremony was also surprisingly orderly, for a ceremony that celebrated resistance. Speakers waited for their turn, standing quietly next to one another, and even the most passionate of the speakers, who gave his speech in Spanish and Nahuatl, followed a strict protocol. One of the speakers mentioned the first time that electricity was brought to the Zócalo, as a clear example of progress. The same site where people celebrated resistance was a display of government-sponsored order, discipline, and progress.

A few weeks before the celebration at the Zócalo, the government of Mexico City renamed a small plaza, also with the intention of emphasizing Indigenous resistance during the conquest. The plaza had been known as *Plaza de la Noche Triste* (Square of the Sorrowful Night). It was reputedly the place where Hernán Cortés, who led the military conquest of Mexico, cried under a tree after losing a battle against the Mexica. The Spanish conquistadors suffered their biggest loss in that battle. The new name of the plaza provides an entirely different way of commemorating the battle: *Plaza de la Noche Victoriosa* (Square of the Victorious Night). A bridge, known as Puente de Alvarado in memory of a Spanish conquistador, was renamed as *Calzada México Tenochtitlan*. A statue of Columbus was moved from its place in Reforma Avenue, and in its place will stand a monument to Indigenous women. These changes are celebrated, criticized, and dismissed by the media and the general public, as they debate the meaning of defeat, victory, conquest, and resistance. They also debate the value of monuments and public ceremonies to capture and communicate truth, and to do so in ways that are meaningful to people today.

Defeat, victory, conquest, and resistance are ideas that capture only a fraction of the complexity of the colonial period in Mexico. These ideas tend to emphasize a clash between two ethnic groups, or between two societies from different sides of the world. Of course, that clash was important. The battles resulted in death and much destruction. The diseases that spread as the Spanish made their way through the Americas, often preceding the colonizers, decimated Indigenous populations. Estimates indicate that between 60 and 95 percent of the Indigenous population died after contact with Europeans due to epidemics, overwork, and violence (Márquez Morfín and Storey 2017). The conquest and colonial period were indeed shaped by this encounter, or clash, between two very different societies, and our ideas about defeat, victory, conquest, and resistance certainly reflect part of what happened in the past. Coercion and violence mattered in the colonial period.

But another aspect that shaped the conquest and life in the colonial period was interethnic alliances. If people saw differences along ethnic lines, they also saw people of similar rank and status across ethnic lines. In other words, Spanish colonizers were quick to recognize who was an elite among Indigenous people, and they struck alliances with them. As they moved across the land on their way to Tenochtitlan, they met and exchanged gifts with Indigenous leaders. By seeking alliances, the conquistadors turned what would have been a small band of Spaniards trying to conquer Tenochtitlan into a giant army made up mostly of Indigenous warriors. In turn, by seeking interethnic alliances, Indigenous rulers built an army that could defeat the mighty Mexica of Tenochtitlan. Sometimes, they bolstered their own status after the conquest by appealing to powerful colonizers, or even the King of Spain, for recognition of special rights and status (Chance 2008; Cline

1986; Haskett 1991; Lockhart 1992; Matthew and Oudijk 2007; Spores 1997; Villella 2016).

Such alliances continued to shape daily life and the material world throughout the colonial period. People found motivation for their actions not just in ethnicity, but also in status, and in creating a life, a material world, and a place to live. In other words, Indigenous people sometimes defended themselves against strangers from other lands who spoke other languages, including other Indigenous groups and Spanish conquistadors. That is the resistance that gets celebrated today, although it mostly refers to resistance against the Spanish. But Indigenous people also looked for ways to create or even improve their status in colonial society. Some fought against a common enemy, and some competed against others of similar status to improve their own situation in the colonial world (Gibson 1964:156; Haskett 1991:161–163; Olko and Szemiński 2018; Ruiz Medrano and Kellogg 2010). Some may not have competed to improve their status, but instead, they worked to create their place in the world. As I will argue throughout this book, some people worked hard to validate themselves as a good builder, or a carpenter, a potter, a tailor or simply a valuable member of their society. Many people worked to forge their place in their community. Some of them probably produced the things that Spanish colonizers owned, and that I study in this book. My focus is on the material worlds of Spanish colonizers, and those worlds were created by people who sometimes competed with one another, sometimes resisted the Spanish, sometimes created the material worlds of the colonizers, and whose behaviors cannot be seen simply as resistance, defeat, victory, or serving an ethnically defined interest.

These celebrations, commemorations, and acts of renaming of public spaces are exciting. They are a reminder that what happened in the conquest and the colonial period, some 500 years ago, is still politically relevant. Those events matter to people today, and people are actively reexamining them. I propose that in addition to viewing life in colonial Mexico as an ethnic clash, or a matter of defeat or resistance, we also examine how people actively shaped the encounter based on interests related to class, social inequality, and to building their own place in the world.

Acknowledgments

Several institutions provided support for this project. A National Science Foundation Doctoral Dissertation Improvement Grant (BCS-0083274) and a Minority Post-Doctoral Research Fellowship (SES-0309796) supported my research at the Archivo General de Indias in Seville. Those two grants made it possible for me to collect the data from the probate inventories that form the basis of this book. A Fellowship from the National Endowment from the Humanities supported part of the writing portion of the project, along with a Supplemental College Research Fellowship from the College of Liberal Arts at the University of Texas at Austin. A Visiting Fellowship from Bard Graduate Center allowed me to continue writing and almost finish the manuscript. I am grateful for the support of these different institutions. Without their support, I may have never finished this project.

My three mentors deserve many thanks for their help in this project. First, I thank Kathy Morrison, who insisted that I look at probate inventories and check whether there was truly a simple, direct relationship between wealth and consumption of Spanish goods among colonizers. At the time, I was sure that there must be such a relationship, and that checking whether it existed was a waste of time, but I decided to look at the probate inventories because I could spend some time in Seville. Kathy was right in making me check (the relationship was neither simple nor direct), and I was wrong, and not only did I get to live in Seville, which has become one of my favorite cities, but I also got to write this book.

Second, I must thank Elizabeth Brumfiel for taking me to the Templo Mayor for the first time and introducing me to some of the archaeologists there. She encouraged me to pursue the analysis of colonial material and helped me formulate part of the research. I am grateful for her years of mentorship, criticism, and encouragement.

And third, I thank Sam Wilson, who really deserves a lot of credit for the completion of this book. He made most of the drawings that you will see in this book, prepared other figures for publication, and gave me feedback on the entire manuscript, chapter by chapter. His work and influence on my work can be seen throughout this manuscript. Without his support and hard work, I doubt that I would have finished this book.

I owe this project also to the archaeologists in Mexico who welcomed me and gave me access to the material they had excavated. They had no reason to offer me such hospitality, other than the fact that they are great people and some of the best archaeologists in the world. I especially thank Raúl Barrera Rivera, Francisco Hinojosa, Flor Rivas García, Alvaro Barrera, Alicia Islas, Socorro Alvarado, María de Lourdes Gallardo Parrodi, and many other archaeologists who worked with the Programa de Arqueología Urbana. Their fine work and publications made this book possible.

Several colleagues and friends read different chapters and provided feedback that improved the manuscript significantly. Franz Scaramelli and Kay Tarble provided much needed feedback on the Introduction. Gustav Peebles, John Millhauser, and Noa Corcoran-Tadd provided feedback on Chapter 2, my first attempt at writing about the confusing world of money. Silvia Saladrigas Cheng was gracious enough to help me correct several errors in the classification of textiles in Chapter 5, even though I reached out to her as a complete stranger, over email. Nancy Whittier replied to some questions that I had about the statistics I used in Chapter 7 and helped me figure out what I was doing. I had conversations about my discussion of materiality with Jonathan Sterne, Kristin De Lucia, and Barbara Voss, and those interactions shaped my thinking significantly. Gwen Ruth Jones, Blair Heidkamp, Anya Gruber, and Zack Scholsberg provided comments on a draft of the conclusion. I also had plenty of conversations on materiality and on the topics that I touch upon in this book with Shannon Iverson, Emily Dylla, Ana María Navas Méndez, and Emmy Dawson. Julia Guernsey read a first draft of the preface and helped me improve it, and the casual discussions I had with her about materiality helped me immensely. I am grateful for their comments and all their feedback. They all have influenced my thinking for this book.

I presented an early version of Chapter 2 at the Archaeological Research Facility, University of California Berkeley, and later at the Archaeological Research Center at UC, Santa Cruz. I thank all the faculty and students who provided thoughtful comments and asked interesting questions at those two presentations, especially Christine Hastorf, Meg Conkey, J. Cameron Monroe, Tsim Schneider, and Chelsea Blackmore for their great conversation and hospitality.

I spent only six weeks at Bard Graduate Center before I left rather unexpectedly because of the COVID-19 pandemic. Still, Bard left a mark on my book, especially through the many conversations I had with people who are interested in the material world. I thank everyone who attended my brown bag lecture, and especially Soon Kai Poh, Hazel Clark, Stefan Heidemann, Meredith Linn, and Casper Meyer for their comments and suggestions. Peter Miller deserves very special thanks for his comments, stimulating conversation, and for welcoming me at such a vibrant and active community as Bard.

A Note on Terminology and Gentilics

Gentilics and other terms used in this book are the result of a good-willed effort in my part to be respectful, to generalize when necessary, and to be specific whenever it is possible and useful. They are my best effort in 2022.

Following the lead of many Indigenous societies, groups, and scholars, I use the term *Indigenous* (capitalized). I use the terms *indio* and *india* in the text only when I feel it is necessary to indicate that the people who wrote the documents used the term. They sometimes appear as *yndio* or *yndia*, as they appear in the original documents.

I use the term *Mexica*, instead of *Aztecs*, to refer to the Indigenous people from Mexico-Tenochtitlan. Both terms have complicated histories, and neither presents a perfect solution to how to refer to the Indigenous people of central Mexico before or after 1521 (Nichols and Rodríguez-Alegría 2017). Although the term Aztec is most popular today in the literature in English, it is not a term that the Mexica used to refer to themselves. They had called themselves the Mexica for centuries before the Spanish arrived. I only use Aztec when it is a proper noun of archaeological ceramics (Aztec II ceramics, for example). When writing about the empire, I will write about the empire of the Triple Alliance, or the Mexica empire.

The term *Spanish* may also be somewhat misleading. The terms Spain and Spanish existed in the sixteenth century (e.g., Mercado 1985), yet the colonizers who appear in the documents I consulted referred to one another by their specific town of origin, rather than by a larger national or even regional gentilic. Still, there is little to gain from referring to individuals by their town of origin in this particular study. I also use the term *colonizers* mostly to refer to Spanish colonizers, even though they came with Black slaves, who were also foreign.

I will use the term *Black* whenever I refer to Africans and Afro-descendants. The documents invariably refer to them as "negros," the Spanish equivalent to "blacks," and they very rarely reveal where the person was born. The term has the advantage of including those born in Spain and those born in the Caribbean, in addition to those born in Africa. It focuses on their common experience as people who were seen as Black, but it has the disadvantage of glossing over the experiences of people from many different backgrounds. Unfortunately, neither the primary documents consulted as part of this study nor the secondary literature give the opportunity to distinguish between Black people from different places, as is characteristic of most of the historical sources of this time period (Velázquez Gutiérrez 2018). I capitalize the term, as many scholars and newspapers do nowadays.

Another term that may cause discomfort among readers is *slave*. Many people today prefer *enslaved person* or *enslaved people* to emphasize their personhood. I sometimes use the term slave because that is how they appear in the documents. Other times I use enslaved people, following the lead of some of my colleagues, to emphasize that we are writing about human beings, not things.

How to Enter the Material and Social Worlds

When Spanish colonizers and their slaves arrived in central Mexico in the sixteenth century—many today would say invaded—they entered a world different from anything they had ever experienced. The variety of temples and houses were unlike those in Europe. The furniture that Indigenous people had was extremely simple, consisting mostly of reed mats (Aguilera 1985), in comparison to the bulkier wooden chairs, tables, beds, desks, and many other pieces of furniture seen in Europe at the time (Aguiló Alonso 1993). The clothing that Indigenous men wore, mostly loincloths and capes, made them look naked to colonizers, who were more accustomed to seeing men in layers of clothing that covered the entire body (Bernis 1962). Yet the Spanish also praised the high-quality cloth woven by Indigenous women (Blum 2006:146–147). The food consisted of an endless variety of dishes and ingredients unrelated to anything they had in Spain at the time. Indigenous people ate corn tortillas and tamales instead of wheat bread, and spiced their food intensely with chilies. Some of the pottery was different from what they knew in Spain. Some of the animals, including the beautiful xoloitzcuintle (often known as Mexican Hairless Dog) and the turkey, and many plants, were simply exotic. The stone tools were quite unlike the metal tools in Europe at the time. It is difficult to overstate the differences between the material world in Mexico City and the material world that colonizers had left across the ocean. Colonizers who wanted to create a material world that resembled the world they were used to, had one big challenge: how to make a new Spain. They had to figure out how to construct the kinds of houses that fit their ideas of proper housing. They had to figure out how to get the kinds of clothes that fit their sense of propriety, decency, and hygiene. They had to figure out how to obtain the foods they missed and wanted to eat, or find local substitutes.

Indigenous people at the time also saw things that they had never experienced before, including the clothing and armor of colonizers, their livestock,

How to Make a New Spain. Enrique Rodríguez-Alegría, Oxford University Press. © Enrique Rodríguez-Alegría 2023.
DOI: 10.1093/oso/9780197682296.003.0001

their steel swords and metal tools, their wooden boxes, and the many other things that colonizers brought with them on their ships. There was a new challenge for Indigenous people: how to make the things that the Spanish brought. Some were enslaved and learned the crafts of the colonizers, including shoemaking, tailoring, ironworking, and others. Some Indigenous people took up that challenge out of their own volition and interest, sometimes in spite of Spanish attempts at preventing them from learning the skills and secrets of their crafts. In a famous passage written in the 1530s, fray Toribio de Benavente (Motolinía) wrote that Indigenous people made all sorts of Spanish goods, including clothing, different kinds of shoes and sandals, whips, furniture, saddles, ironwork, and many others. He claimed that they often learned by stealing goods from the Spanish and figuring out how to make them. He even praised the good quality of the goods, and wrote that the houses of colonizers were full of chairs made by Indigenous people (Benavente 1985:262–263). But it is difficult to generalize from one statement, especially a passage as impressionistic and vague as Benavente's. Did Indigenous people fill the houses of colonizers with their products? Did colonizers reject or embrace their products? How did different people, including colonizers and Indigenous people, create the material worlds of New Spain?

In this book, I present a partial description of the material worlds of sixteenth-century Mexico City, focusing on the archaeological remains found in the houses of colonizers in the center of the city, and on the probate inventories of thirty-nine colonizers. The questions that drive this project forward belong in three interrelated groups. First, I ask what the material world of Spanish colonizers was like: what things did they own? How did they dress, and what did they eat? What were their houses like? Every chapter of this book contains descriptions of the things that colonizers owned, and plenty of quantitative analysis of what was in the inventories. But the answers to these questions do not end at description. Archaeological artifacts and historical documents offer different opportunities to know the origin of the things that colonizers owned, leading to a second group of questions: did colonizers adopt Indigenous things, or did they only own European and perhaps Asian things? Did colonizers adopt Indigenous technologies? The question of whether colonizers adopted Indigenous things has been the subject of much research both in Mexico and in the Spanish colonies in general (e.g., Charlton and Fournier 2011; Charlton et al. 1995; Deagan 1983, 1995, 1998, 2001; Fournier 1998; Fournier García 1997; Hernández Sánchez 2012, 2019;

Jamieson 2000a, 2000b, 2004; McEwan 1992, 1995; Montúfar López 2003; Rodríguez-Alegría 2005a, 2005b, 2016a; Voss 2005, 2008a). Many scholars have also been interested in patterns and processes of change in Indigenous technologies in colonial Mexico (e.g., Alexander 2019; Charlton 1968; Forde 2017; Foster 1960; Hernández Sánchez 2012; Pastrana 1998; Rodríguez-Alegría 2008a, 2008b, 2016a), but the question of whether colonizers adopted Indigenous technologies has not been the subject of nearly as much research. In this book, I provide new insights on the complex process of Spanish adoption of Indigenous technologies.

Finally, a third group of questions brings together the description of the material worlds of colonizers with an analysis of socioeconomic status, wealth, and political strategies among colonizers: what was the relationship between wealth and patterns of ownership and consumption of Indigenous and imported goods among colonizers? Did wealthy colonizers generally reject things made by Indigenous people? Did wealth and socioeconomic status shape patterns of consumption? Or did political strategies, personal connections, and factors other than wealth guide the choices of colonizers? Perhaps colonizers were guided by a sense of ethnic solidarity with each other, and separatism from Indigenous people, but wealth shaped their ability to obtain expensive imports. Or perhaps colonizers recognized power among Indigenous people and were more interested in creating links to powerful Indigenous people and less interested in emphasizing ethnic differences. The patterns that can be seen in the archaeological data and the probate inventories provide fresh insights into the links between the material and the social worlds.

Material and Social Worlds

One only needs to think of foundational works by Marx (Tucker 1978), early ethnographic works by Malinowski (1922) and Mauss (1924), and archaeological work by Pitt-Rivers (1875) to see a long scholarly tradition that has related the material and the social world. But according to Cochran and Beaudry (2006:193), a new wave of scholarship that began in the 1970s resumed in earnest a discussion of the interrelation between the social and the material worlds. Influential works, including Arjun Appadurai's *The Social Life of Things* (1986) and Daniel Miller's *Material Culture and Mass Consumption* (1987) have helped scholars see objects as part of the social world, and reconstitute "material culture studies as a people-centered, relational field of study" (Cochran and Beaudry 2006:193). Plenty of scholars agree today that material culture is part of society and that social life is material (e.g., Acuto 2005; Gosden 2005; Latour 1993, 1996; Miller 2005; White and Beaudry 2009). The literature on materiality is vast, and other authors have provided useful discussions of the historical development of this literature (e.g., Cochran and Beaudry 2006; Hicks 2012). In this discussion, I focus on ideas that I have found useful or important to debate, especially ideas that have been particularly influential in the past twenty years, rather than on an historical take on the development of the debates on materiality.

The idea that people and the material world "mutually constitute" one another has become a mantra among archaeologists in recent years. People and things create one another (Johnson 2010:264). Acuto (2005:211), for example, is among many who see material culture as an integral part of being human. He has argued that viewing objects as an active part of social life is not enough, and we should instead view them as part of who we are as human beings. He proposes a dialectical relationship between people and things, in which both form and transform one another through time. Scholars in other disciplines have proposed a greater integration between people and things. A particularly provocative example is Donna Haraway's "A Cyborg Manifesto." Haraway writes that "we are all chimeras, theorized and fabricated hybrids of machine and organism; in short, we are cyborgs" (1991:150). She argues that twentieth-century society has broken down the boundaries between animal and human, between machines and humans, and between what is imagined and what is material. The strict differentiation between organism and machine is for Haraway part of Western sexist, capitalist, male-dominated science and politics (1991). Bruno Latour also provides provocative ideas about the material and human worlds when he argues that he wants "to end the partition between materialist and culturalist accounts" of technological change (1993:377). He has proposed that people enlist objects into their actions, making society not just a group of people and their beliefs, but a network of human and nonhuman actors. For Latour, things are not simply objects. Society is inseparable from its material and technological projects, and a dialectical approach only obscures the analysis of the actor network that forms society by separating actors (people and things, among them) that are really part of a single whole (Latour 1993, 1996). In a different proposal, Miller (2005) attempts to transcend the duality between subjects and objects. He wishes to set people or society aside as the main focus of anthropology, arguing that there is no distinction between humanity and materiality.

In the past few decades, *agency* has become perhaps the most commonly used concept to propose different relationships between materiality and society. Agency often feels like both a mandatory topic of discussion and a burden on the debate. Twenty years ago, Marcia-Anne Dobres and John Robb had already written that agency had become one of the buzzwords in archaeology, even though "there is little consensus about what 'agency' actually means" (2000:3). They compile a range of definitions of agency, many of which relate explicitly to the material world, including "the imposition of form on material via socially situated creative activity," and "a process of intersubjective engagement with the material and social world" (Dobres and Robb 2000:9). Four years later, Robb (2004) wrote that definitions or ideas about agency hinge around two different criteria. Some definitions emphasize agency as having some sort of effect on human events, which Robb calls "effective agency" (2004:132). Other definitions emphasize agency as resulting in actions that are conscious or intentional, which Robb calls "conscious agency" (2004:132). Regardless of their particular definition, scholars typically use the concept of agency to propose arguments about how people and things shape ideas, actions, and society.

Calls to set society aside in order to make things the center of analysis and to endow things with power or agency seem to be more common than ever (Johannsen 2012). Alfred Gell (1998), and other scholars, including Latour (1993, 1996), have argued that things should be considered agents, just as much as people, and they have inspired much scholarship on this matter. In an influential article, Gosden (2005) asked "What do objects want?" and claimed that things have agency. By arguing that things have agency, he means that things have an effect on people and other things. People are not the only ones who affect things or one another. Things can shape the way we move, how we travel around a city, how we make new things, how we think, etc. The idea that things can affect people's lives and decisions is not new, and seems to me uncontroversial, although I would argue that people knew that things had an effect on human behavior even before these scholars wrote about things having agency. But Gosden's proposal is radical, because he argues that materiality, and not society, should be the focus of anthropological research. He believes anthropologists have reified society, and we should focus instead on materiality. "Things create people," he writes (Gosden 2005:194). Instead of people making things, "objects use human muscles and skills to bring about their own reproduction" (Gosden 2005:194). People in Gosden's approach appear passive and unimportant. The idea of "material agency" (Cochran and Beaudry 2006:196), or the "Inanimate Agency Proposition" (Johannsen 2012), appears in different forms in the scholarly literature as a way of extending the active roles that things can play in society.

Hodder (2012), for example, has argued that a problem with studies of materiality is that they do not focus enough on things. He believes that scholars tend to write about things without going into details of things' appearance, the materials that form them, where they were made, their relationships with other things, and many other aspects of things. He believes many studies are too anthropocentric, focusing too much on what people do with things rather than on what things do, how things relate to one another, and what they are made of. Anthropocentrism, or an approach in which things are part of people's world, and people make things, use them, and are generally the ones doing the action (the ones with agency, for those more comfortable with the term), offers too limited a view of the material world for Hodder.

The current literature on material culture and society presents many ideas that are useful and that I will embrace in this project. The literature shows that studying the material world is important in and of itself, because the material world and society are linked, or intertwined, or one and the same (Acuto 2005; Gosden 2005; Latour 1993, 1996; Miller 2005; White and Beaudry 2009), or because people and things are entangled in complex relationships. Some of those relationships are more difficult to escape than others (Hodder 2012). Our relationship with things is part of daily habits, practices that shape socialization, and the lived experience (Bourdieu 1977; Loren 2015:144). Material things are not just the result of ideas, but also the source of ideas to begin with (Gosden 2005:196; Malafouris 2013; Renfrew 2004). Things can also be created and used to promote ideas and ideologies (DeMarrais et al. 1996), and they can shape people's behavior and expectations even in ways that may go unnoticed. Material relationships can be strongly political and have major consequences. People enter different relationships with things and with one another in terms of production, ownership, and exchange of things, and those relationships have political, economic, and historical consequences (Tucker 1978; Voss 2008a).

The literature also presents some ideas that will be tangential to this work, but that may be useful from time to time. These include the idea that humans cannot necessarily control things, at least not always and not entirely. Things may reproduce on their own, as in the case of livestock, plants, and other living things. Some things can appear or disappear and create havoc in people's lives, as could be the case with volcanic eruptions, droughts, floods, and other environmental and geological phenomena. Things decay on their own, and there is often very little that humans can do about it. In short, the material world is not always and not completely under human control, but its effects on humans can be strong (Hodder 2012; Miller 2005). Control over things and over production of things can depend on human relations and differential access to the material world (Tucker 1978), and on knowledge and skill (Ingold 2013).

Finally, the literature on materiality presents some ideas that I find problematic. The first problem is not so much an idea that is written explicitly, but a result of scholarly practice: the use of agency as mandatory concept in discussions of materiality and society. Sure, the concept has been useful in some ways. Scholars used it to draw attention to human action and intention (although intention is certainly not part of all definitions of agency), and to show that human action is not just part of a structure that determines behavior (Johnson 2000:213). Humans can act in creative ways that are not entirely determined by their surroundings, their social status, their situation, or any other factors external to them, including their material conditions. The concept helped scholars think productively especially in debates that saw agency in its relationship to its recently neglected partner, structure (see papers in Hendon and Joyce 2004). In fact, ideas that I present shortly, about the need to think clearly about who or what is doing the action when we write about material culture, probably formed in my head as a result of reading the literature on agency. But as much as the concept has been useful, it is not necessary to let all discussions of materiality and society hinge on agency or become a contest in which one needs to determine whether humans or things have more agency. A problem with agency lies with the diverse definitions of the concept (Dobres and Robb 2000). The difficulties in defining agency present the distraction of a debate that often ends up focusing on the concept itself. I would argue that it is entirely possible to discuss the material world without coming up with a new definition of agency, or using the concept at all, in spite of the ongoing focus on agency in much of the literature on materiality. We can, in fact, go beyond agency as we think of materiality (Robb 2010).

Another problem with the concept of agency, especially when scholars argue that things have agency, is that inanimate agency is modeled after human agency. In other words, things end up seeming like their agency is just like the agency of humans. Things have projects, they bring about their reproduction, they enlist humans and other things into their projects, and in the end, they lack any "otherness" in their materiality or in their relationship to humans (Johannsen 2012:307). In the rest of this book I purposefully abandon any use of the concept of agency except for when I discuss ideas presented by other scholars that are strongly tied to the concept. My goal is not to examine the agency of things or to define agency at all, but rather to find how people created, traded, used, exchanged, or otherwise related to things and to other people in colonial Mexico City.

A second problematic idea in the literature on materiality, and certainly the most important from the point of view of this work, is the call to set aside the study of society and instead focus on things. As discussed previously, various authors have presented different versions of this idea and tried to endow things with agency (however defined) and to decenter society as our main subject of study. For example, both Hodder (2012) and Gosden (2005) set aside political and historical factors in their musings about things. Gosden (2005), using a case of Roman colonialism, brushed power considerations away. He focused not on the power relationships between people, but on how things, or styles, shaped the production of new things. Hodder (2012), uses several "thought experiments" and anecdotal examples, rather than historical or ethnographic cases. For example, one of the thought experiments involves an impossibility: a child suspended without any contact with any material thing, in the dark, with no sound and no sensory input. Another example focuses on a wheel and how the wooden wheel depends on a metal sheet wrapped around it to be more resistant. In the literature that calls for decentering society and focusing on the agency of things, there is a common thread: society is usually treated as if it were homogeneous. Scholars who are promoting ideas that aim to redirect scholarly focus on the agency of things usually write about "people" as a unitary category, even though in most historical contexts people rarely treat each other as equals. People have created systems of social inequality, slavery, poverty, racism, sexism, homophobia, and many other factors that have shaped the lives of billions of people and their relationships with the material worlds. Many of the examples and thought experiments that convey the idea that things depend on one another or that a thing-centered approach is desirable only seem to work precisely because they leave out social difference and conflicts between people.

In spite of their significant contributions to the field, folks who have promoted ideas about the agency of things often seem to forget that humans have historically not treated one another as equals. In their debates about the relationship between humans and things, they have not shown much interest in the ways that feminist scholars and people of color have found various social groups to shape society in important ways. When discussing these ideas, Ana María Navas Mendez, and archaeologist and graduate student of mine, argued that although saying that we need to redirect attention to the agency of things may sound like a politically neutral statement, it is inherently political, because it ignores important and ongoing debates about social inequality both in the past and in the present (personal communication, January 2020). Thirty years ago, Brumfiel (1992) critiqued a previous generation of archaeologists for focusing on whole populations and ignoring the role of conflict and negotiation between different social groups within those populations. I argue that if we simplify materiality as a relationship between humans on one hand and things on the other, we are reproducing the same problems that Brumfiel noted in previous generations of archaeologists.

I find greater inspiration in scholarship that draws attention to society and how people involve things in their daily lives, often to create, manipulate, or try to erase differences between people. Feminist scholars, and scholars interested in gender from various perspectives, have shown that women and men involve material things in different productive activities, and that they sometimes use things to negotiate power, and create or challenge gender hierarchies (e.g., Gero and Conkey 1991; Joyce 2000; Robin and Brumfiel 2010), and reformulate gender and ethnic identities (Deagan 1983, 2001; Jamieson 2000a, 2000b; Voss 2008a; Voss and Casella 2012). Many scholars have shown that people have shaped urban layouts and architecture to manipulate social relations and power hierarchies, often in racialized ways (e.g., Amaral 2017; Jamieson 2000a, 2000b; Low 1995; Mier y Terán Rocha 2005; Mundy 2015; Nemser 2017; Ortiz Crespo 2006; Sanoja and Vargas-Arenas 2002; Sanz Camañes 2004:33–38; Therrien 2016; Voss 2005, 2008a; Wagner et al. 2013; Wernke 2012; Zarankin and Funari 2020). Many scholars have also shown that everyday household objects are important in how people create and manage ethnic or cultural difference, enforce or resist political and social oppression, and negotiate social relations (e.g., Bauer 2001; Benítez 1993; Deagan 1983, 1998, 2001; Jamieson 2000b; Lister and Lister 1982; McEwan 1991, 1992, 1995; Oland 2014, 2017; Robin 2014; Rodríguez-Alegría 2005a, 2016a; Voss 2005, 2008a). Scholars have shown that people involve dress to control people or to challenge normative ideas of beauty and value or conform to them, and to help form social identities. Many of these ideas and identities are related to power (e.g., Flewellen 2018; Franklin 2020; Loren 2010; Scaramelli and Tarble de Scaramelli 2005; Voss 2008a). This book builds on the work of all of these scholars who have demonstrated the value of studying the relationship between people and things, and to keep differences between people—along lines of gender, sexuality, class, ethnicity, culture, and any other differences—at the center of analysis. The chapters in this book build upon the debates presented by these and other scholars.

Keeping people at the center of analysis, however, can be challenging, perhaps because of the world of concepts and analytical categories that shape the debates. Sometimes scholars write as if abstractions or analytical categories are doing the action (or as if abstractions had agency, for those more comfortable holding on to the term). In other words, the subject of a sentence, the part that is doing the action, is often a concept rather than a person or even a thing. For example, when scholars discuss how social class affects patterns of consumption (Chapter 7), sometimes it is not people who are doing the action, but a concept: class. Class determines what people buy, what people like, and people have little choice and little possibility to enact social change through consumption. Some archaeologists have critiqued the idea that class determines consumption patterns precisely because they feel that such an approach makes people seem passive and as if they were playing out roles that are predetermined for them. These archaeologists prefer to evaluate what people do, or what they consume, independently of a determination of their social class. That way, it is possible to view people as active, rather than projecting all the action onto abstractions such as class or wealth (e.g., Henry 1996; Tarble 2008). The same could be said about other factors, such as ethnicity, gender, educational capital, and many other conceptual categories. On one hand, it is entirely possible that people simply do not have infinite choices, and people are often unaware of choices that they have (Chapter 7). On the other hand, if we want to make people the active part of the story, we should not unwittingly make analytical concepts do the action. We may classify people into social classes, and people may still act in ways that do not conform to what others in their social class are doing.

I find the same problem in approaches that seek to address the function of things, even in scholarship that precedes the literature on the agency of things: sometimes authors let analytical concepts do the work that things could be doing. For example, as I will discuss in Chapter 1, there is a long scholarly tradition in which authors claim that money has three main functions: facilitating exchange, fixing value, and accumulating wealth

(Jevons 1896:13–18; Neale 1976:7; Papadopoulos 2012:265; Vilar 1976:19; Wallace 1987:396–397; Weber [1922]1978:76). At first glance, the question of the functions of money seems to focus on things: money has specific functions that define it. But instead of focusing on things, the agent of the story is an abstraction: money. Money is a concept born out of material things, but it is still a culturally constituted abstraction. In this example, a more concrete way of injecting agency into things would be to explain how specific coins (less abstract that money) were used. And a more anthropocentric way of studying coins would be not to focus on the functions that some coins served, but to focus instead on how people used those coins. Such an approach, as I will show in Chapter 1, can expose the many ways in which people used coins, shaped the coins themselves, reformulated the materials that coins were made out of, built their wealth, and managed socioeconomic relationships.

It is worth examining variation in people's behavior and consumption patterns, rather than letting analytical concepts do the work, and this is a challenge that I take up repeatedly in this book. This idea that we must pay attention to who is doing the action is what I discussed earlier as a probable result of my consideration of the literature on agency, a concept that I will now set aside for the rest of the book. Keeping different individuals and groups of people at the center of analysis, studying how they involved material goods in their struggles for power, and examining how they experienced the material world are themes that I weave together in the following chapters.

From Tenochtitlan to Mexico City

Sixteenth century Mexico City was the site of the many social and material struggles and challenges examined in this book. Indigenous people knew Mexico City as Mexico-Tenochtitlan, Mexico, or Tenochtitlan. It was one of the three capitals of the empire of the Triple Alliance, more commonly known today as the Aztec empire (Berdan 2017; Rojas 2017; see Nichols and Rodríguez-Alegría 2017 for a discussion on the names of the empire). The two other capitals were Texcoco and Tlacopan, two nearby city-states, although it is pretty clear that the elites of Tenochtitlan were dominant in terms of politics and military matters (Berdan 2014:140). In the middle of the city was the great temple of the Mexica, known today as the Templo Mayor, surrounded by Mexica palaces, temples, schools, and other civic and religious facilities (López Austin and López Luján 2017; Rojas 2017). In 1521, many buildings in the city were partially destroyed, after two years of epidemics, encounters, feasts, skirmishes, and major battles between Indigenous people and foreigners, mostly from Spain. In spite of the violence, the city remained largely an Indigenous city into the colonial period (Mundy 2015:3). After the battles of 1521, both colonizers and Indigenous people began a complex process of rebuilding, destruction, change and continuity in the use of space, demographic change, and appropriation (Rodríguez-Alegría 2017).

Scholars traditionally have written about the events of 1521 as the Spanish Conquest of Tenochtitlan, based on the writings of Spanish chroniclers at the time (e.g., Cortés 2003; Díaz del Castillo 1942). Chroniclers eagerly declared victory over the Indigenous armies of Tenochtitlan, and hyperbolically described dramatic battles between very few Spaniards and Indigenous armies that outnumbered them exponentially (Oudijk 2012; Restall 2003). More recently, scholars have shown that the Spanish conquerors were outnumbered by their Indigenous allies. The conquest resembles a gigantic Indigenous insurrection against Tenochtitlan rather than a small band of Spaniards conquering a huge army of Indians (Matthew and Oudijk 2007; Oudijk 2012; Restall 2003). Scholars have pointed out that the term "conquest" and the events of 1521 are often entirely absent from chronicles written by Indigenous people. Susan Schroeder (2007:13) has argued that many Indigenous people saw what the Spanish called "the conquest" as "a nonevent." Some Indigenous books narrate history since before the sixteenth century, and they lack the dramatic narratives of the conquest that the Spanish preferred. In many Indigenous books, Spaniards begin to appear as new characters in the story, without any mention of a dramatic conquest (Boone 2000:229).

Even before scholars questioned the view of the conquest as an epic battle between a few conquistadors and hordes of Indigenous warriors, they were studying aspects of change and continuity in the years after 1521. Their work is vital in assessing the effects and consequences of the conquest. Most agree that catastrophic depopulation was among the most dramatic consequences of the arrival of the Spanish. Scholars often cite Calnek's (1974) estimate of 150,000 to 200,000 people in Tenochtitlan before the epidemics, although it is quite possible that the city was closer to between 72,000 to 108,000. The specific number of Indigenous people in Tenochtitlan at the time is impossible to verify (Márquez Morfín and Storey 2017). Epidemics never before seen in Central Mexico, including smallpox, influenza, measles, and others killed significant fractions of the population. Estimates vary widely, but scholars have argued that between 66 and 95 percent of the Indigenous population was lost to epidemics, warfare, and abuse (Gerhard 1993; Márquez Morfín and Storey 2017). The broad range of this depopulation estimate should not distract from the agreement that depopulation was catastrophic. Márquez Morfín and Storey (2017:195) explain that "to argue about whether the precise figure was 66 or 75%, or even 95%, is less important than grasping the tragedy of the post-Conquest demographic history of Mesoamerica." Population losses in different regions in Mesoamerica impacted labor regimes. Sometimes tribute demands were not reduced along with the populations (Fowler 1993). Reduced populations may have also had an effect on production, sometimes eliminating the elders who could transmit expertise and artisanal knowledge to new generations of producers of items like pottery (Charlton 1968, 1979) and others. The suffering caused by disease and the trauma of death is too big to comprehend.

Another demographic effect of the conquest was mixing between Indigenous people, colonizers and Africans and Afro-descendants. Spanish colonizers and Black people (whether free or enslaved, from Africa or from the Caribbean) made up approximately 1 to 2 percent of the population in the colonial period (Aguirre Beltrán 1981:198), and they mixed with Indigenous folks. People of mixed descent would soon be known as *castas*, and even though it is difficult to estimate how many castas there were with clarity, Valero (1991:163) identified around 3,000 castas in Mexico City in historical documents from before 1560. There must have been plenty more castas whose lives are not part of the documentary record, or whose documents have not been found by modern scholars. In addition, there were people of Spanish descent who were born in Mexico City from immigrant parents. They were known as *criollos*, and their presence reminds us that an easy distinction between Spanish, Indian, and African cannot capture the complexity of the demographic patterns and cultural views of locals, immigrants, and mixed people even just a few years after 1521.

Although castas existed, it is important to remember that the categories of Spanish, Black, and Indigenous are still important and relevant. There were plenty of people who classified themselves under those categories. Entire towns just outside of Mexico City were often made up of Indigenous people only, without much of a colonizer or casta presence, as was the case of Xaltocan (Rodríguez-Alegría 2016a:129) and others. The documents consulted as part of the present study mostly classify people by their city of birth if they were from Spain, and as *yndio* or *negro*. A few casta children appear, usually the offspring of a Spanish colonizer and an enslaved Indigenous woman, as will be discussed in Chapter 6.

In spite of the changes associated in part with epidemics and racial mixing, scholars have shown many continuities in the lives of Indigenous people and in their material worlds before and after 1521 (e.g., Charlton 1968; Gibson 1964; Lockhart 1992). Some material goods produced in the colonial period are often difficult to distinguish from goods produced in the pre-Columbian period, indicating continuities in production processes, traditional knowledge, and technologies (e.g., Charlton 1968; Charlton and Fournier 2011; Charlton et al. 1995). In my previous work, I have argued that there was much change in Indigenous societies and material lives both before and after 1521, making it inaccurate to view the events of 1521 as the only causes of change in Indigenous lives. Paradoxically, constant change was the continuity (Rodríguez-Alegría 2008a, 2008b, 2016a). Indigenous people sometimes adopted aspects of the material culture of the colonizers and incorporated them into their own practices, political strategies, and daily lives.

Perhaps the most important aspect of change and continuity in Indigenous lives in the colonial period, from the point of view of this book, is the continuation of Indigenous political and economic power well into the colonial period. The idea that conquistadors conquered, colonizers ruled, and Indigenous people formed part of a powerless lower class used to be central to scholarship on colonial Mexico but scholars have not found much support for this idea in the archival or material record (Hernández Durán 2017a). Scholars have pointed out that in many places, Indigenous rulers maintained, and sometimes even increased their power well into the colonial period (e.g., Chance 2008; Cline 1986; Haskett 1991; Lockhart 1992; Spores 1997; Villella 2016). Many historical documents contain complaints by Indigenous elites who claimed that they had lost their power and privileges, but Lockhart (1992:112) argues that their complaints were strategic and may have even strengthened their power and legal standing. The Spanish tried to rule over Mexico City and limit Indigenous rulership only to other Indigenous towns, which became known as *cabeceras* (Gibson 1964:166), or "head town of a municipality" (see Ruiz Medrano 2010:52). Still, there were Indigenous kings in colonial Mexico City, and they even built a new ruling house or palace close to the main plaza in the city (Mundy 2015:109), demonstrating that their power had not ended and they were a force that the Spanish had to reckon with.

Indigenous people sometimes made claims of authority by claiming kinship with previous rulers, although descent from politically powerful ancestors did not guarantee political power in colonial Mexico (Schroeder 1991:8–13). Obtaining power could also depend on astute political maneuvering, and even alliance and collaboration with the Spanish. Indigenous people also incorporated different kinds of material culture and practices into their strategies for negotiating and demonstrating status. Sometimes they adopted ceramics, clothing, horses, weapons, and other things associated with the colonizers, and at other times they retained their traditional ways of demonstrating rank through their Indigenous material culture (Charlton and Otis Charlton 1994:248; Gibson 1964:156; Haskett 1991:161–163; Rodríguez-Alegría 2010, 2012a, 2016a:154–183; Terraciano 2001; Von Winning 1988; Wood 2003; Yannakakis 2008). Political maneuvering from both Indigenous people and Spanish colonizers contributed to the constant evolution of Indigenous rule throughout the colonial period (Olko and Szemiński 2018). Indigenous people variously competed with one another for positions of authority, and negotiated with the Spanish (Ruiz Medrano and Kellogg 2010). Spores (1997) has pointed out that some Indigenous lords were even wealthier and more powerful than many Spanish colonizers.

This background of shifting alliances, mixing, and fluctuating status provides the setting for the study of the material worlds of Spanish colonizers in sixteenth-century Mexico City. Some scholarship that focuses on colonizers has relied on the idea that the Spanish were more complex and more powerful than Indigenous people (e.g., Foster 1960). But if we take seriously the idea that some Indigenous people maintained and sometimes enhanced their political power in sixteenth-century Mexico, the next step should be to reconsider how colonizers engaged with Indigenous people. It is time to reexamine the political strategies of Spanish colonizers and the ways in which material culture, from everyday things to special or highly symbolic objects, formed part of their strategies for obtaining and managing power. It is time to reconsider how colonizers used production, exchange, and consumption of many different material things to create the kinds of social, political, and economic relationships that they wanted with Indigenous people, from the very powerful to the oppressed. And it is time to consider how Indigenous people, from the powerful to the oppressed, transformed the material worlds of Spanish colonizers.

Sources and Inspiration

A combination of historical documents and archaeological remains provides a view of the things that the Spanish owned and the spaces where they lived. The main source of data that I introduce in this book consists of thirty-nine probate inventories of Spanish colonizers who were born in Spain and died in central Mexico between 1532 and 1590. Most of them died in Mexico City. Their inventories are held in the *Contratación* section at the *Archivo General de Indias* (AGI) in Seville. The Casa de Contratación was the government branch in charge of managing trans-Atlantic travel and trade with the Americas. When a Spaniard died in the Americas, Contratación officers were supposed to compile an inventory of the decedent's belongings, sell anything not made of gold and silver, and collect the value of the decedent's belongings. They then had to settle the decedent's debts and collect their credit. It was common for those who left a will to request many masses and to purchase objects for churches, chapels, and convents, including candles, crucifixes, and others. Once all the debts and other transactions were settled, Contratación officers sent the inheritance, in cash, to Seville. In Seville, officers announced the death and inheritance in front of the Casa de Contratación and the Cathedral. The families then had the opportunity to claim the inheritance there. If they failed to claim the inheritance within a month, and Contratación officers could not locate any family members, then the Casa de Contratación would keep the money. Even though the Casa de Contratación guaranteed that families would receive the complete inheritance, the process was fraught with fraud and theft, and families were often left without their inheritance (Canterla and de Tovar 1984; Rodríguez-Alegría 2016a:36; Vila Vilar 1983).

The inventories I consulted for this study belong to thirty-seven men and two women. This strong gender imbalance reflects strictly the probate inventories that I could find at the AGI. All of my attempts to come up with more inventories that belonged to women failed, perhaps because the great majority of migrants to the Spanish colonies were men. Boyd-Bowman consulted the Catalog of Passengers to the Indies and compiled information on their gender, place of origin, destination, and occupation. He found that women made up only 6.3 percent of all passengers to the Indies after 1521. The majority of the women who took a chance at sailing across the Atlantic were widows, single women, girls, or women of an unspecified civil status (Boyd-Bowman 1968:xvi). The percentage of women in the probate inventories I present here closely approximates the percentage of women who sailed from Europe to the Americas. Mexico attracted over 4,000 immigrants from Europe after 1523, more than any other destination in the Americas, by far (Boyd-Bowman 1968:xxv). Most of them settled in Mexico City, which resulted in a broad availability of doctors, lawyers, carpenters, tailors, and many other specialists that could be found in Spain at the time (Boyd-Bowman 1968:xix). The decedents whose inventories I examine here reflect the gender imbalance of the colonization process as well as the variety of occupations among colonizers. They include tailors, seamstresses, miners, merchants, carpenters, smiths, muleteers, miners, shoemakers, and religious specialists, such as friars and clerics (Rodríguez-Alegría 2016a:46–47).

Even though the sample of inventories reflects the gender imbalance of the conquest, I did not set out to study a sample that resembled a demographic profile of colonizers in Mexico City. My original intention was to find the probate inventories of the people who lived in the houses excavated by the *Programa de Arqueología Urbana* (PAU) of the *Museo del Templo Mayor* in Mexico City. For my PhD dissertation, I was studying the ceramics found in the different house lots. I planned to study the other belongings of the residents in those houses to create socioeconomic profiles for them and inform my ceramic analysis. Once in Seville, I did not find a single inventory that I could match to any of the house lots excavated by the PAU. I quickly formulated Plan B and began to compile as many probate inventories from sixteenth-century Mexico City as I could find. I studied whatever inventories I could find from anyone who died in Mexico City or nearby during this period. The information could complement the archaeological data by providing a look at many categories of material culture that were owned by colonizers but that my ceramic analysis would not be able to access: clothing, furniture, tools, money, and others. This book is the result of the efforts that I began as a graduate student.

The inventories are at once formulaic and varied, and they fall into three categories that can help understand the information they contain: wills, stock lists, and auction records (Rodríguez-Alegría 2016a:36–38). Wills were usually compiled at someone's deathbed, when illness or injury made it probable that the person would die. Wills tend to have the best information on interpersonal debt, and include the most donations to churches and chapels, as the decedent struggled to secure a path to heaven by purchasing candles, Masses, and rosaries. The very wealthy sometimes even paid for the foundation of a chapel (Vila Vilar 1983:263). Sometimes the wills contain precise information on debt and credit, and sometimes the decedent could barely remember who owed him money or whether he or she owed money to someone else. If someone dictated a will and ended up not dying, they usually created another will the next time they were ill and expected to die (Rodríguez-Alegría 2016a:37). Wills are often the best source of information on slaves owned by the decedent, and children the decedents had out of wedlock, often with their slaves. Wills also contain some information on the personal belongings of the decedent, although the best sources for information on material goods were stock lists and auction records.

Stock lists are different from wills in that they were usually compiled after the decedent's death, by parties who simply created a list of the person's belongings that they could find. They usually contain commentary on the quality of the material goods, and they focus on clothing, household goods, tools, livestock, and small personal items. Sometimes the stock lists include a list of estimated prices or monetary value of the items, although they mostly consist of lists and descriptions without the prices.

Auction records are the third kind of probate inventory consulted. They consist of a list of items sold in auction after the decedent's death, the names of buyers for each item, sporadic comments on the quality of the items, and the price paid for each item sold in the auction. At the end of the list, the scribe typically includes the total money paid in the auction. In the sixteenth century, public auctions were quite common in Iberia, and different kinds of people participated, including the wealthy and powerful (Mercado 1985). King Phillip, for example, obtained some of his furniture in public auctions (Aguiló Alonso 1993:17). Most of the buyers that appear in the auction records I consulted are Spanish men, although I do not have clear information regarding whether women and Indigenous people were usually prevented from participating. In some ways, auction records tend to repeat much of the information in the stock lists, given that they are listing the same items, for the most part. But sometimes they include items not mentioned in the stock lists, sometimes they offer further descriptive details on the same items, and occasionally they quantify differently the same items that have already appeared in the stock lists. For example, I have seen a stock list that included one mule, one horse, and "some mares," whereas its corresponding auction record listed the same livestock as thirteen "equine beasts" (Rodríguez-Alegría 2016a:38). By comparing auction records with stock lists, as well as wills, one can sometimes obtain more details about some of the items that appear in more than one inventory.

The other main source of information for this book consists of the archaeological remains found in the houses of Spanish colonizers in the heart of Mexico City. I focus especially on the numerous publications and excavation reports produced by the archaeologists of the PAU. Since 1990 the PAU has conducted archaeological and historical research in the center of Mexico City, in the area occupied by the sacred precinct of the Mexica. The PAU is in charge of excavations in approximately seven blocks in the heart of the historic center of Mexico City, delimited by San Ildefonso and González Obregón streets to the north, Brasil and Monte de Piedad streets to the west, the northern portion of the Palacio Nacional and the front part of the Metropolitan Cathedral to the south, and El Carmen and Correo Mayor streets to the east (Matos Moctezuma 1999:11, 2003). The research conducted by the PAU is best known for spectacular pre-Hispanic findings, such as a monument depicting Tlaltecuhtli, a Mexica earth deity, the skull rack of the Mexica (*tzompantli*), a building where some of the Mexica kings were buried, and a ballcourt, among many others (Matos Moctezuma 2017). As they make their way down to the Mexica monuments and architecture, archaeologists have to excavate the remains of colonial buildings that are sandwiched between modern construction (including the streets and building that are in use today), and the Mexica buildings below. The scientific goals of the PAU include the study of the material findings in the sacred precinct of the Mexica, and documenting findings from all time periods as well, including the colonial period (Barrera Rodríguez, Rivera García, and Medina Martínez 2003:203). The PAU, being part of the Templo Mayor, also curates and preserves the material findings for future study and public exhibitions (Gallardo Parrodi 2017).

The reasons to excavate and begin a research project in the middle of a high-traffic area in the middle of Mexico City are often tied to problems that result as buildings decay and need reconstruction. Excavations are often rescue excavations. Mexico City is subsiding, as water is drained from under the city and soils are compressed under the weight of the architecture. An estimate from 1994 claimed that since 1948 Mexico City was subsiding at an impressive rate of approximately 12 cm per year (López Arenas 2003:233), although more recent estimates claim the city is subsiding at an incredible rate of 50 cm per year (Chaussard et al. 2021). Beneath the streets and buildings of Mexico City lies a meters-thick heterogeneous mixture of sand, clay, rocks, and ancient architecture that compresses at different rates as the water table gets extracted. The soils, the ruins of precontact architecture, and the ruins of colonial buildings subside and shift at different rates, making for an unstable foundation for modern buildings. As modern buildings subside on their unstable foundation, they tend to tilt, rotate, and fracture, requiring intervention by modern engineers. Archaeologists step in to manage the excavations and study the archaeological remains before engineers conduct their work of consolidating the architecture (López Arenas 2003). Thanks to the generosity of my Mexican colleagues, I was able to work with the colonial ceramics excavated by the PAU (Rodríguez-Alegría 2003, 2005a, 2005b, 2016a). In this book I draw insights once again from the ceramics excavated by the PAU and from the remains of colonial and pre-Hispanic architecture in the center of Mexico City. The many publications of the PAU also offer information on the plant remains and animal bones found in the excavations, helping examine the food that colonizers ate.

Scope and Organization

This book focuses on the sixteenth century. I will reach back to the decades or even centuries before 1521, to provide background information, but the main lines of evidence introduced and examined focus on the decades after 1521. The probate inventories range from 1532 to 1590. The archaeological material has a much broader range, but I focus on the remains from the sixteenth century as much as possible. The focus on the sixteenth century is somewhat arbitrary, in the sense that it is not framed by any specific historical or political event, other than the initial arrival of Spanish colonizers. I am most interested in the earliest decades of colonization, when colonizers, their slaves, and Indigenous people started creating a partly new material world. Although there is much work on colonial material culture in general, I avoid generalizing about the colonial period. Enough scholarship has shown diachronic as well as geographic variation during the centuries of colonialism in Mexico and elsewhere in the Americas. Treating the entire colonial period as a total unit of time could trivialize the many changes and variability in experiences under colonialism (Senatore and Funari 2015:6). The royal pragmatics that tried to control dress in the seventeenth century (Katzew 2004:68), for example, and the world of fashionable and ostentatious people strolling down the streets of Mexico City described by Thomas Gage (Thompson 1958) were part of a world that was different from the world experienced by colonizers one hundred years earlier. A contribution of this study is its focus on the first eighty years of colonialism in Mexico City, when gold coins and cacao beans still circulated more than silver (Céspedes del Castillo 1994; Marichal 2015; Seeger 1978), the Metropolitan Cathedral was still under construction (Bérchez 1999a, 1999b; Marías 1999), many of the temples of the Mexica were still in use (Toussaint 1956:15), Indigenous people lived in the center of the city next to the houses of Spaniards (Valero de García Lascuráin 1991:183), Indigenous populations plummeted to their lowest levels in great part to severe epidemics brought by colonizers (Gerhard 1993; Márquez Morfín 1993; Márquez Morfín and Storey 2017), and there were perhaps more Black people than White colonizers living in Mexico City (Velázquez Gutiérrez 2018).

The first chapter combines a socioeconomic profile of the colonizers whose probate inventories form part of the study with a discussion of the different kinds of media of exchange that colonizers brought, found in central Mexico, and created. It will help the reader get acquainted with the thirty-nine colonizers and begin to understand their varied occupations and how they made their money. And I mean how they really *made* their money: by creating different alloys of gold and copper, and by granting each other certificates of debt, among other ways in which they created different currencies. The chapter will also be the first to discuss the advantages of making humans the active subjects of the story, by asking how different people used coins, rather than asking what functions money served.

The following chapters will begin at the largest scale of material, the built environment (Chapter 2), and move sequentially through decreasing scales until arriving at the body of colonizers (Chapter 5). Chapter 2 will examine the layout of Mexico City, and focus extensively on a description of the houses of colonizers, based on the many publication of the PAU. The descriptions of the houses of colonizers and the different construction techniques used to build them will help go beyond descriptions found in the literature, which tend to focus on facades and on the military appearance of houses. It will provide the first discussion in the book about colonizers' dependence on Indigenous technologies.

Chapter 3 will return to the probate inventories to examine the furniture that colonizers owned and used in their houses. A discussion of the different theoretical approaches to everyday objects will highlight the importance of such objects in everyday experience, social life, and politics. The chapter will then examine how colonizers used different kinds of furniture to create a life that they found acceptable and familiar, and sometimes to show off their power and distinction. Sometimes they even presented highly symbolic pieces of furniture, especially chairs, to powerful Indigenous people. Thus, colonizers used different kinds of furniture in different ways, sometimes to mark distinction, and sometimes to create alliances with powerful Indigenous lords. Chapter 4 will continue the examination of everyday objects in Spanish houses, but this time focusing on pottery and food. The main lines of data include a combination of pottery and food mentioned in the probate inventories with the thousands of fragments of pottery and food remains excavated by the PAU. It will touch upon the same issues as Chapter 3, and examine how colonizers variously used pottery and food to create a material world that they found acceptable, sometimes to mark distinction from Indigenous people or people of lower classes, and sometimes even to show hospitality to powerful Indigenous people and to negotiate social relations.

Chapter 5 will focus on the clothing worn by colonizers. It will show that colonizers mostly used their own Spanish styles, but they also used plenty of Spanish-style clothing made locally in New Spain by Spanish and Indigenous tailors and with cloth produced by Indigenous people. The clothes they wore were often torn and mended. The chapter will show how much recreating a Spanish material world depended on Indigenous work and materials, and how the strategies of distinction of the Spanish often depended on forging economic links with Indigenous people.

Chapter 6 will focus on technologies, tools, slaves, and livestock. The colonizers themselves bound tools, slaves, and livestock in the probate inventories with formulaic language that can roughly translate to "some slaves with all their tools," or "a few head of cattle with their tools," and other similar phrases. Thus, I discuss these categories together as part of the technological systems of colonizers. The chapter will provide demographic profiles of the enslaved, descriptions of the tools, and patterns of ownership of livestock. The discussion will also serve to highlight the cruelty and dehumanization of slavery, in a system in which enslaved people were often exchanged alongside batches of tools. The chapter will bring together these three categories to show that Spanish colonizers maintained their traditional technologies as long as they were the ones using the tools. They adopted Indigenous technologies, not in the sense of having adopted tools to use with their own hands, but in the sense of having adopted the entire sociotechnical system and placing themselves on top, as the people who controlled the tools, the labor, and the techniques. Thus, technological change in the colonial period was not a simple matter of progress, but it involved also enslavement and exploitation.

Chapter 7 will examine the patterns of consumption of imported and locally made goods in comparison to colonizers' wealth. Scholars have debated the relationship between ownership of Indigenous and locally produced goods among Spanish colonizers and different economic, cultural, and social variables. Did the wealthy, for example, own more imported goods than the poor? Did poor colonizers rely mostly on locally made products? Or do consumption patterns indicate that the consumption patterns of colonizers were not dictated by wealth? This chapter will emphasize the value of focusing on people as the decision makers when studying consumption, rather than allowing conceptual categories to make the decisions for humans.

Entering Social and Material Worlds

In an oft-cited passage, philosopher Nancy Hartsock wrote:

> Why is it, exactly at the moment when so many of us who have been silenced begin to demand the right to name ourselves, to act as subjects rather than objects of history, that just then the concept of subjecthood becomes "problematic?" (Hartsock 1987:196)

Hartsock was not writing about materiality, but about the relationship between postmodern theorists and a variety of activist groups, including feminists, that they tended to ignore. Still, her core idea rings true to the ideas that shaped this book. Scholars have worked hard to show that Indigenous people were a force to be reckoned with in colonial Mexico. Scholars have shown that Black people, both enslaved and free, were also an active group in colonial society, and their actions shaped history. It is time to examine how different people created and shaped the material worlds of colonial Mexico City. It is time to reexamine the material worlds of colonizers, now that we know that they interacted with a wide variety of Indigenous and Black people, castas, the wealthy, the poor, and a colonial society that was as diverse as one could imagine. This book is an invitation to keep the social world in focus as we enter the material worlds of Spanish colonizers in sixteenth-century Mexico City.

1

How to Make Money

As we enter the material worlds of Spanish colonizers, we should get to know a little bit about the colonizers themselves. In this chapter, I characterize the economic standing of colonizers, focusing on their wealth and the kinds of things on which they spent or invested their money. To address issues of wealth, it will be necessary to study the kinds of coin and other media of exchange that were in use in sixteenth-century Mexico City. The people compiling the probate inventories that form the basis of this study measured and recorded the value of each item in material terms: the amount of gold that would be necessary to purchase a person's belongings. They translated each decedent's net worth into coin in official documents, with the intent of communicating and sending the value of the decedent's belongings to his or her family in Spain. Calculating the value of a decedent's belongings as gold also helped the church and the Spanish crown collect some revenue from a person's estate, through donations to the church and taxes to the king.

In a sophisticated analysis of the introduction of coinage into the colonial Andes, Noa Corcoran-Tadd (2016) argues that by analyzing everyday practices of coin circulation, "we can begin to consider the actual making of the 'social'" (2016:64). He considers coins not just as symbolically rich objects, but also as objects that depended upon people and other things to be created, regulated, exchanged, provided as tribute, presented as offerings, substituted other material things to measure wealth, considered worthless, discarded, etc. To study coin production, he focuses on techniques of manufacture and the composition of the metal. To study circulation of coins, he focuses on the many contexts of use of coins, especially among Indigenous people in the Andes. He argues that "there is a striking disjunction between the discourses of wealth, glory, and empire and the banality, even crudeness of the coins at the heart of the colonial project" (Corcoran-Tadd 2016:69). His work is thus an invitation to bring together a study of the materiality of coins with an analysis of how people create and amass wealth, a challenge that I take up in this chapter.

How to Make a New Spain. Enrique Rodríguez-Alegría, Oxford University Press. © Enrique Rodríguez-Alegría 2023. DOI: 10.1093/oso/9780197682296.003.0002

Coins, however, are not synonymous with money. They are but one material kind of money that will appear in this chapter. Pierre Vilar (1976) makes a useful distinction between three kinds of money. The first is "money as an object or commodity, an object whose substance and weight give it a realizable trading value throughout the world market" (Vilar 1976:20). The metallic coins discussed in this chapter are precisely this kind of money. The second kind is "token or 'fiduciary' money, a token accepted as of a certain value although it is known that it itself could never be sold at the same value" (Vilar 1976:20). Paper money today would be this kind of money. The paper itself is worthless, but the dollar bill is accepted as legal tender. The third kind of money is "nominal money (or accounting money), an indication of value representing no specific currency" (Vilar 1976:20). The totals added up to represent the net worth of each decedent in the probate inventories are this kind of accounting money.

For well over a century, scholars have argued that money serves three functions: measuring and standardizing value, facilitating exchange, and storing wealth (Jevons 1896: 13–18; Neale 1976:7; Papadopoulos 2012:265; Vilar 1976:19; Wallace 1987:396–397; Weber (1922)1978:76).[1] At first glance, these three functions of money seem perfectly attuned to the functions of money in colonial Mexico City. In the probate inventories of colonizers, money served to measure the value of the personal belongings of decedents, to facilitate exchange of their belongings in auctions, and to store the decedent's wealth before sending it to families in Spain. However, my interest in this book is to learn about how people shaped and interacted with their material worlds. Instead of focusing on the functions of money, I prefer to examine the ways that people used money in colonial Mexico. The shift I emphasize here is from conceptualizing objects as having functions that people follow passively, to thinking of people and how they really used those objects and created varied functions for them. To understand the wealth of colonizers, we must keep in mind the actions, strategies, and practices of colonizers, and Indigenous people and how they used money to shape their material and social worlds.

I begin this chapter with a description of the different media of exchange that existed in Spain and Mexico in the sixteenth century. Then, I discuss the different kinds of coins that colonizers invented and used, followed by a

---

[1] Neale (1976:7) lists a fourth function of money: to serve as a means of payment. I would argue that it is simply a different way of stating that money serves as a means of exchange.

calculation of the wealth of the decedents in this study. Finally, I examine how colonizers distributed their wealth into different categories (cash, real estate, furniture, clothing, and others) to study whether colonizers in New Spain used money to store their wealth. What kinds of coins did colonizers have? How did they spend or store their wealth? How wealthy were they? Neither the gold in the museums, nor the popular image of a wealthy Spanish empire did much to prepare me for the answers I found in the probate inventories of colonizers.

Coins and Media of Exchange

There was a surprising variety of items used as media of exchange in circulation in New Spain. The proliferation of several kinds of coin was in part due to the existence of different media of exchange in Indigenous societies and to the importation and subsequent invention of several types of coin by Spanish colonizers (Céspedes del Castillo 1994). Before the conquest, "several sources indicate that the most common means of exchange was barter" (Berdan 2014:123). Still, people in central Mexico used several items as media of exchange. The most common was apparently cacao beans. Indigenous people used cacao beans in markets to pay for goods, and also to pay for labor in postconquest documents, perhaps in continuity with pre-Hispanic patterns (Berdan 2014:125). They used cacao beans so commonly that Spanish colonizers recognized and used cacao as currency in the colonial period (Seeger 1978:170) and people used them in Mexico well into the nineteenth century (Caplan 2013:337). Another common form of currency in central Mexico before the conquest were lengths of cloth or cloaks (known as *quachtli*), although other items were also used, including gold, tin and copper axes, stone and shell beads (Berdan 2014:124–125; Seeger 1978:168), and salt (Millhauser 2017a). Hernán Cortés commented that copper and tin were made into pieces that were comparable to coins, and he wrote that they were said to come from Taxco (Seeger 1978:168), which later would become one of the most important sources of silver in central Mexico.

If things were complicated in central Mexico, they were not much simpler in contemporary Spain. In the fifteenth century, there were several types of metal coins in circulation in the Iberian Peninsula. The three main coins in circulation, which together formed a sort of unified monetary system, were the *excelente* in Granada, the *ducat* or *ducado* in Castille, and the *principat* in Catalonia (Plate 1; Seeger 1978:173). The monetary system was complex, and among the coins in circulation one finds *marcos, castellanos* (later known as *peso de oro*), *tomines* (one-eighth of a castellano; Céspedes del Castillo 1994:155), and *maravedís* (Figure 1.1). Of these coins, only maravedís will be important in the rest of this book, even though they were never mentioned in the probate inventories that I consulted. Maravedís certainly existed and were used in the Spanish colonies in the sixteenth century, and archaeologists have found maravedí coins in Mexico City (Sánchez Vázquez and Mena Cruz 2004); however, I only use them here as accounting money, or a way of comparing all other currencies to a standard value. I have converted the value of the probate inventories into maravedís, as is done in a main source that I will use for comparative purposes (Rodríguez Vázquez 1995). The

Figure 1.1 Four maravedí coin from Cuenca. Public domain image, https://commons.wikimedia.org/wiki/File:Maraved%C3%ADs_de_los_Reyes_Cat%C3%B3licos_Acu%C3%B1ada_en_Cuenca_Reverso.jpg.

term maravedí comes from *morabati*, the coin used by the Almoravids when they invaded the Iberian Peninsula (Vilar 1976:31–32). Since 1497, Spanish mints achieved some standardization of gold, silver, and silver/copper alloy coins. Based on this system, the *excelente* or *ducado* of gold was worth 375 maravedís, the silver *real* was worth 34 maravedís, and the *vellón* of silver and copper was worth half a maravedí (Vilches 2010:126).

Although the coins in Spain were varied, colonizers did not bring enough coins to circulate in the colonies in the Americas. When colonizers arrived in Mexico, they learned rather quickly the varied items that Indigenous people used as media of exchange in central Mexico. They also invented other coins that were somewhat different from the ones in Spain. The invention of these coins was in part a reaction to the scarcity of coins from Spain, and the desire of colonizers to keep using coins as media of exchange. Colonizers took advantage of the availability of copper in Mexico and used it to dilute the gold, which resulted in different kinds of gold and gold coins of different value.

The coins used in colonial Mexico include no less than four kinds of gold pesos with different composition and value, including the *peso de oro, oro de minas* (also known as *oro ensayado, castellano,* and *oro de ley perfecta*), *oro común,* and *tepuzque,* also known as *oro corriente* (Table 1.1; Céspedes del Castillo 1994; Marichal 2015; Seeger 1978). Tepuzque is an alloy of gold that is so high in copper that its name is derived from the word for copper (*tepuztli*) in Nahuatl (Seeger 1978:175). The story goes that Hernán Cortés himself ordered that a few gold coins be adulterated with additional copper to create more coins for circulation and to be able to pay his soldiers. Debasing the metal resulted in coins that were three karats lower than they were supposed to be, according to the royal stamp with which they had been marked (Seeger 1978:175; Vilches 2010:134). This was the first tepuzque gold in circulation. It was designated as having a value of 272 maravedís as early as 1526, only five years after the conquest, and standardized at 13.6 karats (Céspedes del Castillo 1994:157). Notice that in spite of its reputation for having high amounts of copper, it is just below 14-karat gold, which is happily accepted as gold for jewelry today. Tepuzque was the most commonly used coin in New Spain at the time (Céspedes del Castillo 1994:157), although Marichal (2015:21) has argued that people used tepuzque mostly in local markets, whereas they used castellanos or peso de minas mostly for long distance trade.

If money is supposed to facilitate exchange through the standardization of value, people certainly found ways to defy standardization and ease of use by

Table 1.1 Coins used in the probate inventories.[a]

	Other names	Value	Karats
peso de oro		500 maravedís	
peso de oro de minas	ensayado, castellano, de ley perfecta	450 maravedís	22.5
peso de oro común		300 maravedís	15
peso de tepuzque	oro corriente, oro que corre	272 maravedís	13.6
tostón (de oro)		125 maravedís	
marco de plata	(in objects made of silver)	2,310 maravedís in 1557; 2,250 maravedís in 1572	
marco de plata	(in coin)	2,278 maravedís	
ducado		375 maravedís	
peso de plata	real de a ocho	272 maravedís	
real (plata)		34 maravedís	

[a]Sources: Burzio 1958; Céspedes de Castillo 1994; Luengo Muñoz 1951; Marichal 2015; Riva Palacios 1977; Seeger 1978.

creating different types of coin. In fact, the story of the creation of tepuzque points to Hernán Cortés himself as being involved in the debasement of the gold that was used to make tepuzque. On one hand, the story repeats the same tendency of putting "big men" in the center of everything in the conquest (critiqued in Restall 2003). On the other hand, if we put aside the issue of whether Cortés himself invented tepuzque, the story highlights the active role of people in manipulating money to seek advantage. As much as people quickly adopted the new kinds of coin, they also reacted against them. Payers or users of coins tried to pass their coins as more valuable than they were, given that the gold they contained had been diluted. They entered a constant negotiation with receivers of payments in coin, who constantly tried to lower the value of the coins they were about to receive, or increased the prices of their goods to get the most gold out of each transaction (Céspedes del Castillo 1994: 157–158; Vilches 2010:134).

Two other types of metallic coins are worth mentioning: silver reales and copper coins. The silver real (*real de plata* or *real de a ocho*) was valued at 272 maravedís in the sixteenth century, or the equivalent of eight silver reales in Castile at the time. For that reason, it was commonly known as real de a ocho, which loosely translates to "real of eight." Silver reales appear infrequently in the inventories that form part of this study, in which gold was the standard, and the reasons have to do with the initial search for gold, and the later discovery of abundant silver. In the initial years of conquest and colonization in the Indies, when Europeans were trying to find gold at any cost, most coins in circulation were made of gold. Toward the end of the sixteenth century, the stream of silver from the Americas to Europe increased dramatically, with the discovery of major silver deposits in Mexico and Perú. Estimates claim that in the 1540s, Seville received 177,000 kilos of silver from the Americas. By the last decade of the sixteenth century, Seville was receiving more than 2 million kilos of silver. Silver eventually replaced gold for use in coins, as it became more and more abundant in the colonies (Marichal 2015:22).

Copper coins were the lowest denomination coins in circulation in New Spain, and they are nowhere to be found in the inventories I consulted. People probably used them as small change. Archaeologists have found a small hoard of twelve coins of two maravedís, and twelve coins of four maravedís minted in Mexico in the sixteenth century. In addition, they found one coin of two maravedís probably minted in Spain and meant for circulation in Santo Domingo. Archaeologists found them approximately 2.5 meters beneath the patio of an Indigenous house in Tlatelolco (Sánchez Vázquez and Mena Cruz 2004). I mention them here because they were part of the world of coins in the sixteenth century, and because there are published photos of copper coins, but not of any of the sixteenth century gold coins. Finding coins at all is rare, but one would be more likely to find archaeological specimens of the least important coins (because people discarded them more easily), and less likely to find a single specimen of the most widely used coins (because people held on to them and used them). The publications and collections I have consulted have photos of coins from the eighteenth century, and rarely from the seventeenth century. Perhaps the earliest specimens are nowhere to be found today in part because Indigenous people discarded many of those coins into the lake when trying to manipulate the monetary system (Caplan 2013; Sánchez Vázquez and Mena Cruz 2004).

These copper coins provide the only opportunity I have to discuss the imagery in the coins. Briefly, the coins include images that one would associate exclusively with the Spanish monarchs: crowns, castles or towers that symbolize the kingdom of Castile, lions that symbolize the kingdom of León, columns, and pomegranates. There are no images of anything related to New Spain in these coins, except for the letter M, which stands for Mexico, the location of the mint. Other letters include the words PLVS VLTRA, the letters K, CH, and C, which correspond to different ways of symbolizing the name of King Charles (Sánchez Vázquez and Mena Cruz 2004). The imagery in these coins clearly emphasizes royal authority and completely ignores Indigenous imagery and iconography. The use of images that referenced the Spanish monarchs but ignored any imagery related to New Spain continued through the seventeenth, eighteenth, and nineteenth centuries. Coins from the twentieth century include images of Mexica monuments, portraits of Mexica rulers, and even Nahuatl poetry printed so small that one may need a magnifying glass to read it, but no references to Spain (photographs in Chapa 2015).

In addition to coins, a few non-metallic media of exchange appear infrequently in the probate inventories as payment for goods or for debt. Cacao appears only once in the documents. Historical documents state that cacao was used for everything among colonizers, including for purchasing clothes and other things in the market, and even paying for labor (Berdan 2014:125). Indigenous people sometimes paid tribute to the Spanish with cacao (Gasco 1992:67; Valle 1994). Some colonizers and Indigenous people made a fortune in cacao cultivation and trade (Céspedes del Castillo 1994:151; Gasco 1987). Cacao production was so important in the colonial period that it peaked in the middle of the sixteenth century, and slowly declined for the rest of the colonial period (Gasco 1987:135–137). People continued using cacao as currency until the end of the colonial period (Caplan 2013:337; Seeger 1978:172). Caplan (2013:337) has argued that Indigenous people forced the continued use of cacao as currency as part of "an extremely successful effort undertaken by the Mexicas in the mid-sixteenth century" to get low-denomination minted coins out of circulation and force the use of cacao instead. Indigenous people, according to historical sources, discarded low-denomination copper and silver coins in large enough quantities that cacao survived as a medium of exchange because it was the most available alternative to coins (discussed later).

Conflicts over Coins

Colonizers in all parts of the Spanish empire complained about the variety of coins and the lack of standardization and control over coinage, and called for the establishment of a mint. Peter Martyr D'Anghieria argued in favor of the establishment of a mint as part of the civilizing mission of colonizers. He argued that a mint would promote social and economic well-being, because minted coins would encourage contact between Spaniards and Indians, who would in turn be encouraged to find more precious metals, and their discoveries would be followed by peace and prosperity (Seeger 1978:175). But other intentions reveal conflict and struggle more directly. Some colonizers accused Indigenous people of inflating prices in the market, and argued that only by standardizing the value of minted coins would they be able to prevent inflation. Others wanted to control the flow of coins and who could use them to prevent the loss of gold to Indigenous people, which in turn meant loss of revenue to the crown (Seeger 1978). In 1535, Charles V gave the order to establish mints in three places in the colonies: Potosí, Perú; Santa Fe de Nueva Granada, Colombia; and Mexico City (Pérez Mora and Ibarra Arzave 2014). The mint in Mexico City was established in 1537 (Seeger 1978:168), and it was known as the Real Casa de Moneda and located next to the Palacio Nacional (Pérez Mora and Ibarra Arzave 2014).

In spite of the establishment of the mint, the conflicts over money and the use of different coins continued, especially between Spaniards and Indigenous people. Historical documents from 1544, only nine years after the establishment of the mint in Mexico City, contain accusations from Spanish colonizers that Indigenous people were hoarding gold coins to make them scarce and increase the value of gold, and later using them to bargain with Spanish merchants. The Spanish tried to control ownership of coins and stated that Indigenous people were even using their coins of inflated value to purchase firearms in the black market (Actas de Cabildo 1313, December 22, 1544). The accusations that colonizers made against Indigenous people are often amusing. Colonizers sometimes accused them of falsifying coins, which is exactly what colonizers themselves were doing when they added copper to gold coins to begin with. Colonizers also accused Indigenous people of taking minted coins and melting them to make jewelry (Seeger 1978). Some colonizers even wanted to prohibit Indigenous people from using coins altogether, and allow them to use only cacao, cloth, and maize as currency in the marketplace (Actas de Cabildo 1313, December 22, 1544). Spanish attempts at dictating what media of exchange Indigenous people could use apparently did not work. Lockhart (1992: 177) has argued that Indigenous people dropped the use of cloth as payment in marketplaces, but continued using cacao beans alongside silver and gold coins. Indigenous documents from the sixteenth century frequently express debt, whether it is interpersonal debt or Indigenous tribute to the Spanish, in terms of different kinds of coins (Cline 1986:91; Haskett 1991:61; Lockhart 1992:180).

If Spanish colonizers had their own ideas and strategies about what coins should be used, Indigenous people did so too. Historical documents claim that they reacted overwhelmingly against low-denomination coins of copper and silver and threw those coins away to force people to use other media of exchange (Caplan 2013; Torquemada 1975–1983:370). Some people refused to accept low-denomination (four maravedí) coins, to the point that the Cabildo of Mexico City even decided that people who refused to accept those coins would receive a rather extreme punishment: 100 lashes (Caplan 2013:334). The archaeologists who found the maravedí coins in Tlatelolco mentioned earlier argue that the hoard is associated with the process of discard of coins. They believe an Indigenous person was fearful of punishment for not accepting these coins, and decided to accept them and bury them instead, to remove them from circulation (Sánchez Vázquez and Mena Cruz 2004).

At once, we have a pattern of Spanish colonizers creating a greater variety of coins, using those coins in exchange with Indigenous vendors in the marketplace, using the coins also to assess some of the tribute they received, and sometimes trying to limit the use of those coins among Indigenous people. Colonizers who were intent in controlling the flow of wealth and manipulating value and prices with the use of minted coins saw much resistance from Indigenous people who had their own intentions in using those coins. The historical documents reveal some Indigenous people trying to continue using their own media of exchange, some adopting the new media of exchange, some removing new coins out of circulation, and everyone trying to manipulate the monetary system to gain some advantage. The historical development of coins in Mexico was to some extent related to the scarcity of gold, but it had more to do with how different people manipulated the monetary system in different ways to their advantage. The variety of coins and uses for those coins raise the question of whether some coins were used more commonly than others, and why.

Coins Used in Transactions

A glance at the coins typically mentioned in the probate inventories can give an idea of how familiar colonizers were with the different kinds of media of exchange in colonial Mexico City. Did colonizers use some kinds of coins more frequently than others? The data answer the question in the context of

Table 1.2 Types of gold and other media used for payment in the probate inventories, by count.

Media of exchange	Number	%
tepuzque	386	30.7
oro corriente (tepuzque)	130	10.3
oro de minas	333	26.5
oro común	221	17.6
oro de minas y común	1	0.1
quilates	11	0.9
oro (unspecified)	4	0.3
granos de oro	1	0.1
oro de marca	1	0.1
oro en polvo	2	0.2
silver reales	161	12.8
silver ducados	1	0.1
fanegas de trigo (wheat)	4	0.3
cacao	1	0.1
wine	1	0.1
Total	1258	100

the probate inventories and the auctions of decedents belongings directly. The same data only provide indirect information about other contexts in which coins were used (the marketplace, or in payment for labor being two examples), and other studies may complement or build on the information provided here. Table 1.2 shows the frequency of different media of exchange mentioned as payment in all of the inventories.[2] It is a count of each time that a specific type of coin or medium of exchange appears in the inventories. It is worth noting first that the type of coin is not specified in 89.4 percent of the transactions in the inventories. It seems that the people involved understood what type of coin they were using and the scribe did not feel the need to write it down. The percentages reported in Table 1.2 include the 1,258 instances in which a type of coin was specified.

---

[2] Ideally, I would look for temporal patterns to see if there were changes in the frequency of use of different kinds of coin in the sixteenth century. However, the probate inventories consulted may not be enough to come up with reliable temporal patterns. There may be too few inventories to represent change over time within the sixteenth century.

Céspedes del Castillo (1994:157) argues that oro corriente was the type of gold that was used the most in the sixteenth century, and the probate inventories confirm his assertion. Tepuzque is mentioned in over 30 percent of the transactions, and it appears in 10.3 percent of the transactions as oro corriente, making tepuzque the alloy of choice in 41 percent of the transactions in the sample. The second most used alloy was oro de minas, a type of gold coin that colonizers brought from Spain (Marichal 2015:21). Locally minted coins, including tepuzque, and oro común were used in over 58 percent of all transactions that specify the type of gold used. In the sixteenth century, colonizers used silver reales infrequently compared to other coins, at least in the context of the probate inventories.

Goods other than coins were also mentioned as media of exchange in the documents, including cacao (used only once), wheat (mentioned four times), and wine (mentioned once). The infrequent use of cacao is in contrast to comments by other scholars who write that cacao was used for all kinds of transactions in the market (e.g., Berdan 2014:125; Caplan 2013; Céspedes del Castillo 1994:151). It appears in the probate inventories only to reckon debt and not as payment for any auction items. Wheat appears more than cacao, but also infrequently and as debt, rather than payment for goods in auction. I believe that the discrepancy between my findings and the findings of other scholars is an indication that colonizers strongly preferred using gold coins when engaged in exchange with other colonizers, probably because they were used to gold coins in Iberia. However, when dealing with Indigenous people, colonizers used cacao, probably at least in part because Indigenous people forced the continuation of cacao as a medium of exchange, as discussed before. This finding is a clear indication that one must interpret the data provided carefully. While they are relevant to the context of exchange between colonizers, and they may provide clues about economic transactions in other contexts, one should complement them with other data before making broad generalizations.

The table also shows that colonizers used several different alloys of gold quite frequently. Most of the inventories mention more than one type of coin, even though most of them show a preference for one type of gold and the occasional use of other types. It seems like scribes and the people present at the auctions tended to prefer using one kind of coin, but were flexible enough to use others. The use of different coins in these inventories indicates that people were familiar with the many different coins and were able to use them as needed, and they used locally minted coins even more than coins that were familiar in Spain.

Wealth of the Decedents

Calculating the wealth of the decedents was challenging, in part because scribes used a variety of coins in each inventory. The difficulties were surprising, given that people compiled the probate inventories precisely with the goal of calculating the total worth of each person's belongings and sending their value in cash to the families in Spain. Each inventory typically includes the total sum of the value of the decedent's items as calculated by the scribe, but it is often difficult to reconcile the total written down by the scribe with the total calculated by me as I added them up item by item. The discrepancies between the total reported and the total I calculated were sometimes of a few maravedís, but often they were of hundreds or thousands of maravedís. The discrepancies often defy explanation. They could be due to theft, poor recordation, mathematical errors, and many other causes, some more purposeful than others. After all, poor accounting could somehow help conceal theft and fraud. Another factor that may explain the discrepancies could be that scribes often recorded the value of different items in different kinds of coin in the same inventory, and even though they reported the coin used in many of the transactions, they also failed to report them in other transactions. For example, an inventory may list a shirt that is worth 2 pesos of tepuzque, followed by a shirt that is worth three pesos of oro de minas, followed by three shirts worth ten pesos of an unspecified kind of gold. Sometimes it is easy to infer the kind of coin being used, based on items listed around the item in question, but often I was left guessing whether the coin was tepuzque or common gold or any other type of gold. Scribes always reported the grand total of an inventory in one kind of coin, and that is where the discrepancies between the total calculated by the scribe and the total calculated by me could become apparent. These documents, designed to provide a clear accounting of the worth of a decedent's material belongings, often fail to do precisely that. They are full of errors and inconsistencies, and they miss a lot of information.

To deal with the problem of missing values of gold, I classified the inventories into two categories. One category contains probate inventories that seemed clear, that specified the use of different kinds of gold consistently or used a single type of gold throughout the inventory, and that were complete in the sense of having no missing pages, no holes that obscure part of the inventory, and no unreadable passages. I refer to those inventories as the Grade A inventories and use them to calculate the wealth of decedents and to study the distribution of wealth among different categories that are discussed later. I often use Grade A inventories also to discuss issues related to the cost of different items, given that the Grade A inventories contain the best and most consistent prices of items in different kinds of gold.

The rest of the inventories contain many missing values in the types of coin used and they may have missing pages, unreadable passages, and large discrepancies between the total value calculated by the scribe and the total value I calculated myself. I use these inventories whenever there is no need to study the monetary value of the items involved. They are invaluable in studying the types of items people owned, the quality and place of manufacture of the items, and many other aspects of the material worlds of colonizers not related to the price of items or to the total worth of the decedents' belongings.

The formula I used to calculate the total worth of each Grade A inventory consisted of adding up the following values:

a. the net worth of the decedent's belongings as sold in auction, which I added item by item, plus
b. the money owed to the decedent as declared in the probate inventories (credits, or debts in favor to the decedent), plus
c. any declared properties, including real estate or belongings in Spain that appeared in the inventories, although these were uncommon.

From that total, I subtracted all debt against the decedent, or money the decedent owed others (Rodríguez-Alegría 2016b:45) and arrived at the net worth of the person in question. Whenever I write about the wealth of the decedents, I refer to the net worth of the items in their probate inventories. Logically, the decedents must have had other items that were not sold in auction, either because they were not considered valuable from a monetary standpoint, because they were stolen, not found, or for any other reason. At least one of the inventories, that of Bartolomé González (Cont. 197 N21) mentions that people had started to steal some of the decedent's belongings before they could be sold. I believe that theft took place frequently. Thus, the totals provided here most likely underestimate the total worth of the decedent's belongings consistently. The totals should be seen as an estimate rather than a specific value of a person's material items when they died.

The Grade A category includes twenty-six inventories, and their estimated value varies widely between a low of 6,281 maravedís and a high of 6,704,930 maravedís (Table 1.3). It is worth comparing the value of these inventories with a study of wealth in Seville done by Rodríguez Vázquez (1995). In his study, Rodríguez Vázquez divided the population of Seville into groups depending on the worth of their inventories. "Popular classes" were the poorest, with inventories that were worth 1 million maravedís or less. They made up 60 percent of the population in Seville. "Middle classes" had fortunes between 1 million and 10 million maravedís, and they made up 25 percent of the inventories consulted in Seville. The rest were the rich, whose inventories in Seville amount to more than 10 million maravedís.

Table 1.3 Grade A inventories and the wealth of decedents.

Decedent	Occupation	maravedís
Bartolomé Hernández	carpenter	6,281.00
Pedro de Madrid		14,737.50
Alonso García		27,114.00
Juan Bautista	cabin boy	33,825.00
Salvador Franco	scribe	36,709.38
Juan Díaz Caballero		38,069.98
Juan de Campomanes	merchant?	48,654.00
María de Espinosa		65,475.00
Pedro Vázquez		68,901.25
Juana Bautista	seamstress	79,762.50
Francisco de Sigüenza	tailor	84,238.25
Baltasar Godínez		99,450.00
Miguel Rodríguez	tailor	105,454.50
Martín López		107,698.50
Bartolomé de Prado	merchant	107,762.45
Juan Gómez		115,075.00
Alonso de Castro	muleteer	178,753.00
Andres de Plasencia		190,980.75
Juan Gutiérrez de Grado		201,731.28
Diego Delgado	smith	206,144.25
Maese Gregorio de Heredia	carpenter	351,351.50
Martín Carrasco	cleric	441,257.65
Bartolomé González		516,588.75
Alonso Serrano		716,933.75
Antonio Martínez	presbyter	1,597,950.00
Hernán Núñez Caballero		6,704,930.00

Comparing the value of the inventories in Mexico with those in Seville should be done carefully, because the cost of living and the price of gold and silver varied between Mexico and Seville. By law, coins were valued differently on either side of the Atlantic. "According to the royal prerogative of 20 December, 1505, the legal value of money in the Indies was 29.4 percent higher than in Spain" (Vilches 2010:127). A castellano of gold was worth 580 maravedís in Castile, but only 480 maravedís in the Indies, and the difference in value was meant to cover transportation and related expenses (Vilches 2010:127). The increase in prices of different items between Seville and Mexico City inspired Tomás de Mercado (1985) to write his volume on the economy of Seville in the sixteenth century. The literature is clear: things were more expensive in Mexico City than in Seville (Mercado 1985; Vilar 1976:11; Vilches 2010). In spite of these caveats, Seville emerges as a logical place for comparison for compelling reasons. Most colonizers came from Spain, and Seville was one of the major cities in Spain at the time. For many colonizers, Iberia remained a main point of reference in terms of their economic life. Seville also had close commercial and administrative ties to the Americas, given that it was the point where most ships entered and left Spain with items for transatlantic trade. Finally, Seville was the place where colonizers sent the money collected in the auctions of decedents' goods, and the place where the letters and other documents related to the probate inventories were kept. The wealth of the decedents was measured precisely to send money back to their families in Seville. If there is a place that can serve as a comparison for the social and economic lives of colonizers in New Spain, it would be Seville.

All but two of the inventories from Mexico City would fall into the category of popular classes in Seville in terms of net worth, given that they are well below a million maravedís. Almost half of the inventories, or twelve out of twenty-six, are worth under 100,000 maravedís. The highest two inventories are worth approximately 1.6 million and 6.7 million maravedís, significantly more than the rest of the inventories consulted. With the important exception of these two very large inventories, the colonizers in this data set belong in the popular classes category, which is to say that they were poor, although not destitute. Only one of the inventories, that of Bartolomé Hernández, a carpenter, is valued below 10,000 maravedís. The decedents in this category had a series of specialized (or unknown) occupations, and they include carpenters, a cabin boy, a scribe, merchants, tailors, a seamstress, a smith, and a cleric. Among the two wealthiest inventories there was a presbyter and a knight. Thus, the inventories analyzed as part of this study mostly include commoners, although there are a few examples of wealthy colonziers. The general impression is one in which many or most colonizers in this sample did not achieve or even get close to any goals of great wealth in Mexico City.

Distribution of Wealth

The way that people generally distributed their money, belongings, and investments can help us understand the material worlds of colonizers in New Spain, especially in comparison with the distribution of wealth in Seville. By "distribution of wealth," I refer to how a person's or population's wealth was divided into the following categories:

a. *cash*, mostly declared by decedents in their wills;
b. *silver and jewelry*;
c. *credit*, defined as debt in favor of the decedent;
d. *household items and clothing*;
e. *cultural items*, including mostly books, paper, ink, and other writing instruments;
f. *agricultural products*, including food, salt, spices, the occasional barrel of olives, a jug of wine, or box full of cacao beans;
g. *livestock*, including cattle, horses, sheep, and goats;
h. *slaves*, whether Black or Indigenous;
i. *real estate*, including houses in New Spain or Spain,
j. *unidentified miscellaneous*, including items that were not legible in the documents or not identified clearly by the scribe.

I adopted these categories from the study of wealth and private property in sixteenth-century Seville by Rodríguez Vázquez (1995) to facilitate comparison between our results and understand the differences and similarities between the material worlds of people in Seville and in Mexico City.

The analysis I present here is not based on direct comparison of the raw data, but rather on comparisons between Rodríguez Vázquez's (1995) published results and similar statistics done by me. Still, there are important differences between the categories we use. First, a potential difference is between my category of "unidentified miscellaneous" and Rodríguez Vázquez's category of "otros." Both categories imply that they include items that are difficult to categorize, but it is impossible to tell whether they items are equivalent across our studies. This category accounts for a small percentage of the data, and probably makes little difference for our inferences. Second, Rodríguez Vázquez makes a distinction between urban real estate and rural real estate, and I lump both into a single real estate category, given that there are few instances of houses and farms in the inventories from Mexico. Third, Rodríguez Vázquez uses some categories that are not present in my study, including *censos, oficios, dotes, pasivo,* and *colaciones.* These are all financial investment categories of very low liquidity (they were difficult to sell), and they do not appear in the inventories I consulted in Mexico. Censos refers roughly to taxation on real estate. It is a contract in which a person paid taxes to another person or to the state for the right to use a property (Rodríguez Vázquez 1995:85). I did not find any items in my data that could belong in those categories and therefore, I left them out of the analysis. Finally, there may be differences in what specific items Rodríguez Vázquez and I placed into any of the categories, although I assume that those differences are minimal and do not account for a great percentage of the estimates. After all, a shirt must logically be classified as clothing and not debt, and a cow must be livestock and not clothing.

The first observation that surprised me is the prevalence of credit and debt in these inventories. Table 1.4 shows that about half of the total value in the Grade A inventories is credit. Such a high proportion of credit in the inventories is astounding, especially when compared to Seville, where credit

Table 1.4 Distribution of wealth among colonizers in New Spain in the sixteenth century.[a]

	maravedís	%
cash	576,771	10.07
silver and jewelry	14,151	0.25
credit	2,947,028	51.46
household items and clothing	1,417,358	24.75
cultural items	36,733.50	0.64
agricultural products	98,312	1.72
livestock	143,852.75	2.51
slaves	254,894	4.45
real estate	174,880	3.05
unidentified miscellaneous	62,680.75	1.09
Total	5,726,661	99.99

[a]The categories are presented in descending order from greater to lesser liquidity.

in the sixteenth century amounted to approximately 15.4 percent of people's belongings (all comparisons with Seville are from Rodríguez Vázquez 1995:33). Based on his data from Seville, Rodríguez Vázquez (1995:54) commented that personal debt in Seville was surprisingly high, especially considering moral judgment from the medieval church, which equated debt with greed. But debt in the probate inventories from Mexico City is much higher, over 51 percent, morally scandalous or not.

Household items and clothing form the next biggest portion of the wealth, making up roughly 24.75 percent of the total. Colonizers in Mexico City held a greater portion of their net worth on clothing and mobile goods than people in Seville at the time, where household items and clothing made up a mere 3.24 percent of their net worth. The third category that made up the largest proportion of the net worth of this group of decedents was cash, which at 10.07 percent was higher than in Seville, where it made up a mere 4.29 percent of people's net worth. In general, the categories that made up the greatest proportion of people's net worth in Seville at the time were the same as the ones in Mexico City. An important exception may shape these percentages strongly: in Mexico City, real estate made up a very low percentage of the total (3.05 percent), assuming that these inventories are a good sample of the population of colonizers in the city, whereas in Seville the proportion made up by real estate is 20 percent of the wealth in the inventories. Perhaps some of the colonizers in Mexico City owned real estate in Spain and it does not appear in these inventories, especially if the inventory lacks a will, or perhaps the inventories reflect a real lack of real estate ownership, whether in Spain or New Spain, among colonizers.

It is important to note, however, that the data discussed so far include people of different occupations and radically different fortunes, in terms of wealth; therefore, it is worth considering briefly the distribution of wealth among the inventories from Mexico that total less than 1 million maravedís, in comparison with popular classes in Seville, as defined by Rodríguez Vázquez (1995:56).

Table 1.5 summarizes the distribution of wealth into different categories among popular classes of colonizers in Mexico City (eliminating the two inventories with the highest net worth in the sample). Just as with the general population of colonizers, the same three categories emerge as accounting for most of the wealth among popular classes only: first, credit; second, household goods and clothing; and third, cash. If one compares the popular classes of colonizers in Mexico City with popular classes in Seville (all data from Rodríguez Vázquez 1995:57), the patterns can be revealing. Credit emerges

Table 1.5 Distribution of wealth among colonizers in New Spain in the sixteenth century in the inventories that are worth less than 1 million maravedís.

	Total in mrvds	%
cash	518,855.75	15.97
silver and jewelry	14,151	0.44
credit	1,447,027.75	44.53
household items and clothing	649,194	19.98
cultural items	28,708.50	0.88
agricultural products	155,011.50	4.77
livestock	121,052.75	3.73
slaves	89,100	2.74
real estate	174,880	5.38
unidentified miscellaneous	51,580.75	1.59
Total	3,249,562	100.01

once again as remarkably higher in Mexico City (44.5 percent of the wealth in the inventories) in comparison to Seville (16.2 percent). Household goods and clothing formed a higher percentage of the sample from Mexico City (19.9 percent) than in Seville (14.7 percent), and cash was not too different between Mexico City (15.9 percent) and Seville (17 percent) among popular classes. Important differences include that both agricultural products and livestock made up almost twice as much of the personal wealth of people in Mexico City as they did in Seville, albeit both categories made up less than 5 percent of the wealth of popular classes among colonizers in Mexico City. Another important difference is that real estate ownership in Seville represented a much higher percentage of people's belongings (21.1 percent) in comparison with the probate inventories from Mexico City (5.38 percent). Two categories that were almost equal among popular classes in Seville and Mexico City in terms of percentage of the total wealth of the population were cultural goods and slaves. Even the poor sometimes owned enslaved people, as will be discussed later, and nobody invested much in books or writing instruments, which made up less than 1 percent of the net worth of decedents. Books and writing instruments are very rare in the probate inventories by count.

In the rest of the book, I will examine the many things that belong in the different categories used so far. In this chapter, I will only focus on two kinds of items that fall most clearly in the category of money: coins (already discussed), and debt.

Debt

The prevalence of debt in these inventories deserves some attention. Anthropologists have long noted the importance of debt and credit in society. Founding figures of the discipline, including Mauss and Malinowski, observed that debt can help build relations of hierarchy and power, but that it can also help build solidarity and group cohesion (Peebles 2010:226). More recently, Graeber has argued that "consumer debt is the lifeblood of our economy" (2011:4). Apparently, debt was the lifeblood of the economy of colonizers too. Vilches (2010:30) writes that "Spain's colonial expansion was built upon credit," and the probate inventories are provide compelling support to her argument.

I make a distinction here between credit and debt. Both terms refer to a relationship of debt, and the only distinction between them is from the point of view of the person who owes and the person who lends. Credit refers to interpersonal loans and debt in favor of decedents; that is, money that others owed to the decedent. It makes up approximately half of the wealth that was declared among the colonizers in the Grade A inventories. It accounts for 2,947,028 maravedís in the documents consulted, or five times as much as the total money held in cash by the same group of people. Of course, theft and fraud most likely made part of the cash disappear from the inventories before it could be accounted for, but some of the credit might also be left out of the documents due to fraud and poor recordation.

Debt, on the other hand, refers here to money that decedents declared that they owed others, or that other people showed up to claim after a decedent's death. It accounts for a total of 194,660 maravedís in these documents. In other words, people declared credit approximately fifteen times more than they declared debt. According to ethnographic reports people everywhere in the world "describe credit as power and debt as weakness" (Peebles 2010:226). If this were true, then colonizers presented themselves as powerful even in their deathbeds. The Catholic Church has been known for its hard stance against money lending, and especially against charging interest (Graeber 2011:10). But it seems that in the case of colonizers in sixteenth-century Mexico City, economic interests (recovering the money) took precedence over any fear of being judged for lending money or for trying to recover it.

If we look at each debt declared in the entire data set (including every item that is debt that has a clear value in pesos written next to it), the value of each item of debt ranges from 150 maravedís to 1,500,000 maravedís. The average debt is of 34,582 maravedís, if we take into account all of the data; however, the highest five instances of debt are significantly larger than the rest. The lowest of these five items is 250,950 maravedís. In comparison, the next largest item of debt is 67,500 maravedís. The jump in value is significant. If we remove the five highest debt items, because they skew the average value of debt by virtue of being much larger than other debts, we can see that the typical debt was an average of 11,779 maravedís. Among the items listed in auction records as having sold for approximately the same price one may find an imported cape, a lot of ten pairs of wool socks, and a gold chain. With the value of an average item of debt, one could purchase about twenty shirts, or nine pairs of hose. Colonizers accumulated small debt after small debt, until they had half of their net worth locked in debt.

There may be different reasons for the prevalence of debt in these documents. First, debt was simply a part of broader economic processes at the time. Vilches (2010) argues that credit was an indispensable part of conquest and colonization in the Americas, with the crown and merchant class becoming engulfed in debt. The conquistadors themselves were deep in debt. Bernal Díaz del Castillo, one of the chroniclers of the conquest, "describes Hernán Cortés as 'head and ears in debt' at the Conquest's start and notes that, by the end, most soldiers were deep in debt to Cortés and to the Spanish barbers and surgeons who accompanied them" (Millhauser 2017b:269). Conquistadors had to buy their own weapons on credit (Vilches 2010:134), showing how much the process of conquest depended on credit from the beginning. Millhauser has argued that people use debt "to manage risk and hardship" (2017b:263), an explanation that rings true to the uncertainties and risks of the process of conquest. A second explanation in the literature is related to the availability of money. Scholars have argued that there were not enough small-denomination coins to use in exchange in the Spanish colonies. People had to borrow money to be able to make small market transactions (Céspedes del Castillo 1994:170; Martínez López-Cano 1995:51).

I offer two additional explanations for the prevalence of debt and credit in these inventories. These explanations are not mutually exclusive with the previous two. First, another reason for the prevalence of debt was the search among colonizers for community in addition to money. People loaned money to one another, partly as a way of supporting each other and building ties that were at once social and economic. Graeber (2011:329) has described debt as "the very fabric of sociability." He argues that in many societies throughout history people did not see market transactions and debt as cold and impersonal. Instead, they saw them as a matter of mutual aid, especially in societies in which debt and credit prevailed in market transactions over money. Through time, people have come to see debt as a moral problem only because relationships that are founded on violence have been reframed in the language of debt and credit, but not because there was any moral judgment against debt to begin with (Graeber 2011:5). The idea of building a community was probably central to credit/debt among colonizers. Plenty of scholars have shown that lending money to someone or allowing someone a delayed payment for goods can form a bond of debt that can also transform into social ties and community (Peebles 2010:229). Millhauser argues that "the social ties of debt are paradoxical because debts and obligations can just as readily foster social solidarity as they can enforce hierarchies and inequalities. Some debts generate and reinforce social ties" (2017b:264). Today, even proponents of Bitcoin cite trust and community among the factors that make the cryptocurrency appealing. Although cryptocurrency is not credit/debt, citing community shows an awareness among its users that monetary transactions have a social component (Mauer et al. 2013). Therefore, credit/debt could also help form bonds between people that variously translated to indebtedness, friendship, support, family, and even tension between lenders and those who repeatedly failed to pay them. There are instances in the probate inventories in which decedents declared that they do not remember whether they owe money to a specific person that they name, or whether that person owes them money, and order the debt to be settled after their death (e.g., Cont. 235 N1 R20, Cont. 5575 [1492–1550]). These instances reveal that the main concern was not simply monetary, but also social.

A second explanation that I propose is that credit and debt were also ways of creating wealth. The letters that recorded debt in paper and ink were a material form of something that did not exist. The money loaned did not exist because it had been used already if it was cash, or it had never existed as money if it was goods or services provided for future payment. The money owed did not exist either because neither the debtor nor the creditor had it. It existed in the future. According to the data, half of the net worth of the decedents in this study was money they did not even have. It was credit. In his review of anthropological scholarship on credit and debt, Peebles (2010:227) comments that Marx saw credit as "fictitious capital" because it was capital that the person could declare in the present, but depended entirely on receiving it in the future. Peebles comments in that in relations of credit/debt both the creditor and the debtor are trading resources today "in exchange for speculative gains in the future" (Peebles 2010:227). Just like creating coins by diluting gold with copper, debt was another way of creating wealth. In this instance, the wealth was materialized with slips of paper that documented the debt, and the future held the promise of realizing the wealth, and probably earning interest as well. Legislation may have forbidden charging interests in interpersonal debt, which may explain why interest is not documented in writing; however, Martínez López-Cano (1995:54) provides examples that show that interests were sometimes charged on interpersonal loans.

Interethnic Debt

The question of community building and debt brings up an important and related question: do the inventories show that there was what we could call "interethnic debt," that is, debt between Spanish colonizers and Indigenous or Black people? An attempt at determining whether the people in relationships of debt to the decedents were Spanish (identified when their town of origin is mentioned) or other ethnicities will have to depend on the names of people and any information on ethnicity provided in the documents.[3] Out of a total of 263 instances of credit/debt recorded in all of the inventories there are

---

[3] The probate inventories often mention the person in debt to the decedent, but the names themselves make it a challenge to identify Indigenous people and others with certainty. Lockhart (1992:117–130) discusses naming patterns among Nahuas in the sixteenth century. His discussion makes clear some of the difficulties in determining ethnicity based on names alone. Soon after the conquest, many Indigenous people were baptized and they received a Spanish name, often without a surname. They sometimes had a Spanish first name, and an Indigenous second name. Lockhart lists many examples of Spanish-Nahuatl name combinations, such as Domingo Tecuetlaca (Domingo He Hurls People's Skirts Down), Gerónimo Tlaxcalcecec (Gerónimo Cold Tortilla), and Doña Ana Cihuanenequi (Doña Ana Imagines Herself a Woman). Of course, there are less humorous names in the list. By 1550, some Indigenous people were adopting Spanish surnames also, often Christian surnames in reference to saints. In spite of the adoption of Spanish surnames by some, the tradition of having a single name without a surname continued among others, making it difficult to identify Indigenous people in a list of names that includes last names also. Sometimes, "not infrequently," Lockhart (1992:122) writes, Spaniards referred to Indigenous commoners plus "Indio" to indicate the person's ethnicity, as is seen in the documents consulted. This is the clearest indication of ethnicity in the data set. The matter of naming is made complicated by class, as elite Nahuas sometimes adopted Spanish surnames held by conquerors and other prominent political and religious figures. Lockhart (1992:123) writes: "a Cortés was much more likely to be an Indian than not, and if he bore the "don" it was almost a certainty." "Don" (fem. "doña") was an honorific term associated with the highest Spanish nobility and adopted quickly by many Indigenous people who did not hesitate to use it because of its classy ring. In Spanish language documents, however, the term don appears infrequently applied to Indigenous men because scribes refused to use it in reference to them. Sometimes, the lack of a last name in Spanish documents reflects that Spanish scribes simply did not know how to write an Indigenous second name correctly.

fourteen items in which the scribe clearly mentioned Indigenous or Black people, or castas. There are two instances of credit with "negros," six with "yndios" (two of whom received two loans each), one involving a mulatto, one involving a Moor, and one involving a probable casta ("un tal moreno"). In addition, one case involves a woman from Tultepeque, who I assume is Indigenous because her name is not mentioned and because she is from Tultepeque. Another case involves a servant ("su criado") who I assume is either Indigenous, Black, or casta based on his social status and the lack of a first or last name. That makes it fourteen instances of debt involving anyone other than a Spaniard, out of 263 debts recorded in the documents, or 5 percent of all instances of debt by count.

However, this statistic may underestimate interethnic debt. The data reveal eight instances in which a first name appears for the person involved in the debt with the decedent, but there is no last name, as was frequently the case with Indigenous people. These people may have been Indigenous, or maybe the scribe simply did not write the last name of a Spaniard for other reasons that we may not know. There are also five cases in which the scribe wrote down the first name, followed by "algo" (something), which may indicate that the last name was a Nahuatl name and the scribe did not know how to write it. The lack of a second name may also mean that the decedent forgot the name or that the scribe did not write it for some other reason, making it difficult to tell with certainty whether the person was Indigenous or not. There were also two cases in which the term Doña appears, making it likely that the person was Indigenous (see Lockhart 1992:123). Finally, there were eleven cases in which the person was not mentioned by name. It is impossible to tell whether the scribe simply did not know how to write the Indigenous person's name, or whether the person was Spanish and the decedent could not remember their name. The person's name each time was listed as "a woman," or somebody ("alguien"), or "un tal harriero" in reference to the person's occupation as a mule driver, or with a simple statement that they do not know the person's name. It is possible, but difficult to prove that these twenty-six cases are cases of interethnic debt. After all, they all fit the naming patterns discussed by Lockhart for Indigenous people in some ways. If they are cases of interethnic debt, we would have 40 cases out of 263 (or 15 percent of all cases of debt mentioned in the documents) in which there was interethnic debt in this data set.

Not all interethnic debt was credit in favor of the decedent: six out of the fourteen cases that are most likely interethnic debt are against the decedent.

Miguel Rodríguez, a tailor whose inventory was worth approximately 105,000 maravedís, owed money to a woman in Tultepeque. Unfortunately, the total worth of the other decedents who had interethnic debt was not calculated because their inventories lacked data on the type of gold used in their transactions or because there is no record of the auction of the decedents' belongings. Thus, it is difficult to know whether there is a correlation between wealth and interethnic debt. Among them, Lorenzo Hernández owed money to a mulatto. Juan de Oliva owed money to an Indigenous woman not because she had loaned money to him, but because he felt indebted to her for services she had done for him, unpaid, as the wife of his servant. Two loans made to one person, Salvador Márquez who owed money to an Indigenous man and a "man of black color." Finally, Rodrigo Ruano owed money to his own servant, who I assume was Indigenous or Black, based on his status as a servant (perhaps an incorrect assumption). Several of the instances of debt had to do with Spaniards prepaying other people for work to be done for them in the future. Alonso de Zapardiel (Cont. 203 N4R8) had prepaid at least one Indigenous person and one mestizo, and two other men, for services, and he provided details of the amount of gold he had loaned to them and declared that they had to pay it back after his death. Still, the data do not support the idea that interethnic credit may have been part of an attempt to create a relation of indebtedness that benefited only Spaniards.

The total credit in favor of the decedents in the fourteen cases that are most surely interethnic debt amounts to 40,138 maravedís, not counting the 50 fanegas of wheat. The total interethnic debt against the decedents adds up to 12,324 maravedís. Similar to the total debt in all of the documents, credit declared in favor of the decedent is significantly higher than debt against the decedent; however interethnic credit in favor of the decedent is 3.25 times greater than interethnic debt against the decedent. Earlier I reported that the total credit declared in favor of the decedents is fifteen times greater than the debt declared against them. In spite of the differences in these two ratios, it is clear that interethnic credit in favor of decedents far outstrips debt declared against them. It is simply a pattern in which Spanish colonizers are declaring credit in their favor as much as possible, and they were either reluctant to borrow from Indigenous or Black people or castas, or they were reluctant to declare those debts and pay them back.

In spite of the difficulties presented by the data, especially the difficulty in identifying ethnicity, some patterns are clear. First, debt was mostly between Spaniards, although it sometimes included other people. Roughly between

5 percent and 15 percent of the credit/debt in these documents, by count, are instances of interethnic debt. There may be more interethnic debt in the documents, but the naming patterns do not help identify it. When there was interethnic debt, the money owed was not significantly lower than debt between Spaniards.

An important question is whether the inventories of Indigenous and Black people, which are not part of this study, would reveal more interethnic debt than the inventories of Spanish colonizers. Lockhart (1992:182–185, 301–303) has studied the adoption of vocabulary related to debt among Nahuas, and argues that during the sixteenth century, the vocabulary reveals "the formation of concepts without exact parallels in pre-conquest times (though not without precedent in a general fashion)" (Lockhart 1992:183). The loans found in the documents Lockhart consulted are typically small (between 10 pesos and 1 peso [Lockhart 1992:184], or 5,000 to 272 maravedís). Lockhart argues that the changes in vocabulary and the associated concepts of borrowing and debt, and the appearance of debt in Nahuatl documents are evidence of the penetration of loans and debt into Indigenous society to a level that would affect such conceptual and practical changes. The colonial Nahuatl vocabulary related to debt studied by Millhauser (2017b:267–268) reveals sophisticated distinctions between loans, loans for profit, collateral, debtors, lenders, paying one debt with another debt, and many other concepts related to debt. Millhauser argues that among Indigenous people, the main innovation in the colonial period was lending money rather than staple goods.

Summing Up

The data on the economic lives of these thirty-nine Spanish colonizers, in spite of their challenges, omissions, and ambiguities, reveal interesting patterns. First, colonizers used several kinds of coin, and even invented some of their coins, creating an economic world with coins of different value. They were familiar with the use of different kinds of coin, and used them as needed. When they found little gold in New Spain, they simply created new alloys to stretch the value of gold. They altered the material properties of the things they were using as coins. Later, they would complain about the variety of coins and the difficulties in using and exchanging them. By creating new alloys, they really created part of their wealth.

A second important finding is that the people whose inventories I have studied were generally poor. If we place the value of their inventories in the categories formulated by Rodríguez Vázquez (1995) for the people in Seville, most decedents in this data set would fit in the category of popular classes, or poor people. Still, their wealth varied significantly, ranging from 6,281 maravedís to 6,704,930 maravedís, making for a highly varied lot of colonizers. Many of them lived in debt, although some claimed not to have any debt at all. As a group, their debt made up approximately half of their total worth. They came to the Americas most likely in search of wealth, some of them perhaps lured by stories of gold and riches. Instead of simply finding gold, they ended up creating relations of debt with one another. They sometimes entered relations of debt with Indigenous and Black people, castas, and Moors. The data indicate that at least 5 percent of the cases of debt in the documents consulted were cases of interethnic debt. It is likely, but difficult to prove, that 15 percent (or even more) of the cases of debt were interethnic debt, based on the naming patterns in the documents. Therefore, interethnic debt brought together Spaniards and others in socioeconomic bonds. Even when using data that most likely underestimate the frequency of interethnic debt, it is clear that economic interaction between Spaniards and other people were not limited to the cold and quick transactions in the marketplace or to tribute, but they also involved the bonds of debt in all of their positive and negative aspects. Debt accounts for a much higher proportion of people's wealth than money in these inventories. Thus, people created wealth not by finding gold, but by creating wealth out of copper and paper, through the creation of debt and different kinds of coin.

The ways that people actively shaped money and debt in colonial Mexico can build on the literature on the functions of money in important ways. At the start of the chapter, I mentioned the three functions of money discussed by many scholars: measuring value, facilitating exchange, and storing wealth. If one focuses on the active role that people played in colonial Mexico when using and manipulating money, the uses of money were much broader. Colonizers used money to measure, stretch, and negotiate value, in part by creating coins of different value in spite of the availability of media of exchange in Mexico. They also used money to facilitate exchange with some people but also tried to leave others outside of spheres of exchange by not allowing them to use certain kinds of coin. They sometimes even tried to force people to use some kinds of media of exchange and not others. They sometimes used money to store surplus wealth, even though these inventories show that they were not storing much money at all. They sometimes tried to create and manipulate social connections with others by creating relationships of credit/debt. I would argue that money does not really have functions. People use money with different goals in mind, some of which are economic and some of which have social aspects to them.

Now we know a little about the colonizers whose inventories I discuss in this book. Ironically, I have discussed the last aspect of anyone's life that one tends to know today upon meeting people: how much money they have. We also know a little about their occupations and where they were from. In the next chapter, we will learn more about their material worlds, starting from the built environment that existed when the conquistadors entered Tenochtitlan, and focusing on the houses where colonizers lived.

2

How to Build Houses

This chapter focuses on the largest scale of the material worlds of Spanish colonizers: the built environment. Recent comments by scholars who study sixteenth-century Mexico City inspire this chapter. First, Barbara Mundy, in her excellent volume on the transformation of Tenochtitlan into Mexico City, reviews some of the literature on Indigenous government and politics in colonial Mexico. She observes that in spite of the focus on Indigenous government, "no one has focused extensively on the role of Indigenous peoples in shaping the built environment and lived space in sixteenth-century Mexico City" (Mundy 2015:15). Second, Ivonne del Valle (2009) observes that early colonial chroniclers sometimes wrote as if the canals that crisscrossed the city were part of the natural landscape. Instead of recognizing those canals as feats of Indigenous engineering, the Spanish often saw them merely as natural features that brought canoes into the city. In this chapter, I examine the role of Indigenous people in building colonial Mexico City, not simply as a source of labor or brute force, but also as providing intellectual work, engineering skills, and knowledge of architecture. As I will show, Indigenous people were in charge of building the houses where colonizers lived, playing a stronger role than has been recognized in shaping the material worlds of Spanish colonizers.

Scholars studying Spanish colonialism have long seen an important relationship between power and two aspects of the material world that I consider in this chapter: the layout of cities, and domestic architecture (e.g., Amaral 2017; Deagan 1983, 2001; Jamieson 2000a, 2000b; Low 1995; Mundy 2015; Nemser 2017; Therrien 2016; Voss 2005). Many scholars have focused on whether the grid pattern and the central location of plazas and churches in colonial Latin American cities are a result of Spanish design and colonial policy, or a continuation of Indigenous building traditions (Low 1995; Mier y Terán Rocha 2005; Ortiz Crespo 2006; Sanz Camañes 2004:33–38; Wagner et al. 2013). The link to power in this literature is related not just to who made the decisions on how to build the city, but also to the idea that the organization of the cities was a way of creating and imposing order among the

How to Make a New Spain. Enrique Rodríguez-Alegría, Oxford University Press. © Enrique Rodríguez-Alegría 2023.
DOI: 10.1093/oso/9780197682296.003.0003

population. Archaeologists who have studied architecture in Latin America view the built environment as a product of the struggle for power (Zarankin and Funari 2020).

The literature on domestic architecture has posited different ways of relating houses to power. Some scholars have seen domestic architecture, especially the houses of colonizers, as an expression of power, or a symbol of ethnic identification with Spain. In this approach, scholars argue that colonizers used Spanish styles and construction materials in part to show that they belonged among a powerful class (e.g., Deagan 1983, 2001). This approach often focuses on house facades and the outward appearance of houses (Jamieson 2000b:10). Other scholars have gone beyond the symbolic aspects of houses and studied their economic value, the varied construction materials used, the size and shapes of houses, the organization of production of architecture, and the way that space was used and controlled within houses. The value of houses can be related to economic status, and perhaps even social status and strategies of display. The variability in materials used can be related to the presence or absence of centralized control of house construction and to the management of labor and resource extraction. The size and shape of houses can also be related to economic status and the presence or absence of centralized control, and to the strategies of display of the owners. Finally, the use of space in houses can be related to the desire for privacy, attempts at controlling behavior, and the segregation of people by status and by activities they perform (e.g., Jamieson 2000a, 2000b; Voss 2005, 2008a).

Scholars who have drawn attention to the relationship between power and the varied aspects of houses and house construction have followed different approaches, both theoretically and methodologically. For example, Jamieson (2004) emphasized the way that house plans constrained and encouraged movement and access through space within houses. Voss (2005), on the other hand, emphasized variation in construction materials, the organization of production of architecture, and house size and enclosure. Still, what these approaches have in common is that they do not consider houses only as symbol of power, but instead, they study architecture to obtain clues about how people managed labor in house construction, about how people managed the use of space, and about homogeneity, variation, and control over symbolic expressions in architecture.

In this chapter, I emphasize that as people managed construction projects or participated in them, they often participated in a division of labor, in which some people make decisions, others execute those decisions, others learn, and some do specialized tasks. As they worked, they all forged part of their identities as laborers, members of construction teams, leaders, subalterns, equals, etc. Participating in these construction projects also meant participating in building a society of people engaged with the materials of construction, and with one another, and there were dimensions of power at play. In short, while building houses, people also built their social worlds.

The archaeological remains of the houses of colonizers yield some clues about who participated in construction projects and what their participation meant in colonial society. The work of the PAU illuminates our understanding of the early colonial city in at least two main ways. First, it provides an understanding of changes in the use of space at a small scale. Instead of studying entire sections of the city, at this smaller scale we can see how the space beneath contemporary architecture was used through time. Second, the work of the PAU provides information on the construction techniques used in pre-Conquest and colonial buildings and the aesthetic aspects of different buildings. Studying the buildings excavated, the materials used to build walls and floors, the types of surface finish used, the color of the surface finish, and other details can provide ideas of changes in aesthetics and engineering technology in the conquest period.

I begin this chapter with a brief history of how people built Tenochtitlan, the great city of the Mexica, followed by a discussion of the different patterns of change and continuity as people transformed Tenochtitlan into Mexico City in the colonial period. Many scholars have discussed the layout of the city and the major changes that took place after the conquest, and I present here only a brief summary. The main contribution of the chapter will come later, when I address the architecture and engineering of the houses of colonizers. I compile information on the architecture of the many early colonial houses excavated in Mexico City to address questions of the aesthetics and engineering of early colonial houses. Were the early colonial houses Spanish in appearance? Or were they Indigenous in terms of engineering and aesthetics? Thanks to a wealth of archaeological data, we can enter the material world of colonial Mexico City with a renewed understanding of the built environment.

The City in the Swamp

The largest scale I use to study Tenochtitlan/Mexico City is the scale of the city and its surrounding environment. At this scale, the city emerges as an epic struggle between humans and nature. The setting is an internal drainage basin in central Mexico, and a system of lakes and marshes that grew during the rainy season (June-September) and became interconnected, and then shrank during the long dry season (October-May) to become five different, smaller lakes (Figure 2.1). The lakes were shallow, and the water was saline

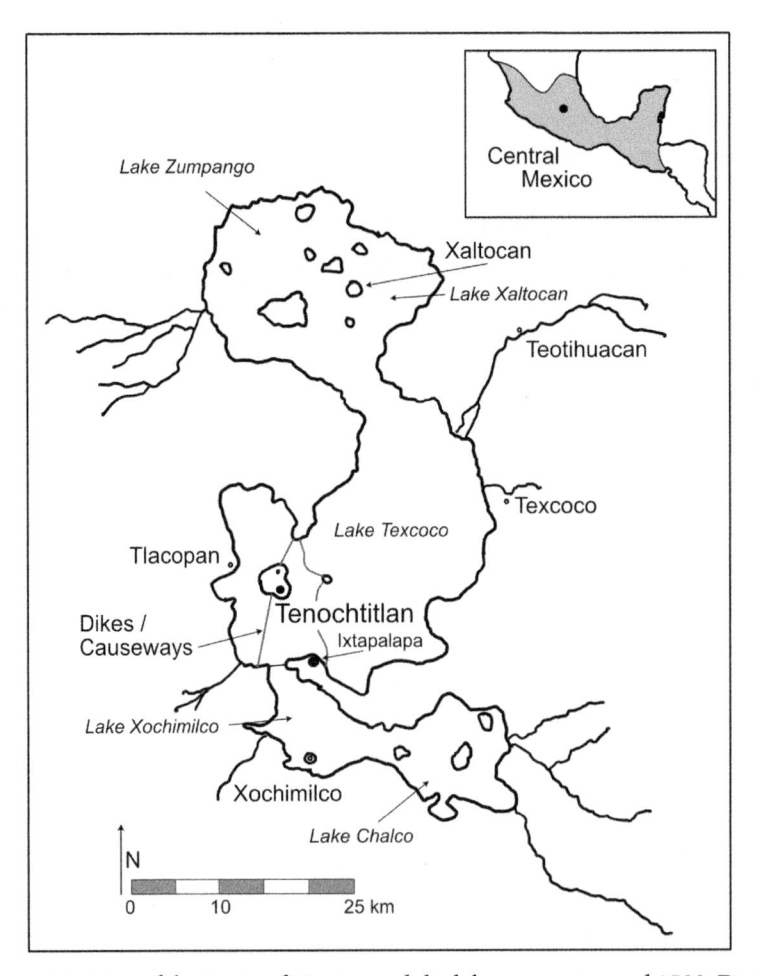

Figure 2.1 Map of the Basin of Mexico and the lake system around 1500. Drawn by Samuel Wilson.

(Millhauser 2017a). In a small island in the middle of this lake system, people decided to settle and slowly they built their city.

The natural environment presented opportunities, including water for agriculture, household tasks, and transportation; abundant flora and fauna; salt; and many other resources (McClung de Tapia and Martínez Yrizar 2017; Millhauser 2017a; Morehart 2017). It also presented challenges, including floods, salty water, and limited land for settling, among others. The water of the surrounding lakes was too salty for human consumption, although it could be used for household tasks, and for obtaining salt (Millhauser 2017a; Sanders 2008). People brought fresh water from a spring in the nearby city of Chapultepec, for which they built a great aqueduct that transported the water into the middle of the city (Berdan 2014:77–79; Sanders 2008:68). Rojas has described the city and how humans engaged with its watery milieu quite vividly, when he states that the city was created by "building artificial islands, and connecting them with channels and bridges in an engineering feat that would become one of the city's highlights: streets alongside canals, streets that served as canals, and packed earth streets" (Rojas 2017:219–220; Figure 2.2). People kept building the city, rock by rock, enlarging its land area, and building canals and other features that helped control the surrounding lakes. They used canoes for transporting goods, including food and water, throughout the city. They also built large causeways that connected the island city to the shores of the lakes to the north, south, and west (Sanders 2008; Figure 2.1). To manage water in and around the city, the people of Tenochtitlan built dikes, including among them a great dike that protected the eastern side of the city, commonly known as Ahuitzotl's Dike, after the king who was in power during its construction (Mundy 2015:74–75; Sanders 2008).

By the time the Spanish arrived in 1519, the city covered an area estimated between 13 to 15 km². The population of the city is a matter of debate. Estimates range between a low of 60,000 to as many as 1 million people (Rojas 2017:219–220), and beyond such a wide range, there is little agreement among scholars about the size of the population. Lourdes Márquez Morfín and Rebecca Storey (2017:191) state that "the most popular estimate is Calnek's (1974) figure of a residential density of 12,000 per km . . . which would result in a population of about 150,000 to 200,000" for Tenochtitlan. Sanders believes that at the time, Tenochtitlan was one of the ten biggest cities in the world (Sanders 2008:68). Thus, the environment presented challenges and opportunities, and human ingenuity transformed that environment into a great city that grew to be the densely populated capital of an empire.

Figure 2.2 Detail of mural by Diego Rivera at the Palacio Nacional,
Mexico City.

Space and the City

Most of the city, approximately three-quarters of its area, consisted of house
lots and adjacent agricultural plots surrounded by canals. These were the
house lots where most commoners lived and worked (Calnek 2003; Sanders
2008:81). Their houses consisted of several structures for living, storage,
cooking, and conducting all sorts of daily activities. Most activities, including
craft production, took place in patios that were surrounded by the different
structures of the house (Sanders 2008).

At the center of the city, where the Centro Histórico is today, was the ma-
jestic sacred precinct of Tenochtitlan. The sacred precinct is best known
today for the Templo Mayor, the main temple of the Mexica, excavated as
part of one of the great urban archaeological projects in the world in terms of
the monumentality of discoveries and the incredible preservation of remains
(Gallardo Parrodi 2017; Matos Moctezuma 1988). In the fifteenth century,
the sacred precinct was surrounded on four sides by a platform. The platform measured approximately 340m on its north to south sides, and 360m

on its east to west sides. It had walls, balustrades, and stairways on both the outside and inside, and three or four entryways that helped control access to the precinct (López Austin and López Luján 2017:606). Archaeologists have found portions of that wall, as will be discussed later. Inside the wall, there were dozens of buildings, with the Templo Mayor being the largest (Figure 2.3). The first construction of the Temple was small in comparison to a lot of the later architecture, but the Temple was expanded at least thirteen times in 130 years by rulers who used the architecture to display their power and to celebrate successful war campaigns (López Austin and López Luján 2017:610). At least five of those reconstructions consisted of building a larger pyramid that enveloped the previous temple entirely (Matos Moctezuma

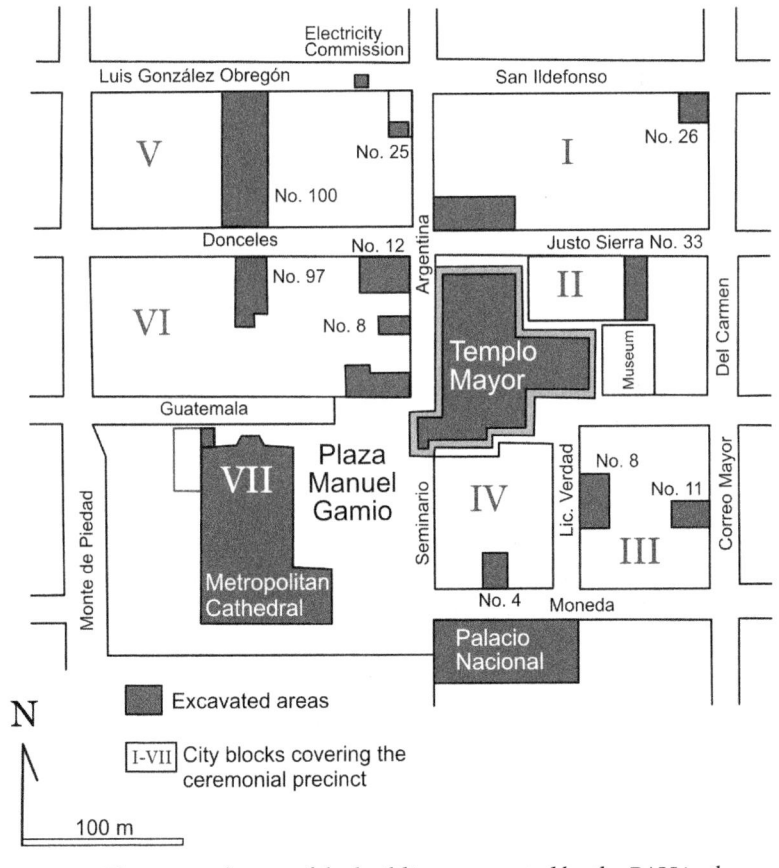

Figure 2.3 Plan view of some of the buildings excavated by the PAU in the sacred precinct. Redrawn from Matos Moctezuma 1999:12 by Samuel Wilson.

1988), and that by the time the Spanish arrived, the Templo Mayor was about 45 meters tall (López Austin and López Luján 2017:605). Many other buildings surrounded the Templo Mayor. Scholars most often cite Sahagún's claim that there were seventy-eight "towers" or buildings inside the sacred precinct, although historical sources mention anywhere from forty to seventy-eight buildings (López Austin and López Luján 2017:606). López Austin and López Luján (2017:607) provide a concise description of the area:

> The interior space of nearly 20 ha. was occupied by pyramids of all sizes crowned by temples; *momoztli* (small ritual platforms); priestly quarters; oratories (areas devoted to fasting and penance by the most important people); *calmecac* (temple-schools for the nobility); *tlachtli* (ballcourts); *tzompantli* (palisades where the skulls of sacrificial victims were displayed); *tlachcoalco* (storehouses where weapons acquired sacred powers); *Yopilcalco* (the temple where visiting foreign sovereigns stayed when they traveled to Tenochtitlan to witness the great ceremonies); ritual monoliths like the *techcatl, temalacatl,* and *cuauhxicalli* (the sacrifice and the offering of blood and hearts); and springs and other replicas of the sacred geography (including a grove), all separated by wide plazas or smaller patios.

Moctezuma had two palaces (known as the old palace and the new palace) in the heart of the sacred precinct. The buildings mentioned provided the setting for many of the encounters, ceremonies, feasts, battles, and massacres that took place during the Spanish conquest.

The main plaza has been an important feature of the city, from pre-Hispanic times, through the colonial period, until today. Before the conquest, the main plaza served many civic, religious, social, and economic functions, including that of a *tianguis* or marketplace. The main marketplace in Tenochtitlan rivaled that of Tlatelolco in terms of size and importance, and they were known for the endless variety of goods sold there, including all kinds of produce, cooked food, pottery, stone and stone tools, cloth and clothing, luxury goods, gold, animal skins, shells, silver, copper ornaments, pigments, and many other goods. People brought produce, water, salt, and other goods to the southern end of the main plaza by canoe, and sold them right there in the tianguis (Matos Moctezuma 2012). Although archaeological evidence of marketplaces can be difficult (but not impossible) to find, given that such places were routinely cleaned, there is some archaeological evidence that confirms that a marketplace was located in the main plaza.

Excavations have unearthed two stone carvings with the glyph for tianguis in the main plaza of Tenochtitlan (Barrera Rodríguez et al. 2012), although the glyph that can also be associated with precious greenstones and lordly houses (Mundy 2015:82).

Some Traits of Mexica Architecture

A combination of ethnohistoric and archaeological data can help reconstruct some traits of Mexica architecture, whether domestic or monumental. Ethnohistoric documents remain the main source of information on houses in Tenochtitlan, given that most of the residential areas remain buried under the modern city. Still, archaeological remains excavated in several sites in the basin of Mexico can give a broader idea of architectural and engineering traditions at the time (De Lucia 2017). These traits can help us understand how people in colonial Mexico City used Mexica engineering and architecture when building the houses of Spanish colonizers. I focus here on the materials used by the Mexica, on construction techniques, and on finishing techniques, rather than on overall architectural form and decorative elements and designs.

The materials used to build the houses of commoners among the Mexica included wood, adobe, thatch for building roofs, and stone. They sometimes used wood for building walls, roofs, and for house foundations. Adobe was probably the most common material used to build house walls. The floors of houses were most often dirt floors, or made of plaster (De Lucia 2017; Valero de García Lascuráin 1991:61–86). Sahagún (1981:272, Book 11, Chap.XII) describes a variety of houses of commoners, although his descriptions are mostly value judgments ("It is a little squat, low, crude, unfit, unfinished; small and not finished; a humble house") rather than precise descriptions of the architecture and engineering. Still, his descriptions are useful in understanding the value placed on the houses made for colonizers, especially when compared to the descriptions he provides for elite houses.

The materials used in building Mexica architecture in the sacred precinct, including elite residences and palaces as well as pyramids, were varied. Stone is the material most associated with monumental sculpture in Mesoamerica, and archaeologists have observed that the Mexica used basalt, andesite, and tezontle. Tezontle is a highly porous and oxidized volcanic rock, often seen in red and black varieties in Mexica architecture (Viart Muños and Martínez

Meza 2003:121). Given the high porosity of this rock, it is lightweight but hard, and it remains to date a commonly used material in construction in Mexico. The Mexica used basalt blocks and andesite slabs to pave their floors. In one of the lots excavated by the PAU, Argentina #15, excavations revealed a Mexica floor made of andesite that was then covered with fill during a remodeling episode. The Mexica laid out another floor on top of the fill, this time using basalt, which the authors claim was better quality than the andesite (Barrera Rodríguez and Rivas García 2003:168).

Sometimes the Mexica covered floors made of pink andesite or basalt blocks with a layer of well-polished stucco (Barrera Rodríguez 2006; Viart Muñoz and Martínez Meza 2003). They also used stucco to finish walls and water boxes, and often painted it a distinctive red color (Hinojosa Hinojosa 2003:23). Finally, wood was an important construction material. The Mexica often used pilings or stakes made of wood as part of the foundation of buildings or in the interior of construction walls. They arranged pilings vertically and parallel to each other to support walls and floors and distribute the weight of structures to manage subsiding and shifting in a city with such a high water table (Sanders 2008; Valero de García Lascuráin 1991:80; Figure 2.4). Sahagún (1981:270, Book 11, Chap.XII) describes the palaces of Mexica lords and the combination of materials used to build them, in clear contrast with the description of commoner houses cited above: "It is not just an ordinary place; it is in some way good, fine. It is something embellished, a product of care . . . the product of carved stone, of sculptured stone, plastered, plastered in all places: a plastered house; a red house."

To build their monumental constructions of stone, the Mexica often laid out dressed stones: stones with one worked side facing out of the structure. They joined the stones with plaster, concealing the unworked side of the stones inside the structure. Different types of Mexica buildings (platforms, monumental walls, and others) were solid constructions, and people used different techniques to build them. A technique known as *entortado* was common. It consisted of laying out a layer of mortar made of lime and sand, then laying pieces of tezontle on top of it, and repeating the layering process several times before covering with a façade (Barrera Rodríguez 2006:280; Barrera Rodríguez and Rivas García 2003:161). Another construction technique consisted of making adobe bricks and joining them with a mixture of clay and lime (Barrera Rodríguez 2006:285). A third widely used technique is known as the *cajones* system. This stress-inducing name is derived from the Spanish word *cajón* (pl. cajones), which means box. It consisted of building

Figure 2.4 Pilings in front of the Templo Mayor Museum. Photo by author.

square boxes using stone and mortar, and then filling up the boxes with loose rocks and more mortar. In the mixed rocks used to fill out the boxes, archaeologists have sometimes found rocks that had been used in the facades of previous constructions, evidence of recycling of construction materials in the pre-conquest era (Barrera Rodríguez 2006:279; Hinojosa Hinojosa and Barrera Rodríguez 2003:149).

The Mexica are known for having constructed, destroyed, and reconstructed their buildings repeatedly. The best-known example of construction and reconstruction is the Templo Mayor. The Mexica built and expanded it several times, in what are typically considered seven construction phases (López Austin and López Luján 2017; Matos Moctezuma 1988). To accommodate new construction, sometimes the Mexica demolished some buildings, whether completely or partially, as seen in the excavations in the sacred precinct (Barrera Rodríguez and Rivas García 2003:164). Sometimes, to prepare for new construction, they laid down thick layers of fill. For example, in González Obregón 25, archaeologists unearthed three pre-Hispanic floors. One of the floors is separated from a previous floor by no less than 1.3m of fill (Barrera Rodríguez 2006:279; Figure 2.5). The motive behind building new architecture sometimes included preparation for state religious and political ritual. Mexica kings commissioned enhancements and renovations of the Templo Mayor as part of their kingly ceremonies. Religious ceremonies and reconstructions of the Templo Mayor affected other buildings too. Builders partially destroyed some of the buildings underneath the Plaza Gamio, right in front of the Templo Mayor, to expand the forecourt of the Templo Mayor. Also, in Donceles 97, archaeologists found a structure that was demolished and then covered with rubble to facilitate construction of a new structure that corresponded to Phase VI of the

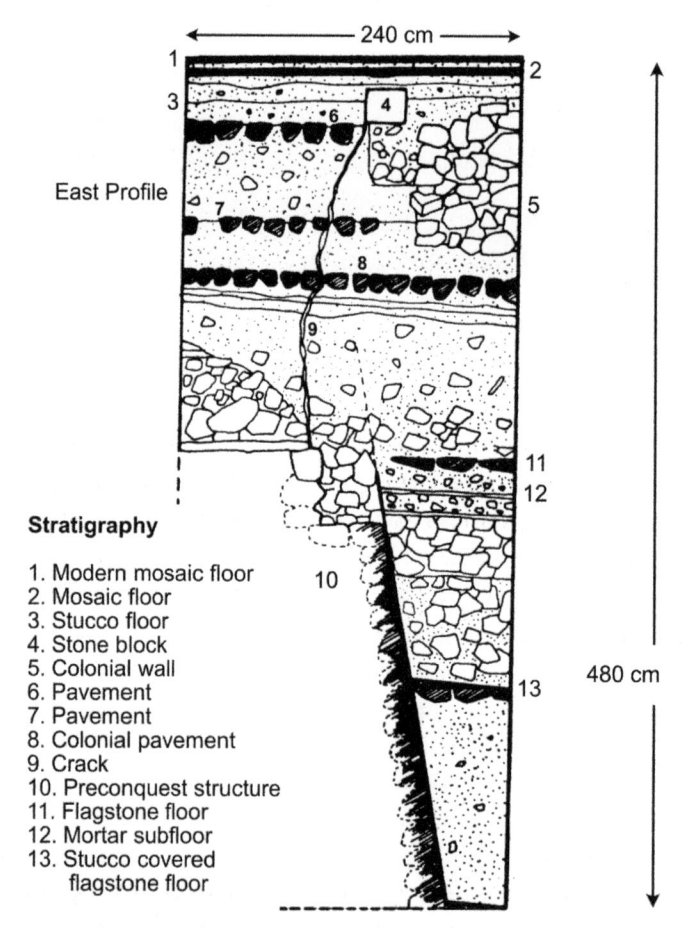

Figure 2.5 Profile of excavation in González Obregón #25, Block V, Room 3, Unit 1. Redrawn by Samuel Wilson after Barrera Rodríguez 2006:278. Used by permission from the Instituto Nacional de Antropología e Historia.

Templo Mayor construction. Perhaps this remodeling episode was directly related to the kingly ceremonies at the time, although this is a matter of speculation (Barrera Rodríguez and Martínez Meza 2010, Barrera Rodríguez et al. 2012).

Other times, the Mexica began destruction and remodeling projects to manage flooding. People raised floors, even several meters higher than previous constructions, in a way that suggests they were trying to escape the waters of the lakes surrounding the city (Hinojosa Hinojosa and Barrera Rodríguez 2003:153). Finally, the Mexica faced the same problems of subsiding, turning, inclination, and cracking on the sides of their buildings that the PAU addresses today. The engineering problems of today have been present in Mexico City for centuries. Some of the architecture underneath the Metropolitan Cathedral shows cracked facades, and it also shows that the Mexica were aware of changes in orientation as buildings subsided and turned, and they corrected the orientation of buildings as they laid out new architecture on top (Barrera Rivera 1999).

There is little information on how construction was organized before the Spanish conquest, but among the many specialists described in the *Florentine Codex*, Sahagún (1950–1982 Book 10, Chapter VIII) describes good and bad carpenters and masons. Among the qualities of good masons he includes the ability to cut stone, work the stone diligently, make arches, draw the plan of a house, make good foundations, and build a house correctly. Among the qualities of good carpenters, he includes cutting wood well, making sure that it is well measured, and laying out wooden beams correctly. Sahagún's comments are of somewhat limited usefulness to understand preconquest masons and carpenters. He wrote them decades after the Spanish conquest and the specializations on construction arts appear alongside some specializations that are uniquely colonial, such as ironworking. However, his comments are still useful in establishing that there were Indigenous specialists involved in working stone and wood for construction, that they could be well-trained and expert enough to do a good job, and that they were skilled enough so that we should not think of them as just brute force. I speculate that the unskilled masons and carpenters worked on commoner houses, although perhaps all commoners worked on their own houses, whereas the highly skilled ones worked on elite houses and palaces. But I acknowledge that my speculation is only based on the quality of the results rather than well-documented knowledge of the division of labor at the time.

After 1521

On 1521, after the Spanish conquest, the city was partially destroyed. Some buildings suffered much damage, as did some of the infrastructure that helped manage water and flooding in the city. During the conquest and soon thereafter, conquerors demolished most of the Templo Mayor, including the construction phase that could be seen in 1521 and some of the previous construction phases that had been buried beneath it. The only construction phases of the Templo Mayor that did not suffer damage were the first and second phases, the ones protected by at least five larger temple constructions on top (Matos Moctezuma 1988). Colonizers would soon refer to Tenochtitlan as Mexico City, the capital of New Spain, and the main destination for Spanish colonizers in the Americas.

Still, Barbara Mundy argues that Tenochtitlan remained largely an indigenous city in spite of the conquest and the influx of Spaniards into the city. Claims that city was destroyed during the conquest are exaggerated: "while the Conquest changed an indigenous New World capital . . . it did not destroy indigenous Tenochtitlan, either as an ideal, as a built environment, or as an indigenous population center. Instead, indigenous Tenochtitlan lived on" (Mundy 2015:3). Many of the Indigenous temples were still visible and in use for Indigenous rituals for decades after the conquest (Toussaint 1956:15). Many of the religious sculptures of the Mexica were visible and formed a part of the daily life of colonizers after the conquest. Archaeologists have found vivid evidence of it in the form of two monumental sculptures that were found in an archaeological context surrounded by Chinese porcelain and majolica (Chapter 4) at Donceles 97. The sculptures depicted the Mexica deities Xiuhtecuhtli, lord of turquoise, and Mictlantecuhtli, lord of the underworld (Barrera Rodríguez and López Arenas 2008).

The Spanish decided to settle mostly in the center of the city, in the area occupied by the sacred precinct. Their decision to settle in Tenochtitlan was controversial even among colonizers. Some opposed living there for different reasons, including that they had partially destroyed the city during the conquest, and that the city presented problems of flooding. Transportation by canoe was also a challenge for people who were not used to the marshy conditions of Tenochtitlan. The city also lacked much land for cattle grazing, and it could be surrounded and sieged by Indigenous people, just like the Spanish had done to the Mexica (Gibson 1964:368; Kubler 1948:69; Marroqui 1969:21–24; Valero de García Lascuráin 1991:141–144). Initially,

Hernán Cortés himself was among the people who thought that nobody should live in Mexico City, but only a few months after the conquest he began to see some advantages that made the city attractive (Kubler 1948:70). The city was already a great city, and conquistadors had been bedazzled by its canals and beauty. People brought revenue and food into the city every day, in part due to the existing tribute system and in part because of its marketplace. Furthermore, Cortés thought that taking over Tenochtitlan would be a powerful psychological blow to the Mexica and discourage rebellions, as Indigenous people saw their city taken over by others who must have been more powerful (de Gante 1954:45; Martínez 1988; Valero de García Lascuráin 1991:143). Christians had a long tradition of settling by the ruins and towns of Moors in Spain, in an effort to identify with the grandeur of former seats of power (Kubler 1948:70). In fact, Cortés himself took residence in Moctezuma's palaces. The palaces also housed the viceroys and the audiences of New Spain until 1562 (Toussaint 1956:16), placing the most powerful colonizers squarely in spaces built by Indigenous people and with Indigenous aesthetics. By 1522, Indigenous workers were hard at work in rebuilding the destroyed parts of the city, and scholars tend to remember the masses of Indigenous workers that made up the work force (Kubler 1948:71; Martínez 1988), but to overlook the skills and knowledge they provided.

Drawing the Colonial City Plan

The reconstruction, and especially the creation of the historic center, took advantage of the layout of the existing city. Many scholars today mention that Cortés assigned the task of drawing the plan of the new city to Alonso García Bravo, also credited with being the first city planner ("urbanista") (Toussaint 1956:1). But the emphasis on García Bravo and his contributions to the shape and plan of Mexico City are overstated. Scholars have even pointed out that the master plan of the city had already been laid out by the time that he was brought in to serve as the city planner (Low 1995:757). Instead, I argue that the city plan is the result of Indigenous work and planning, both before and after the conquest. The generous credit offered to García Bravo for planning the city, and the trivialization of Indigenous people who participated in designing the city began during the conquest, and they are the result of how things are remembered, expressed, forgotten, and omitted in historical documents.

In 1561, García Bravo himself claimed credit for having drawn up the plan of the city (Kubler 1948:73). Over eighty years after the conquest, in 1604, a second round of historical documents conspired with García Bravo's claim to support the idea that he was the main urban planner and the big man in this story. The documents record the testimony of several residents of Mexico City who wanted to prove García Bravo's achievements, in support of doña Violante de la Serna Guzmán, a descendant of García Bravo.[1] Guzmán, of course, stood to benefit from any recognition of García Bravo's legacy. One witness after another claimed that García Bravo designed the layout of Mexico City all by himself and without anyone's help. They repeatedly deny that anyone else was involved in the process. Nobody mentioned Indigenous people at all, given that it was in nobody's interest to give them any recognition for their work (Mantecón Navasal 1956).

The witnesses served to prove the merits of García Bravo, in a manner similar to a *probanza de mérito* or proof of merit, a genre of documents that served to document or claim achievements and contributions in front of the crown. People used probanzas to petition for different rewards, including status, coats of arms, grants of labor, and others (Restall 2003:12). Those who wrote this sort of claim often exaggerated their own actions and contributions and left out the contributions of others, trying to obtain the biggest reward possible from the crown. The exaggerations contained have contributed to the creation of big men, including Christopher Columbus and Hernán Cortés, and of many myths of the conquest that upon further analysis can be understood to be the result of processes and of the actions of many people, including Indigenous people and Africans (Restall 2003). The documents from 1604 are part of this process of exaggeration in colonial Mexico to obtain social and economic rewards.

Scholars have found evidence that at least three others helped García Bravo. The first, and apparently the only one mentioned by name, is Bernardino Vázquez de Tapia, another Spaniard. In addition, two Indigenous men were part of the team of urban planners (Mier y Terán Rocha 2005:82; Sodi Miranda 1994:17), although I have not managed to find any sources that mention them by name or offer any other information about them. The anonymity of the Indigenous contributors helps trivialize their participation.

---

[1] In 1596, doña Violante de la Serna Guzmán married licenciado Pedro Martínez. In 1604, Martínez sought what could be considered a retroactive dowry. As part of this dowry, he wanted to benefit from any titles or rights associated with his wife's ancestors. The witnesses testified to provide evidence of the achievements of her ancestors, including those of García Bravo (Toussaint 1956:7).

I would argue that they were vital to the design of Mexico City and perhaps they were the most knowledgeable members of the team associated with García Bravo. As locals, they must have had a more intimate and thorough knowledge of the city than the two colonizers, and they contributed their knowledge to the design of Mexico City. I admit that I do not have proof of how much they contributed, but given the insistence that García Bravo completed the map of Mexico City without any help that is found in the documents, I believe that the memory of García Bravo's overwhelming role in drawing the map of Mexico City is greatly exaggerated.

In 1933, José R. Benítez wrote in disbelief that nobody remembered Alonso García Bravo and his significant contributions to the history of Mexico City. At a time in which history focused squarely on big men, Benítez did not see any problem with not mentioning the other men who participated in planning the city. Almost 100 years later, I write in disbelief that nobody remembers the other men, two of them Indigenous, who contributed their expertise into the design of Mexico City. My impulse is not one of creating big men. Instead, I am interested in understanding the contribution of Indigenous people to the formation of the city, because it can have significant implications on how we view colonialism and power in the sixteenth century. I argue that Indigenous people were the vital intellectual force in creating the urban plan, before and after the conquest, and finding the Indigenous folks who worked alongside García Bravo can support the idea.

One can easily see the Indigenous contributions to the urban plan. The colonial city maintained several important aspects of the Mexica capital. It kept the city's orientation to the cardinal directions, with streets running north to south and east to west. The maintained orientation should not be a surprise, given how challenging it would have been to make significant changes to the city in that respect: the easiest way to lay down streets would be to put them where there were already streets. Historical documents indicate that colonizers often used the streets that were already in existence. Tovar de Teresa (1985:10, note 21) has consulted over 1,792 documents pertaining to the streets that were mapped and named by García Bravo and his team. Based on those documents he has argued that García Bravo named only ten streets (Table 2.1). Of those, Tovar de Teresa argues that three already existed before the conquest, and another two were laid out adjacent to Moctezuma's Palaces, which became Cortes' houses in the years following the conquest. It is not clear whether he believed the other streets named by García Bravo

Table 2.1   Streets named by Alonso García Bravo and his team.

Sixteenth century name	Modern name	Comments
Del Agua	Acequia	In existence before the conquest
Los Ballesteros	Cuba and Allende	
Los Bergantines	Guatemala	
De la Carrera de los Caballos (later San José el Real)	Isabel la Católica	Adjacent to Moctezuma's palaces, which became Hernan Cortes' houses.
De la Celada	Venustiano Carranza	
Donceles (later known as de Chavarría, then Monte Alegre, Cordobanes, Canos, and Puerta Falsa de San Andrés)	Donceles	
De Diego Orgaz	nknown	
Ixtapalapan (later divided into two parts, with the southern part named Flamencos, then Porta Coeli, del Hospital de Jesús, Rastro, and San Antonio Abad, and the northern part named Seminario and Reloj)	Pino Suárez, Palacio Nacional, and Seminario	In existence before the conquest
San Francisco	Madero	Adjacent to Moctezuma's palaces, which became Hernan Cortes' houses.
Tacuba	Tacuba	In existence before the conquest

were in existence also before the conquest, or whether García Bravo and his team designed them entirely anew.

Some modern scholars have argued that the chosen orientation of the streets was as an attempt by colonizers to impose order on an Indigenous world. Others claim that the straight streets and their orientation, as well as the presence of plazas that were integrated into the urban design, should be seen at least in part as a continuation of their pre-conquest design (Low 1995:449; Rodríguez-Alegría 2017:662–664; Tovar de Teresa 1985:17). Wagner and his colleagues (2013:41) even suggest that plazas in Spain may have had their origin instead in New Spain, reversing the direction of influence over the layout of cities. Archaeological remains may help examine and give nuance to arguments about continuity in street layout and orientation. In maps and photos published by the archaeologists working in Mexico

City (e.g., Barrera Rivera and Domínguez 2018; Matos Moctezuma et al. 2017) one can see that the temples of the Mexica sometimes lay, at least partially, under modern streets. The correspondence between Mexica, colonial, and modern streets and temples could be studied further, taking advantage of the archaeological evidence to understand continuity, change, and how human action has changed the layout of the city through time.

The Use of Space: Segregation, Appropriation, Continuity, and Change

The central part of Mexico City, including the area occupied by the sacred precinct of the Mexica, became an area nominally occupied by Spanish residents. The area covered some 100 city blocks, or approximately one-fourth of Tenochtitlan. Indigenous folks were supposed to live in barrios that surrounded the central area, after Cortés' decree in 1534 that the Spanish and Indigenous populations were to live separately (Martínez 1988; Tovar de Teresa 1985; Valero de García Lascuráin 1991:150). However, segregation was never complete, due to four separate patterns. First, Indigenous people lived in the center of Mexico City for most if not all of the sixteenth century, and Spanish officials, including the Viceroy, sometimes protected the right of Indigenous occupants to live there. In 1537, the viceroy ordered that Spanish colonizers could not displace Indigenous families out of their houses in the center of the city as long as there were empty plots of land that could be assigned to other Spaniards. This is not to say that Indigenous people lived in the area free of harassment or evictions. In the second half of 1563, colonial authorities expelled at least thirty-seven Indigenous families from the center of Mexico City. Historical records indicate that throughout the sixteenth century colonizers continued expelling Indigenous families from the center of the city (Valero de García Lascuráin 1991:183). Of course, this also means that there were Indigenous families living in the center of Mexico City throughout the sixteenth century, and interacting with colonizers in various ways.

A second pattern that made segregation in colonial Mexico City only partial and never complete was that Spanish colonizers did not always live in the central part of the city (Sodi Miranda 1994:18). We may refer to the center of Mexico City as a focus of Spanish colonization, but Spanish colonizers did not always settle there. They lived, although in smaller numbers, in other areas of the city as well. A third pattern was the influx of Black people into Mexico City, whether enslaved or as free colonizers. The Black presence in the city should not be underestimated. Meza (2013:43) has argued that there were at least 8,000 Africans in Mexico City by 1555, only thirty-five years after the conquest. I provide a greater variety of estimates in Chapter 6. Many Black people lived in the houses of Spanish colonizers as urban slaves, although others were conquistadors or had other occupations (Chapter 6).

Finally, a fourth pattern is perfectly logical: where there are people, people mingle. Mixing between Europeans, Black people, and Indigenous people was a fact since the beginning of the colonial period. Mexico City became a place full of castas, or people of mixed descent, challenging the possibility of dividing the population along any clear-cut lines. People also lived together without mixing in the biological sense. For example, Cosme de Orrantía, one of the decedents whose inventory forms part of this study, declared upon his death that he had lived in the house of an Indigenous man named Pedro. My interpretation of the document is that they lived together in the house, in part because Orrantía declared that they were compadres (a term of fictive kinship) and that he had received a lot of good service from Pedro. Orrantía left all of his belongings to Pedro except for his weapons, and specified that Pedro should receive his gold, silver, and precious stones (Cont. 209, N.2, R.2).

In the center of Mexico City, right above the partially destroyed Templo Mayor and other buildings (whether complete or in ruins), colonizers and Indigenous people built their city. At times, it is difficult to disentangle processes of appropriation and of continuity in the early history of the colonial city. Appropriation of space could be defined as "the act of taking over a space and continuing its previous function for personal gain or for the advantage of one group over another" (Rodríguez-Alegría 2017:662). Continuity in the use of space could be defined as "the existence and persistence of any space, in the absence of major changes in use" and without an intent from a group of people to benefit exclusively from that area (Rodríguez-Alegría 2017:662). Many of the apparent continuities in terms of the design and layout of the city and in terms of the use of space could be either appropriation or continuity, depending on how they were related to struggles of power in the past. The center of Tenochtitlan became the center of Mexico City and the site of the most important civic and religious buildings, including the Metropolitan Cathedral, the houses of Hernán Cortés, houses for religious elites, the mint, the vice regal palace, and houses for Spanish colonizers.

An important pattern of continuity is the persistence of Indigenous temples and rituals right in Mexico City. In 1537 the bishops of Mexico wrote a letter to the king of Spain complaining that Indigenous people would go to their old temples and practice their rituals at night. Even though they did so at night, which the bishops suspected was done to practice their rites in secret, colonizers were well aware of the rituals taking place (Tovar de Teresa 1985:3). Many of the temples were in existence and in full view until at least 1538, and probably later, when the Spanish crown decreed that they should be torn down and the stone used to build churches and monasteries (Tovar de Teresa 1985).

An important pattern of change accompanied the process of appropriation of space by the Spanish: Indigenous rulers built their own *tecpan* or ruling house close to the center of the city, near the modern metro stop at Salto del Agua, or southwest of the main plaza. Mundy (2015:108) has argued that around 1541, only two decades after the conquest, Indigenous people built their tecpan. An Indigenous scribe painted it in the Codex Osuna as a large building with decorations of *chalchihuitl* or precious green stones. This sort of decoration is typically found in Indigenous tecpan and other important buildings in the colonial period and before (Mundy 2015:109; see also Evans 2005, 2017; Figure 2.6). The tecpan also had arch and keystone construction, which was new in central Mexico at the time, as well as its own courtyard plaza. It was adjacent to a market, ideally situated for Indigenous rulers to observe the people and even supervise market activities (Mundy 2015:110). In the drawing, one can see Viceroy Luis de Velasco sitting on a *silla de caderas*, a type of chair discussed in Chapter 3 as a symbol of power.

The exact location of the tianguis may have changed in the years after the conquest, according to evidence presented by Mundy (2015:81–86). Initially, Hernán Cortés wrote that the marketplace had moved close to the houses of Spanish colonizers. Although Cortés may make it seem like this location benefitted Spaniards only, in fact the market was also next to the house of an Indigenous ruler, Tlacotzin. In the colonial period, the marketplace was divided into three sections. To the west was the Manila Market, known also as the *parián*, established in 1533 (Marías 1999; Rubial García 2012:40). Parián was a term used to refer to marketplaces that sold in all kinds of items, but not food (Mundy 2015:85), and this particular parián sold goods imported from Asia, including porcelain, jewelry, clothing and many other items. Another section of the market was known as the *Baratillo* or flea market, specializing in used goods, clothing, tools, items made of stone, and

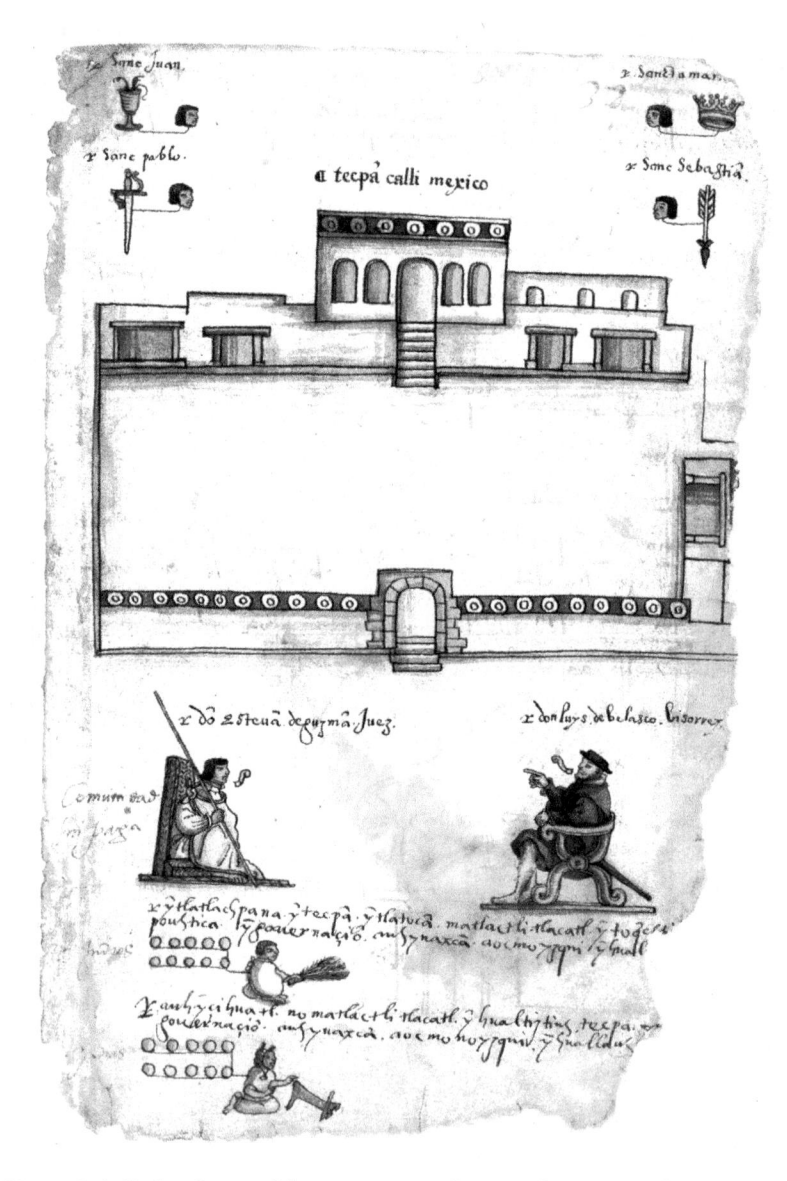

Figure 2.6 Codex Osuna, fol. 38r, ca. 1565, showing the tecpan of Mexico-Tenochtitlan.

pottery, and selling its share of contraband and stolen goods as well (Katzew 2004:56). Finally, the Indigenous tianguis continued to sell all kinds of goods, including agricultural produce, cooked food, mats, water, wood, and other goods. Additionally, one could find other services in the tianguis, including barbers, and porters. The tianguis of the main plaza is a good example of continuity in terms of the location of a marketplace, but also change in terms of the kinds of material goods sold there. Thus, at the scale of city planning, the city retained its general layout, in a complex mixture of continuity and appropriation that defies any clear division between the two categories.

Perhaps the most striking example of appropriation is the Metropolitan Cathedral. The first cathedral was located near the southwest corner of the atrium of today's cathedral (Figure 2.7; Virchez 2003). It was already partially built and in use by 1525, only four years after the conquest, although its construction was not completed until 1532. The building was oriented East to West, and eight of the bases of columns inside the building had reliefs of monumental snake bodies or snake heads underneath them. Mexica sculptors carved the images of snakes, which may have been obtained from the ruins of the Templo Mayor (García Moll and Salas Cuesta 2011; Virchez 2003). Interpreting the presence of these images in a Christian church is complex, given that they could signify appropriation of space and building materials for the imposition of religion from the Spanish, but they could also be interpreted as resistance, or even reinterpretation of religion by Indigenous people. Construction of the Metropolitan Cathedral, still in use today, started in 1573, and the first Cathedral remained in use until it was demolished in 1626. At that point, the partially built Metropolitan Cathedral replaced it as the principal church in Mexico. Construction of the Metropolitan Cathedral continued for a long time after it was already in use, until 1813 (Bérchez 1999a, 1999b; Marías 1999).

The Metropolitan Cathedral was built on top of not just one, but several Mexica structures. The structures buried under the Cathedral include a circular temple most likely dedicated to the Mexica god Ehecatl, the god of wind, a structure that archaeologists named the Temple of the Sun for the solar glyphs displayed prominently on its side, and part of a ball court (Barrera Rivera 1999; Islas Domínguez 1999), among other buildings (Figure 2.8). But the temples that lay under the Cathedral had probably not been in use for decades. It is unclear whether they were visible at all. Since 1527, Spanish colonizers had owned the land where the Cathedral was built. The Cabildo of Mexico City granted the land as house plots to three Spaniards,

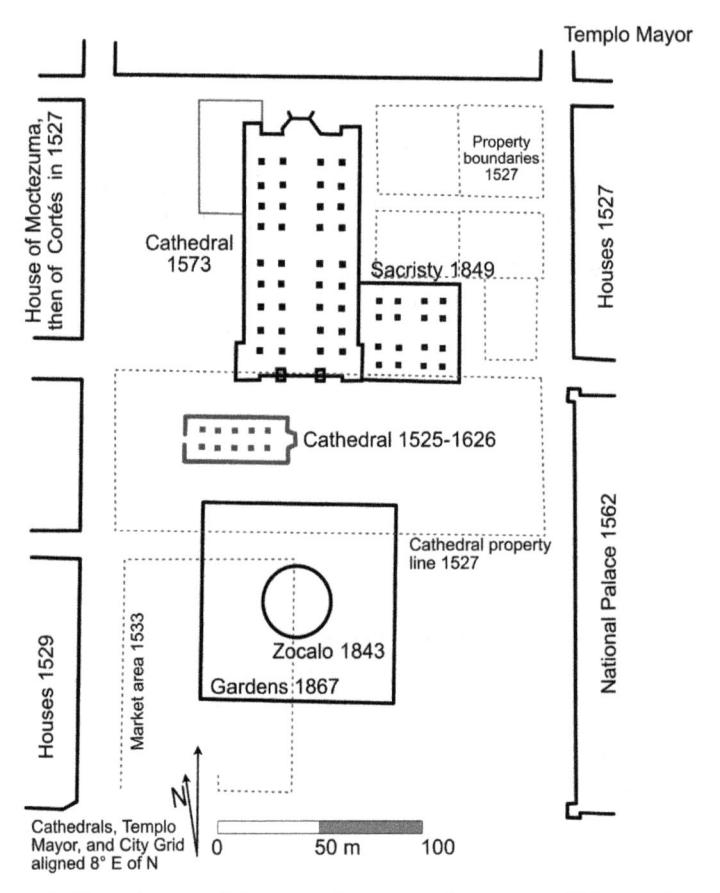

Figure 2.7 Plan of some of the major features at the center of Mexico City after 1521, drawn by Samuel Wilson.

although there is no evidence that they ever built any houses there. It was usual for plots of land in Mexico City to remain empty for years after being assigned to colonizers. Thus, the land went from being the site of several Mexica religious structures and open space, to being assigned as house lots for the Spanish and remaining empty, to being the site of the Metropolitan Cathedral.

Historical sources reveal that when building the Cathedral, colonizers were well aware of the problems presented by the high water table underneath Mexico City. They wanted to build a cathedral modeled after the cathedral in Seville, and no smaller in size. Archbishop Zumárraga wanted the Cathedral to be "like another Rome for Indians" and to accommodate all

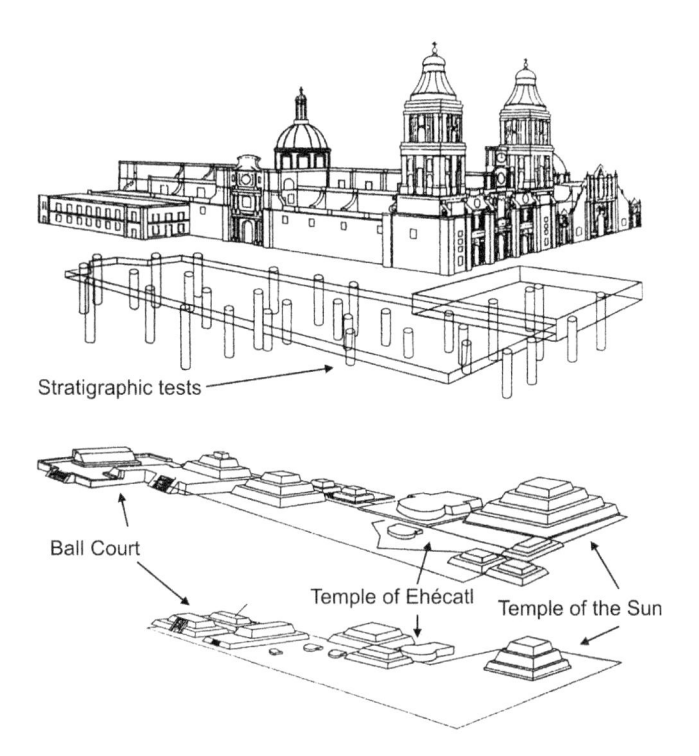

Figure 2.8 Drawing of the Metropolitan Cathedral and Tabernacle, with the stratigraphic tests and Mexica ruins beneath it. Courtesy of the Templo Mayor Museum and INAH. Used by permission.

vecinos (colonizer landowners) and natives in the city. Yet even before the building project started, colonizers expressed concern that the soils and the high water table would never be able to support such a large construction (Bérchez 1999a:244).

Other spaces in the city were not appropriated to be used for public ritual and religion. Several of the colonial houses excavated by the PAU were built on top of what were once buildings dedicated to Mexica state religion, politics, and education. The houses at Donceles #97 were built directly on top of a building that may have served as a *calmecac* or school for teaching religion and militarism to elite children (Barrera Rodríguez and López Arenas 2008), and other structures that contained numerous monumental braziers and sculptures of human crania, claws, and animals (Terreros Espinosa 2003; Figure 2.3). The houses at Guatemala Street #38 were built directly on top of some of the impressive offerings in front of the Templo Mayor, including the colossal Tlaltecuhtli monolith (Gallardo Parrodi 2011; López Luján 2009). The houses at Argentina #15 were built on top of a section of the precinct of the Eagle Warriors, north of the Templo Mayor (Rivas García and Barrera Rodríguez 1997).

The Plaza Gamio is a good example to show that changes in the use of space took place in the sixteenth century and in every century thereafter, and that such changes can take one space in a long trajectory from being open space, through several lives as different buildings, to open space again (Figure 2.3). The Plaza Gamio is directly west of the Templo Mayor, right against its front stairs. Before the conquest, the Mexica partially destroyed some of their religious buildings to make room for an expanded forecourt for the Templo Mayor. In the sixteenth century, people built houses for Spaniards there. In 1688 the houses were demolished and construction for the Conciliar Seminary began. The building was later used as a hotel and for other commercial purposes. Then it was demolished in 1933, becoming a street, then public restrooms, and then part of a plaza once again. At the beginning of the twenty-first century, archaeologists from the Templo Mayor excavated the space in part to prepare a new entrance to the archaeological zone (Barrera Rodríguez and Martínez Meza 2010; Barrera Rodríguez et al. 2012). Setha Low (1995) remarked that she did not feel comfortable arguing that the plazas we see today in many colonial cities were European but she also did not feel comfortable arguing that they were Indigenous. In the case of the Plaza Gamio, which has gone from Indigenous architecture, to the forecourt of a great temple, to many different kinds of buildings, and then to plaza, I would agree with Low. I would add that neither tradition determined the creation of this space fully. Instead, contingent human decisions that took place at many different times over the centuries are responsible for creating this space.

Mexica Engineering in Spanish Houses

Historical documents contain some information on the domestic architecture of Spanish colonizers. Based mostly on these documents, scholars have described colonial architecture in the sixteenth century as simple, lacking in decoration, and military or fortress-like in appearance (de Gante 1954:163–167; Tovar de Teresa 1985:12). The city was not fortified, but some colonizers fortified their houses and built watchtowers in fear of attacks by Indigenous

Figure 2.9 Houses as drawn in the Codex Tepetlaoztoc, Folio 41 recto. The British Museum, used by permission.

people. The houses drawn by Indigenous people in the Codex of Tepetlaoztoc consistently depict the houses of Spaniards with a plain, military aesthetic, and made of stone blocks (Valle 1994; Figure 2.9). The military appearance of the houses lasted until the 1580s, when colonizers started building houses with a less-military aesthetic (Kubler 1948:77–80). The descriptions tend to emphasize the exterior of houses, making it clear that they were orderly, laid out in straight rows, and that the houses received plenty of sunshine and air. Houses were also uniform in height. This sort of order took some effort in the part of local authorities. By 1538 the viceroy declared that Spanish buildings had to respect the city layout and the streets, and that house facades had to be built out of stone and mortar (*cal y canto*) (Kubler 1948:75–76; Tovar de Teresa 1985). The authorities commanded that porticoes that extended beyond the dimensions required by law be torn down and rebuilt to maintain uniformity and to respect the layout of the streets (Kubler 1948:76).

Archaeology can furnish more details about house construction and materials. All of the materials mentioned above as being part of Mexica architecture, including wood, andesite, red and black tezontle, plaster, adobe, and basalt were used in the houses of Spanish colonizers. Wood was used to lay the foundation of many walls and floors of colonial houses, with the same system of vertical, parallel pilings that the Mexica used to manage shifting and subsiding. Among the house lots that contain clear evidence of the use of this system, one may find González Obregón 25, Licenciado Verdad 2, Donceles 97, and probably others (Barrera Rodríguez et al. 2003:207; Mundy 2015:194). Hundreds of pilings also hold up the Metropolitan Cathedral (Bérchez 1999b). The use of wooden pilings is perhaps the most frequently mentioned adoption of pre-Hispanic engineering in the colonial period. The technique was known in Europe at the time, and used in cities like Venice. But the people who built Mexico City were Indigenous people who used the techniques they already knew.

The people who made the houses of Spanish colonizers also used andesite slabs to make some of the floors, just like in pre-conquest times (Barrera Rodríguez and Rivas García 2003). They also used andesite slabs to line a well in Donceles 97, and perhaps other wells in the center of town (Terreros Espinosa 2003:244; Figure 2.10). In other houses nearby, one may find stucco used to finish floors and walls. In the house located at Argentina 15 builders used andesite slabs and then finished them with a layer of polished stucco. Builders of sixteenth-century houses also used plaster to finish the interior

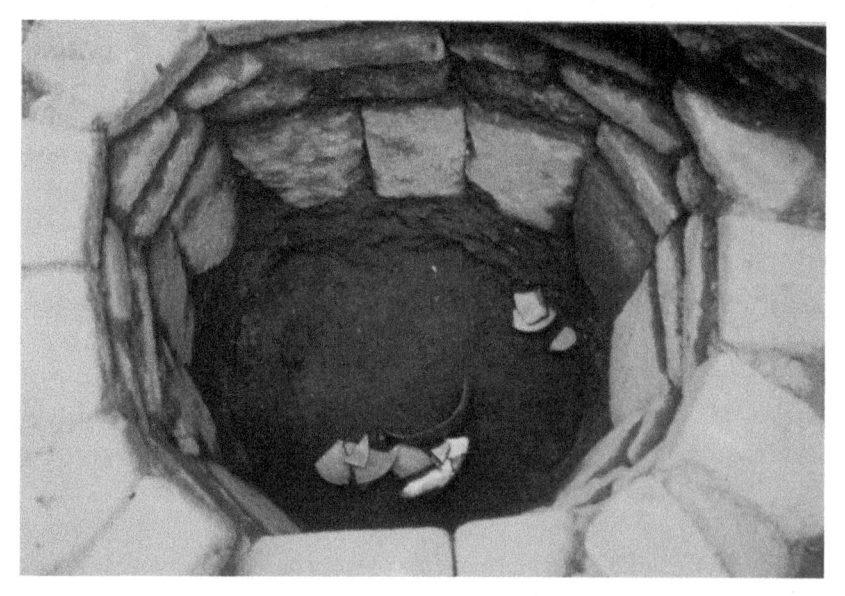

Figure 2.10 Well lined with andesite slabs at Donceles 97, Mexico City. Photograph courtesy of the Templo Mayor Museum and INAH. Used by permission.

of water boxes, such as the one found in Justo Sierra 33 (Hinojosa Hinojosa 2003:23). In yet another house lot, Donceles 97, one of the colonial floors was made up of seven layers of polished stucco just like in preconquest times (Terreros Espinosa 2003:243).

Builders often used the different materials in combination. Archaeological evidence shows that floors in the early houses of colonizers were sometimes made of different materials in different areas of the house. It is unknown whether the use of different materials and finishes on floors is the result of piecemeal construction of the houses, remodeling with different materials, or for any other reason. In Donceles 97, for example, archaeologists found a sixteenth-century room with stone slabs obtained from a pre-Hispanic structure (probably basalt) and brick (Figure 2.11). Another room in the same house had a floor made of pink andesite. Another room has a floor made with brick covered with a thin layer of lime. Yet another room in the same house had a floor made of adobe, and there was also a patio paved with andesite slabs. The walls of the house also had different types of finish. Some of the walls had a single finish of plaster, whereas other were finished with two layers of plaster: a white layer, with a second layer decorated in red (Terreros Espinosa 2003).

Archaeological evidence shows plenty of recycling of old materials in the colonial period. At times, people recycled building materials from the later phases of pre-conquest Mexica buildings and turned them into houses for colonizers. Some of the andesite slabs used in colonial floors in Argentina 15 have clear indication of having been used in previous constructions and finished anew in the colonial period (Barrera Rodríguez and Rivas García 2003:164). The earliest mint in Mexico City, the Real Casa de Moneda, was located adjacent to the Palacio Nacional or what once were the houses of Hernán Cortés. The tezontle stones used in the earliest construction of the original mint also show clear indication of being reused from a pre-Hispanic construction (Pérez Mora and Ibarra Arzave 2014). Hernán Cortes' house, at Monte de Piedad #7, is among the most dramatic examples of reuse of preconquest materials. It was built directly on top of the ruins of the palace of Axayacatl, one of the Mexica kings. Archaeologists found not only the use of tezontle and basalt recycled from Axayacatl's palace, but also several stones that contained Mexica reliefs. The reliefs display images of plumed serpents, a feathered headdress, and the glyph for market or Chalco, among others. These stones were visible in Cortes' house (Barrera Rodríguez and García Guerrero 2017).

Figure 2.11 Excavations by the Programa de Arqueología Urbana at Donceles 97, Mexico City. Photograph courtesy of the Templo Mayor Museum and INAH. Used by permission.

Ray Hernández Durán (2017b) has argued that the reuse of pre-Hispanic construction materials and monuments in the colonial period was motivated by reasons that were both practical and ideological: materials were used because they were available right there, and because they served to demonstrate the imposition of Spanish power. Demonstrating Spanish imposition of power would be especially salient when using Mexica religious monuments as construction materials, such as the column base that obscured beneath it an image of the god Tlaltecuhtli (Hernández Durán 2017b:691). Building on Duran's interpretation, one could also think of the motivations that Indigenous builders had when reusing symbolically rich materials to build colonial architecture. Perhaps Indigenous people did not consider having their monuments buried under colonial construction simply a result of Spanish imposition. They may have seen it as a preservation of their ancient sacred space. The reuse of materials from earlier construction, and the practice of burying monuments in spaces that remained sacred—in part precisely because the monuments were buried there—were certainly not a colonial innovation; they may be as much a pattern of continuity of pre-conquest practices, although in a new political and social context.

Lockhart coined the term *double mistaken identity* to refer to processes in which both Spaniards and Nahuas (or any two different groups) assume "that a given form or concept is essentially one already known to it, operating in much the same manner as in its own tradition, and hardly takes cognizance of the other side's interpretation" (Lockhart 1992:445). Burying Mexica monuments under colonial structures or reusing their pieces in new architecture may be an example of that process at work. Over time, the use of Mexica monuments in colonial architecture changed in an interesting way. In the eighteenth century, people used Mexica carvings to decorate architecture in ways that were clearly visible (López Luján and Sánchez Reyes 2012).

Colonial builders used pre-conquest architecture in ways other than just as recycled building blocks. Sometimes they used Mexica architecture as foundations for walls and floors of colonial buildings. In Justo Sierra 33, for example, sixteenth-century arches and columns were laid on top of Mexica walls and structures (Hinojosa Hinojosa 2003:23). In the Palacio del Arzobispado, archaeologists found two pre-conquest walls that served as colonial wall foundations, and four colonial columns supported on top of the steps of a pre-conquest stair. Also at the Palacio del Arzobispado, archaeologists found three circular scars on a pre-conquest floor, probably the result of using wooden pilings to support the colonial construction (Del Olmo Frese 2003). Sometimes, colonial builders simply dumped rocks on top of preconquest floors and then placed wooden pilings between the rocks to serve as foundation for colonial floors (Hinojosa Hinojosa 2003:23; Viart Muños and Martínez Meza 2003:121). The house at Donceles 97 shows evidence of this technique in use even in the seventeenth century. Archaeologists found the circular scars associated with wooden pilings on a sixteenth-century floor, which supported a seventeenth-century construction (Terreros Espinosa 2003:248).

The many examples of the use of pre-conquest architecture as foundation for colonial houses should not give the impression that colonial builders always preserved Mexica architecture to use it as foundations, nor should it give the impression that the pre-conquest city determined the construction of the colonial city. Sometimes, colonial builders destroyed pre-conquest architecture to make room for new buildings. For example, a profile from Luis González Obregón 25 shows that the pre-Hispanic structure was once taller, but it was partially destroyed in the colonial period and dismantled for new construction (Barrera Rodríguez 2006:278; Figure 2.12). In Argentina 15, colonial builders filled up the House of the Eagle Warriors with rubble, and then built colonial structures on top (Barrera Rodríguez 2006:282). In Donceles 97, there is evidence of destruction of three structures to build colonial houses and a colonial well (Terreros Espinosa 2003).

The use of Mexica building techniques and materials can be seen in seventeenth-century contexts as well, providing evidence of the long continuity of Mexica technologies. In Argentina 15, for example, a floor was made of a combination of tezontle, basalt fragments, and andesite. The fill beneath this floor contained glazed ceramics, Mexican tin glazed ceramics, Chinese porcelain, and tin enameled ceramics from Puebla (Barrera Rodríguez and Rivas García 2003:166), marking this floor as a late sixteenth or early seventeenth century floor. The continued use of the same building materials for such a long time is remarkable. In another house lot, Donceles 97, archaeologists have argued that two rooms were remodeled in the seventeenth century and they have walls made of tezontle and plaster. One of the rooms has a floor made of pink stone, much like in pre-Columbian times (Terrero Espinosa 2003:248).

It is worth discussing the house lot located at Licenciado Verdad 2, directly south of the Templo Mayor Museum, as an example of how the varied patterns discussed previously can come together in a single site. Archaeologists conducted extensive excavations at Licenciado Verdad 2, complemented by historical research (Barrera Rodríguez 2002). Excavations at Licenciado Verdad 2 found a monumental platform, and they have argued that it is part of the wall that surrounded the sacred precinct of Tenochtitlan (Barrera Rodríguez 2002:105, 2003:175). The platform runs north to south along what is today called Licenciado Verdad Street, and it was enormous: no less than 30 meters wide, with stairs to the east and west and a bench on top

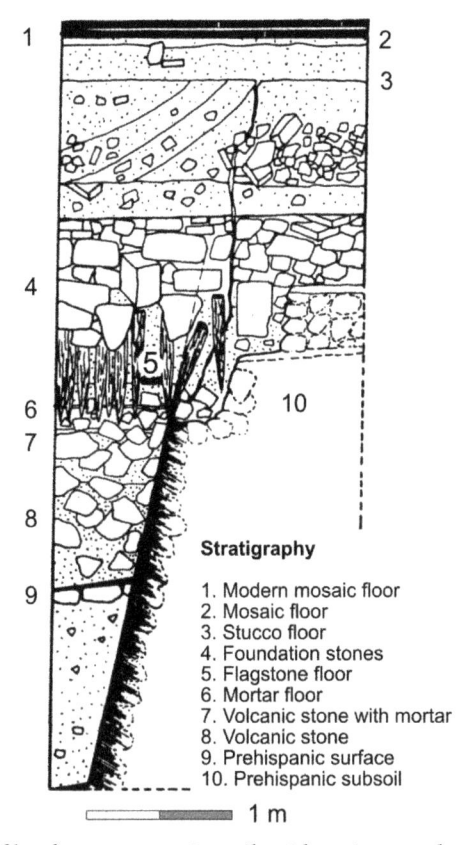

Stratigraphy
1. Modern mosaic floor
2. Mosaic floor
3. Stucco floor
4. Foundation stones
5. Flagstone floor
6. Mortar floor
7. Volcanic stone with mortar
8. Volcanic stone
9. Prehispanic surface
10. Prehispanic subsoil

1 m

Figure 2.12 Profile of structure at González Obregón #25, showing a partially demolished pre-Hispanic structure, wooden pylons and a series of floors. Image courtesy of the Templo Mayor Museum and INAH. Used by permission.

that was 40cm tall and 1.86m wide. The floor of the platform is made of volcanic rocks joined with cement, and a thin layer of well-polished stucco on top (Barrera Rodríguez 2003:177). There were no living quarters or any other type of pre-conquest contexts, other than the wall and fill at Licenciado Verdad 2 (Barrera Rodríguez et al. 2003).

In the sixteenth century, the lot at Licenciado Verdad 2 went from being a monumental wall, to being the site of colonial houses. The lot belonged to Juan Luis de Ribera, but it seems that Juan Luis de Ribera did not live there for long, if ever, and that the people who lived there were poor and not very influential in the political life of the city. The archibishop and the police evicted them violently in 1614, and historical sources state that they

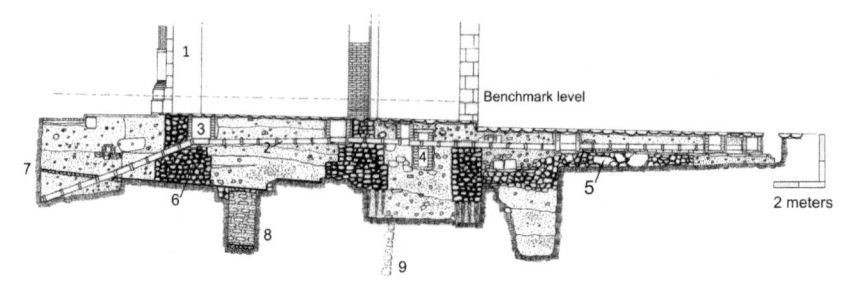

Figure 2.13 Stratigraphic profile in Licenciado Verdad #2, showing the main façade of the convent resting on top of the Mexica wall. Image courtesy of the Templo Mayor Museum and INAH. Used by permission. (1. Modern walls. 2. Drain. 3. Twentieth-century register. 4. Nineteenth-century register. 5. Drain. 6. Foundation of seventeenth-century Church of Sta. Teresa. 7. Mexica platform. 8. Substructure of Mexica platform. 9. Possible exterior limit of Mexica platform.)

were partly naked and some were only covered with blankets or shirts as they ran out of the houses screaming (Barrera Rodríguez et al. 1999). Ribera had donated the lot and 4,000 pesos to Carmelite nuns, who began demolishing the houses in 1615 to build their convent (Barrera Rodríguez et al. 2003:199). They built the main façade of the convent facing west, using the eastern side of the Mexica monumental wall as a foundation (Figure 2.13). But the Mexica wall did not serve as a foundation for the entire convent. Elsewhere, builders dug a deep trench that destroyed part of the wall and then laid out the foundation of an internal wall for the convent (Barrera Rodríguez 2002:106, 2003:177). Some of the internal walls of the convent used the remains of the walls of the sixteenth-century houses as foundation (Figure 2.14). Wooden pilings surrounded by rock, lime, and sand served as support for some of the convent's walls (Barrera Rodríguez et al. 2003:208).

To build the walls of the convent, they used some of the traditionally Mexica materials and construction techniques. One of the rooms excavated had walls with red and black tezontle fragments joined with lime and sand, and a flat surface with red paint. The builders in this convent also used wood pilings to hold walls together and to serve as foundation for walls and floors. They also built the walls of a portico, walls that were 90 cm thick, out of rocks held together with cement made with lime and sand, perhaps an example of the continued use of the entortado technique mentioned earlier. Archaeologists also found the foundations of three limestone columns

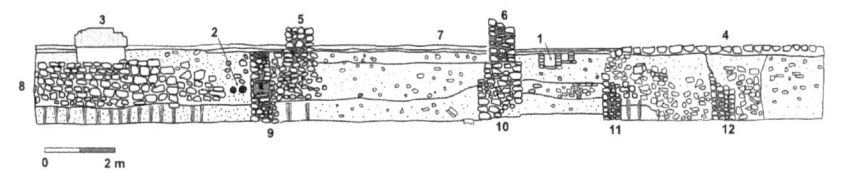

Figure 2.14 East profile at Licenciado Verdad #2, showing the colonial architecture in relationship to the Mexica architecture. Image courtesy of the Templo Mayor Museum and INAH. Used by permission. (1. Red brick drainage, twentieth century. 2. Clay pipe drainage, twentieth century. 3. Wall of convent, seventeenth century. 4. Paving, eighteenth century. 5. Convent, seventeenth century. 6. Convent, seventeenth century. 7. Convent floor, seventeenth century. 8. Mortared stone, seventeenth century. 9. House, sixteenth century. 10. House, sixteenth century. 11. House, sixteenth century. 12. House, sixteenth century.)

in the portico, built with the same materials and technique. The surface of the columns was made of a mixture of ground red tezontle, lime, and sand. Elsewhere in the convent, they built columns using the same technique of joining pieces of tezontle with lime and sand cement, sometimes with colorful tiles that provided decorative accents. The tiles seem to be the only colonial innovations incorporated into the seventeenth-century columns (Barrera Rodríguez et al. 2003).

Just like the walls and the columns, the floors were made using Mexica materials and techniques. Archaeologists found four superimposed floors in the convent and of those, three were made of andesite slabs, whereas the top (most recent) floor was made of red brick. The floor of one of the rooms that archaeologists excavated was finished with a layer of stucco, and other floors in the convent were most likely also finished with stucco. Even though archaeologists only found the footprint of the slabs that made up the floor of the floor of the portico, they are certain that the floor was made of andesite slabs. A second floor in the portico, separated from the first by 30 cm of fill, was made of andesite slabs of the same size and shape as the ones whose print remains where the first floor was. It is clear that they reused the materials to lay out the second floor. Archaeologists also found a large water box, 3.60 m wide, 60 cm tall, and estimated to be over 7.80 m long. The water box was lined with andesite slabs and it also had a decorative frame at the bottom of colorful tiles laid in a square that was approximately 1m wide on each side (Barrera Rodríguez 2003:179–181; Barrera Rodríguez et al. 2003:208). Andesite, tezontle, lime, sand, plaster, and reused materials were among the most commonly used materials in Mexica architecture, and they were used to build the seventeenth-century convent of Santa Teresa. The builders began incorporating tiles into their decorative elements, but even a whole century after the conquest, the building materials and techniques used in the convent remained traditionally Mexica.

In Ciudad Vieja, El Salvador, archaeologists have found a different pattern. The architecture there shows Spanish designs and architectural elements, including walls of roughly one *vara* (83 to 84 cm) in thickness, adobe tapia walls, ironwork, and roof tiles (Card and Fowler 2019:194). In sites in the Caribbean, including St. Augustine and Puerto Real, archaeologists have found that house construction methods and technology are mostly Spanish (Deagan 1983, 1995). The difference in findings may reflect regional differences among the Spanish colonies. Perhaps in places like Mexico City, where there was much available and expert Indigenous labor, colonizers depended more on Indigenous engineering. The differences may also be due to data collection and the observations made by archaeologists. For example, I have found no easy way to compare the wall thickness that Card and Fowler (2019) reported with any similar data on walls in the colonial houses of Mexico City. I have not found a way to compare the ironwork or use of tiles in the earliest Spanish houses either, whether it is due to data presentation in the secondary literature, or simply to their absence in the archaeological record. Still, the differences between the two sites are important, because they may point to regional variation, and because they may encourage future research that can us to compare patterns more thoroughly.

Conclusion

Colonial Mexico City, from its general layout to the houses of colonizers, was the product of Indigenous knowledge, intellectual work, urban planning, and engineering, in negotiation with colonizers, even if the historical record sometimes overemphasizes the role of colonizers in building the city. Destruction, reconstruction, change, continuity, and appropriation can all be seen at the small scale of the house lot in the heart of Mexico City. There were instances of appropriation. Sometimes people turned religious spaces of the Mexica into Christian spaces. Other times, they turned the religious spaces into houses of Spaniards. As the pre-conquest city guided the construction of the colonial capital, humans sometimes put a lot of energy and work to transform small spaces in the city. The built environment guided human decisions to some extent, but people with their creativity, hard work, and perseverance transformed spaces repeatedly through time.

Previous texts have described the houses of colonizers as simple and military in appearance, as a result of the lack of engineers, architects, and books on architecture among colonizers (de Gante 1954:163–167; Kubler 1948:77–80; Tovar de Teresa 1985:12). The archaeological evidence from the houses excavated by the PAU is enough to argue that the houses of colonizers who lived in the center of Mexico City were also similar to Indigenous palaces in terms of the engineering techniques used and the aesthetics of their finishing techniques, at least in the interior part of the houses. The houses of colonizers did not resemble the houses of Indigenous commoners, described by Sahagún as crude and made with little care. Instead, they had the stonework that was previously seen in Mexica palaces, the polished red plaster, and other aspects of the high quality Mexica engineering that had been seen previously in elite architecture. Most of the techniques used by the Mexica were adopted to make the houses of Spanish colonizers. In fact, it seems like the only pre-Hispanic techniques not documented by archaeologists in Spanish houses are related to building solid constructions, such as cajones, and filling buildings with rubble that included adobe blocks. Of course, this may be due to the use of those techniques primarily for building massive solid constructions, whereas colonial buildings were voluminous hollow constructions instead. The houses may also have been built piecemeal, with different kinds of surfaces and surface finishes in different rooms. In some houses, the use of Mexica engineering techniques continued into the seventeenth century, as people slowly incorporated Iberian embellishments into the architecture, including the now-famous glazed tiles that are commonly associated with colonial architecture today.

The argument that Indigenous people participated in engineering and architecture in the colonial period may seem familiar to scholars who know the literature on religious architecture and public works (e.g., Edgerton 2001; Mundy 2015:194). But I extend the argument here to show that Indigenous engineering and architectural skills were also deployed in the houses where Spanish colonizers lived. Extending the roles of Indigenous people into Spanish houses matters in at least three ways. First, it matters because archaeologists have related colonial household architecture to the power of colonizers and to their strategies of display. An emphasis on appearing very Spanish and on Iberian construction techniques may have been the case elsewhere in the Spanish colonies, but it was not the case in Mexico City, at least not in the sixteenth century. Colonizers were forced to confront the reality of living in an Indigenous material world even in the private spaces of their houses, and even in the main destination for colonizers, Mexico City. But it is not clear whether colonizers saw anything remarkable or unacceptable about living in spaces built with Indigenous craftsmanship and aesthetics. Dean and Leibsohn (2003) have argued that in colonial Latin America people mixed items of disparate origins and they often found nothing remarkable or unacceptable about it. They simply participated in a material world of mixed origins.

Second, the Indigenous construction of colonial houses matters because it reveals the continuation of Indigenous work groups and their hierarchies in architectural production. Don Fernando Ixtlilxochitl, lord of Texcoco in the early sixteenth century, and Tlacotzin, high priest of Tenochtitlan at the time, famously managed the labor and work parties involved in reconstructing the city after the conquest (Kubler 1948:71). Indigenous work parties often involved thousands of workers who were part of a hierarchy of workers (Mundy 2015:38, 202), and a contemporary description by Motolinía emphasizes the enormous crowds of workers (Kubler 1948:71). It is not clear whether Ixtlilxochitl and Tlacotzin were involved in building the private houses of colonizers in addition to public buildings, but still, there must have been similar, even if smaller hierarchies in charge of building those houses. As they worked, Indigenous builders were not just part of a hierarchy that placed Spaniards on top and Indigenous people as an undifferentiated mass of workers. Instead, as they built the houses, Indigenous people built their social worlds. They formed their own identities as builders, masons, carpenters and other specialists. They rebuilt their own hierarchies of experts and apprentices. They could earn reputations as good or bad workers, as described in the Florentine Codex (Sahagún 1981 Book X, Chapter 8). They could pass their knowledge to the new generations. And they built the social worlds of Indigenous people, as they built the material worlds of Spanish colonizers.

Finally, colonizers adopted Indigenous engineering and technologies when building their material worlds. Perhaps colonizers did not apply the engineering techniques and tools of Indigenous builders with their own hands, but they certainly adopted the products of those technologies even in their own houses. I would argue that the adoption of the products of technology is not a limited or less important way of adopting technology when compared to adopting the techniques and tools. In this case, colonizers were adopting the entire technosocial system (Chapter 6) of Indigenous engineers, including the hierarchies, the materials they used for construction, the tools, and the final products. This is a true testimony of the adoption of Indigenous technologies among Spanish colonizers, an aspect of change in colonial Mexico that remains underestimated in modern scholarship. The following chapters will show other ways in which the Spanish adopted Indigenous technologies and created entirely new aspects of the material world in colonial Mexico City.

3

How to Furnish a House

Houses are full of the objects of everyday life that people often take for granted, yet they have great importance in shaping people's lives. Miller addressed the importance that a close familiarity with everyday objects can have when he wrote:

> objects are important not because they are evident and physically constrain or enable, but often precisely because we do not "see" them. The less we are aware of them, the more powerfully they can determine our expectations by setting the scene and ensuring normative behavior, without being open to challenge. (2005:5)

Objects can seem familiar and guide our expectations, knowledge, and behavior. In contrast, Cynthia Robin (2014) emphasizes a different aspect of the material world by showing a more active role for humans: people can also use everyday objects to change the world. She builds on decades of social theory to show that commoners in their households have the potential to be inventive, to change politics and religion, and to use production and consumption to challenge the power of large social and political units. Commoners, in their everyday material lives, can also be conservative and maintain the status quo. The work of the many scholars who have focused on households and everyday material culture reveals the importance of the mundane things found in a house (e.g., Brumfiel 2005; Carballo 2011; De Lucia 2013, 2017; Deagan 1983, 1995, 2001; Flannery 1976; Hendon 1996, 2004; Jamieson 2000a, 2000b; Manzanilla 1986; Voss 2008a, 2008b, 2008c, 2012).

In the Spanish colonies specifically, some scholars have argued that colonizers used household goods to reproduce a Spanish way of life, preserve cultural unity among colonizers, and distinguish themselves from Indigenous people through their practices and material culture (Bauer 2001; Benítez 1993; Deagan 1983, 1998, 2001; Lister and Lister 1982; McEwan 1991, 1992, 1995). Some scholars tend to view colonizers as carriers of culture traits (including material culture) that they then selectively imposed

How to Make a New Spain. Enrique Rodríguez-Alegría, Oxford University Press. © Enrique Rodríguez-Alegría 2023.
DOI: 10.1093/oso/9780197682296.003.0004

upon colonial subjects or otherwise brought to colonial households where culture traits and ethnicities mixed and created local identities (Bauer 2001; Deagan 1983, 1995, 1998; Foster 1960).

Other scholars have proposed that people in the Spanish colonies used domestic material culture for reasons other than only preserving their traditional ways of life. Jamieson has drawn attention to the potential that household goods had for challenging or naturalizing relationships of power between Spaniards and Indigenous people: "household items were used in mediating between these groups, both as objects used to control social action and to resist European hegemony" (Jamieson 2000b:161–162). He has argued that the struggle for power was "not just at the level of state intervention, but permeated all aspects of colonial life, including the role of objects in the colonial home" (Jamieson 2000b:xii). Colonizers used furniture, for example, to try to control the daily life of Indigenous people and to convert them to Christianity. They considered it essential that Indigenous people use European tables and beds (Jamieson 2000b:166). Alejandro Cañeque (2004) argues that chairs and cushions were integral parts of rituals that shaped power in New Spain. They were not just ephemera that symbolized power. They were central to how people negotiated and demonstrated their power. Other scholars have also examined the political potential of everyday objects sometimes to minimize difference between colonizers but accentuate differences between colonizers and natives (e.g., Voss 2005), or sometimes to negotiate social relations and power between both groups in contexts of hospitality (Rodríguez-Alegría 2005a, 2016a). These scholars examine people's goals, strategies, social relationships, and broad patterns of labor, production, and trade, to begin to understand how people used domestic material culture in colonial situations (Cañeque 2004; Jamieson 2000b; Rodríguez-Alegría 2003, 2005b, 2016a; Silliman 2004; Voss 2005, 2008b; Voss and Casella 2012).

This chapter focuses on furniture in order to examine how people used different kinds of domestic material culture to recreate familiar material worlds and to negotiate social relations and identities. The analysis also shows that people adjusted how they furnished a colonial house depending on changes in broad patterns of production and trade. The questions that drive the chapter echo those of previous chapters: what furniture did colonizers have in their houses? Was it imported, made locally by colonizers, or made by Indigenous people? Did colonizers adopt furniture associated with Indigenous people? To answer these questions, I consider all kinds of furniture and related items (such as cushions and bed linens), comparing items found in the probate inventories with museum pieces and furniture drawn in Indigenous manuscripts. I begin with a quick look at furniture in pre-Hispanic central Mexico and in Spain, and then continue with an examination of the furniture found in the probate inventories.

Mexica Minimalism

Archaeologists working in central Mexico rarely find furniture in their excavations, probably because Indigenous people made furniture out of perishable materials. Historical sources provide information on the kinds of furniture that existed in central Mexico. Two words come to mind when thinking about Mexica furniture: simple and minimal. Mexica houses barely had any furniture at all, besides reed mats used for sitting, sleeping, and even for getting married, boxes made of the same material as the mats, and censers used for heating. The mats, known as *petates*, were made by weaving together reeds in a crisscross pattern. People sometimes covered sleeping mats with blankets to provide some cushioning, and perhaps used rabbit fur or down to provide further cushioning (Aguilera 1985:17).[1] They rolled their mats and placed them in a corner during the day. Nobles sometimes appear in historical documents sitting on a woven reed seat with a back (Berdan 2014:67–69; Valle 1994; Figure 2.6). Towns like Xaltocan, Zumpango, Citlaltepec, and other towns around the lakes were the main producers of reeds and woven reed furniture (Gibson 1964:336). In the Codex Mendoza (Berdan and Anawalt 1992:127), a couple gets married kneeling on a petate, while elder men sit on petates and women kneel on the floor (Figure 3.1).

The Mexica also had boxes made of woven reeds, which they called *petlacalli*, and sometimes depicted them in their books, such as an illustration in the Codex Mendoza in which a thief steals items from a petlacalli (Berdan and Analwalt 1992:145; Lockhart 1992:70). Finally, some historical sources mention *tolicpalli*, which were prismatic cushions made of woven reeds and sometimes wrapped with animal hides and used for sitting (Carrillo and Gariel 1969). Mexica furniture seems very scant even in comparison to today's minimalists. The minimal use of furniture continued into the colonial period (Gibson 1964:336), although it seems that some, or perhaps many

---

[1] Aguilera (1985) does not cite a source for the claim that Indigenous folks in Central Mexico would use fur or other materials to create cushioning between blankets. The claim may be correct, but I have not been able to verify it.

Figure 3.1 Petates as shown in the Codex Mendoza, Folio 61r. Bodleian Libraries, University of Oxford.

Indigenous families adopted the use of Spanish-style chests, which they had to purchase in the market (discussed later; Lockhart 1992:70).

Spanish Variety

Furniture available in Spain at the time was radically different from that of the Mexica. Studying the variety of the furniture has been difficult because not too much furniture anywhere can survive for five centuries. There is also limited historical information on furniture across all social classes. For those reasons, Aguiló Alonso (1993:10) has proposed that the best approach to furniture of that time is to study inventories, other historical documents and descriptions, and the physical and stylistic characteristics of the furniture that survived in museums and private collections. Most of the furniture available belonged to the nobility and survived in their palaces and storage.

The furniture of the lower classes is mostly lost, but at least the furniture of the elite presents much variety and can give us a partial look at the furniture of the time. The inventories present a similar challenge, given that most of the inventories available belong to the nobility. Most of the inventories that Aguiló Alonso cites contain very little information about the furniture itself, besides naming what piece it is. Still, she emphasized class differences whenever she found enough information to do so, in spite of the limitations of the texts and the furniture itself.

Thanks to the efforts of Aguiló Alonso and other scholars (e.g., Enriquez 1951; Feduchi 1957), there are three general observations that can help approach Spanish furniture of the sixteenth century. First, the furniture was quite varied. In Spain, one could find innumerable items, including beds with posts, and chairs of different kinds. Most of the chairs seem quite bulky and ornate in comparison to chairs today. There were benches, tables, armoires, boxes of different sizes, chests, pillows, and cushions. There were desks that seem so complex and have so many boxes and drawers that it is hard to recognize them as desks today (Aguiló Alonso 1993; Enriquez 1951; Feduchi 1957). The variety seems infinite, especially in contrast with the central Mexican petate. Even though most of the evidence that Aguiló Alonso consulted pertains to the nobility, she argues that all houses, from the noble courts all the way to the houses of the lower classes, contained a variety of furniture. She has argued that even those who were not rich had beds, tapestries, rugs, tables, pillows and smaller pieces of furniture (candelabra, for example) made of silver (1993:24–25). Of course, the nobility would have much more furniture, but the less wealthy classes would also have a variety of furniture in their houses in many regions in Spain. The differences and similarities between the furniture owned by people in different social classes is an aspect of the research on furniture worth developing further in future studies.

To add to the variety of forms, the furniture was often ornate. Even the simpler pieces that remain in museums seem well-decorated (Enriquez 1951). One may find geometric patterns, floral imagery, and even reliefs or three-dimensional carvings of human figures, animals, and architecture. The techniques used to decorate the furniture included carving, inlaying wood of different colors, inlaying other materials, painting, and covering the furniture with metals, leather, and textiles. The materials used at the time to make furniture were varied as well. Furniture makers used wood of many different kinds, and decorated the finest pieces with silver and gold. Smaller pieces, including candlesticks, candelabra, and small boxes, among others, were often made out of silver (Aguiló Alonso 1993).

The variety of materials used leads to the second observation that can help understand the world of furniture in Spain at the time: a lot of the furniture required the coordinated effort or at least the products of specialists of different kinds, including woodworkers, smiths, leatherworkers, tailors, and others. They belonged to different guilds of specialists, but often one finds their work on a single piece of furniture. For example, one may find a box made of wood, covered in leather, and reinforced with iron hooks, nails, and a lock and key. *Arcas ensayadas* (cloth-covered boxes) are defined precisely by the combination of cloth and wood. Some furniture was painted with naturalistic scenes. Aguiló Alonso (1993) presents detailed information on the organization of the many guilds that supported different aspects of furniture production in Spain at the time.

A third observation about furniture in sixteenth-century Spain is that the furniture was made in different regions in the Iberian Peninsula, and imported from Italy, France, Flanders, and Germany. People did not think of furniture from different parts of the Iberian Peninsula as "local" furniture. They made distinctions between furniture made in Cataluña, Salamanca, Castilla, Lisboa, and many other regions. Some of the Iberian furniture, especially in Andalucía, had Moorish influence. Starting in the sixteenth century, one could find furniture imported from the Americas and an increasing number of items from East Asia all over Spain (Aguiló Alonso 1993).[2] Therefore, the furniture in Spain does not seem to have been strongly Spanish in flavor, or perhaps it would be more accurate to state that the furniture in Spain at the time was characterized by a combination of items from different parts of Europe, with some items from Asia and later, from the Americas. However, what was characteristically Spanish were some of the ways that people used the furniture. Historical evidence shows that women in Spanish courts sat on the floor, on rugs or cushions, to rest and eat. Travelers from elsewhere in Europe remarked on this curious custom. Sitting on chairs at a table was reserved for the gentlemen of the Spanish courts (Aguiló Alonso 1993:19, 22). It is difficult to know whether this gendered pattern extended

---

[2] The information provided by Aguiló Alonso (1993) is impressionistic because her sources did not allow her to do a statistical analysis to see how much of the furniture was of local production in different regions in Spain and how much of it was imported. It is difficult to tell also whether the proportions of imported and locally made items varied across social classes. One would suppose that elites owned more imported furniture than the lower classes, although such an assumption should be an empirical question rather than taken for granted, as I will show in Chapter 7.

to the lower classes in their own houses, or whether they shared chairs and tables or the floor. Perhaps there were other characteristically Spanish uses of furniture, and future analyses may help discover them.

The Furniture of Colonizers

Furniture is among the most abundant items in the inventories. It includes beds and bedding, tables, chairs, boxes, and many other items that show that the long trip across the Atlantic was not enough to stop people from bringing bulky furniture. They also brought techniques and tools necessary for woodworking, metalwork, leatherwork, and textile production, all of which formed part of furniture production. Wood joiners were important crewmembers when sailing across the Atlantic because they repaired and maintained ships, which were made mostly of wood. In the Americas, they put their skills to use in making temples and other public buildings, and soon enough, they began making furniture. By 1548, there was a joiners' guild in Mexico. Indigenous people soon began learning to use the tools and techniques of Spanish furniture makers. Initially, they copied Spanish models and conventions, but they also began to develop their own styles all over the Americas (Rivas P. 2006:477). Thus, the furniture of colonizers was initially imported, and then locally produced by Spanish and Indigenous artisans.

Boxes

Among the first items of European furniture seen in Mexico were boxes, listed in the probate inventories as *cajas* (boxes) or *cofres* (chests). Typically, boxes are a container with a hinged lid, whereas chests are containers with a convex hinged lid, but the inventories provide little basis to tell whether the distinction between the two was consistent and whether it was based on the shape of the lid. Perhaps what appeared as a box in one inventory could appear in another inventory as a chest. Aguiló Alonso (1993:81) has argued that even though scholars have provided definitions to distinguish between boxes and chests and between different kinds of boxes and chests, the people who compiled inventories in Spain seem to have used the vocabulary quite loosely. I suspect the same lack of standardization or precision in the vocabulary was true in the inventories in Mexico.

Colonizers used wooden boxes to transport goods across the Atlantic and over land to central Mexico. Boxes appear in an Indigenous drawing in the Florentine Codex, introducing Book XII, which relates to the Spanish conquest (Sahagún 1950–1982; Figure 3.2). The drawing shows the Spanish arriving in Mexico, disembarking from one of four ships. There are horses, pigs, sheep, and a cow already ashore, and in the lower central part of the drawing, one can see two boxes with hinged locks. One of the boxes is a flat white box, and the other a box with a semicylindrical lid. Perhaps this drawing shows how curious Indigenous people found the boxes of the Spanish as soon as they arrived. The white box may be what appears in the inventories listed as *caja blanca*, known also as *arcas blancas* at the time. This type of "white

Figure 3.2 Spaniards disembarking in Mexico, Florentine Codex. Florence, Biblioteca Medicea Laurenziana, Ms. Med. Palat. 220, c. 406r. By permission of the MiC. Any further reproduction by any means is prohibited.

box" was simple, had a single lock, and was used for transporting all kinds of objects, including other, more delicate or precious boxes (Aguiló Alonso 1993:85). Twelve of the boxes that appear in the probate inventories are listed as white boxes, and they were probably like the one shown in the Florentine Codex, although it is difficult to tell with certainty because of the lack of any further description. The box that appears next to it in the Florentine Codex seems like a chest with a semicylindrical lid. The Spanish called this type of chest *cofre tumbado* or *cofre de tumba* at the time because of its curved lid (Aguiló Alonso 1993:81).

The inventories contain a total of 107 boxes that are listed individually as caja, and 38 that are listed as cofre.[3] I discuss boxes and chests separately just in case future research allows telling with certainty that they were indeed different. The inventories give some indication of variation among the boxes in terms of materials and features such as locks and keys. Only 22 out of the 107 boxes had any indication of what material they were made of, and of those, 18 were made of wood, one of leather (probably in combination with a wooden frame), one of hemp (which probably refers to wood rather than fiber), and two were apparently made of gold. I believe they were probably gilded. Notice that the combination of materials produced by different guilds is apparent in the inventories. The main concern in the descriptions of these boxes was whether the box had a lock, a key, or neither one.[4] The second most frequent way of describing the boxes was by size: eight boxes are listed as small, seven as large, and only one as medium, although the inventories provide no precise measurement of the different sizes.

An incredible example of a box at the Franz Mayer Museum shows that boxes were not always simple. A box could turn out to be quite fancy and luxurious once opened (Plates 2a, b). It is labeled as an *arca de novia* (bride's ark), and said to have been made in the sixteenth century. The outside looks fancy enough, with its polished wood and delicately carved surface with

---

[3] There are more boxes listed as containing other things, such as a box of combs, for example, or a box of tin rings. When the emphasis in the entry was on the things contained in the box, I did not count the box, in an attempt to focus only on boxes that functioned as household furnishings. I discuss the items contained in such boxes in their appropriate sections (scissors along with other tools, knives with other knives, ribbons with other items of cloth, etc.).

[4] Eight of the boxes were listed as having a lock but not a key. The mention of a lock without a key either means that the box had some sort of closing mechanism that did not require a key to open, or that the box had a locking mechanism that was not useful anymore, given the absence of the key. In addition, four boxes are listed as having both a lock and a key, and ten are listed as having a key, which probably means that the box had a lock and a key. Only seven boxes are listed as not having a lock and key.

architectural motifs and floral details painted in gold, but the inside is most impressive. Once opened, one can appreciate the extensive gilding on the many smaller drawers on the inside of the box. Even the underside of the top lid is painted in floral motifs. This sort of luxurious box probably contained clothing and maybe smaller boxes with jewelry. The probate inventories do not mention any such boxes, although perhaps there is one in there, hiding behind the lack of detail and listed simply as a box.

There are thirty-eight chests listed in the inventories, including twenty-six that are listed simply as chests, two that are listed as chests for mail, seven that appear as small chests, one as a chest for spices, and two as chests with a lock. Only one of the chests is described in terms of the material it is made of, and oddly enough, it is made of crystal. The rest of them were most likely made of wood and metal. Exactly half of the chests are described in terms of their quality. The descriptions emphasize the same attributes as the descriptions of boxes, having to do with the presence or absence of keys, and with the size of the chests. Scribes listed three of the chests as having a key, and two as not having a key. Scribes listed one of them as big, and three as small, without providing a clear definition of the sizes. Scribes described three of the chests as *cofre tumbado*, in reference to the curvature of the lid. The Franz Mayer Museum has a wooden chest from the sixteenth century, with silk lining and iron (Plate 3a). The interior is simple, but the red lining gives it a luxurious feel (Plate 3b). It was brought from Castile, and it could be an example of the beautiful workmanship of the chests that are simply labeled as cofre in the inventories. Then again, as I look at the boxes that people have chosen to protect and curate over five centuries, I wonder whether we are missing many examples of simpler boxes that perhaps existed but nobody deemed worthy of saving.

Chairs and Other Seats

A second item that Indigenous people saw when the Spanish arrived and throughout the conquest was the wooden chair. Chairs are perhaps the most evocative of the sixteenth century, especially the *silla de caderas*, with its S-shaped legs that interlock to form an hourglass figure in the front and back of the chair. It could be folded by pressing the sides of the chair toward the center, giving the chair another of its typical names *silla de tijeras*, or "scissors chair." As if two names were not enough, this chair was also known as *jamuga* (https://tallerymedio.com/tag/silla-de-caderas/). Folding the chair was easy, given that the seat and backrest were typically made of leather or velvet, and they hung from the frame without any cushioning. It was one of the most common pieces of furniture in Spain during the sixteenth century, although it was not invented in Spain. Its hourglass shape and folding seat are derived from the *sella curul* of Rome, and it seems that in Italy it also had several names: *sedia di campo*, *sedia Dantesca*, and *sedia Savonarola* (Feduchi 1957:21; Garbana 1969:8). Even though it was known in ancient Rome, this type of chair was not used in Spain until the beginning of the fifteenth century (Aguiló Alonso 1993:136–139).

Bernal Díaz del Castillo, writing about the conquest some fifty-five years after the fact, narrates how Cortés sent to Moctezuma several presents as he made his way to Tenochtitlán. The presents included a silla de caderas with wood inlays, as well as a hat with a medallion of St. Michael, and some precious stones (Díaz del Castillo 1942:127). This gift underscores that the Spanish thought of sillas de caderas as symbolically charged and did not hesitate to use them as presents to powerful Indigenous rulers during the conquest. The chairs certainly made an impression on Indigenous people, who sometimes depict colonizers sitting in those chairs and talking to Indigenous officials in pictorial manuscripts. In a fragment of the *Lienzo de Tlaxcala* painted in the mid-1540s, Cortés appears sitting on a silla de caderas (Plate 4). Xicotencatl, lord of Tlaxcala, is also sitting in a silla de caderas next to Cortés, underscoring the association with power that such chairs quickly gained among the people of Tlaxcala (*Lienzo de Tlaxcala*). Indigenous writers painted plenty of images of Spaniards sitting on sillas de caderas, as can be seen in the Florentine Codex (Sahagún 1950–1982), the Codex Mexicanus (Diel 2018: plate 39), in different scenes in the Lienzo de Tlaxcala, the Codex of Cuetlaxcohuapan, and in the Codex of Tlatelolco (Martínez del Río de Redo 1985). One of the scenes in the Lienzo de Tlaxcala shows no less than sixteen Spaniards sitting on their chairs (Figure 3.3). Due to the chair's powerful symbolism, Diel (2018:141) has called it "a European equivalent to the woven reed thrones occupied by native rulers."

The fifty-nine chairs found in the inventories are mostly sillas de caderas, which total thirty, plus one *silla de costillas*, a similar style of folding chair discussed under the general category of silla de caderas in some of the literature (e.g., Aguiló Alonso 1993:139). The rest of the chairs include twenty-one chairs of unspecified style, two that are labeled as *silla de corrida*,[5] and five

---

[5] I suspect these are horseback riding saddles, but I have not been able to verify it.

Figure 3.3 Spaniards sitting on sillas de caderas. Detail from the Lienzo de Tlaxcala, redrawn by Samuel Wilson.

that are labeled as *silla de espaldas* (roughly, chair with a back rest). The Franz Mayer Museum has a few chairs from the sixteenth century, catalogued as *silla de brazos* (arm chair). It is difficult to know how flexible the different categories of chair were, and whether these chairs could be classified under any of the categories that appear in the inventories. These chairs help us see some of the variation in terms of luxury that one of the categories could imply. The sixteenth-century chairs at the Franz Mayer are not folding chairs. One example shown here (Plate 5) is made of wood, with a red velvet seat and back rest. It has adornments of bronze. The velvet, although luxurious, seems modest and perhaps even plain in comparison with another example from the Franz Mayer collection (Plate 6). Similar to the previous example, it was made in Spain in the sixteenth century, and it has a wooden frame with velvet seat and backrest; however, the seat is cushioned, and the velvet includes an image of St. Paul and other motifs woven in gold and silver thread. By virtue of its more complex and detailed seating, the chair seems richer and more luxurious, although it lacks the bronze details of the previous example. I suspect that there were plenty of chairs that did not approach these two in terms of workmanship and luxury.

Looking at what colonizers did with chairs forces me to reconsider the range of uses that colonizers gave to furniture. They did not only use chairs to rest, to reproduce a Spanish life, or to seek distinction from Indians. They also sometimes gave them away to powerful Indigenous people, in search of alliances, although the few examples I have provided do not facilitate an analysis of how frequently chairs were provided as gifts to Indigenous lords. Still, these examples show that conquistadors, and by extension colonizers, knew that their chairs could have symbolic uses, and they mobilized that symbolism, on occasion, in recognition of Indigenous power.

In addition to chairs, colonizers rested their weary legs on benches, which are typically defined simply as seats for two or more people (Feduchi 1957:23). There are eighteen benches in the inventories, under various names: *banqueta*, *banco*, *banca para asentarse*, and *bancal de mesa*. The term *banco* by itself may be misleading because it had at least two different meanings. It could be used to refer to a bench or it could be used to refer to the thick legs of a table, which often resemble columns. Contemporary descriptions of tables sometimes emphasize the legs (banco) and not the top surface of the table (Aguiló Alonso 1993:126), and in some cases, the legs of benches were quite similar to the legs seen in tables (Feduchi 1957:24). Given that six of the bancos are left without any information as to whether they were supports for beds or for sitting, we are left with between twelve and eighteen benches for sitting. Benches for sitting were typically boxes with a low backrest and armrests, or simply a wide seat, and they were used typically for receiving guests or for sitting in lieu of individual chairs (Aguiló Alonso 1993:143–144).

Cañeque (2004:629) has argued that in public ceremonies, people used chairs and benches to show rank. In the meetings for the Cabildo of Mexico City, only viceroys, bishops, and a few other high-ranking officials could sit in chairs. Members of the cabildo had to sit together in benches. Violating these seating arrangements and customs could create conflicts, so much so that the amusing clashes sometimes appear in historical documents from the sixteenth and seventeenth centuries. Cañeque argues that the conflicts are no mere anecdotes. Displays involving material culture were integral to the negotiation of power in New Spain. Whether people used chairs or benches to display rank in domestic contexts is speculative and could be researched further in the future.

Finally, another seating element found in the inventories are forty-one *cojines* or cushions. Only one of them is described as *labrado*, which loosely translates to "wrought." The rest of them are not described, or simply described as new, old, or dirty. Only one of them is described as being imported, and the rest of them lack any information on where they were made or who made them. Cushions were typically square and used for sitting, although the descriptions in the inventories do not provide any information about shape or decoration. Cañeque (2004:609–610) also describes how cushions were part of disputes between a viceroy and members of the cabildo of Mexico City. Sometimes people resented that the viceroy used a cushion to appear to sit higher than government officials at a meeting. Other times people complained that the viceroy had banned the use of cushions at church among cabildo officials. These conflicts were not a question of comfort, but rather a struggle for authority, comparable to wearing insignia of power. Just as was the case with chairs and benches, I do not know whether conflicts over the use of cushions extended into households in New Spain.

Tables

The inventories also contain thirty-one tables. As tends to be the case with the inventories, the descriptions lack details. Fifteen of them are simply listed as tables. Another table is listed as *mesa de pies*, which simply refers to a table with its legs fixed to the top permanently. This type of table could not be disassembled or folded (http://tesauros.mecd.es/tesauros/mobiliario/1175097.html). The rest of them are tables with their bench, in reference to their ornamental legs, but lacking any other details of what they looked like. The tables do not contain information on where they were made. Only one listing mentions that the table was painted in Valladolid, and offers no other information on its origin. Thus, the descriptions provide no opportunity to tell whether at least some of the tables were locally made. Martínez del Río de Redo (1985:52) claims that colonizers started making tables early in the sixteenth century, and that the earliest tables were simple boards of wood over four legs. The legs were joined by curved pieces of iron that formed an hourglass figure underneath the table and provided stability to it. Three of the tables in the inventories are described as painted, but there is no other information on color or any other qualities of the tables. Only three tables are described by size: one big, and two small. Thus, the inventories offer little data on what the tables in question looked like or where they were made. At the time, tables in Spain were quite varied, and they were made of different materials, including different kinds of hardwood, ebony inlaid with ivory, bronze, or shell, lacquer, marble, and any of the previous materials inlaid with jasper or silver. The tables could be quite fancy, especially in the carvings all over their legs (Aguiló Alonso 1993:131–136; Enriquez 1951: photos 28–34).

It is interesting that there are no examples that are specifically described as folding tables. Folding tables made up the majority of tables in the inventories in Spain in the sixteenth century. There are also no buffets (*bufetes*) listed in the inventories. The intended function of buffets at the time was to serve as a portable table.[6] Like folding tables, buffets were very common in Spain at the time, and they were used for eating, writing, and many other purposes during travel. Many houses in Spain had several buffets (Aguiló Alonso 1993:127–128). One would think that these two kinds of tables, by virtue of their portability, would be found in the inventories. There is some evidence that folding tables were seen in Mexico in the sixteenth century. In an illustration in the Codex of Yanhuitlán (1550), one can see a friar writing on a folding table with scissor legs (Martínez del Río de Redo 1985:50). Another, similar table appears later in the Codex, this time with two men writing on paper places atop it. This Indigenous codex is from the town of Yanhuitlan, Oaxaca (http://bdmx.mx/documento/codice-yanhuitlan). Perhaps Indigenous people had seen plenty of tables like the one depicted there, but I do not have much evidence to support this statement. Either the portable tables are present in the inventories under the general category of tables, but not identified as folding tables, or they were not found at all among the belongings of these thirty-nine decedents.

---

[6] The word buffet, like some other terms used in furniture studies, can be misleading. Buffets can also be chests with many small drawers. They are found in the literature on seventeenth century furniture in Mexico, and they were quite common. They could be fancy, with wooden inlays, as well as inlays of shell, turtle shell, and other materials (Martínez del Río de Redo 1985).

A seventeenth-century table at the Franz Mayer museum (Plate 7) may give us an idea of what some tables in the sixteenth century could be like. The seventeenth-century table at the Franz Mayer Museum was made in Spain out of carved walnut wood. The design is simple, although the legs and the beams that hold them together are ornamented with much attention to detail. The result is a beautiful table that straddles the line between simple elegance and ornamentation. Unfortunately, one table cannot possibly capture the variety of tables that existed at the time, and it cannot tell us much about how tables may have changed from one century to another. Further research could help understand the variety of tables in the sixteenth century and its social implications.

Beds, Pillows, and Sheets

Other items that appear frequently in the inventories include beds and bed-related items. Beds with a wooden frame were considered by Spaniards in the Andes essential for civilization (Jamieson 2000b:166), and the same was likely the case in Mexico and elsewhere in the Spanish colonies. It has been difficult to learn much about beds in general, but especially the beds of the lower classes, because people tended to burn the beds of those who died of an illness, leaving very few surviving examples today. Still, there is information in the historical literature that can help learn about beds. In Spain in the sixteenth century, beds were made in pieces. Some parts were of wood, and some were of iron. Woodworkers, organized in guilds, were in charge of the manufacture of the different parts in some cities, including Madrid, whereas workers in other cities, especially Seville and Málaga, were in charge of making the beds with the pieces furnished by others. Beds were made to be pulled apart easily and transported in boxes. Wooden planks typically supported the sleeping surface, although beds that were made for travel had canvas instead of wooden planks as a support for the mattress. Some beds, usually for lower classes, had ropes that crisscrossed underneath the mattress, creating a net for support. Beds had four legs, one in each corner. The legs usually also formed a column that went well above the sleeping surface and served to support fabric that enclosed the bed like a tent. The upper classes enjoyed draping fabrics that were expensive and embellished with gold and silver thread over their beds. Expensive beds had fancy headboards throughout the sixteenth century, although cheaper beds must have been a lot simpler and plain (Aguiló Alonso 1993:144–145).

There are only thirty-one beds listed in the inventories. One is listed as *cama de lienzo* or canvas bed, and the other as *cama de ropa*, or cloth bed, in reference to the use of canvas or other cloth to support the mattress. Another one is listed as a *cama de red*, probably in reference to the net of ropes used to support the mattress. That leaves us with fewer beds than people in the documents, but expecting a one-to-one correspondence between beds and people would be unrealistic. Many people must have slept in beds that they did not own, especially if they did not have a house or room of their own. Even though there are only thirty-one beds, there are forty *colchones* or mattresses. Mattresses back then were quite different from the type of rigid mattress seen today. They were usually two pieces of cloth, usually linen, that had the same dimensions as the bed. Wool, down, or other soft material was placed between the two pieces of cloth, and they were then sewn together to contain the cushioning material. People often used one, two, or three mattresses at a time to enhance the cushioning and comfort of their bedding. In seventeenth-century Seville, and probably earlier as well, some of the poorest people did not own a bed and instead just placed a mattress on the floor to sleep at night (Martín Morales 2016:21–22). Twenty people owned the forty mattresses in this sample of inventories, further indication that many people must have slept in beds or mattresses that belonged to others. The inventories provide very little in terms of descriptions of these beds. Martínez del Río de Redo (1985:52) has claimed that beds were probably extremely simple in the sixteenth century, which may have been the case; however, the inventories include seven *paramentos de cama*, a term that refers to the cloth that was usually draped over the beds when sleeping. The presence of the paramentos de cama suggests variety, probably ranging from simple beds to beds with fancy cloth draped over its columns.[7]

Other items related to bedding were much more frequent in the inventories. The inventories contain 103 pillows listed among the belongings of 21 decedents. A few people owned five or six pillows. Sheets appear in the inventories frequently, and under different names that may suggest different uses or slightly different designs or sizes. One may find eighty-one sheets (*sábanas*), plus another thirty-one *paños de cama*, which were probably sheets or bed cloths in general. In his glossary of household items in

---

[7] Additionally, there are twelve items labeled simply as paramentos, without specifying that they were for beds. The term paramento could refer to decoration for beds or for a horse, or a house, and the vocabulary in the inventories is not enough to claim that these were made specifically for beds. Another five items are listed as paramentos de la tierra, specifying that they were locally made, but leaving in doubt whether they were for beds or for something else.

seventeenth-century Seville, Martín Morales (2016:27) writes that he was not able to narrow down a definition for paños de cama. The historical documents that he consulted did not contain enough information to tell whether there was any way to distinguish between paños de cama and any other kind of sheets, blankets, or cloths related to beds.

Another item that is found even more frequently than sheets is blankets. Mexico City can be cold in the evenings for most of the year, even in the summer when the daily afternoon rains cool the city down all night and into the morning. Blankets were therefore highly desired, as indicated by the presence of 150 of them in the inventories. Of these 150 blankets, 144 were labeled only as *mantas* and do not contain information on use, but they were most likely used for sleeping. One of them was sold along with a pillow, another one with a mattress. Two of the blankets were *mantas fresadas*, which can translate to thick or milled blankets. There are fourteen other mantas in the inventories, but those are labeled specifically as *mantas de carga*, which indicates they were likely used to wrap goods and carry them, much like one would use a bag.

Missing Items: Desks, Tapestries, and Petates

Three items that do not appear in any of the inventories are worth mentioning. First, it seems as if none of the decedents owned a desk. There were desks in Mexico in the sixteenth century, but perhaps they were rare in the first few decades after the conquest. Perhaps people simply used tables and *escribanías* to write. Escribanías were boxes that held writing instruments, paper, knives, scissors, ink, and other items related to writing. There are thirteen cajas de escribanías in Juan Bautista's inventory (Cont. 200, N.2, R.2), and all of them were empty. There are four others in the inventories, and they are listed as having a knife or scissors, but there is no mention of other tools or writing instruments. Perhaps the only valuable items worth mentioning were the cutting tools.

A second item that is notably absent from these inventories is tapestries. They are ubiquitous in the historical documents about Spanish furniture and household decorations consulted by Aguiló Alonso (1993), and they were found in 15 percent of the houses in seventeenth-century Seville (Martín Morales 2016:46). Judging by those documents, Spanish courts covered their walls with tapestries and used them to decorate even when they traveled, although the lower classes did not have access to such luxuries. In New Spain, Cortés and Doña Juana de Zúñiga, his wife, decorated their palace in Cuernavaca with tapestries that had images of lions, birds, and other creatures. When their belongings were inventoried in 1549, they had no less than fourteen rugs at their palace. Martínez del Río de Redo claims that tapestries are present in many inventories in sixteenth-century New Spain, although she only provides Cortés' inventory as an example (1985:52).

The presence of such tapestries and rugs in the inventory of Cortés' palace, and their complete absence in the thirty-nine inventories consulted for this study, shows that tapestries and rugs were a rare luxury in New Spain in the sixteenth century. Not even the very wealthiest of the inventories I consulted contain a single tapestry. There was only one rug in all of the inventories. It belonged to the wealthiest inventory, that of Hernán Núñez Caballero. His rug was made in Europe and it was sold in auction for 11 pesos, probably of oro común. About thirty shirts in his own inventory were sold for almost twice as much (18 pesos) each. It was definitely not an expensive rug. Unfortunately, there is no more descriptive information about this rug, making it impossible to know its size, materials or any details about what it looked like, but given its low price, it must have not been a luxurious rug by any means.

The furniture listed in the probate inventories does not include an item found in Indigenous houses all over central Mexico: the petate. Perhaps colonizers owned petates, or perhaps they found no use for them, but the inventories do not provide enough information to know. A pattern that seems clear, however, is that the Spanish brought a lot of European furniture and used it when there was no Indigenous equivalent. They brought beds, tables, sheets, and mattresses. A petate was apparently not enough of an equivalent to a Spanish bed or mattress. When Indigenous producers began making similar items, such as boxes and chairs, they adopted those. Importation of furniture was not determined by the cost or trouble of importing, but rather by the perceived need for the items. The demand for furniture that the Spanish considered appropriate engaged with patterns of trade and production, and very likely altered those patterns, as Indigenous people began to produce some wooden furniture for the Spanish and ships sailed across the ocean with loads of mattresses, sheets, and wooden furniture.

Owners and Producers

Questions of ownership of the items are paramount in this study. The probate inventories include information on the origin of the furniture and sometimes even comments about the identity of the producers. Of course, information on the origin or manufacturer of plenty of items in the inventories is missing. The lack of information may be due to disinterest among the people compiling the inventories in pointing out matters of origin, a lack of knowledge, or many other possible reasons. Still, the probate inventories are the best source we have for learning where the furniture was made. In this section, I address both, the origin of the furniture and who owned the different items, to continue examining issues of wealth, ethnicity, power, and their relationship to materiality.

Only 5 of the 107 boxes contain any information of provenience, and of those, 2 are designated as de la tierra, 1 from Michoacán, and 2 from Castile. None of the boxes is listed as being made specifically by Indigenous producers. As usual, it is hard to know whether any of these figures, especially the provenience of the items, is a reliable indicator of where the rest of the items were made. I speculate that many of the boxes probably came from the various countries that supplied furniture to Spain at the time, but the documents are mostly silent on this matter. Still, it is interesting that some of the boxes were made in the Americas, and that most of the boxes do not contain information on their origin. Perhaps colonizers were not too concerned about the origins of boxes.

Only six of the chests contain any indication of their origin, and they are all made in Flanders. Along with Italy and Germany, Flanders supplied a lot of the furniture used in Spain at the time, judging by its frequent appearance in the documents cited by Aguiló Alonso (1993). There is no clear agreement as to what distinguished chests from Flanders from others (Aguiló Alonso 1993:81). None of chests in the probate inventories are listed as made in the Americas, let alone by Indigenous producers.

Perhaps the most symbolically charged item of furniture was the chair. The silla de caderas became associated with luxury in Spain during the fifteenth and sixteenth centuries (Aguiló Alonso 1993:138), and they were mobilized as a symbol of power and authority during the conquest, as discussed previously. Chairs appear in only thirteen of the inventories. Among this group of colonizers, chairs in general, and chairs that are listed specifically as silla de caderas, show a tendency to be associated with the wealthier decedents, although not exclusively (Table 3.1). The three wealthiest men in this table (who are ranked 1, 2, and 4 in terms of wealth in the Grade A inventories) owned twenty of the fifty-nine chairs. Six of the top ten wealthiest men in all of the Grade A inventories owned thirty-five of the fifty-nine chairs.

They also owned eighteen of the thirty chairs that are marked specifically as silla de caderas. However, there is another way of looking at the data that can reveal the complexity of the pattern: four of the ten wealthiest decedents did not own chairs at all (or at least they are nowhere to be found in the inventories), and some of the poorest men owned chairs also, including sillas de caderas. One of them was Bartolomé Hernández, who was so poor that the value of his inventory would fall below the poverty line in contemporary Seville (Chapter 2). Nevertheless, he owned five chairs, of which four are listed as silla de caderas and one as silla de costillas. He was a carpenter, which means that he could have made the chairs, whether for others or for his own use, or that he obtained the chairs through his personal connections to other carpenters. Four of his chairs are described as being locally made ("de la tierra"), lending support to the idea that he made them himself. The only other chairs that contain any information on their place of manufacture are the five chairs owned by Martín Carrasco, also described as being made locally. The pattern of ownership of the chairs shows that if it is true that sillas de caderas were associated with luxury in Spain, in the sample consulted from Mexico City they could be found among the belongings of some of the wealthiest people and sometimes also among the belongings of

Table 3.1 Owners of different types of chairs.

	Rank by wealth	Silla	Silla de caderas	Silla de corrida	Silla de costillas	Silla de espaldas	Total
Hernán Núñez Caballero	1	5	0	2	0	0	7
Antonio Martínez	2	5	3	0	0	0	8
Martín Carrasco	4	0	5	0	0	0	5
Maese Gregorio de Heredia	5	1	0	0	0	0	1
Juan Gutiérrez de Grado	6	0	6	0	0	0	6
Andrés de Plasencia	7	0	8	0	0	0	8
Alonso García	22	0	1	0	0	0	1
Bartolomé Hernández	24	0	4	0	1	0	5
Alonso de Zapardiel	na	0	3	0	0	0	3
Alonso Serrano	na	0	0	0	0	4	4
Hernando Ladrón	na	0	0	0	0	1	1
Juan de Oliva	na	1	0	0	0	0	1
Salvador Márquez	na	9	0	0	0	0	9
Total		21	30	2	1	5	59

some of the poorest. Access to this luxury, and perhaps other luxuries, could perhaps be related to wealth, and it could be related to other social factors and contingencies, including the occupation of the person, their contacts, and perhaps even their social goals (Chapter 7).

The patterns of ownership of cushions support the findings of ownership of chairs. Hernán Núñez Caballero, the wealthiest of the decedents, owned most of the cushions, with eighteen. Only three other decedents are listed as owning cushions. Of those, the only one who appears in the Grade A inventories is Juana Bautista, who owned seven cushions. She was certainly not among the wealthiest, ranking fifteenth among the Grade A inventories in terms of wealth. But she was probably a seamstress, judging by the items she owned. Although I have no solid proof, it is possible that she made the cushions herself, showing how a person's occupation could offer them access to items that were rare or that most others did not own.

Although the documents do not contain much information on the origin of tables,[8] there is much more information about the origin of the beds. Nine out of the thirty-one beds had information on its origin. Of those, five are listed as locally made, three as imported, and one specifically as "made by Indians." The latter bed belonged to Antonio Martínez, who owned the second wealthiest inventory in this study. The imported beds belonged to Andrés de Plasencia, ranked seventh in terms of the value of his inventory, and to Juan de Oliva, whose inventory is not among the Grade A inventories. Still, the presence of a locally made bed among the belongings of one of the wealthiest men in the sample confounds the expectation that the wealthiest would stay away from things made locally and especially things made by Indigenous people. Only ten of the forty mattresses contain information on origin. Of those, eight were made in Europe, and only two were made locally.

---

[8] The inventories do not contain much information on the origin of the tables; however, they contain better information on who owned the tables: twelve of the decedents owned all of the tables. Martín Carrasco (Cont. 197 N.21 (10)), a cleric, owned the most tables, with seven. He is also the fifth wealthiest decedent in the inventories consulted (Chapter 2). Juan Negrete (Cont. 211 N.2, R.7), a friar, owned the second most tables in the sample, with six tables, although I was not able to calculate his overall wealth due to missing data, as discussed in Chapter 2. The third person to own several tables was Salvador Márquez (Cont. 5575 N.13), a tailor who may have used his four tables for work and whose wealth, just like Juan Negrete's, I was unable to calculate, making it difficult to associate ownership of this type of furniture with wealth. Finally, Andrés de Plasencia owned four tables. His inventory declares that nobody knew where he was born and nobody knew his occupation either (Cont 473 n2 r1/1), but his total worth was rather high, making him the ninth wealthiest person in the inventories that I was able to add up with confidence. Thus, the information is not enough to provide a clear association between wealth and ownership of tables. In fact, wealthier colonizers seemed more likely to own chairs than to own tables, assuming that the probate inventories are a close reflection of real-life patterns.

As is usually the case, it is difficult to tell whether the indications of the origin of these mattresses are random and representative of all mattresses.

There are only seven paramentos de cama, and all seven were from in Mexico. They all belonged to Salvador Márquez, a tailor whose inventory is not included among the Grade A inventories. The fact that all of the paramentos belonged to one decedent and that I could not calculate the net worth of his inventory in a reliable manner makes it difficult to check any relationship between wealth and ownership of this type of bed ornamentation. However, his occupational specialization as a tailor is a reminder that occupation could be among the factors that granted people access to items associated with Spain but made locally. Perhaps he made his own paramentos, in between making billowy shirts and hose.

Only seventeen of the pillows contain information on origin, and of those, ten were imported from Europe and seven were made locally. If the information is representative of all pillows owned by colonizers, it means that one would have a greater chance of finding a locally made pillow than of finding a locally made mattress. Given that it must have been more difficult (bulkier) to import a mattress, this finding challenges the idea that ease of transportation strongly determined which items were imported. Perhaps Indigenous people and colonizers adopted pillow production more readily than mattress production.

It is surprising that more than half of the eighty-one sheets, forty-two to be exact, contain some comment on origin. Of those forty-two sheets, thirty-six were imported from Europe and only six were made locally. If the numbers are representative of all sheets, that means that most of the sheets, or 85.7 percent, were imported from Europe. This percentage is far higher than the percentage of clothes imported from Europe in the inventories (Chapter 5), and I find it surprising, given that colonizers expressed admiration for local cloth. Perhaps European examples met the expected measurements of a sheet or some other qualities of sheets, but those produced by Indigenous makers did not.

Two of the blankets were described as *mantas con las que se cobijan las indias* or blankets that Indigenous women use to cover themselves, indicating that they were made by Indigenous makers. As tends to be the case with bedding items, only about half of the decedents, sixteen to be exact, are listed as owners of the blankets, and only three of the decedents had more than five blankets among their belongings. The origin of the blankets is of interest. Whereas 62 of the 144 items labeled simply as "manta" do not indicate where they were made, 36 of them are labeled as *de la tierra*, or made in the Americas, and another 46 are labeled specifically as made by Indigenous producers. None of them are labeled as imported from Europe. This means that even if the information is not representative of all blankets, at a very minimum over half of the blankets were made in the Americas and many by Indigenous producers. Indigenous blankets depicted in the Codex Tepetlaoztoc tend to be fancy and colorful. They often have geometric or floral designs, although some of them can be almost entirely white, except for a few lines or zig-zags (Valle 1995; Plate 8). Although the descriptions provided in the probate inventories are not enough to tell whether the blankets were similar to the ones depicted in the codex with absolute certainty, it is quite possible that they were. Archaeologists and other scholars have found striking similarities between clothing and other objects found in Indigenous codices and existing examples of the same objects (e.g., Gallardo 2014). There are even fancier blankets depicted in the Codex Tepetlaoztoc, with richly colored design, most of them geometric, but they are specifically labeled as made with feathers (Plate 9). I believe that most of the blankets owned by colonizers were not feathered, because they did not specify that in the probate inventories. Still, there is enough information in the inventories to state that while the mattresses and sheets were predominantly European, the blankets were mostly, if not all, local and made by Indigenous hands. If it is true that Spaniards associated sleeping in beds with civilized behavior (Jamieson 2006b:166), they certainly incorporated an Indigenous product, the blanket, into their civilized practices.

If one considers the bedroom a private context, or at least a context that is not commonly visible, then it is interesting that it was a context where imported and local or Indigenous products were used in combination. But bedrooms and beds were hardly private contexts. Much socializing, even quite intimate socializing, can take place in beds, including through sex (if they ever had sex in beds at the time, which I do not know) and when receiving guests when sick. Colonizers dictated many of the wills that form part of this study from their beds. Thus, beds were sometimes contexts of socialization where a Spanish colonizer could lay on top of a European mattress, and underneath a cozy Mexican blanket.

Conclusion

At first glance, it may seem that Jamieson was exaggerating when he argued that the struggle for power in the Spanish colonies involved even household objects (Jamieson 2000b:xii). But this brief study of patterns of ownership and use of furniture in colonial Mexico shows he was right. Colonizers and Indigenous people sometimes involved furniture in their negotiation of power. The silla de caderas emerges as an example of how colonizers may have used furniture to reproduce their daily life in Spain, and maybe even to distinguish themselves from Indigenous people using material culture. But they also used the silla de caderas to create bonds with powerful Indigenous people. Sending a silla de caderas to Moctezuma, and sitting in sillas de caderas with Xicotencatl in Tlaxcala were dramatic gestures that recognized Indigenous power and sought commonalities, rather than distinction, between powerful Indigenous people and colonizers or conquistadors. Thus, the furniture could serve to mark distinction, but not necessarily and not always between Spaniards and Indians. It could also mark commonalities between those with power, and distinction from those who were left out of positions of leadership and power.

The information on furniture also challenges the idea that domestic objects were consistently part of the private facets of people's lives. People certainly saw the boxes and chairs of colonizers in public, and Indigenous people were apparently curious about those objects. The beds of colonizers, even though they were used inside the house, were sites of interaction and socialization if and when people had sex on them, invited guests to visit them, and received scribes and others who came to visit when they were ill and ready to dictate a will. Although there are objects that are more commonly associated with public life, beds and other household furniture were not consistently stuck in the private world. They could be powerfully symbolic when they crossed to the public sphere, as we have seen with the sillas de caderas.

If people used household objects to reproduce a Spanish way of life, furniture can also help add complexity to the idea of what it meant to reproduce a Spanish lifestyle. The furniture was hardly Spanish. It included items from different kingdoms in Spain, Portugal, France, Flanders, Italy, Germany, and Asia. People also started to incorporate items made in Mexico, even items made by Indigenous producers, into their furniture. A favorite example of mine would be the use of Indigenous blankets to lie on top of a Spanish mattress, on a Spanish bed, with locally made drapery. Of course, this means that furniture in Spain was characteristically a combination of furniture form different places, but my point is that the people did not feel particularly against using furniture from other places or regions. They incorporated a variety of traditions into their furniture, and they started to do so in Mexico as well, even though the variety of furniture was very little in comparison to the variety of furniture in Europe at the time.

The patterns of furniture are also a reminder that to say that someone wanted to reproduce a Spanish material world sounds simple enough, but any attempt at doing so involved hard work by many occupational specialists. It involved the work of carpenters, smiths, tailors, and leather workers from different parts of Iberia and different countries in Europe. Making a bed involved creating the wooden pieces of the bed in one place, and often assembling the bed in an entirely different city. It involved transporting items across the Atlantic, and up the mountains into central Mexico. Reproducing a material world takes a lot of work from specialists and people of different social rank, probably including enslaved people.

Finally, the patterns in the inventories show that associating some types of furniture with the upper classes and creating a clear dichotomy between the wealthy and the poor does not capture all the meaningful variation in patterns of ownership of furniture. Class or wealth are not the only factors that can explain who owned certain items of furniture and why. The general tendency of ownership of chairs, for example, was that they appear in the inventories of the wealthy, but not all of the wealthiest people in the inventories owned chairs. In fact, four out of the top ten wealthiest did not own chairs, and some of the poorest people owned chairs. Similar patterns are true for cushions. Ownership of tables is not clearly associated with wealth in this sample. The second wealthiest colonizer owned a bed made by Indigenous producers. Thus, ownership of different items of furniture was not consistently associated with wealth or social status. Sometimes people owned certain pieces of furniture because their occupation or social connections provided them access to some products. In sum, to understand the world of furniture in sixteenth century Mexico City it is necessary to think of people as active participants in shaping the material world, and not just as people who occupy certain positions of socioeconomic status and play out prescribed social roles. Discovering their actions and figuring out their goals can help understand variation in material patterns and in social and political life in this colonial situation.

4

How to Get Pottery and Food

Archaeologists pull thousands of pottery fragments out of the ground in any archaeological excavation in Mexico City. Finding these pieces of broken pots reminds us that people used ceramics in both, mundane activities, and in symbolically charged contexts. People used globular ceramic jars in colonial Mexico to store food and water, and to cook. They made cylindrical jars to store medicines and herbs. People still admire the beauty of some of these jars, known typically as *albarelos*, displayed in old pharmacies in Mexico City. Colonizers transported oil, olives, and wine across the Atlantic in ceramic jars, quite similar to amphorae with their convex base and rough surfaces. They used ceramic cups to drink, and they used bowls and plates to serve food. Some of those bowls and plates were quite plain, and people used them to eat in everyday contexts. Others were beautifully decorated, sometimes with intricate motifs painted in fine lines, and sometimes in thick brush strokes and splatters. Some of these ceramics were fine enough to show off in a feast with pride. In an era before indoor plumbing, people also used ceramic chamber pots that look like a glossy bucket hat. They remind us of the underrated luxury of flushing toilets. People used ceramic pots to wash, and to do many household activities. Given the varied uses, forms, quality, decoration, and origins of pottery, and its ubiquity in archaeological contexts, it is no wonder that archaeologists have found much to write about colonial ceramics (e.g., Charlton 1968, 1970, 1976, 1979, 1996; Charlton and Fournier 2011; Charlton et al. 1995; Deagan 1983, 1987, 1995; Fournier 1990, 1998a; Fournier García 1997; Goggin 1968; Hernández Sánchez 2012, 2019; Kuwayama 1997; Lister and Lister 1982, 1987; López Cervantes 1976; McEwan 1991, 1992; Oland 2014, 2017; Sodi Miranda 1994; Van Valkenburgh et al. 2018).

Scholars have also written much about food, which was commonly served and stored in ceramic pottery in early colonial Mexico City. Food appears in many historical documents, starting with the letters and chronicles of conquistadors and colonizers who sometimes marveled at the variety of ingredients and foods that Indigenous people ate and offered them

How to Make a New Spain. Enrique Rodríguez-Alegría, Oxford University Press. © Enrique Rodríguez-Alegría 2023.
DOI: 10.1093/oso/9780197682296.003.0005

(e.g., Durán 1994:510–511, 523; Sahagún 1950–1982, Book 12, Chapter 26). Some scholars have emphasized the cultural history of different foods, and the reactions, positive or negative, that Europeans had to food from the Americas (e.g., Coe 1993). Rebecca Earle (2012) has argued that colonizers ate Iberian foods not just to preserve their traditions or to maintain a diet that seemed familiar to them, but also as a way of preserving the bodies of Spanish colonizers. She argues that colonizers believed that eating the food of Indigenous people too much would change their bodies and make them resemble the bodies of the Indigenous people they sought to dominate. Archaeologists have also found plenty of food remains in houses in Mexico City, in the form of botanical and faunal remains, especially seeds and bones that have survived decomposition for centuries. These discoveries have provided glimpses of diet and food associated with individual households, and they can help see the combination of American and Old-World ingredients in the houses of colonizers (e.g., Guzmán and Polaco 2003; Montúfar López 2000, 2003; Montúfar López and Valentín Maldonado 1998; Valentín Maldonado 2003).

In the previous chapter, I explained that the furniture that colonizers grew up with in Spain was radically different from the minimal Indigenous furniture in central Mexico. In contrast, pottery and food provide an opportunity to study household items that both the Mexica and the Spanish produced prolifically. Indigenous people made a wide variety of pottery, and they had markets with plenty of food. Instead of a situation in which colonizers could not find functionally equivalent Indigenous products, pottery and food present a situation in which colonizers found functional equivalents to the products that they had. Thus, the questions that framed the previous chapter, related to the adoption or rejection of Indigenous and imported everyday goods in the houses of colonizers, are worth examining in relationship to pottery and food.

Pottery, containers made of other materials (mostly glass and metal), and food appear in the probate inventories infrequently and with a frustrating lack of detail. They are much more accessible in archaeological remains and in other historical sources. Therefore, I begin this chapter with a few insights from the probate inventories and then expand upon those insights considerably with the archaeological and historical literature available. Scholars have written entire books about both pottery and food in colonial Mexico. I provide only an expedient summary here, emphasizing what we can learn from the probate inventories and from the archaeological remains.

Pottery and Other Containers in the Probate Inventories

Two patterns stand out as I study the pottery in the probate inventories: (1) how little they mention pottery at all, and (2) how different the information they provide is from the information that archaeologists typically gather. The infrequent mentions of pottery do not mean that it was unimportant, and the differences between how pottery is mentioned and how archaeologists write about it do not mean that archaeologists are collecting the wrong information. They both simply mean that those who compiled the inventories and archaeologists have different interests in the pottery, and that the information from the probate inventories can be enriched significantly with archaeological data.

It is surprising that pottery appears so little in the inventories. Pottery was everywhere at the time; thus, it is important to study it as a ubiquitous aspect of the material world. Yet only 373 items of pottery and containers of any kind (including ceramic, metal, glass, and gourds) appear in the inventories (out of 11,639 total items), including a tray for cups (Table 4.1). On one hand, 373 seem like few containers. On the other hand, 373 is nearly 10 containers per person, which may not be such a small number.

When they provide information on pottery, the information looks quite different from the data that archaeologists collect. People often verbalize some meanings and ideas about objects, but leave many other meanings and ideas unexpressed. They may even be unaware of all the meanings of things in a particular context, but use things in activities that provide things with meaning. "Even if people cannot answer what the pot means, they can use the pot very effectively in social life" (Shanks and Hodder 1995:17; see also Hodder 1992:16). Thus, the ideas that people express in the inventories are only a fraction of the meanings that they gave to the objects that appear listed. The inventories do not always mention a bit of information that is of paramount importance to most archaeologists: the material that makes up the containers. A total of 61 items mention the material that they were made of (Table 4.1), and the different materials include:

   A. Silver: 32 items made of silver[1] (*piezas de plata*),
   B. Gourds: 18 probable gourds, including 15 *jícaras*, and 3 *tecomatillos*,

---

[1] The silver items were mostly serving vessels, listed as "plates, bowls, jars, cups, candle holders, salt shakers, and a tecomate" ("platos, escudillas, jarros, tazas, candileros, saleros, y un tecomate de plata"). All 32 items made of silver belonged to Juan de Oliva (Cont. 235, N.1, R.16). He was a cleric. His probate inventory only consists of a will, with no record of sale of his belongings, providing no opportunity to calculate his net worth. The silver itself is neither weighed nor priced in the

Table 4.1 Pottery listed in the probate inventories.

	English name	Material	Frequency	%
bacín de barbero con servilleta de acofar	barber's pot with tin brim	tin brim	1	.3
bacineta, bacinica, bacinilla	chamber pot		6	1.6
bateas	bats		6	1.6
batejuela de limpiar oro	bat for cleaning gold		5	1.3
botijas	bats		4	1.1
caldera	boiler		1	.3
caldereta	stew pot		2	.5
caliz	chalice		1	.3
caliz con su bacín en su vasera	chalice with its basin in its own tray		1	.3
cazuela	casserole		1	.3
copa	cup		3	.8
cubeta	bucket		1	.3
cubilese de yndios del Perú	beaker of the Indians of Perú		1	.3
cubiletas, cubiletes	beakers		11	3
escubilla de limpiar	bowl for cleaning		14	3.7
escubillas de limpiar ropa	bowls for washing clothes		3	.8
escudilla	bowl		44	11.8
frasco	jar		3	.8
frasquillo	small jar		1	.3
jarra	pitcher		1	.3
jarro	pot		10	2.6
jarro de vidrio	glass pot	glass	3	.8
jícara, xícara	gourd	gourd?	15	4
lebrillo	basin		2	.5
maceta	pot		3	.8
olla	jar		9	2.4
olla con sal	salt jar		1	.3
ollita	small jar		2	.5
paila, payla	pot		12	3.2
paileta, paililla	small pot		2	.6
payla de acoffar	tin pot	tin	1	.3
pichel	tankard		7	1.8
piezas de peltre	pewter pieces	pewter	2	.5

(*continued*)

Table 4.1 Continued

	English name	Material	Frequency	%
piezas de plata	silver pieces	silver	32	8.6
pileta	basin		1	.3
plato	plate		72	19.3
plato y escudilla	plate and bowl		2	.5
platonsillo	plate		3	.8
platos de estaño y salseros	tin saucers	tin	5	1.3
porcelana	porcelain	porcelain	1	.3
porcelana de la China	Chinese porcelain	porcelain	2	.5
redoma	flask		4	1.1
redomillas	flasks		5	1.3
sahumador	censer		1	.3
salero, salerillo	salt shaker		14	3.7
salsericas	saucers		6	1.6
sartén	pan		3	.8
taza	cup		12	3.2
tazón	cup		1	.3
tecomate	neckless jar		1	.3
tinaja	jar		15	11.2
tinaja de agua, de tener agua	water jar		3	.8
tinajas e lebrillos	jars and basins		3	.8
tocomatillos de tomayaca (?)	gourd	gourd	3	.8
vaseras de vidrios	tray for glasses		2	.5
vaso	cup		3	.8
Total			373	100.0

C. Tin: 6 vessels made of tin, including 5 *platos de estaño y salseros* (tin plates and saucers), 1 *payla de acoffar* (tin pile), and 1 *bacín de barbero con servilleta de acofar* (barber's pot with a tin brim)

D. Glass: 3 glass jars or flower pots (*jarros de vidrio*),

E. Porcelain: 3 items made of porcelain of unspecified form, and

F. Pewter: 2 pots of indefinite shape (*piezas de peltre*).

inventory, providing no opportunity to calculate its value. Thus, it is not possible for me to associate his silver with any specific calculation of wealth. Several other items could be made out of metal, but the documents do not specify the material they are made of. For example, the *sartén* (pan) could be made of metal. The same could be said of the *pileta* (basin), the *pailas* (pots), and several others.

The probable gourds include 15 jícaras, which are named after *xicalli*, lacquered gourd bowls made by Indigenous producers before and after the Spanish conquest. They could be painted with flowers and gilded, and they were usually red. Unfortunately, the name jícara is too vague to determine much, besides the idea that they were containers. Jícara could also refer to ceramic chocolate cups made in the colonial period to imitate the shape of the gourds (Pierce 2003:253–254). The probate inventories sometimes specify that the jícaras were for washing, or for storing medicines; therefore, I hesitate to argue that they were definitely gourds or that the term refers to a specific shape. It is probable that the rest of the items, or 310 containers, are simply ceramic pottery, most likely earthenware, some glazed, some not glazed, some made by Spanish colonizers, some imported, and some made by Indigenous potters. The lack of interest in the material is a striking contrast with the interest that archaeologists have in it.

Pottery and other containers in the inventories are sometimes listed in a way that emphasizes form (plate, bowl, basin), sometimes material (porcelain, gourd, silver), and other times a combination of form and use (basin for cleaning gold, barber's bowl). The categories of form and use show the varied uses of these containers in the houses of Spaniards, which can be separated into three general categories with permeable boundaries:

A. Food service: 72 plates, 44 *escudillas* or bowls of unspecified use (although as can be seen below, many could be used for cleaning), 3 *platonsillos* or small plates, 12 cups, and 11 jars or pitchers.

B. Cooking and storing food and liquids: 9 *ollas* or cooking jars, 1 olla full of salt, 13 salt shakers, between 17 and 20 *tinajas* or water jars of which 3 were listed as *tinajas y lebrillos*, 4 *redomas*, which were flasks or glass vials (Deagan 1987:191) and 5 *redomillas*, which were probably small flasks.

C. Cleaning: 14 *escudillas de limpiar* (cleaning bowls), 3 as *escudillas de limpiar ropa* (basins for washing clothes), 7 basins and 6 *bateas* or pans, 5 pans for washing gold, 15 *pailas* or large pans.

Many of these uses are what people today would relegate to plastic buckets and reused plastic containers, but in the sixteenth century, they were mostly containers made out of clay. Separating the containers into these three categories should not imply that each form had a unique function. Colonizers probably used the same form for different purposes. Further, the three categories do not capture all of the functions of containers. Chamber pots, for example, are conspicuously absent from the probate inventories. Did nobody find a reason to leave a used chamber pot listed in their will?

Archaeologists often classify pottery into specific and ever-more-detailed categories of form. For example, a plate may be a brimless plate, or a compound-silhouette plate with an annular support. A bowl may be a hemispherical bowl or a porringer with a leaf-shaped handle and a flat bottom. The categories of shape can be specific, sometimes even measured with calipers or rulers to arrive at a precise classification. All of these classifications may become useful or not in interpretation, depending on the interests of the analyst. Some of the detailed information on pottery attributes that archaeologists collect may be useful to determine the origin of a pot, to determine when it was made, or simply to be able to compare pottery assemblages with other archaeologists. Sometimes, the ability that archaeologists have to collect information on pottery outpaces our ability to know what the information means (Braun 1983:107–108), but that information may become useful in the future, when someone figures out how to use it. The categories of form in the probate inventories are strikingly different, and would be considered vague and maybe even worthless or untrustworthy if they had been used by an archaeologist. None of the forms are as specific as those that can be found in an archaeological typology. Still, the forms mentioned reveal what was important to the people writing the classification: the implied use of the form, regardless of details that may make the pot finer or nicer.

Another category of information that is of paramount importance to archaeologists, and basic for the present study, the place of manufacture, is rarely mentioned in the inventories. Only 8 out of 373 items mention where they were made. Six of them were made in the Americas (one of them in Perú), and two porcelain items were listed as specifically made in China. The other porcelain item in the inventories must have also been imported from China, given that porcelain was not made in the Americas or in Europe at the time.

The inventories contain very few assessments of another issue of importance to archaeologists: the quality of pottery and how people evaluated it. If we look at the number of comments that assess the quality of the objects, it seems like a lot of commentary on quality: 157 items (42 percent of all of the pottery) include some assessment of quality (Table 4.2). But most of the comments are related to the size of the container in question, to its weight, age, and to whether it was broken. None of the comments offer any hint of the decoration of the pottery or other containers, or even whether they were

Table 4.2 Comments about the quality of the pottery.

	English translation	Frequency	%
No comment		216	57.9
chica	small	1	.3
con los maniles dorados	with golden handles	12	3.2
con salero	with a saucer	2	.5
con una medalla	with a medal	1	.3
de limpiar	for cleaning	23	6.2
dorado en partes, pesó 4 marcos y cinco onzas y dos reales	part golden, weighing 4 marcos and 5 ounces and 2 reales	1	.3
dorado por dentro que pesa 2 marcos y 5 onzas	golden on the inside, weighing 2 marcos and 5 ounces	1	.3
en platos, escudilla, jarros, tazas, candileros, saleros, y un tecomate de plata	in plates, a bowl, jars, cups, candlesticks, saucers, and a silver tecomate	32	8.6
en que había un cascalote	with a cascalote plant	1	.3
Grande, grandes	big	11	2.9
grandes de tener agua	big, for keeping water	2	.5
hierro	iron	1	.3
labrado	worked	1	.3
llana	shallow	1	.3
mayor	large	1	.3
Medianas, medianos	medium	17	4.6
muy vieja	very old	1	.3
para obradas pequeñas	small, for work	1	.3
Pequeña, pequeños	small	13	3.5
pesa tres marcos menos media onza	weighs three marcos minus one ounce	1	.3
pesó cinco marcos y cinco onzas y 6 reales	weighed five marcos and five ounces and six reales	1	.3
pesó un marco y un real	weight one marco and one real	1	.3
quebrado	broken	2	.6
vidriado grande	glazed and big	1	.3
Vieja, viejo, viejos	old	24	6.4
viejas con tinta	old with ink	4	1.1
Total		373	100.0

decorated at all, which is precisely the kind of information that archaeologists would collect with diligence. Only one item specifies that it was glazed and none of the items offer any evaluation of the workmanship or fineness of the containers. Plates were plates and bowls were bowls, and they were big, medium, or small, new, old, or chipped, and the people who compiled the inventories saw little else to comment about the containers, besides their form, use, and sometimes the material that they were made of.

Archaeological Pottery

Archaeology can help us understand the pottery in the houses of colonizers from a different perspective that enhances the information provided in the inventories. Archaeologists and other scholars have written extensively about colonial pottery, and I focus here on aspects of origin (including who made it) and quality of the pottery, and their association with wealth and ethnicity. These are precisely the kinds of information left out of the probate inventories, but also information that can help understand the material worlds of colonizers and the importance of pottery in their daily life. I focus here mostly on ceramic pottery, given that there are far fewer studies of glass and other kinds of containers, which are found in much lower frequencies than ceramics.

Indigenous Pottery

Indigenous people in central Mexico, and the rest of the Americas, had been making ceramic pottery for thousands of years by the time the Spanish arrived. In the sixteenth century, Indigenous potters in central Mexico produced several types of earthenware for cooking, serving food, storage, sculpture, and sumptuary goods (Hernández Sánchez 2012; Minc 2017; Parsons 1966). They made plain earthenware globular jars for cooking stews and tamales, and to prepare maize drinks. They also used jars to ferment *pulque*, their best-known alcoholic beverage, made from *aguamiel*, or maguey sap. They stored and transported water in globular jars. A very different kind of ceramic pot was the *comal*, a very smooth circular griddle. They used comals for cooking dry foods, including tortillas, and for toasting and cooking seeds, grains, and vegetables (Brumfiel 1991; Fournier 1998b).

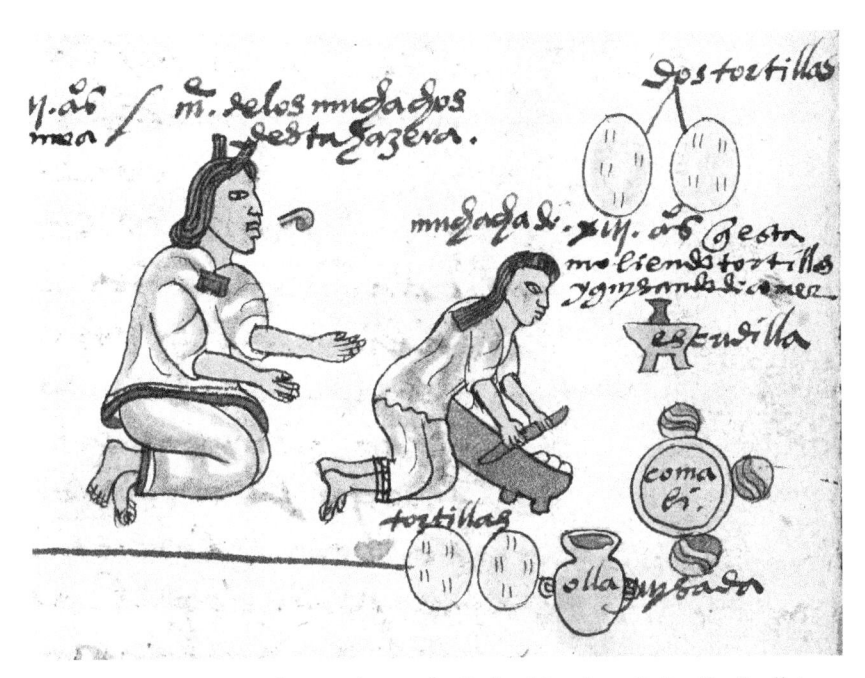

Figure 4.1 Woman teaching girl to cook. Codex Mendoza, Folio 60r. Bodleian Library.

Many central Mexican women used jars and comals together to cook different dishes in a meal or to take different steps in cooking a single dish. And they used these pots every day. For example, a cook could use a jar or a large bowl in the *nixtamalization* process, in which maize is soaked in hot water and mineral lime to soften and prepare for grinding (Biskowski 2000; Katz et al. 1974). After grinding the maize, the cook could shape and season it to make tortillas on a comal, or to make tamales in a jar. The Codex Mendoza (Berdan and Anawalt 1997:165, Folio 60r) shows a woman teaching a girl to grind maize next to the ceramic pottery that was essential in every house in central Mexico at the time: jars and comals (Figure 4.1).

Archaeologists find jar and comal fragments in abundance in sites all over central Mexico (Figures 4.2 and 4.3). In a pioneering study of gender in Late Postclassic central Mexico, Elizabeth Brumfiel (1991) studied changes in the proportions of jars and comals in archaeological assemblages to estimate whether people were eating more stews, more tortillas, or even taking dry provisions with them when they went to work and had to eat far from the house. By studying the proportions of these forms, she was able to detect

Figure 4.2 Jar fragment from Xaltocan, Mexico. Photo by Kristin de Lucia, digitized by Samuel Wilson. Used by permission.

Figure 4.3 Comal fragment from Xaltocan, Mexico. Photo by Kristin de Lucia, digitized by Samuel Wilson. Used by permission.

change through time in cooking practices, and to study regional variation in cooking. The women in some sites in the basin of Mexico cooked more dry foods and made less stews after they were conquered by the Mexica, perhaps to send food to men who were working away from the house in military campaigns or providing tribute labor to the Mexica.

Indigenous people in central Mexico traded widely in cooking vessels before and after the Spanish conquest. The places where people from a particular community obtained their cooking pottery sometimes changed historically before the formation of the empire of the Triple Alliance, and under Mexica and later Spanish control. These changes underscore that the work of potters, the patterns of exchange, and the work of women in the house could all be affected by broad political changes. Studies of trade in archaeological pottery have also revealed much trade between rural Indigenous communities. Such a pattern was not revealed with any clarity in the existing historical documents (Charlton et al. 2008; Nichols et al. 2002; Rodríguez-Alegría et al. 2013; Rodríguez-Alegría and Stoner 2016).

Among the serving vessels that Indigenous potters made, some of the most ubiquitous are Black-on-Orange pottery and Red Ware, and they are exactly what they sound like. Black-on-Orange consists mostly of orange dishes, hemispherical bowls, jars, and other forms used for serving foods. Potters painted them with repetitive geometric or calligraphic designs and patterns in black. In the colonial period, potters painted Black-on-Orange ceramics with images of birds, fish, flowers, and other natural things. In addition to food service, there were also Black-on-Orange *molcajetes*, or dishes with striated bottoms used for grating vegetables and making and serving salsas (Plate 10; Minc 2017; Parsons 1966).

Red Ware was a deep, bright red, and potters made it mostly into serving vessels, including plates, bowls, and copas (goblets), although one may also find Red Ware jars and other forms. Its surface decoration varied within a few characteristic color combinations. The most common decorative treatments of Red Ware are black motifs on red or black and white motifs on red (Plate 11). In addition to these wares, Indigenous potters in central Mexico also made polychrome vessels and a range of other ceramic types that are found all over the empire of the Triple Alliance as a result of widespread production and trade in ceramics (Charlton et al. 2008; De Lucia 2018; De Lucia et al. 2020; Hernández Sánchez 2012; Hodge et al. 1992, 1993; Minc 2017; Nichols et al. 2002; Nichols et al. 2009; Parsons 1966). Six towns in early colonial Mexico were known for being major centers of ceramic production: Cuauhtitlan, Azcapotzalco, Huitzilopochco, Tenochtitlan-Tlatelolco, Texcoco, and Xochimilco (Barlow 1951; Gibson 1964:350). Archaeologists have used chemical characterization methods and compared the chemical composition of pottery fragments found all over central Mexico to discover that many other towns made pottery, including Chalco, Huexotla, Otumba,

Tepetlaoztoc, Xaltocan, Cerro Portezuelo, and other sites in the southern basin (Hodge and Neff 2005; Hodge et al. 1992, 1993; Neff and Hodge 2008; Nichols et al. 2002, 2009). It is clear that very many people were involved in pottery production all over central Mexico.

Indigenous potters continued making plain orange ceramics, Black-on-Orange, and Red Ware into the colonial period. Colonizers did not try to eradicate Indigenous pottery production, or production of any crafts, and Indigenous producers continued working independent of colonizers (Gibson 1964:335; Hernández Sánchez 2012:91). They continued making Red Ware for more than a century after the conquest (Charlton 1979; Charlton et al. 1995). This long continuity in ceramic production was an important discovery, given that it showed that not everything changed in the lives and material worlds of Indigenous people after 1521 (Charlton 1968, 1970). Potters continued making long-handles censers used for burning incense in religious ceremonies through the sixteenth century in some cities and rural towns. There is one censer in the probate inventories, but it lacks a description; therefore, it is hard to know whether Indigenous potters made it. With the religious changes and oppression associated with the conquest, they stopped making such censers by 1620. They stopped making vessels with Mexica religious iconography as well, but continued making different types of ceramics for daily use. On top of making Indigenous-tradition ceramics, they took up production of Spanish-style ceramics, and other products, especially in urban areas (Hernández Sánchez 2012:92–94).

Archaeologists have found Red Ware and other Indigenous ceramics in the houses of colonizers (Charlton et al. 1995; Rodríguez-Alegría 2005a, 2016a). Potters did not incorporate many changes in form or decoration that would suggest an adoption of Spanish aesthetics into most of the Red Ware found in the houses excavated by the PAU. It was simply Red Ware pottery, with its old forms and decorative treatment (Rodríguez-Alegría 2016a:88). The proportion of Red Ware found in the houses of colonizers in the center of Mexico City is significant. In fact, Red Ware serving vessels make up 21.6 percent of all the serving vessels by sherd count in the houses of colonizers excavated by the PAU.[2] An additional 25.9 percent of the pottery classified is made up

[2] This statistic includes only ceramic collections from the houses I analyzed, which are discussed in some detail in previous publications (Rodríguez-Alegría 2002:170–195; 2016a:73). All of those houses were excavated before 2000. More recent research by the PAU in other houses may alter those statistics simply because the sample keeps growing. The houses are named by their street address, and they include Justo Sierra 33, Licenciado Verdad 8, Guatemala 38, Donceles 97, Argentina 15, Correo Mayor 11, González Obregón 25, and the Metropolitan Cathedral and Tabernacle.

of Red Ware sherds that were too difficult to classify into specific forms, and could therefore be storage vessels, serving vessels, or a combination of both (Rodríguez-Alegría 2016a:87).

A few historical documents also show that colonizers sometimes commissioned pottery from Indigenous potters for their own use. In 1564, the Indigenous potters from Cuauhtitlan presented a document to a judge to protest that the *alcalde mayor*, or major of their town had commissioned pottery from them but did not pay for part of the pots. The document is known today as the *Códice de los Alfareros de Cuauhtitlan*, and it even depicts pottery with modeled faces of Africans, Spaniards, and birds (Barlow 1951; Hernández Sánchez 2012:96, 211–213). Some of the pots drawn in this manuscript are made in the shapes used before the conquest, and some "show formal attributes of Spanish origin . . . such as ring bases and cover lids" (Hernández Sánchez 2012:213). In addition, historical documents claim that Martín Cortés, son of Hernán Cortés, used ceramics also from Cuauhtitlan for the celebration of his son's baptism (Charlton et al. 1995; Suárez de Peralta [1589] 1990:185). These two documents, although rare, show that the Spanish had an appreciation for Indigenous ceramics, and even incorporated it into their own meals and special occasions. This is not to say that colonizers did not appreciate and even highly desire European ceramics. Instead, it seems like they appreciated Indigenous ceramics in addition to their European wares.

Archaeologists have proposed different kinds of explanations for the presence of Red Ware in the houses of colonizers. Fournier (1997:134) has argued that Spanish colonizers liked it, probably because it resembled *terra sigillata*, a kind of pottery they had in Iberia at the time (also Fournier García and Otis Charlton 2019:43). Charlton and Fournier (2011) believe that simple economic reasons explain why some Spaniards adopted less expensive local goods, including Indigenous pottery, instead of using more expensive imports. Briefly, Spaniards who could afford expensive imports would purchase them, and poorer colonizers would only be able to afford less expensive, local ceramics. These explanations fall on the side of explanations that view people as carriers of culture traits whose taste and consumption patterns are determined mostly by economics.

In contrast, I have argued that some colonizers used Indigenous pottery and food in feasts or other meals with Indigenous people. They certainly used Indigenous ceramics for their own purposes and for specific functions, such as the residents of the house lot located on Guatemala Street #38, who predominantly used Red Ware jars, probably to store and serve water or other liquids. But colonizers, I argue, sometimes adopted Indigenous ceramics and food to show their hospitality to Indigenous people and negotiate favorable social relations with them, in recognition of their social and political power. The idea is based on the presence of Indigenous serving vessels in some Spanish houses excavated by the PAU, and on historical documents that narrate that some Spaniards ate "like Indians" and "with Indians" (Rodríguez-Alegría 2005a, 2016a). Other historical documents show that they used meals and feasts to bond with Indigenous folks and obtain social and economic benefits (Lockhart 1991:62). Other documents show that they staged a theatrical feast at least once when they declared independence from Spain in alliance with Indigenous lords (Orozco y Berra 1853; Ruiz Medrano 2010). My explanation aligns better with a view that emphasizes how people use material culture to negotiate social relations. I will return to this issue of factors that can explain consumption of Indigenous and imported objects in Chapter 7.

Imported and Locally Made Colonial Pottery

Colonizers really liked their traditional glazed earthenware. In addition to using Indigenous ceramics in their houses, colonizers also began to import pottery from Europe, especially Iberia and Italy, and to make their own pottery in the Spanish colonies (Deagan 1987; Fournier 1990; Goggin 1968; Lister and Lister 1982, 1987). A few decades after the conquest, they also began importing porcelain from Asia. By 1573 ships were sailing the Pacific regularly, and in 1574, the first two ships from Manila arrived in Acapulco, carrying 22,300 pieces of porcelain, inaugurating trade that would bring Asian ceramics and other goods to Mexico regularly until 1815 (Fournier and Junco Sánchez 2019; Kuwayama 1997:11–13).

Most of the ceramics that colonizers brought from Europe and Asia were very different from Indigenous pottery. Potters in many places in Europe glazed their serving vessels with lead and tin, which gave the ceramics their characteristic glossy surface. This type of pottery is commonly known as majolica (also staniferrous or tin-glazed pottery), and it can be easily distinguished from Indigenous pottery by its glossy surface and its colors (Figure 4.4). Majolica was typically white or off-white, and less commonly blue, gunmetal, or yellow. Potters or decorators painted it with designs in blue, green,

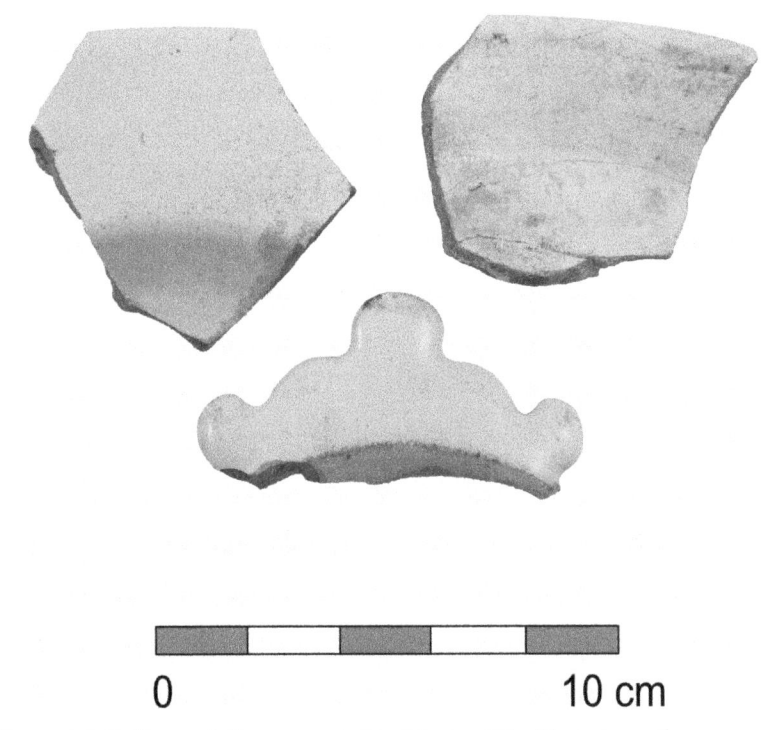

0   **10 cm**

Figure 4.4 Italian majolica excavated in Mexico City. Photo by author.

and orange, although over time they began using black, brown and other colors in lower frequencies (Figure 4.5; Deagan 1987; Fournier 1990; Goggin 1968; Lister and Lister 1982, 1987). In addition to bringing majolica from Europe, colonizers started making it in the colonies, including in Mexico City (Gámez Martínez 2003; Lister and Lister 1982, 1987). Hernández Sánchez (2012:103) argues that potters in Mesoamerica made the first glazed wares of the region around 1529, and that by the 1570s production of glazed pottery was common. Gámez Martínez (2003:231) argues that Indigenous potters had adopted glazing technologies before 1540 in Mexico City, and they made European forms, including chamber pots, candle holders, and casseroles. She cites archaeological evidence from several sites in Mexico City where archaeologists have found colonial kilns and majolica fragments. Thus, it is clear that potters began producing majolica and lead-glazed earthenware soon after the conquest.

People who saw majolica could potentially distinguish visually between majolica imported from Europe and local majolica, and between majolica of greater

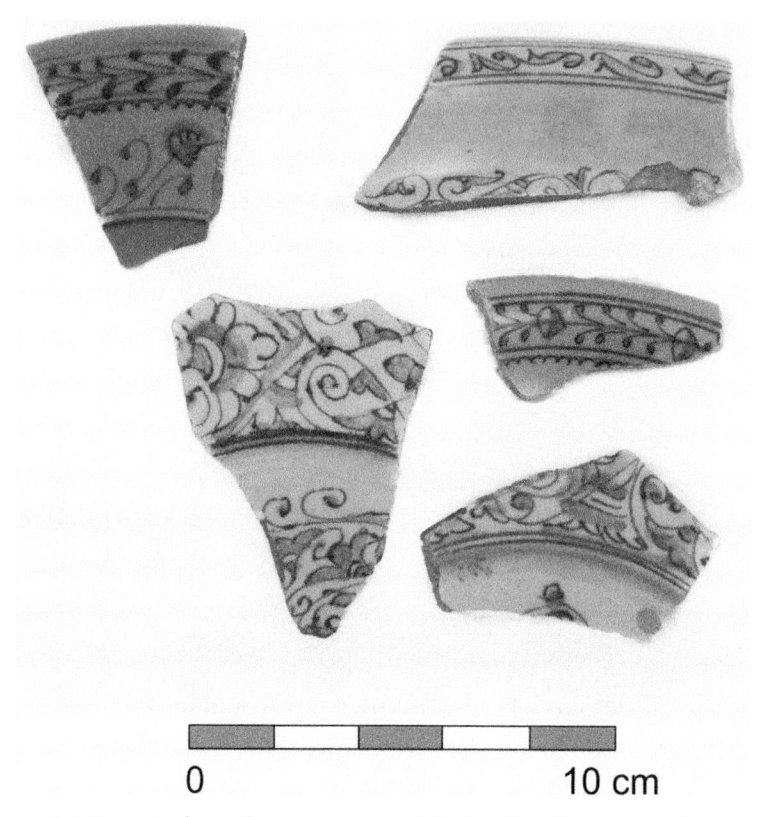

Figure 4.5 Imported majolica excavated in Mexico City. Photo by author, digitized by Samuel Wilson.

or lesser quality. The color of the glaze could furnish clues about provenience and quality, as could the opacity of the glaze (whether one could see the color of the ceramic body through the glaze), the visible imperfections of the surface (ranging from pristine smoothness, through cracked glazes, to friable glazes full of bubbles and imperfections), the range of forms, and the thickness of the pottery. For example, very white glazes were often associated with European imports and with fine local majolica. In contrast, off-white, cream, or yellowish glazes were often associated with lesser quality majolica (Lister and Lister 1982, 1987).

Mexican majolica can be split into more than two major categories that provide information on provenience and quality, including what Lister and Lister (1982) called Mexico City fine grade, and Mexico City common grade majolica (Figure 4.6; Plate 12). A main characteristic of fine grade is its very opaque white glaze, although off-white glazes are also possible. The opacity

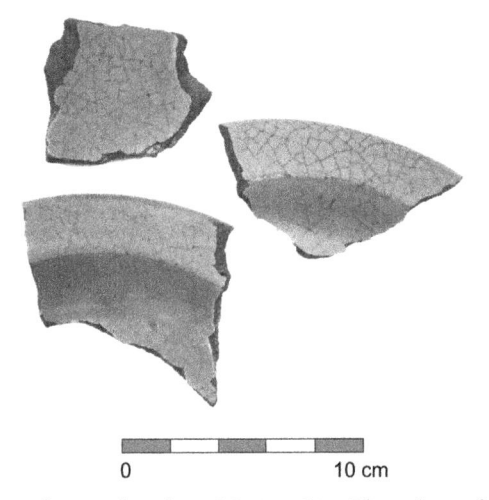

0   10 cm

Figure 4.6 Fine grade majolica from Mexico City. Photo by author, digitized by Samuel Wilson.

of the glaze hid the bright red color of the ceramic body quite well. Mexico City fine grade majolica was made into a range of shallow dishes, hemispherical bowls, and other service forms, and it compared in quality with the finest imports from Seville and Italy (Figure 4.7).

Common grade majolica, on the other hand, tended to have an off-white, cream, or yellowish glaze that was not opaque enough to hide the color of the ceramic paste beneath it. It was whitish, but translucent, and the color of the cream paste beneath could be seen through the glaze. The forms of common grade majolica were not as refined as the forms of fine grade majolica (Figure 4.8). The sherds were thicker, and the surfaces often a bit rough in spite of the glaze (Lister and Lister 1982). All of these attributes, whether the color of glazes or details of form and thickness of the vessels would have been visible to people back then as well, and I speculate that some folks cared more than others about the quality and specific look of their pottery. Potters certainly cared about the different quality of their products. The guild ordinances in seventeenth-century Puebla distinguished between fine grade, common grade, and yellow pottery (Hernández Sánchez 2012:104), although archaeologists have not typically used the yellow majolica category in their typologies. Most likely, the archaeological category of common grade majolica includes pottery that would have been classified as yellow majolica back then but archaeologists today have not managed to distinguish between common grade and yellow majolica.

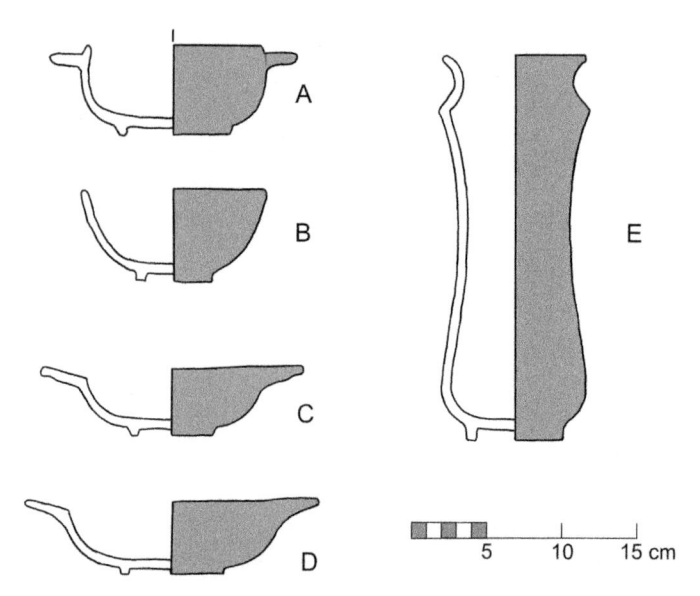

Figure 4.7 Some common forms of fine grade majolica excavated in Mexico City. Drawing by Samuel Wilson, after Lister and Lister 1982.

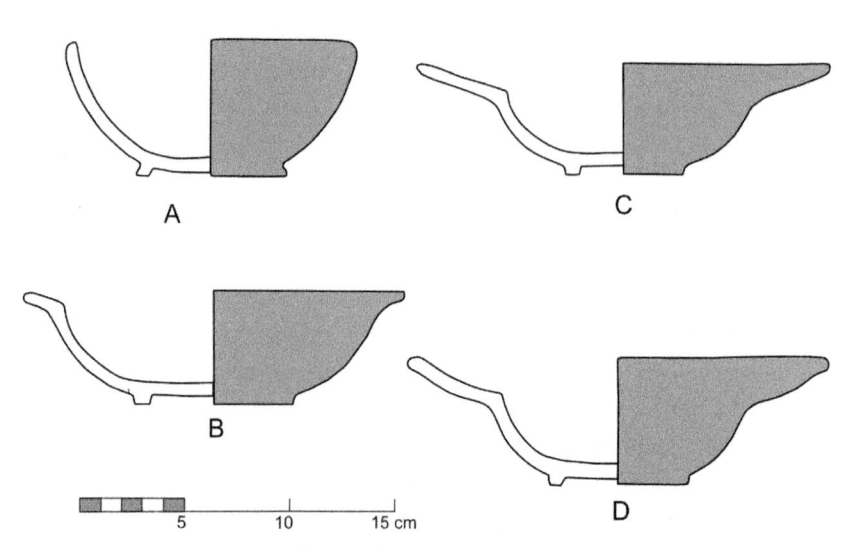

Figure 4.8 Some common forms of common grade majolica excavated in Mexico City. Drawing by Samuel Wilson, after Lister and Lister 1982.

There were other types of majolica produced in Mexico and in the other Spanish colonies, and even a kind of pseudo-majolica, known today as Indígena Ware, which has been found in Mexico City (Plate 13; Lister and Lister 1982). Indígena Ware was made in Michoacán (Iñañez et al. 2010). Instead of glazing it with a mixture of lead and tin, potters created the white and glossy surface by slipping it with white clay, burnishing it, and then glazing it with lead. The result was a surface color similar to majolica, although one can distinguish it easily from majolica if one is paying attention. Potters sometimes carved designs through the white slip to reveal the red paste beneath, in a tradition that goes back to the ninth century CE in Europe and the Near East (Kuleff and Djingova 2001). Scholars have examined and described the variety of majolica and other serving vessels imported or made locally by colonizers (e.g., Deagan 1987; Fournier 1990; Gavin et al. 2003; Goggin 1968; Lister and Lister 1982, 1987). They have also studied changes in potting traditions in the colonial period, the incorporation of glazing and other European techniques into local pottery production, and the adoption of majolica and other glazed pottery among Indigenous people (Charlton and Fournier 2011; Fournier 1997; Fournier García and Otis Charlton 2019; Hernández Sánchez 2012; López Cervantes 1976; Oland 2014, 2017; Rodríguez-Alegría 2003, 2005b, 2010, 2016a).

Another kind of ceramic that colonizers introduced is lead-glazed earthenware (Plate 14). It is different from majolica because potters did not add tin to the glaze, creating a translucent glaze that was never white. The pottery often looks green or brown, and it is decorated with splotches of glaze, stamped designs, incisions, and paint. Potters made it into a seemingly infinite variety of cooking and serving forms, including jars, molcajetes, basins of many different sizes and shapes, bowls, pitchers, candlesticks, and more. Cooks evidently loved lead-glazed earthenware, judging by its ubiquity in central Mexico, and potters in many places all over Mexico adopted the glazing techniques. Indigenous potters began using lead glaze by the middle of the sixteenth century, if not earlier (Hernández Sánchez 2012:117). It seems like the only pre-Columbian tradition form that they did not glaze was the comal. Chemical characterization of lead-glazed pottery indicates that it was probably made in many production centers all over central Mexico (Rodríguez-Alegría and Stoner 2016). Lead-glazed earthenware is depicted in many works of art from the seventeenth and eighteenth century (e.g., images in Katzew 2004), perhaps as a show of pride in the colorful tools of everyday life.

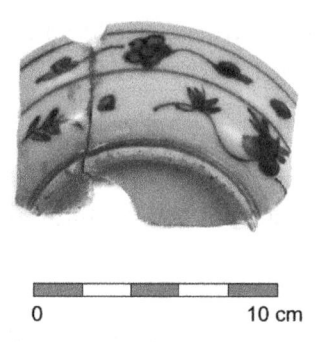

0   10 cm

Figure 4.9 Chinese porcelain excavated in Mexico City. Photo by author, digitized by Samuel Wilson.

Finally, perhaps the finest of all ceramics introduced by colonizers was Asian porcelain, especially Chinese porcelain (Figure 4.9). Porcelain has a completely vitrified body, which is often translucent. Chinese and Japanese porcelain can be found in many of the Spanish colonies, beginning in the early sixteenth century, and especially after 1574, when the Manila Galleon began to cross the Pacific on a yearly basis, connecting Manila to the port of Acapulco (Kuwayama 1997; López Cervantes 1974:50). The purpose of the galleon was not to supply the Spanish colonies, but to bring porcelain, textiles, spices, and other goods that would then be sent to Spain. Still, colonizers managed to keep much merchandise for themselves in the colonies and porcelain is distributed widely in many sites in the Spanish colonies (Deagan 1987:96; Fournier and Junco Sánchez 2019). The majority of Asian porcelain found in the Spanish colonies is of the blue-and-white varieties, although one may also find polychrome varieties (Deagan 1987:98). For the most part, archaeologists have found porcelain plates, cups, small bowls, and many other service vessels, often with delicate forms and fine line decoration in blue. The beauty and decoration of porcelain impressed Spanish potters, and they thought of it as the best quality. In 1653, an ordinance from a potters' guild in Puebla instructed potters to imitate Chinese porcelain. They were to make pots that resembled the colors, surface finish, and even the motifs found in porcelain, even though many of the motifs were meaningless in traditional Mexican pottery (Kuwayama 1997:24). In spite of the desire for Chinese porcelain, it is only found in low frequencies in houses in colonial Mexico City, probably because it was rare in comparison with local products. Porcelain forms only about 6.1 percent of colonial serving vessels in the houses excavated by the PAU (Rodríguez-Alegría 2016a:87). The admiration that colonial potters expressed for porcelain is in contrast with the lack of detail in the probate inventories. They simply mention porcelain, without stopping to describe or admire the pottery.

Pottery Assemblages in Different Houses

The variety of serving vessels available to colonizers thus ranged from Indigenous pottery, to European imports, and Spanish-tradition ceramics made in the colonies. Besides bringing pottery from different places, colonizers also classified serving vessels into different quality grades. Archaeological excavations by the PAU have found a mixture of different types of pottery in the houses at the center of Mexico City. The proportion of Indigenous and imported pottery varied widely. Some colonial households had a much higher ratio of Red Ware to majolica than other households. Different households had different mixtures of porcelain, imported majolica, and local fine grade and common grade majolica, but a general tendency was to have a variety of all or nearly all kinds of pottery. It is possible that households mixed different kinds of pottery in a single meal, or that they used different types according to the situation, the need to show hospitality, or the standing of the person being served. The mixture of a range of imported and local pottery of different kinds does not indicate a consistent association between wealth and the use of fine imports and the avoidance of locally made pottery. Some of the wealthier households excavated by the PAU had Red Ware. Some of the poorest households had the most porcelain (Rodríguez-Alegría 2003, 2005b).

For example, Licenciado Verdad #8, one of the poorest households excavated by the PAU (Rodríguez-Alegría 2016a:74–75; Figure 2.3), had plenty of majolica and porcelain. Together, these two wares make up 78 percent ($n = 180$) of the serving vessel fragments found at the house lot by count (Rodríguez-Alegría 2016a:89). This proportion of porcelain in this house lot is higher than in any of the houses excavated by the PAU that I studied, including the houses of wealthy people in the center of the city. Perhaps the residents of this household obtained majolica and porcelain at a discount or as presents from other colonizers, or even at the kinds of public auctions that provide the data for this study. Perhaps they were very focused on their appearances because of their impoverished status. They made sure to build material worlds that were very different from the material worlds of

Indigenous people. They may have had more at stake in showing off Spanish material goods than many wealthier colonizers.

In contrast, the people who lived at Justo Sierra #33, had more Red Ware than all other wares combined: 61 percent (n = 174) of all serving vessel fragments excavated in the house by count (Rodríguez-Alegría 2016a:90). Two prominent Spanish colonizers lived at this address in the sixteenth century: Diego de Soria, a conquistador, and Lic. Gerónimo Gutiérrez de Montealegre, a government figure (Mariscal 1998). In the house of these two powerful colonizers, located in one of the streets with the wealthiest and most powerful colonizers at the time, they used mostly Red Ware (Rodríguez-Alegría 2016a:90–91). There is still the possibility that Indigenous servants, rather than colonizers, were the ones who used the Red Ware in this house, although the Red Ware found here is highly decorated, including polychrome pots, which probably were not in everyday use among servants. Also, equating the presence of Red Ware with Indigenous people would require ignoring historical documents discussed earlier, in which colonizers showed an appreciation of Indigenous pottery and even commissioned it for their own use.

Other houses conform to a pattern that shows a strong preference for majolica. At Guatemala #38, majolica and porcelain make up 68.9 percent (n = 151) of the serving vessel fragments by count. At that house, most of the Red Ware sherds were fragments of small jars, probably used to store and serve water. Perhaps the porosity of Red Ware served to keep the water cool. The priest who lived at this house probably preferred majolica and porcelain, had access to both, and maintained or displayed a Spanish identity in part through the use of different kinds of Spanish material culture, including ceramics. The three house lots that I have discussed here are but three examples of the range of variation of different wares that could be found in the houses of colonizers. I discuss these and other house lots in greater detail elsewhere, showing the varied patterns of pottery use and discard in the houses of colonizers (Rodríguez-Alegría 2003, 2005b, 2016a:89–91). In Chapter 7 I will address the association between wealth and consumption in more detail.

Food

Food may not be something one associates with a will or with the things expected to be distributed upon a person's death, but it is found in the inventories

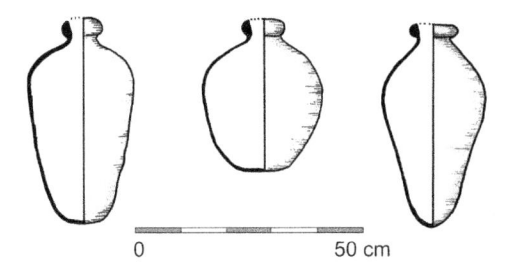

0   50 cm

Figure 4.10 Some common shapes of olive jars in the Spanish colonies. Drawn by Samuel Wilson, after Goggin 1960.

in higher frequency than pottery. The food listed in the inventories consists mostly of items with a long shelf-life: salt, wine, oil, vinegar, and spices. Most of these items were probably imported. Wine appears a total of 31 times, most often as pipes or butts of wine (*pipa* or *bota*); thus, when decedents left wine, it was usually not a small bottle but a barrel with up to 650 l of wine.[3] Vinegar appears much less frequently, whether as a bottle of vinegar (*n* = 2) or a pipe. Oil appears much more frequently than vinegar, in a total of 25 oil jars and three redomas. The oil jars are not described in the inventories, but archaeological specimens abound. Archaeologists typically call them *botijas* or olive jars, and they were generally wide bottles with a short, narrow neck, and sometimes glazed with lead in the interior, exterior, or both (Figure 4.10; Deagan 1987:31; Goggin 1960:28). The olive jars found in Mexico come from many different places around the world, including Iberia, Southeast Asia, and South America, and some were made in Acapulco (Guerrero-Rivero et al. 2020), indicating that the contents of the jars were widely traded, and not just with Spain. Even though oil appears nearly as frequently as wine, the latter was probably much greater in volume, as is implied in the use of pipes for its storage.

Cheese is another European item that appears in the inventories, although in much lower frequencies than the rest of the food items. It appears only fifteen times as cheese, and as twenty loads of cheese, although there is no specific information on what a load of cheese was. Although it is hard to imagine modern Mexican cooking without dairy, especially cheese and cream, dairy

---

[3] Pipes and butts are both vague terms for measuring wine, but the idea is that the wine was in a barrel. The capacity of pipes today ranges between 550 and 620 l, depending on the region where they are made (Robinson 2006:532). The capacity of a butt today ranges from 600 to 650 l, although small butts or shipping butts may be as small as 500 l (Robinson 2006:116).

production began in Mexico after the Spanish conquest as soon as cattle arrived. By 1531 there was enough production so that the *cabildo* or city government set a price for cheese, and by 1532, a price for milk (Coe 1993:231–232). Other dairy products were also for sale in Mexico by 1549, including "fresh cheese, aged cheese, milk, cream, and *requesones*" (Coe 1993:233), a milk dessert made by heating milk with rennet and removing the whey (Coe 1993:231).

Spices appear in the inventories, in small quantities both in terms of the times they appear and in terms of their weight or volume. The spices mentioned only once include anise, saffron, rosemary, and a small box with spices. "Spices" are mentioned an additional three times without any indication of what they are or how much there was. Cinnamon appears once mentioned individually, twice as sticks of cinnamon wrapped in cloth, and twice as bags of cloth with cinnamon, with no indication whether the bags were big or small. Pepper appears three times, once mentioned as a bit of pepper wrapped in folded paper. The idea that someone would keep a bit of black pepper in a piece of folded paper, and that it was valued enough (regardless of its price) to be put in a probate inventory is fascinating. Sugar appears twice and honey once. Both were at times considered spices and often enjoyed as sweeteners (Mintz 1985). All of the spices mentioned, with the exception of honey, were imported from Spain or Asia (Stoopen 1997). Markets in Mexico City had plenty of spices available, including chili peppers of many different kinds (Coe 1993:92–93). Perhaps the spices that appear in the inventories were exotic and difficult to come by, and colonizers were glad to buy them in auction after someone died.

The difference between the spices that appear in the documents and the intense flavor provided by chilies is difficult to exaggerate. Colonizers put a lot of effort to bring these familiar flavors to their palates. They often sold a mixture of equal parts saffron, cinnamon, cloves, and black pepper, although they also sold each one of those separately. They also imported cumin, ginger, caraway, and sesame seeds across the Atlantic, and soon across the Pacific as well (Coe 1993:239). And soon, of course, colonizers began enjoying the fire and flavor of chili peppers, which continue to feature prominently in Mexican food today.

Cacao stands out at the local food product that is most frequently mentioned in the documents. It appears measured in *cargas* of cacao. Different authors have estimated a carga of cacao to be between 50 and 62 lb. (Gasco 2018:225). In Chapter 1 I discuss cacao, how its price changed through the sixteenth century in Mexico City, and how people used cacao before and after the conquest as a medium of exchange. Even though some sources claim that cacao was used in all sorts of transactions in marketplaces in Mexico, cacao appears infrequently in the inventories as payment for any goods. It appears most frequently as an item that belonged to a decedent. This does not mean that the idea that colonizers used cacao as a means of payment is wrong. Instead, it means that they did not use cacao as a means of payment in the context of the auctions associated with these inventories. The inventories include a total of seventy-eight cargas of cacao (an additional twelve are repeated in one inventory after having appeared in a will), plus 1,400 units of cacao (probably beans). They belonged to only four men, and one of them was a tailor who owned twelve cargas of cacao. The information provided makes it difficult to know whether this tailor owned the cacao for his own consumption or whether he was looking to sell it. Another of the cacao owners was probably a merchant, a conclusion based on the range of items in his inventory, and he owned the 1,400 units of cacao. There is no clear indication of the occupation of the other two decedents, making it hard to tell who owned cacao for his own consumption, who was trading in cacao, and who was doing a little of both. It is even possible that the men who owned cacao had accepted it as a form of payment from Indigenous people and intended to sell it later.

There is plenty of literature on cacao, in part due to our contemporary interest and consumption of this delicious food. In pre-Columbian times, cacao was reputedly a drink reserved for the Mexica nobility, and it is mentioned in some of the descriptions of the feasts of king Moctezuma (Coe 1993:101; Gasco 1987). Indigenous people in the Soconusco area produced cacao with a variety of techniques, from managed forests to "full/sun agricultural plots and fallow fields" (Gasco 2018:212). They provided tribute in cacao to the Mexica, sending between 200 and 400 cargas of cacao annually, which is at least 10,000 lbs. of cacao. Transporting that would have been a major effort, although cultivating it would not have (Gasco 2018:210–211). People poured cacao from a height from one vessel to another repeatedly to create the desired and flavorful foam on top of the beverage. In colonial times, people began using wooden whisks called *molinillos*, which one must spin by placing the handle between the palms and rubbing them quickly back and forth to create the froth (Pierce 2003:249). Thomas Gage famously narrated a scandal in which Spanish women in seventeenth-century southern Mexico made their servants bring them chocolate in the middle of Mass, causing interruptions, scandal, and much friction with the clergy (Thompson 1958:143). In colonial times, majolica producers even developed a vessel form specifically for serving chocolate. It is called a *mancerina*, and it is a plate with a ring in the middle, designed to hold a jícara in place. Colonizers also adapted the form of large Chinese porcelain jars, and made them out of majolica with an added iron lid with a lock and key to store chocolate safely inside (Pierce 2003:254).

The food products that appear in the inventories are limited in comparison to the ones that appear in other historical sources, which include "beef, veal, pork, wine, oil, wheat, olives, onions, garlic, lettuce, radishes, parsley, carrots, eggplant, spinach, chickpeas, lentils, cauliflower, asparagus, melons, cantaloupes, squashes, cucumber, rice, citrus fruits, tea, and spices such as cinnamon, black pepper, and saffron" (Stoopen 1997:28; see also Bauer 2001:63–68, Coe 1993). The spices that can be added to the list based on the inventories are anise and rosemary, in addition to sugar and honey. One may also add pork fat and cheese to the list of ingredients (Coe 1993:232–234). The fact that the inventories present only a limited list of ingredients and foodstuffs is a reminder that they only contain information on whatever was preserved, both in the sense of not decaying and not being stolen or consumed, and whatever was deemed valuable enough to sell.

Archaeology can contribute more information regarding the foods consumed by Spanish colonizers. Except for the cheese and a few other animal products, such as pork fat, most of the items that appear in the inventories are plant based and processed to last a long time. Faunal remains excavated in Mexico City, mostly bones, can provide a better idea of the role of animals in the diet of colonizers. Faunal analysis in Donceles 97, one of the house lots excavated by the PAU (Figure 2.3), reveals that colonists preferred imported fauna, although they certainly consumed local fauna as well. In the pre-Hispanic strata at the site, turkey was the predominant animal; however, in the colonial strata, turkey became much less popular in comparison to other fauna. Still, the frequency of turkey remains at the site is almost as high as that of chicken (Barrera Rodríguez et al. 2008:24) the most popular animal among those imported by the Spanish (Gibson 1964:344).

Faunal analysis in Justo Sierra 33, another of the houses excavated by the PAU (see Chapter 2) revealed a preference for imported animal species in that house. The faunal remains found there include pig (*Sus scrofa*), goat (*Capra sp.*), sheep (*Ovis aries*), and cattle (*Bos taurus*). All of these animals appear in some detail in Chapter 6. Cat (*Felis domesticus*) bones are also present in the faunal remains there, and it is the only animal found in that house that was not used as food. Less than half of the animal bones classified at this site were of local origin, including rabbits, turkeys, and different kinds of waterfowl. All of the local species were widely available at local markets in Mexico City, and all of them were hunted or raised traditionally by Indigenous people. Spanish colonizers probably bough them from Indigenous vendors at the market, or that they had Indigenous cooks that bought these items (Valentín Maldonado 2003). Broad patterns indicate that Spanish colonizers tended to consume animals that seemed familiar to them due to the availability of similar species in Europe. Mexican hares and many species of fish seemed familiar to colonizers, and therefore fit for consumption. The diet of Spaniards was therefore a combination of Indigenous and imported foods, including animals that were purchased locally and that were brought across the Atlantic (Guzmán and Polaco 2003; Montúfar López 2000; Montúfar López and Valentín Maldonado 1998; Valentín Maldonado 2003).

Archaeologists have also provided evidence of the consumption of different plants by studying botanical remains. Once again, the evidence shows a combination of imported and native plants among colonizers. In Justo Sierra #33 archaeologists found olives, cantaloupes, peaches, and grapes among the plants that were imported from Europe. The local plants at the site include corn, amaranth, chili, tomatoes, Mexican hawthorn, black cherry, pine nuts, and prickly pear fruit (Montúfar López 2003). Notice the presence of chilies at the site. Chilies can be thought of as a vegetable if the entire chili pepper is consumed as part of a dish, or as a spice, if the chili is dried, powdered, ground, or otherwise added to a dish to give it flavor and heat. Chilies were certainly available at markets in Mexico City at the time, and their presence in the archaeological remains in this house indicates that they were consumed by colonizers, or at least some colonizers. However, they are not present at all in the inventories, whether because they were not considered valuable enough to be listed, or for any other reason. The archaeological data show a greater presence of local plant foods in the diet of colonizers than can be gleaned from the inventories alone.

Conclusion

In contrast to furniture, for which the Spanish barely found functional equivalents in Mexico, pottery and food presented many similarities between Mexico and Spain in terms of function and form. The pottery and food that

Spanish colonizers found in the markets of Mexico City could, at times, look and taste drastically different from their familiar pots and foods. Indigenous potters produced a wide variety of sophisticated ceramics for cooking, storage, and serving. Indigenous ceramics were not glazed, and they were mostly orange or red, in contrast with the usually white ground of Spanish serving vessels. Still, Spanish colonizers adopted the pottery of Indigenous people and went through great efforts to bring majolica from Europe, porcelain from China, and to produce majolica and other pottery in the colonies. The pattern is not a pattern of rejection of Indigenous pottery. Instead, it is a pattern of adoption in combination with much effort to obtain pottery that was traditional and familiar to the Spanish, and also exotic pottery, in the case of Asian porcelain.

To some extent, the same can be said about the different fauna that Spanish colonizers ate. Many colonizers incorporated central Mexican fauna into their diets, especially animals that looked similar to those in Europe: certain kinds of fish, hare, and waterfowl. They also incorporated some of the plant foods available in Mexico, including cacao, among others. Sometimes colonizers also adopted the gourds that Indigenous people used to drink it, and created new ceramic forms to drink or store chocolate, such as the mancerina and jars with locking lids.

The probate inventories provide vague descriptions of the pottery, other containers, and food owned by the colonizers. They barely ever mention Indigenous pottery, although terms like jícara and tecomate indicate the possibility that they were referring to Indigenous wares. Even if they were not referring to Indigenous wares, the use of the terms indicates new knowledge and familiarity with Indigenous pottery. Archaeological data show much more Indigenous pottery in the houses of some colonizers than what can be gleaned from the documents. This is an indication that the probate inventories severely underrepresent the proportion of Indigenous pottery in the houses of colonizers, and that perhaps the documents also underestimate the proportion of other kinds of Indigenous things that the Spanish owned. The information presented in this book should always be taken as just one more step in learning about the material worlds of colonizers, rather than the final word on their consumption patterns. I cannot emphasize this idea enough. Archaeology can help discover more about material categories that preserve well after discard, and sometimes documents provide information on items that archaeologists find very rarely. Silver, which people would keep because it was valuable, and gourds, which decompose in the ground, are quite uncommon as archaeological findings in colonial Mexico, but the inventories mention items made of silver, glass, pewter, and gourds. Thus, a combination of archaeology and history can help provide a more complete view of the domestic material worlds of colonizers.

Two patterns should be emphasized in terms of pottery and food consumption in the houses of colonizers. The first is variability. The houses of Spanish colonizers show variation in terms of the pottery they had, and so do the probate inventories. Some houses contained a lot of Indigenous pottery, whereas some houses barely had any. Some houses had more Asian porcelain than others. One of the houses examined here briefly had mostly ceramics imported from Spain, but it also had several Red Ware jars. I speculate that the owners liked the jars because they were porous, which can help keep liquids cool as the water soaks into the vessel walls and evaporates, thereby cooling the vessel. Variation can also be found in terms of the food that people in different houses ate. This variation can only be explained partially due to processes of preservation, the formation of archaeological contexts, or recording in the inventories. Regardless of the explanations, whether they favor cultural, economic, or political factors, the material worlds of colonizers were hardly uniform in the sixteenth century. Generalizations about colonizers and their patterns of consumption are useful only when they take variation into account.

Finally, a second pattern shows that consumption depended on much labor and on changes and continuities in production, exchange, and distribution. This chapter emphasizes consumption or ownership of pottery, other containers, and food, but it is clear that colonizers intended to trade in some of the pottery they desired. They brought it from across the Atlantic and the Pacific Ocean, and even set up pottery workshops in their colonies (Fournier 1990; Hernández Sánchez 2012; Lister and Lister 1982). Indigenous people learned some of the techniques that the Spanish brought with them, especially glazing, and produced new types of pottery in the colonial period, in addition to their traditional wares. They continued producing some of their traditional wares, and Spanish colonizers used them in their houses. Sustaining the colonial enterprise and the patterns of consumption of colonizers created change inside the households of colonizers, among the people that surrounded them in Mexico and other colonies, but also across the oceans.

5

How to Dress the Part

Different sources present glimpses of the way people dressed in colonial Mexico City. They range from pictorial manuscripts to letters, clay figurines, paintings, and others (Blum 2006; Katzew 2004; McKim-Smith 2006; Von Winning 1988). Thomas Gage is among the writers who provided some of the most vivid descriptions of clothing. He wrote of the "excessive" fashions of men and women as he traveled through colonial Mexico City in the early seventeenth century. They wore "more silks than stuffs and cloth" (Thompson 1958:68). They wore jewels on their hats. Even enslaved people wore pearls and earrings. Gage mentioned silk, gold, silver, fine Chinese linen, and a long list of other luxurious clothing (Thompson 1958:68–70). In addition to verbal descriptions, casta paintings figure prominently in the rich corpus of images used to study textiles and clothing, from the luxurious to the torn and tattered (Katzew 2004). These descriptions and images are at once evocative and rich in detail, but also challenging if we wish to understand colonizer dress in the sixteenth century. First, most of the descriptions that are typically cited date to the seventeenth century or later, including Gage's, which he wrote when he traveled in Mexico and Guatemala a full century after the conquest (Thompson 1958). They may portray a colonial world that had changed significantly in over a century of Spanish colonial presence. Second, the descriptions are impressionistic and often meant to impress. They lack detail, and they privilege a sense of awe regarding the opulence of clothing over the less impressive but still important thorough description of all kinds of clothes, from the new and fashionable to the old, tattered, and unimpressive. Gage seemed to be impressed with everything, including the abundance of food, of sweets, the carriages, the opulent housing, and the beautiful people. Perhaps his descriptions of clothing were exaggerated as well. Was clothing opulent and fashionable among colonizers in the sixteenth century? Were the colonizers in the probate inventories an elegant bunch? How did colonizers dress in the sixteenth century, and where did their clothes come from?

How to Make a New Spain. Enrique Rodríguez-Alegría, Oxford University Press. © Enrique Rodríguez-Alegría 2023.
DOI: 10.1093/oso/9780197682296.003.0006

A related question has to do with the possible adoption of Indigenous cloth, clothing, and accessories among Spanish colonizers. Most Spanish colonizers wore their traditional clothes for reasons that are not surprising, including habit, tradition, a sense of decency, the desire to display rank, and others. Some colonizers in many parts of the Spanish empire even tried to control the dress of Indigenous people and prevent them from wearing Spanish attire. They wanted to keep Indigenous people apart from colonizers, and prevent them from gaining access to powerful colonizers' strategies of display. Other colonizers, however, were happy to grant permission to some Indigenous elites to wear Spanish clothing, as a way of fostering alliances with powerful Indigenous rulers and calming Indigenous resistance with incentives (Haskett 1991:161–162). Indigenous people often combined both their traditional clothes and insignia of power with those provided by the Spanish (Olko 2014).

It is useful to look beyond New Spain, even if momentarily, to understand the different possibilities and variation in the use of imported and Indigenous clothing and accessories among colonizers. In spite of the general maintenance of traditional clothing among colonizers, some of them adopted items of Indigenous clothing or jewelry in the Andes, as was the case of the popular topos. They were needle-like clothing fasteners, as large as a knitting needle or larger, and they became an accessory that colonizer women, even African women, could wear as decoration while keeping the rest of their less-indigenized ensemble (Jamieson 2004). People in the Andes sometimes wore clothing made out of both Indigenous cloth and imported cloth, and tailored according to both local and foreign tastes (Dean and Leibsohn 2003). Adopting items of Indigenous dress was not unique to the colonial Andes. Loren has studied how different people in North America "transformed clothing traditions through processes of cultural exchange" (2010:4). She describes fashion as "a patchwork, a mixture of local and imported, Native and non-Native, handmade and manufactured. The strategy of combining locally made and imported goods created a new language of appearance that individuals used to communicate self and identity in an often-contentious colonial world" (2010:4). The cases from the Andes and North America remind us of the possibility that some colonizers adopted items of Indigenous dress and jewelry, and present an invitation to research the issue further. Did Indigenous people in central Mexico produce items of clothing for the Spanish? Are those items identifiable in the probate inventories?

Studies of Clothing

For a long time, archaeologists and other scholars have associated clothing and bodily adornment with wealth, social class, strategies of display, and many other aspects of social and cultural life, such as ethnicity, occupation, religious beliefs, productive skills, and sexuality (Gallardo 2014; Joyce 2000, 2005; Loren 2010, 2015; McKim-Smith 2006; Roach and Eicher 1973; Sousa Congosto 2007; Wobst 1977). Clothing has a strong association with the body, serving as a "second skin" (Turner 2012) that embodies many aspects of social and economic life, and that often protects the body (Gallardo 2014). But more than protection, the aspect of clothing that has attracted the most attention from scholars is communication, or the idea that clothes communicate to the world "status, prestige, gender, society, politics, and religion" (Loren 2010:7–8; see also Beaule 2015; McKim-Smith 2006). Pasztory (2005:10) argues that "it is impossible to dress in such a way as to convey no meaning. Every fabric, color, and cut has socially and perhaps even biologically determined meaning." And those meanings are no joking matter in society. Turner (2012:487) argues that taking matters of clothing and appearance lightly is often considered evidence of "a 'serious' disposition or of serious psychological problems."

The probate inventories provide the opportunity to expand how we think about communication through clothing in a specific direction: how we think about the perception of clothing. Gallardo (2014:16), based on previous work by Kaiser (1990), shows that different theoretical approaches to the study of clothing share an important view of communication through clothing: the production of meaning is not just in the hands of the person who wears the clothes and sends a message, and it is not an intrinsic part of the clothes. Instead, the production of meaning or of information through clothing is produced socially, by people who interact. It is not just those who wear clothes, but also those who observe them, who engage in communication through clothing. However, the aspect of communication that is often emphasized in the literature is that clothes send a message. The literature emphasizes much less the ways in which that message is interpreted.

Instead of thinking of a message that is sent by someone through their clothes and then interpreted uniformly by viewers, we should think of viewers as having different abilities and motivations to perceive, understand, and interpret the many different aspects and attributes of clothes. My point is not just that clothes send messages that are polyvalent. My point is that polyvalence should be explained whenever possible. People everywhere have different knowledge about clothes, different levels of expertise, different interest in the details of clothing, and different motivations to pay attention or not to others' clothing. From this variable ability to perceive the different details and aspects of clothes, people can form widely-shared ideas about clothing and the people who wear them. People can also form more specific ideas that depend on knowledge, perception, and attention. For example, many people in sixteenth-century Mexico City may have seen a Spanish man dressed in a shirt, hose, boots, a cape, and a hat. Some of those people, but not all, may also have noticed that the man's shirt was made with cloth made by Indigenous weavers but then cut and sewn together by a Spanish tailor, even though the boots were certainly imported from Castile. Some people may not have cared at all about those distinctions. Some people may have used them to assess the quality of the person, and also to calculate the exchange value of their clothes. In the case of the probate inventories, there is evidence of the use of judgment value of the clothes of decedents, assessment of their place of origin, and commentary on the materials used to make the clothes. All of these factors can help us understand what colonizers wore, and what they thought of each other's clothing.

A second contribution in this chapter takes us beyond communication and into the realm of experience and daily life. For decades, archaeologists have noted that the relationship between the human body (including clothing) and society is more complex than just communication. Joyce writes that "the biological person is both the medium and product of social action" (Joyce 2005). She argues that human bodies are not merely the site of communication or inscription, but are also a site of habits, practices, and social action that shape the body. People wear clothes and bodily adornment, and engage in repetitive practices and performances. All of these activities together produce a person that embodies different aspects of their identity, including sex, sexuality, gender, age, ethnicity, social connections, power, and any other aspect of social and economic life (Joyce 2005:149). As part of experiences and practice, people can feel transformed by clothing, or use clothing to transform other things. In some contexts in the pre-Columbian and colonial Americas, clothes could endow a person, an animal, or an object with life (McKim-Smith 2005:155). In the Orinoco region, bodily adornment and beads were "essential for the constitution of 'self' and the acquisition of value" as people moved through different stages in life (Scaramelli and Tarble de Scaramelli 2005:150). In the Aztec world, putting clothes on an animal or a flint knife could make it an appropriate offering to the gods or even a representative of the gods (Chávez et al. 2010). In the colonial Presidio in

San Francisco, native families that were recruited to live in spaces ruled by colonizers received their initial compensation in clothing, as a way to dress them and with the goal of "transforming the recruits' social identities and stabilizing their place in the colonial order" (Voss 2008b:256). Thus, it is productive to think of clothes not just as a medium of communication or a surface veneer, but also as part of the lived experience and the being of a person, and perhaps even animals and other things.

People wear the specific clothes they wear for a variety of reasons, and communication may be a minor goal when choosing what to wear and perhaps when making what to wear. Habit and experience play a strong role in shaping what people wear, delimiting their choices, giving the impression that they are choosing when they may not be choosing at all, or giving the impression that they have no choice but to wear specific clothes, when in fact they may have choices. People may wear specific clothes because they are traditional or because the people are used to the clothes. People may wear specific clothes out of a sense of identity, in its many dimensions of self-attribution and external influence, whether ethnic, age-related, gender, occupational, or any other. People wear some garments out of a sense of decency or hygiene, or to negotiate or deny the possibility of sex. The reasons to wear clothes may also be related to a person's social or personal connections. A person may wear specific clothes because they were a gift, or because the person has personal connections with the seller and they buy their clothes there. Or they may inherit clothes and wear them. Economic reasons also come into play, and people may wear some clothes because they were affordable, or save up their money for new clothes that are not quite affordable. Aspirations are also important in choosing clothes, and people may wear specific clothes because they are trying to belong in a specific group. Clothes may also have their own reputation after having been worn by specific people in public events. Sometimes the history and reputation of clothes may increase the desire to wear them, but simultaneously limit the possibility of doing so. Many or all of these factors may come together when a person decides what to wear, and people may only be aware of some of those reasons, or maybe none of them at all, when choosing what to wear. In fact, a person may not even think they have a choice of what clothes they are wearing, as the weight of their traditions, personal connections, ideas about hygiene and other factors guides a person strongly to wear what they wear. Communication or sending a message about oneself by choosing clothes may be one of those reasons, but it may not explain all, or perhaps even much, about why someone owns or wears specific clothes.

To study issues of the perception of clothing and the lived experience of wearing clothes in Mexico City, it will be necessary to begin by describing the clothing owned and left behind by colonizers.

Clothes Everywhere

Clothing and items used to repair clothes are among the most ubiquitous items in the probate inventories. In Chapter 1, I used a category called "household items and clothing" that lumped together all kinds of clothing, furniture, and mobile goods that colonizers owned. It is worth subdividing that category further, to distinguish between clothing, items used to make and repair clothes (which I will call "miscellaneous clothes"), jewelry, and furniture and household goods. Of those categories, clothing, miscellaneous clothes, and jewelry are most relevant to the discussion in this chapter.

The category of items with the greatest ubiquity in the inventories is "miscellaneous clothes." It includes items related to clothing repair and manufacture, such as lengths of cloth, string and thread, pins, buttons, pieces of leather (whether for shoes or other items of clothing), ribbon, and all kinds of decorations used for clothes. It includes 3,015 items, or approximately 25 percent of all items in the probate inventories by count, a true testimony of the importance of mending and making clothes in colonial Mexico City in contrast with the modern tendency to discard torn clothes and buy new clothing. The second category in terms of ubiquity is less relevant to this chapter, and it is discussed in Chapters 3, 4, and 6: furniture and household goods. The third category is clothes, with 2,246 items, or 18 percent of all items in the inventories by count. The category includes all sorts of finished garments and shoes, such as shirts, hose, hats, gloves, capes, sleeves, socks, and others.[1] Clearly, clothing and items related to clothing are by far the most ubiquitous items in the probate inventories. If we add clothing and all the items used to repair clothes, they account for 5,261 items, or 43 percent of

---

[1] The category does not include weapons, although arguably, weapons were seen as part of a person's outfit. Loren (2010) has argued that armaments of different kinds should be considered among items of dress. In addition, historical documents from colonial Mexico reveal that sometimes Indigenous people requested permission to wear Spanish clothes and carry swords and knives as decoration (Rodríguez-Alegría 2010). I consider the category of weaponry separately in Chapter 6, only because for the most part the inventories do not offer any indication of which weapons were displayed and worn on the body, although it is quite probable that most of them were.

all the items in the inventories by count. The abundance of items related to clothing and to repairing clothes is impressive.

Men's Clothes

In sixteenth-century Spain, a basic male outfit consisted of a doublet (*jubón*) worn over a shirt (*camisa*) and covering the torso down to the waist (Figure 5.1). The shirts were billowy and long, and they had long sleeves. The doublet

Figure 5.1 Basic male outfit with the doublet, shirt, hose. Original composite sketch based on sixteenth century drawings and paintings, copyright S. Wilson (2020).

was attached to hose (*calzas*) that fit the legs snugly. The hose were much thicker than today's tights or nylon hose. They were typically more than one layer of cloth, including an inner layer made of canvas or another strong cloth, and an outer layer made of silk or velvet. Instead of calzas, some men wore *calzones*, or *zaragüelles*, which resembled loose pants worn today and could go all the way down to the ankle or to the knees. Calzones tended to lack any lining, and to be simpler than calzas. Loose calzones were also associated typically with artisans, shepherds, sailors, or workers, whereas tighter calzas were associated with the upper classes. Zaragüelles were quite similar to calzones, and they were made of linen. The difference between zaragüelles and calzones may have been minimal, although the term zaragüelles comes from the Arabic term *sarawil*, perhaps indicating that they were associated with the pants worn by Moors in Spain and thus, distinctive (Bernis 1962:15–16, 80, 109–110). For the most part, socks (*medias*) went up to the knee, although some continued up to the thigh. Some covered the foot, and some only had a strap to secure the hose to the heel. All of these basic items of clothing are found abundantly in the probate inventories from Mexico (Appendix 5.1).

Although it already seems like men wore enough clothes, a man who only wore his shirt, doublet, and hose was said to be nude. To be fully dressed required wearing a smock or tunic (*sayo*) on top of the rest of the clothing (Figure 5.2). As if those were not enough layers, on top of that men could wear additional layers, including a coat with sleeves, often made of leather, worn open in the front. It was typically called simply *ropa*, or *ropa de cubrir*. As an alternative to the ropa, men could wear a cape. Essentially, a *ropa* was a cape with sleeves, or a coat that was open in the front, whereas a cape was sleeveless. Finally, an *herreruelo* was a short cape that went down to the waist, covering only the shoulders, the back, and the upper part of the chest (Figure 5.3). Sixteenth-century writers, including the scribes that wrote down the probate inventories consulted here, may not have made a consistent distinction between capes, ropas, and herreruelos, making it difficult to quantify the use of one versus the other (Bernis 1962:15–16).

Spanish men used different kinds of shoes. They included shoes that were worn directly on the hose and covered only the feet (*zapatos, zapatillas*; Figure 5.4a, b, c, d, j), boots, or shoes that covered part of the leg (*botas*), and *botines*, which typically covered only the foot and ankle (Figure 5.5). In addition to those, there were shoes that were made of very flexible leather and meant to be worn between the hose and the shoes or boots. These included

Figure 5.2 Basic smock. Public Domain image from the *Trachtenbuch* by Christoph Weiditz, published in the 1530s. https://commons.wikimedia.org/wiki/File:Weiditz_Trachtenbuch_137-138.jpg, accessed June 14, 2020.

borceguíes, which went from the foot all the way up to the knee, and *servillas*, which covered only the foot (Figure 5.4e; Bernis 1962:15–17). *Alpargatas* were rope-soled cloth shoes, similar to the ones still worn today in Spain during the hot summer months (Figure 5.4g, h). There were other shoes in the inventories too, including *chapines*, which were sandals wrapped in cordovan leather, and they often had very tall cork soles (Figure 5.4i, k, l).

Plate 1 (A): Doble excelente de Granada; (B): Principat from Catalunya-Aragón; (C): Doble principat, Juana y Carlos, Barcelona, 1531. Photos used by permission from Soler y Llach, Barcelona.

Plate 2a Arca de novia (Caixa Catalana), early sixteenth century, Cataluña. Polychromed wood and gold leaf. Franz Mayer Museum, Mexico City. Photograph by Gerardo Landa Rojano (copyright), used by permission.

Plate 2b Arca de novia (Caixa Catalana), early sixteenth century, Cataluña. Polychromed wood and gold leaf. Franz Mayer Museum, Mexico City. Photograph by Gerardo Landa Rojano (copyright), used by permission.

Plate 3a Chest with curved lid, early sixteenth century, Castile. Wood, silk, and iron. Franz Mayer Museum, Mexico City. Photograph by Gerardo Landa Rojano (copyright), used by permission.

Plate 3b Chest with open curved lid, early sixteenth century, Castile. Wood, silk, and iron. Franz Mayer Museum, Mexico City. Photograph by Gerardo Landa Rojano (copyright), used by permission.

Plate 4 Cortés and Xicotencal sitting on sillas de caderas, Lienzo de Tlaxcala. Benson Latin American Collection, LLILAS Benson Latin American Studies and Collections, The University of Texas at Austin.

Plate 5 Silla de brazos. Carved wood, velvet, and bronze. Spain, late sixteenth century. Franz Mayer Museum, Mexico City. Photograph by Gerardo Landa Rojano (copyright), used by permission.

Plate 6 Silla de Brazos. Carved wood, red silk embroidered with silver and gold thread with an image of St. Paul. Spain, sixteenth century. Franz Mayer Museum, Mexico City. Photograph by Gerardo Landa Rojano (copyright), used by permission.

Plate 7 Table. Walnut wood. Spain, seventeenth century. Franz Mayer Museum, Mexico City. Photograph by Gerardo Landa Rojano (copyright), used by permission.

Plate 8 Blankets as drawn in the Codex Tepetlaoztoc, Folio 15v. The British Museum, used by permission.

Plate 9 Blankets as drawn in the Codex Tepetlaoztoc, Folio 21v. The British Museum, used by permission.

Plate 10 Black-on-orange molcajete fragment from Xaltocan, Mexico. Photo by Kristin de Lucia, digitized by Samuel Wilson. Used by permission.

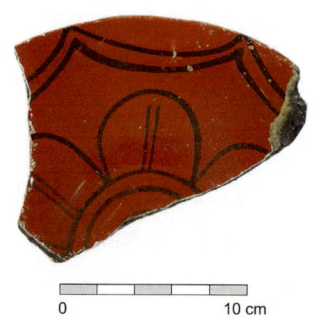

Plate 11 Red Ware plate. Photo by author, digitized by Samuel Wilson.

Plate 12 Green on Cream, common grade majolica from Mexico City. Photo by author, digitized by Samuel Wilson.

Plate 13 Fragments of Indígena Ware excavated in Mexico City. Photo by author, digitized by Samuel Wilson.

Plate 14 Lead-glazed earthenware from Xaltocan, Mexico. Photo by author, digitized by Samuel Wilson.

Plate 15 Eagle pendant, as depicted in the Codex Tepetlaoztoc. Folio 18 verso. The British Museum, used by permission.

Plate 16 Jewel with *xicalcoliuhqui* (stepped fret motif) from the Codex Tepetlaoztoc. Folio 16 verso. The British Museum, used by permission.

Figure 5.3 Man wearing an herreruelo or short cape. Original composite drawing based on 16th century drawings and paintings, copyright S. Wilson (2020).

Slippers (*pantufos*) left the back half of the foot exposed (Figure 5.4e, f). Evidently, colonizers did not lack access to a variety of shoes, boots, sandals, and socks in the sixteenth century.

Head coverings were also popular at the time, and Bernis (1962:17) classifies them mainly into hats, used for protection, and caps, used for adornment. Hats had a brim and tended to be simple. Men often wore hats

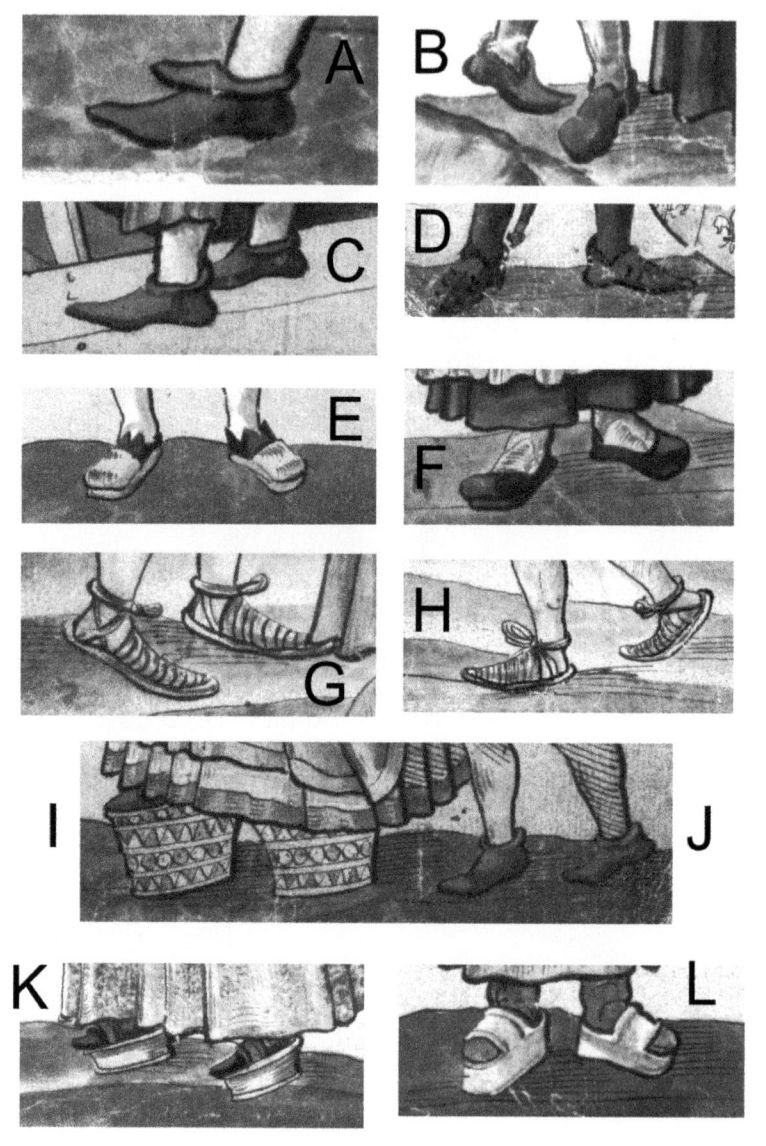

Figure 5.4 Different styles of shoes. Composite of several modified public domain images from the *Trachtenbuch* by Christoph Weiditz, published in the 1530s. Cropped and modified to highlight details of the shoes. https://commons. wikimedia.org/wiki/Trachtenbuch_des_Christoph_Weiditz, accessed June 14, 2020.

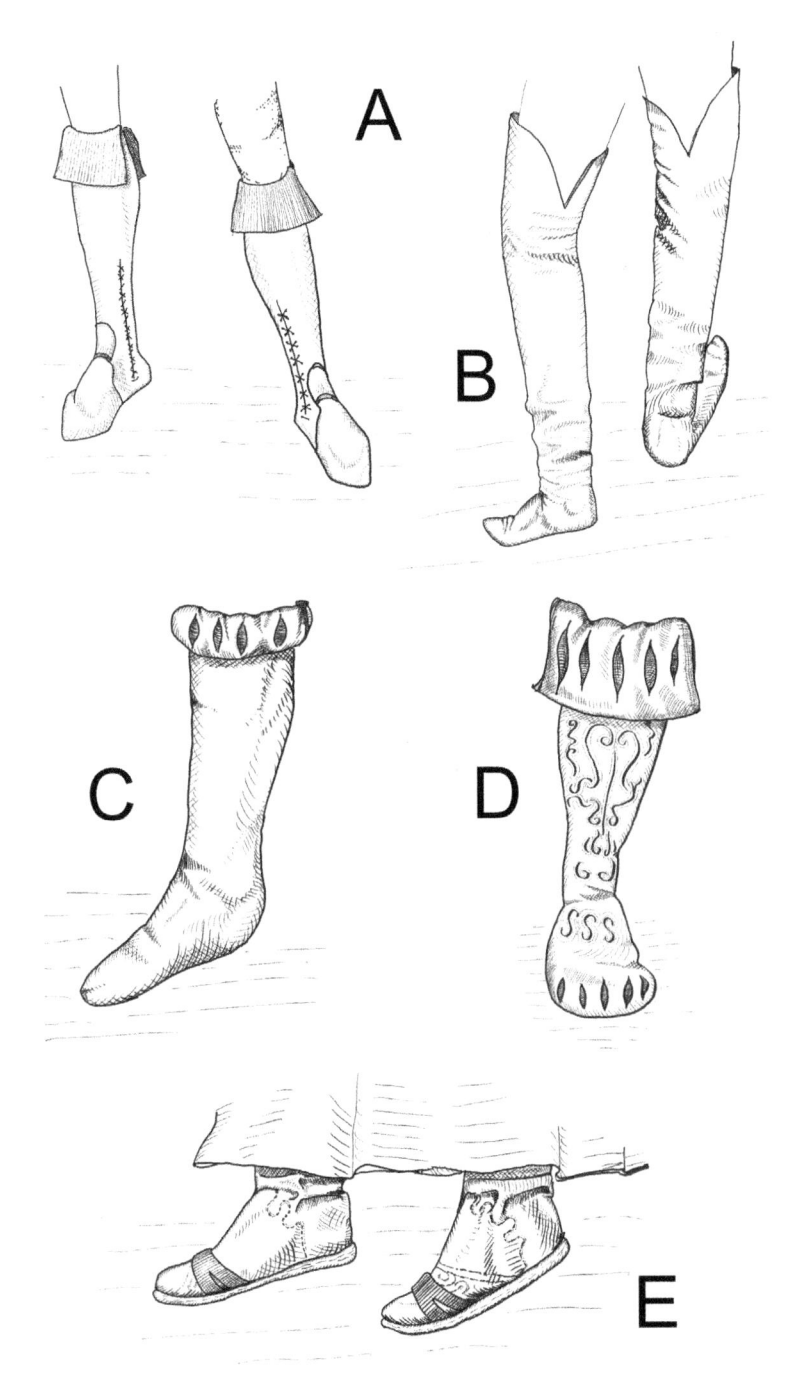

Figure 5.5 Composite of boot designs. Original composite sketches based on sixteenth-century drawings and paintings, copyright S. Wilson (2020).

on top of their cap. The vocabulary used for caps indicates a distinction between caps that were broad and resembled a modern beret (*gorra*) and
simpler caps that fit the head more closely (*bonete*). Writers in the sixteenth
century may have often written about them both as bonetes, instead of dis-
tinguishing between the shapes, much as one could talk about a hat today
to refer to a baseball cap or a brimmed hat. There were separate guilds for
hat makers and for cap makers at the time (Bernis 1962:17, 92, 104). There
are 35 caps (*bonetes*) in the probate inventories, plus several others that are
listed under different names, including *caperuza, capirote, toca,* and *toquilla
de gorra*. Bernis (1962:17) presents definitions for each one, although it is
not clear whether people distinguished between them consistently when
compiling the inventories.

Christoph Weiditz's famous *Trachtenbuch* (1994), or book of dress,
provides illustrations of the fashions worn by Spanish men and women in the
sixteenth century, as well as images of Afrodescendants and Amerindians.
Drawn between ca. 1500–1529, it is the oldest known book on European
dress. Weiditz drew the 154 illustrations for the book during a visit to Charles
V's court, providing images of people of different social classes, ethnicities,
occupations, and regions of Spain.[2] The fourth illustration in the book
(Weiditz 1994: Plate IV) shows Hernán Cortés wearing a hat, a smock tied
around the waist, puffy sleeves, hose covering his legs, and shoes. The entire
outfit is very dark gray (Figure 5.6). He carries a sword tied to his hip. The
clothes were probably quite similar to what Cortés and other men wore when
they arrived in central Mexico.

Other images in the *Trachtenbuch* depict men with different occupations,
and probably of different social classes, in clothes that are very similar to the
ones worn by Cortés. They wore smocks tied around the waist, hose, shoes
and hats (e.g., Weiditz 1994: Plates VI, XXVIII, XXIX). Notice the loose
calzones worn by an owner of a Spanish ship, in comparison with the tighter
hose worn by Cortés (Figure 5.7). As discussed earlier, loose calzones were
associated with sailors and other working folks. Puffy long sleeves were all

---

[2] A critical review of the illustrations in the *Trachtenbuch* is beyond the scope of this chapter, but
it is worth keeping in mind that recent work by Boone (2017) has shown that the illustrations of the
Mexicas who visited the Spanish court are not based only on what Weiditz saw. He incorporated
elements from images, descriptions, and objects from the Americas that were circulating in Europe at
the time, producing more exotic and extravagant Indigenous subjects, rather than trying to adhere to
a more faithful representation of the Indigenous folks that he saw. Although the images of Spaniards
may not have been as strongly shaped by a desire to show exotic subjects, they could still include
elements that are inaccurate.

Figure 5.6 Image of Cortés in full outfit, after the public domain image from the *Trachtenbuch* by Christoph Weiditz, published in the 1530s. Cropped and modified to highlight clothing details of the man on p. 77. https://commons. wikimedia.org/wiki/File:Weiditz_Trachtenbuch_077-078.jpg, accessed October 7, 2021.

the rage. An image labeled "Negro slave with a wine-skin in Castile" (Weiditz 1994: Plate XLVII; Figure 5.8) is peculiar for emphasizing the ragged quality of the man's hose or pants, and for depicting him with only one shoe and without a hat. The image also depicts the man with a chain that goes from his

Figure 5.7 Image of sailor, after the public domain image from the *Trachtenbuch* by Christoph Weiditz, published in the 1530s. Cropped and modified to highlight clothing details of the man on p. 84. https://commons. wikimedia.org/wiki/Category:Trachtenbuch_des_Christoph_Weiditz#/media/ File:Weiditz_Trachtenbuch_083-084.jpg, accessed October 22, 2021.

waist to his ankle, emphasizing his status as an enslaved person. Still, just like others, the enslaved person is pictured wearing a tunic tied around his waist with puffy long sleeves. Other enslaved people in the book, whether African or European, are also depicted barefoot, but wearing long puffy sleeves, and

Figure 5.8 Image of enslaved man, after the public domain image from the *Trachtenbuch* by Christoph Weiditz, published in the 1530s. Cropped and modified to highlight clothing details of the man on p.22. https://commons.wikimedia.org/wiki/File:Weiditz_Trachtenbuch_022-023.jpg, accessed October 2021.

breeches instead of hose (Weiditz 1994: Plates LXIII, LXIV, LXV, and LXVI). The hats depicted in the *Trachtenbuch* stand out as showing the greatest variation in terms of men's clothing, and many of the hats were likely regional and ethnic styles. Another item of clothing that appears quite frequently in the book is the cape in its many designs (Weiditz 1994: Plates XLII, LXVIII, LXXIII, LXXIV), sometimes enveloping the entire body of the person depicted (Weiditz 1994, Plate XXIV).

Women's Clothes

The probate inventories present the challenge of belonging mostly to men. This sample includes only two inventories of women. They may offer but a glimpse at the clothes that colonizer women wore in colonial Mexico City, and they may not be representative of colonizer women's clothing in general. Only 25 items of clothing appear in the probate inventory that belonged to Juana Bautista, a woman who was born in Seville and died in Mexico in 1581 (Cont. 219, N.2, R.3) (Table 5.1). She was apparently a seamstress. Another 31 items of clothing appear in the probate inventory that belonged to María de Espinosa, who was also born in Seville and moved to Mexico when her husband died. She died in 1565 (Cont. 210 N1, R74). Very few of the items are specifically described as being women's clothes by adding the comment "de mujer" after mentioning the item. Perhaps scribes found little reason to clarify that they were women's clothes because the inventories were written up with full knowledge that they were describing clothing that belonged to women. There was probably little need to specify that they were women's clothes, although given than Bautista was probably a seamstress, some of the items of clothing that belonged to her may include clothes she owned as part of her trade.

Bernis (1962:17–19) provides a description of women's clothes at the time. Women wore a bodice over an undershirt as a first layer that would remain mostly covered by other clothes. Bernis (1962:18) lists the bodice as *corpecico*, *corpiño*, and *cos*, but these do not appear in either woman's inventory. They appear in the probate inventories as *corpezuelos*. On top of the bodice, women would wear a *saya*, similar to the tunic or smock worn by men, appearing three times in each of the women's inventories. The related term *sayuelas* may refer to these smocks as well and it only appears in women's inventories. On top of the smock, women could wear loose dresses (*monjil*), or *ropa*. And on top of their dress, they often wore a *manto* or *mantilla*, which was similar to a shawl and could be worn as a covering for the head and shoulders, or for the shoulders and the torso.

Other items found in the inventories that belonged to women include items that have a high frequency in men's inventories, including shirts

Table 5.1 Clothing in women's inventories.

		Juana Bautista	María de Espinosa
camisas	shirts	4	2
camisas de mujer	women's shirts	3	0
chapines	cork-soled leather sandals	0	2
coquillas	codpieces	0	6
gorra	cap	0	2
jubón	doublet	5	0
jubón de mujer	women's smock	2	0
manto	mantle	1	4
manto de mujer	women's mantle	1	0
mantón	shawl	0	1
monjil	dress	1	0
piernas	hose	0	6
ropa	coat	2	0
ropilla	rags	2	0
ropilla de mujer	women's rags	1	0
saya	smock	3	3
sayuela	smock	0	3
sombrero	hat	0	2
Total		25	31

($n = 9$), and doublets ($n = 7$). It is probable that these items were worn by the women, although the women's inventories include some items that were probably not worn by women at all. For example, codpieces (*coquillas*) appear in María de Espinosa's inventory but not in Juana Bautista. Codpieces were associated with men and the presence of the codpieces in a woman's inventory has led me to fantasies (happy or unfortunate, depending on how you view the world) about how they got there. *Piernas* most likely hose, also appear in María de Espinosa's inventory ($n = 6$) but not in Juana Bautista's. As a term, piernas has a very low frequency in all of the inventories ($n = 29$, including the six that were in María de Espinosa's inventory). There are also two hats listed in María de Espinosa's inventory, whereas there is none in Juana Bautista's. Finally, it is surprising that there are no shoes listed in these inventories, besides the two *chapines* in María de Espinosa's belongings. The fact that there are several items one would expect to appear in both lists but they only appear in one list or the other suggests that these two inventories are not reliable as a thorough description of women's clothes. They only offer a glimpse of some of the clothing women could own at the time, but they do not give a well-rounded view of the clothes that they wore on an everyday basis. Perhaps some of the clothes were too deteriorated to be sold in auction, although I am speculating based only on their absence.

The *Trachtenbuch* contains images of women's clothes, including one image of a Sevillian woman (Figure 5.9). She is shown with a long braid, large earrings, a dress cinched at the waist and puffy sleeves. Her dress goes all the way up to her neck, and only her face and hands peek out of the dress. Her shoes are quite tall, thick soled, and her feet are covered in hose (Weiditz 1994: Plate XCII). This particular dress is unique among the illustrations in the *Trachtenbuch*. The women portrayed in the volume are from different regions in Spain, and the images offer a glimpse of the similarities and differences between regional dress at the time. There are many similarities in their manner of dress including big long skirts, puffy sleeves, dresses that are cinched at the waist, and the almost complete coverage of the body. Normally one can only see the woman's hands and face, as is the case in the illustration of a woman from Barcelona (Figure 5.10). But the differences between the dress of different regions are striking, whether one focuses on the hats, or on the design of skirts and shirts. The book does not provide enough information to gauge whether the differences in regional dress are portrayed accurately in the illustrations, or whether there was more overlap between the dress of the different regions. Further, the limited information in these two probate inventories does not allow identifying whether regional differences in Spanish dress continued among colonizer women in Mexico, even if for a while. It is also possible that the dress of colonizer women gained its own local Mexican flavor in the sixteenth century. Further research is needed to gain a better understanding of women's dress in early colonial Mexico.

Indigenous Clothes

Whether one focuses on men or women, most of the clothes in the inventories were Spanish styles, and radically different from the clothing worn by Nahuas in central Mexico. Indigenous clothes appear in the inventories but in low frequencies. The Indigenous item with the highest frequency is *naguas* ($n = 40$), which roughly translate to skirt, slip, or underskirt, whether for

Figure 5.9 Image of Sevillian woman, after the public domain image from the *Trachtenbuch* by Christoph Weiditz, published in the 1530s. Cropped and modified to highlight clothing details of the woman on p. 60. https://commons. wikimedia.org/wiki/File:Weiditz_Trachtenbuch_059-060.jpg, accessed October 2021.

women or men. Naguas is a Taíno term that the Spanish then used to refer to Indigenous clothing in New Spain. When mentioning naguas, Alvarado Tezozomoc (2012:160–161) explains that people in Mexico had different names for them and mentions *chiconcueitl* and *tentacanconcueitl*, although

Figure 5.10 Image of woman from Barcelona, after the public domain image from the *Trachtenbuch* by Christoph Weiditz, published in the 1530s. Cropped and modified to highlight clothing details of the woman on p. 68. https://commons. wikimedia.org/wiki/File:Weiditz_Trachtenbuch_067-068.jpg, accessed October 2021.

most sources refer to them more simply as *cueitl*. Tezozomoc's use of the term nagua shows that the Spanish had adopted the word in the Caribbean, and they used it for other clothes elsewhere. All of the naguas are in the inventories of men, and thirty-seven of them appear in Martín García's inventory (Cont, 197 N 21, 6). I believe that he owned those naguas as items he intended to sell rather than items he would wear. They are described as new

Figure 5.11 Woman wearing a huipil, Codex Mendoza, Folio 68r. Bodleian Libraries, University of Oxford.

and well-made ("nuevas, muy buenas") and of different colors. There is little that indicates that he had used any of them.

In addition to the naguas, there are eight Indigenous women's shirts (one *camisa de yndia* and seven *huipiles*) (Figure 5.11), three *mastiles*, a corruption of the term *maxtle* or loincloth for men (Figure 5.12), and one *escaupil*, or Indigenous cotton vest used as armor (Chapter 6). The two women whose inventories I consulted apparently did not own Indigenous clothes at all. All seven of the Indigenous women's shirts were found in men's inventories.[3]

<hr>

[3] One shirt belonged to Salvador Márquez, who was married to a local woman ("mujer de esta tierra"), probably an Indigenous woman (AGI Cont. 5575 N.13). Seven huipiles were found in Lope Hernández's inventory (AGI Cont. 197 N.21 (18)). His belongings and the commentaries in his inventory suggest that he worked in mining and as a merchant. He owned many slaves, although the number is not specified. He had several children with several of his slaves. His ownership of these Indigenous women's shirts could be an indication of a man's ownership over things that were used by his wife or other women. It is also possible that he sold goods, including Indigenous clothes that he sold to his own slaves and perhaps others.

Figure 5.12 Boys wearing maxtles, and man wearing a maxtle and cape. Code Mendoza, Folio 60r. Bodleian Libraries, University of Oxford.

Two of the mastiles were in Hernando Ladrón's inventory and they were described as worthless ("cosa sin provecho"; Cont. 197 N.21). Based on these inventories, there is no reason to think that colonizers wore Indigenous items of clothing, and I believe they had those items as curiosities or as merchandise they were hoping to sell. Even though it does not look like they adopted Indigenous clothing, there is still the possibility that they used Spanish-style clothing made by Indians, as I discuss later.

Materials

The materials used to make the clothes in the sixteenth century were quite varied. Herrero García (2014) provides descriptions of over 150 different textiles produced in Spain during the sixteenth and seventeenth centuries. As is traditional among textile scholars, he classified them into silk, wool, linens, and blends. Each of those categories can be broken down into a number of different textiles based on the techniques used in production, the weight of the fabric, and other technical factors (see also Dávila Corona et al. 2004). Linens include more than just textiles made of linen. It was made up of a variety of vegetal fibers, including linen (*Linum usitatissimum*), cotton, hemp, and others. In addition to woven fabrics made of silk, wool, and linens, people made clothes, shoes, hats, and many accessories out of leather in Spain.

In central Mexico, Indigenous weavers produced cloth mainly out of cotton and maguey, although in Mesoamerica more broadly they wove cloth using yucca, palm, hemp, and other vegetal fibers. Cotton was softer than maguey, and reputedly reserved for elites in central Mexico, whereas everyone had access to maguey cloth. In addition, they used leather, especially jaguar, rabbit, and hare skins, and animal hair (especially rabbit) and feathers (Anawalt 1981; Blum 2006; Brumfiel 1991; Gallardo 2014; Mastache 2005). Soon after the conquest, Indigenous people started selling some of the foreign textiles in markets, including silk (Mundy 2015:93). They also provided cloth as tribute to Spaniards (Brumfiel 1996).

Given this pattern of adoption, coupled with the importation of clothing and cloth from Europe, there is much to learn about the use of these different materials among colonizers. I focus here on a narrow question: did the men who compiled the inventories mention Indigenous textiles, or did they only mention European textiles? Did they mention maguey? Notice that the question asks what textiles they mentioned. It is one step removed from asking what textiles they used. The probate inventories provide information on what the colonizers thought or at least wrote about their clothes. There is no way to verify whether they reported the different kinds of cloth correctly, or consistently. What we have is a record of what they thought they were looking at, whenever they felt like identifying the cloth. I assume that for the most part, they probably got the names of different textiles right. It would be easy to tell leather apart from silk, for example, or to tell silk apart from linen. However, I have no way of verifying their identification of different materials, and there are probably errors in the inventories.

Approximately half the clothes in the inventories have a clear mention of the material out of which they were made (Table 5.2). The material with the highest frequency was leather ($n = 373$). The abundance of leather should not be surprising, given that shoes and boots are ubiquitous in the inventories. Leather was used primarily for shoes, boots, and gloves, and in much lower frequencies for hose ($n = 5$), chaps ($n = 1$), smocks ($n = 2$) and a cape. Archaeologists working at the Palacio Nacional in Mexico City made an unusual finding: enough leather soles and pieces of leather to fill two plastic bags that were 80 cm wide and 120 cm tall (Jiménez Badillo 2003:101–102). There must have been a shoemaker living nearby, and maybe even supplying some of the leather goods that appear in the inventories.

Table 5.2 Textiles and other materials mentioned in the inventories.

Material	Name in the inventories	Comments	Frequency	%
cotton or blend	fustán	Possibly cotton,[1] although before the seventeenth century it could be a blend[2]	2	0.09
cotton or blend total			2	0.09
leather	badana		1	0.04
	cordobán		59	2.63
	cuero		259	11.53
	venado		49	2.18
	gamuza		5	0.22
leather total			373	16.61
wool	anascote		3	0.13
	bayeta		14	0.62
	escarlatín		1	0.04
	estameña		2	0.09
	fieltro		3	0.13
	grana		20	0.89
	lana		33	1.47
	lanillas		1	0.04
	londres		3	0.13
	paño		164	7.30
	paño de perpiñán		1	0.04
	paño leonado	"Leonado" likely refers to the color.	1	0.04
	perpiñán		2	0.09
	refino	Possibly refers to a type of paño.[3]	3	0.13
	telillas		1	0.04
wool total			252	11.22
linens (from a variety of vegetal fibers)	angeo	also, anjeo[2]	3	0.13
	cañamazo	typically, hemp or linen.[2]	3	0.13

Table 5.2 Continued

Material	Name in the inventories	Comments	Frequency	%
	cotonía	typically cotton, although often a blend of cotton and silk.[1,2]	9	0.40
	damasquillo	linen, silk, wool, or blend[2]	1	0.04
	hilo	Typically, linen, although sometimes it could be hemp.[2]	5	0.22
	holanda	linen or cotton[2]	11	0.49
	lienzo		120	5.34
	lienzo de Castilla		5	0.22
	presilla		3	0.13
	ruán	linen, cotton, or wool[2]	185	8.24
	ruán y presilla		15	0.67
	sábana		1	0.04
linens total			361	16.07
silk	damasco		2	0.09
	raso		32	1.42
	seda		26	1.16
	terciopelo		42	1.87
silk total			102	4.54
silk and wool	terciopelo y lana		2	0.09
	paño con seda		1	0.04
	paño y tafetán	Paño is typically wool, whereas tafetán is silk.[2]	1	0.04
	sayal	Could be wool or a blend of wool and silk.[2]	3	0.13
silk and wool total			7	0.31
linen and silk	lienzo y tafetán		1	0.04
leather and silk	gamuza y terciopelo		1	0.04

(continued)

Table 5.2 Continued

Material	Name in the inventories	Comments	Frequency	%
miscellaneous fabrics	brite	Does not appear in the dictionaries consulted.	2	0.09
	camargo	Does not appear in the dictionaries consulted.	1	0.04
	chamelote	Could be wool, silk, or different blends.	2	0.09
	coleta	Fabric used normally for an outer shell or cover.[2]	9	0.40
	friseta	Could be a blend of linen and cotton, or wool.[2]	1	0.04
	fuchimile	Probably a corruption of a Nahuatl term.	4	0.18
	hecho de pedazos	"made of pieces"	1	0.04
	jerga	Either a thick and rough cloth, or cloth made out of wool.[2]	2	0.09
	malla	possibly a net	1	0.04
	manta	either wool or cotton.[2]	12	0.53
	pelo de rata	Refers to the gray color of the material.	7	0.31
				0.00
	piel de rata	Refers to the gray color of the material.	2	0.09
	pinto	Possibly refers to the color.	1	0.04
	raja	silk or wool[2]	1	0.04
	sarga	May refer to the material (wool, silk, or blend) or to the technique of fabrication.[2,3]	2	0.09
	tafetán	May refer to the material (wool, silk, or blend) or to the technique of fabrication.[2,3]	18	0.80
	tafetán despuntado	May refer to the material (wool, silk, or blend) or to the technique of fabrication.[2,3]	1	0.04
	tapetados	Typically refers to a dark color.[4]	1	0.04
	tela		2	0.09

Table 5.2 Continued

Material	Name in the inventories	Comments	Frequency	%
miscellaneous total			70	3.12
unidentified			1077	47.95
Total			2246	100.00

[1] as classified by Herrero García.

[2] as classified in Dávila Corona et al. 2004.

[3] Sílvia Saladrigas, personal communication, June 2020.

[4] Diccionario de la Real Academia Española, https://dle.rae.es.

Twelve of the textiles mentioned can be classified as linens, making it the category with the second highest frequency in the inventories ($n = 361$). *Ruán* was perhaps the most important of all woven fabrics, judging by its frequency. It is a kind of cloth that resembles a very fine canvas, usually made out of cotton, although it could be made out of linen and wool. It was mostly used for shirts and hose, probably because its softness made it comfortable against the skin. It has been the most important cloth in Spanish commerce and fashion since the sixteenth century. In addition to being used for clothing, it was the material used for making sheets, bed covers, to wrap mattresses, and as the interior shell of many items of clothing (Dávila Corona et al. 2004:171; Herrero García 2014:231–232).

The material with the third highest frequency is wool ($n = 252$). It was among the most varied and important fabrics in Spain at the time, and colonizers brought different kinds of wool to New Spain. Herrero García (2014:133–175) lists at least forty-five different fabrics, each with its unique name, among the varieties of wool described in Royal Pragmatics of the Catholic monarchs in 1500 and 1501. Some of the different categories are based on the number of threads of pure wool per unit of length. Other categories refer to blends of wool and cotton, linen, or silk, and also to wool of different colors. In the inventories I consulted, wool appears under 15 different names. By far the most common was *paño*, the fabric with the third highest frequency in the inventories, behind leather and ruan. It was used for skirts (*faldellín*, $n = 26$), smocks ($n = 23$), short capes without a hood (*herrerruelo*, $n = 11$), hose ($n = 8$), and an endless variety of clothes. It is clearly one of the most versatile fabrics in the inventories. *Sayal*, a fabric that could sometimes be made of wool and sometimes of silk, was one of a few kinds of Spanish cloth sold also by

Indigenous people in the market (Mundy 2014:93). The frequency of wool in the inventories is no surprise, given that the Basin of Mexico can be cold, even on summer nights, and that colonizers introduced a variety of sheep during the sixteenth century (Blum 2006:148). Thus, people who wanted warm clothes found a ready supply of wool quite early in the colonial period.

The material with the fourth highest frequency is silk, which was among the preferred materials for hose, hats, doublets, and sleeves. The fact that sleeves appear mentioned as individual garments in the inventories indicates that they sometimes were made separately and attached to other garments that covered the torso. Silk appears less frequently as a material for shoes and other garments. Among the fabrics made with silk one may find velvet (*terciopelo*, $n = 42$), and *raso* ($n = 32$). Raso is a lustrous silk with more body than taffeta and less body than velvet. The different categories of silk were determined by the weight of the cloth per length, as codified in the ordinances of weavers' guild in Toledo since the sixteenth century (Herrero García 2014:29). Colonizers introduced sericulture to New Spain very soon after the conquest, and by 1526, they already had a silk workers' guild. Domestic silk production developed between 1531 and 1580 in New Spain (Blum 2006:150; Urquiola Permisán 2004). Colonizers faced almost immediate competition from Indigenous people, who started making and selling different kinds of textiles used by the Spanish, including silk. Mundy observes that six out of seven words in a plan view of the Indigenous market of Mexico City, drawn in the 1580s, had to do with cloth and clothing, including "sayal, seda, frazada, cordon, sombrero, and capan" (2014:93). But the main competition for local silk production may have come from around the globe. Urquiola Permisán (2004:204, 217–218) argues that local silk production diminished as a steady flow of silk cloth from Asia reached New Spain once trade with Phillipines was established.

The absence of any explicit mention of maguey, one of the fabrics produced by Indigenous people in central Mexico before and after the conquest, is surprising, given its importance in production of domestic cloth in the Aztec world (Brumfiel 1991). It may be that the people compiling the inventories could not tell maguey apart from other, more familiar fabrics, and simply identified the fabric used for some of the items incorrectly by giving it more familiar names. Or perhaps the probate inventories are not wrong, and the Spanish simply did not use maguey, a fabric that Indigenous people considered fit for commoners, but not for elites. *Fuchimile*, one of the fabrics mentioned in the documents, could perhaps be an Indigenous textile. I only base this idea on the fact that I could not find it in any of the dictionaries

I consulted, all of which focus on Spanish textiles, and on the ending of the word in -ile. I speculate that the ending could be a corruption of a Nahuatl term ending in -tle or -illi, which Spanish speakers may have turned into -ile, a more natural or common pronunciation in Spanish. For example, mastil, mentioned earlier, is a Spanish way of writing maxtle. Fuchimile, if it is indeed an Indigenous textile, appears only four times in the inventories, but my attempt at identifying fuchimile as an Indigenous textile may be entirely wrong. Regardless of whether they used maguey, whether fuchimile is an indigenous textile, and regardless of whether they mentioned Indigenous cloth explicitly in the inventories, Indigenous people actually made some of the clothes that the Spanish wore, a matter to which I now turn to.

Where Were the Clothes Made?

The fashions may have been Spanish, but the place where the cloth or clothes were manufactured could have been in Spain or elsewhere. Only 389 items of clothing, or close to 17 percent of the items of clothing, have their origin stated clearly in the inventories (Table 5.3). It is difficult to explain with certainty why such a low percentage of the items has a provenience, although I believe it is due to several factors in combination. Maybe the people compiling the inventories did not know where the clothes came from. Maybe they did not care, and indifference toward the place of manufacture of the clothing would be important. And maybe they did not think that reporting the origin of the clothing would have any important effect on the price of the clothing, so they did not report it. In spite of the missing information on approximately 83 percent of the items, the data on provenience of this small sample of items is the best data we have to determine where the clothes were made. The information may or may not be random, but we can still glean patterns from it.

Table 5.3 Origin of the clothes in the inventories.

	Frequency	%
American	148	38
Made by Indigenous producers	32	8.2
Imported	209	53.7
Total	389	99.9

I divided the items into four broad categories based on the information provided. The first is items with no provenience at all, and they are not used in most of the analysis. The second category is "American" items, which includes items made in the Spanish colonies that do not specify that they were made by Indigenous, European, or Black producers. Scribes typically labeled these items as *de la tierra*, *de las indias*, or, rarely, with a more specific name for a city or region where they were made. The third category consists of items that are specifically labeled as being produced by Indigenous hands with labels such as *de indios*, *hecho de indios*, or *de los indios de* followed by the name of a specific region or town. Finally, the category "imported" includes all items that were said to be made in Europe, and very few items made elsewhere, whether in Asia or Africa. Sometimes scribes would mention specific cities where the items were made, including Castile, Seville, London, Paris, and others. Other times, scribes would only write *traído* (brought over), or *de la mar* (from the sea), to designate an item as an import.

Of the items of clothing that specify an origin, 38 percent (n = 148) are labeled as made in the Americas, and 8.2 percent (n = 32) are labeled as made specifically by Indians, for a total of 46.2 percent (n = 180) of items made in the Americas, whether by Indigenous producers or Spanish colonizers or both (Table 5.3). Another 53.7 percent (n = 209) of the items were imported. The items made in the Americas include boots, hose, shirts, capes, doublets, gloves, shawls, smocks, and a jacket, as well as Indigenous clothes that I do not believe were worn by the colonizers, such as naguas, huipiles, and mastiles. Most of them are in very low frequencies, except for shirts (n = 35). There are different ways of interpreting this information. If we assume that the designation of provenience is random (an assumption that may or may not be correct), one can say that Spanish colonizers certainly used a lot of clothing made in the Americas. About half of the clothing owned by Spanish colonizers was made in the Americas, and about 8 percent made by Indigenous producers, although we must remember that most of the items said to be made by Indigenous producers were naguas and mastiles, which were not really worn by colonizers.[4]

---

[4] If we assume that all of the items made in the Americas were pointed out in the inventories (an unlikely assumption), then 8 percent of the clothes owned by the decedents (180 items labeled as made in the Americas out of a total of 2,246 items of clothing found in the inventories) were made in the Americas. This last statistic is unlikely, because it assumes that absolutely all of the items made in the Americas were labeled as such in the inventories, and that all of the items that are left with an unspecified provenience were imported from Europe. I bet that the proportion of items made in the Americas is much higher, closer to the 46.2 percent reported in Table 5.3.

Of course, the patterns also show that approximately half of the clothes with a stated provenience were imported from Europe. Many of the people represented in these inventories may have been poor, as discussed previously, but they had access to imported clothes, whether because they bought those clothes in Mexico or because they brought some of those clothes, or both. Thus, colonizers used both, imported clothing and locally made clothing that conformed to Spanish fashions. What initially seemed like a world of fashion made in Spain now seems like a world of Spanish fashions made about half in Spain and half in the Americas, some by Indigenous producers. Dressing with distinction depended as much on importing items as it did on obtaining items from Indigenous people, including cloth and finished clothing.

The Quality of the Clothes

The probate inventories include commentary on the quality of items of clothing. Those who compiled them noticed what was new, or old, torn, ragged, mended, what would have been impressive to others (e.g., "impressive to Indians but not to me"), and what was, simply put, worthless. Travelers in the seventeenth century sometimes expressed admiration for the clothing and fashions of people in Mexico City, as discussed previously. The probate inventories provide us with another opportunity to examine the quality of the clothing of colonizers, focusing now on the sixteenth century. These inventories eliminate the problem of the bias of the traveler and the inclination to describe the wealth and grandeur and ignore the uglier aspects of daily life. The descriptions written by scribes may be biased in ways that are difficult to discern, but at least they were free of the goals of impressing readers just for the sake of impressing them.

Indifference comes across in these documents more than anything else. A total of 776 items of clothing (or 34.6 percent of all clothing) have some sort of evaluation of quality (Table 5.4). Items were more likely to be evaluated in terms of their quality than to have a designation of their origin, probably because the quality of the item was more readily visible to any observer, whereas knowing the origin required more detailed knowledge of the items in question. The descriptions are often what I consider neutral, which means that they focus on explaining aspects of the composition, size, color, or use of the objects in question without offering a value-laden or critical assessment of the object: "with sleeves, with two velvet stripes, for children,

Table 5.4 Quality of the clothing, as stated in the probate inventories.

	English translation	Frequency	%
que es provecho de ellos	to their benefit	1	0.1
bueno	good	112	14.4
con oro	with gold	4	0.5
de indios bueno	of Indians, good	22	2.8
de indios, sin provecho	of Indians, worthless	2	0.3
neutral	neutral	220	28.4
no son nada	that amount to nothing	7	0.9
nueva	new	1	0.1
roto	torn	25	3.2
viejo	old	338	43.6
viejo con oro	old with gold	2	0.3
viejo y remendado	old and mended	3	0.4
viejo y roto	old and tattered	39	5
Total		776	100

fancy (*labradas*), etc." Of course, these kinds of descriptions are not exactly neutral, because depending on a person's tastes, needs, and interests, these descriptions increase or diminish the value of an object. Still, the point of having a category that includes all neutral descriptions is to draw attention to the other descriptions: those descriptions that are value-laden and present an evaluation of quality that is subjective ("very good, good, poorly made," etc.) or that is related to the manufacture, deterioration, or repair of an item ("new, old, old and tattered, mended, worthless," etc.).

Almost a third (28.4 percent, $n = 220$) of the items of clothing with a description are described in neutral terms related to the size or details of workmanship of the clothes (Table 5.4). More useful for the present analysis are the value-laden categories. Only one category surpasses the neutral descriptions in terms of numbers: items described simply as old (43.6 percent, $n = 338$). It is difficult to know whether "old" refers to clothing that was deteriorated, or clothing that was a bit out of fashion or could otherwise be seen as something old. I can neither assume that fashion turned as quickly as it does today, nor can I assume that fashion was stable in the sixteenth century. The related categories of old and torn ($n = 39$), old and mended ($n = 3$), and my favorite, old with gold ($n = 2$) bring the percentage of items described as old in one way or another to 49.3 percent, or practically half of the clothes described in the inventories. In addition, there is a category of torn clothes that makes up another 3.2 percent ($n = 25$) of the clothing. This total of old and tattered clothes is quite different from the descriptions of fancy people in the latest fashions in the seventeenth century (Thompson 1958). Of course, there is always the possibility that these were old clothes that nobody used anymore. Still, the fact that people bought them in auction means that being old and torn was not necessarily the end of the valued life of a garment. Most likely, people would mend or have clothes repaired, and they would wear them again. We should also remember that there were new clothes for sale in Mexico City, and these inventories mostly contain used clothes, given that they had belonged to someone. In fact, only one item of clothing is described as new, and 14.4 percent (n = 112) items of clothing are described as "good." The fact that we have hundreds of items of used and tattered clothes selling in auction reveals that the clothes that people wore in sixteenth-century Mexico City included a lot of used and old clothing.

The question whether colonizers thought positively or negatively of clothing made by Indigenous producers is another important aspect of the material worlds of Spanish colonizers. Gallardo (2014) provides extensive citations of several times when colonial chroniclers, including Sahagún, Durán, and Alvarado Tezozomoc, wrote commentaries about the cloth and clothing of Indigenous people. The chroniclers lavished praise, but it is difficult to tell whether such praise is admiration for products that the chroniclers admired but did not want, or whether they were products they wanted to own and use. When Hernán Cortés wrote to Charles V, King of Spain, in the middle of the conquest (1520), he expressed admiration for the quality of cotton textiles presented to him by the Mexica king Moctezuma, and even compared the quality of such cloth, its colors and beautiful workmanship, with silk (Blum 2006:147). Bernal Díaz del Castillo described some of the presents brought to the conquistadors as being "the finest cotton cloth" (Díaz del Castillo 1966:57), echoing the impression given by Cortés. His description of cloth follows an incredibly lavish list of presents, written to impress any reader with the opulence and riches of Mexico. The presents include, among others, plates made of gold and silver and said to be larger than a wheel of carriage, helmets full of pieces of gold, animal figurines made of gold, jewelry, feathers made of gold and silver, green feathers, and the fine cloth, as well as other things that Díaz could not remember. But it is possible that Cortés and Díaz presented such an overwhelmingly positive view of Indigenous cloth because they were interested in securing more support for the conquest, and in the glory of having conquered a splendid land. Exaggeration could only help their cause.

After the conquest, colonizers obtained tribute cloth from Indigenous producers. Brumfiel (1996) cites some documents in which colonizers provided a rather different opinion of Indigenous cloth. They sometimes complained about the quality of tribute cloth, finding that the cloth was woven loosely and that it was shoddy. Colonizers requested that the cloth be woven with a tighter weave. The documents cited by Brumfiel raise the possibility that some colonizers were not, after all, so impressed by Indigenous cloth.

The probate inventories complement the information in the chronicles and other colonial documents. They provide comments about the quality of Indigenous cloth in contexts in which colonizers were not necessarily trying to exaggerate the quality of Indigenous things. They were simply trying to describe items in an inventory. The appreciation of Indigenous craftsmanship of clothes is unmistakable in these inventories. The descriptions of quality in this data set include 22 instances in which clothes were described as good and made by Indians ("de indios, bueno"), whereas only two items describe clothes as made by Indians and worthless ("de indios, sin provecho") (Table 5.5). One of the descriptions of an Indigenous-made item is both positive and distancing at the same time, explaining that the item is of worth to Indians ("que es provecho de ellos"). The inventories are generally positive in their evaluation of the craftsmanship and quality of things (clothes and other items) made by Indigenous producers.

A second pattern is that items made in Europe or in the Americas receive rather similar evaluations to one another in most other categories. Things are almost as likely to be evaluated as good, whether they come from the American colonies or from Europe, and they are equally described in neutral terms regardless of where they were made. A third pattern is that the only category in which there are some differences are "old and tattered" or "tattered," where items made in Europe are the ones mostly found to be old and tattered. Perhaps those items had been in use for a longer time than those made in the Americas and they were tattered simply for that reason. But overall, the table offers little reason to think that Spanish colonizers thought poorly of the quality of clothes made in the Spanish colonies in general, whether made by Spanish or Indigenous tailors. They seem, in fact, to have viewed those clothes positively.

Table 5.5 Commentary on the quality of different clothes compared to the origin of the clothes.

	American	European	Indigenous	na	Total
"que es provecho de ellos" (to their benefit)	1	0	0	0	1
bueno (good)	21	18	0	72	111
con oro (with gold)	1	0	0	3	4
de indios bueno (of Indians, good)	0	0	22	0	22
Indios, sin provecho (of Indians, worthless)	0	0	2	0	2
neutral	18	18	0	186	222
no son nada (nothing)	1	0	0	6	7
roto (torn)	2	8	0	22	32
viejo (old)	20	23	0	238	281
viejo con oro (old with gold)	0	0	0	2	2
viejo y remendado (old and mended)	0	0	0	3	3
viejo y roto (old and torn)	1	15	0	22	38
Total	65	82	24	554	725

In an earlier publication, I reported that a total of 363 items in the inventories (including clothes and any other items) have both a description of quality of the items and also a clear indication of the provenience or place of manufacture of the items. Of those, only seventy-three items were made by Indigenous producers, and 93 percent of them (n = 68) are evaluated positively. Only two items, mentioned previously, are made by Indigenous people and evaluated negatively in the entire data set. It is important to note that all of the items described in positive terms are from only one inventory, that of Martín García, a merchant who died in 1545 (AGI, Cont. 197, N.21[6]; Rodríguez-Alegría 2016a:53–54). Even though the explicitly positive evaluation of Indigenous goods appears only in this document, I argue that in general, colonizers thought highly of Indigenous craftsmanship. There are very few explicitly negative evaluations of Indigenous products, providing little reason to think that the Spanish thought of them in any negative light.

Jewelry

Jewelry is also an important part of dress, often impressive to the wearer and sometimes even to others. In a description of Hernán Cortés' jewelry, Díaz del Castillo mentions a simple gold chain of fine craftsmanship, a medal with religious imagery, a diamond ring, and a medal on his hat. The chain impressed him not for its size or weight, but because of its fine craftsmanship. But one of the medals did not impress him enough to remember what image it had (Díaz del Castillo 1966:480). Jewelry could be of value both as an item of display and because of its high exchange value in comparison to its size, if it was made of fine metals or precious stones. It is thus surprising that there are only forty-nine entries that mention jewelry in the inventories. This does not mean that there were only forty-nine pieces of jewelry. It just means that jewelry is mentioned forty-nine times, whether as an individual ring, jewel, or chain, or as a box full of rings, beads, or other jewels. Thus, the information makes it clear that there were many more individual jewels, but it does not show exactly how many. Besides the lack of specificity in the inventories, another reason why the count of jewelry seems low must be due to how easy it would have been to steal and sell jewelry for a good price. I speculate that scribes and other officials who worked on the probate inventories, as well as people who had access to decedents' belongings, stole small jewels made of gold and silver on occasion. A more benign possibility is that the owners gave away jewelry as they got closer to the end of their lives.

The jewelry that is mentioned is but a sample of the jewelry that these colonizers owned. It includes items of gold, silver, tin, and beads of different materials. The stones that are mentioned include an emerald ring, and an unspecified number of amber beads. Gold makes up almost half of the items mentioned, appearing as the primary material in twenty-four of the items, not including one item that is made of something that looked like gold ("algo que parece oro"). Silver is mentioned as the primary material only five times, and there are ten boxes of tin rings (assuming that they were used as jewelry) included in the inventories.

The different designs of jewelry are only hinted at in the inventories, showing that the attention was often squarely on the material and its value rather than on the specific design or style of the jewelry. Still, we have some general idea of what people wore. Rings are the most ubiquitous items, with a total of 20 entries in the inventories that mention rings. Ten of those items were boxes of rings, making it difficult to know how many rings there were in total. It is telling that the ten boxes of rings contained rings made of tin. If the rings had been made of gold, I bet they would have been counted or weighed. Ten entries mention jewels without specifying what they were (*joyas, joyuelas, alhajas, joyeles, joyitas*). Seven entries in the inventories mention unspecified numbers of beads, sometimes made of amber, gold, and perhaps other stones. The inventories also include three eagles, small chains of gold, a chain of glass (likely a chain of gold with glass pendants or beads), and two medals of unspecified imagery. Both medals probably had religious imagery, and each one belonged to a different priest.

A quick glance at the jewelry provides indication that the Spanish owned at least some Indigenous jewelry. Out of forty-nine items of jewelry that appear in the inventories, only a handful are identified as being made by Indigenous people. The descriptions are frustratingly skim. The first one is some jewels of gold (*joyuelas de oro*), and the only description associated with them, besides that they were made by Indians, is that they were old. I speculate that they were pre-Columbian, given that the inventory dates to 1545 and that it describes the jewels as old. They belonged to Hernando Ladrón, mentioned previously as the owner of the "worthless" loincloths (AGI Cont. 197 N.21). Another two items of jewelry specifically described as being made by Indigenous producers belonged to Juan Negrete, a friar of the order of Santiago (AGI Cont. 211, N.2, R.7). One of them is an unidentified jewel made of gold and engraved with an image that is not described in the document. The other is a golden eagle. Juan Negrete owned two other eagles made of gold that are otherwise not described in the inventory. I speculate that the other two eagles were also made by Indigenous people, just like the first one, which is the only one described specifically as being made by Indians. In the description of the presents brought to Hernán Cortés cited above, Díaz del Castillo (1966:57) lists several heads of animals and animal figurines made of gold. Even though he does not specifically mention eagle heads, these types of heads were probably similar to the figurines described by Díaz.

The Codex Tepetlaoztoc gives us an idea of what these jewels probably looked like. Several pages of the codex depict gold beads, pendants, and other jewels given to the Spanish as tribute. Among the pendants, there is a golden eagle, depicted with details of the feathers, head, and legs, and suspended from a red tie (Plate 15). Although the description in the probate inventories is skim, the eagle depicted in the codex probably resembles the golden eagles mentioned in the probate inventories. After all, archaeologists have found golden jewelry that is identical to Indigenous depictions of jewelry in other media, including stone sculpture and pictorial manuscripts

(Vela 2015). Other images of jewelry in the codex depict bells, beads, and pendants similar to archaeological examples. A particularly fancy jewel in shape of a shield with arrows (Plate 16) resembles an archaeological example made of gold and turquoise and attributed to the Mixtecs from the Late Postclassic period (Vela 2015:87). The shield, minus the arrows, and the stepped fret on the interior part of the shield, appear in other illustrations of jewelry in pictorial manuscripts (Hermann Lejarazu 2017; Herrera Meza and Ruiz Medrano 1997:22). The various designs of the jewelry in the Codex Tepetlaoztoc appear in other codices as attributes of different Mesoamerican deities (Hermann Lejarazu 2017). All of these examples suggest that the jewelry illustrated in the codex likely resembled the jewelry mentioned in the probate inventories, including the golden eagles, and the golden beads.

Two other items are described in a way that strongly suggests they were made by Indigenous producers. The first is a lot of gold beads made of *oro baxo*, which most likely stands for *oro bajo*. The second is a lot of amber and gold beads, also specifically made with *oro baxo*. The expression *oro bajo* refers to *oro de baja ley*, considered by the Spanish to be an inferior metal with a low content of gold. Spanish colonizers used the expression *oro bajo* to describe *guanín*, a gold alloy made and used by the Taíno in the Caribbean (Bray 1997), and I argue that the expression is used in these documents to describe gold alloys produced by Indigenous people in central Mexico. If that were the case, then between 5 and 7 items out of 49, or between approximately 10 percent and 14 percent of the items that mention jewels were made by Indigenous people.

It is interesting that none of the jewelry is identified as being European. My feeling is that the gold and silver jewelry identified in the documents was mostly American in origin, and valued mostly for its metallic content and not for its design or quality as jewels. I believe, but cannot prove, that there are other unmentioned items of Indigenous manufacture in the jewelry, but their importance rested not on the design of the items, but on the value of the metal. This is in contrast with the importance given to topos in Peru, where colonizer and criollo women wore these traditionally Indigenous items in part for their exotic beauty (Jamieson 2004).

Conclusion

Several patterns emerge from the information on clothing in the probate inventories of Spanish colonizers. Colonizers certainly wore their traditional

Spanish clothes, with their puffy sleeves, hose, leather shoes and boots, tight bodices, capes, and hats. Their clothes were made out of leather (especially for shoes and boots), linen, cotton, silk, and wool. The two women in the sample also wore Spanish fashions, although a larger sample of female decedents would be necessary to find out more details about women's clothing, especially about variety. Colonizers owned very few Indigenous garments, such as naguas, loincloths, and huipiles, or women's blouses. This group of colonizers did not go native. They held on to their own traditional dress. Thus far the information could be entirely compatible with a study of clothing as communication, or more specifically, the choice of clothing to send information: colonizers used their traditional clothes to communicate their ethnicity and belonging in a group with power in colonial Mexico. But I have argued that studying clothing just as items used to send information is too narrow. We can also study the way that clothes were perceived, which is an undeveloped aspect of the study of clothing as information exchange. We can study the experience of wearing clothes (were they new, tattered, old?) and the commercial and social connections that are implied in the place of manufacture of cloth and clothing.

Even if the fashions were European, people sometimes distinguished between imported and locally-produced clothes. The inventories reveal that a lot of the clothes that colonizers wore were imported from Spain and to a lesser extent, other cities in Europe. The lower-class colonizers that form the bulk of the decedents included in this study had access to European imports, whether because they brought most or all of their clothes when they sailed across the Atlantic, or because they bought imported clothes in Mexico, or probably both. These options are impossible to tell apart with the data in the inventories. Still, the information indicates that the same colonizers who wore Spanish fashions incorporated Indigenous products into their daily wear in an important manner: they sometimes wore clothes made with fabrics produced in the colonies, cloth made specifically by Indigenous people, and they also wore garments made by Indigenous people. Exchange with Indigenous people is, of course, well-known among scholars. But in this case, it is worth emphasizing that colonizers were obtaining from Indigenous people the clothes that colonizers would use to maintain a sense of tradition and decency (by wearing their traditional clothes) and perhaps to display their own ethnic difference from Indigenous people. Even after trading with Indigenous people in items made in Castile was prohibited, colonizers continued trading with Indigenous people in items that looked just like those made in Castile. In this way, distinction from Indigenous people through display was a process that simultaneously required integration with Indigenous people through exchange and socialization.

Colonizers spoke quite highly of Indigenous textiles and clothes. The probate inventories are more likely to contain negative commentary on European textiles than Indigenous cloth. The abundantly negative commentary of European cloth is mostly not meant to be a criticism of the initial quality of the cloth, or the beauty of the designs, but rather a commentary on the fact that clothes were old and sometimes torn. Commentary on the old and torn quality of many clothes is another aspect of daily life and the experience of wearing clothes among colonizers that people perceived. Clothes in sixteenth-century Mexico were apparently quite different from the world of spotless and fabulous fashions described in the travel literature of the seventeenth century. These old and tattered clothes make up approximately half of the clothes sold in the auctions recorded in the probate inventories, and they were presumably worn again by the people who bought them. Materials used to make new clothes or fix old clothes (thread, pieces of cloth, pieces of leather, buttons, and many others) make up the largest category of things in the probate inventories. Thus, people wore old clothes, tattered clothes, used, and mended clothes.

The descriptions of opulence and fashion that travelers wrote in the seventeenth century may indicate different possibilities. First, it is possible that in the sixteenth century, people wore clothes that were older and in worse shape than later into the colonial period. Perhaps as colonizers settled in greater numbers in Mexico City, there was a greater availability of tailors, seamstresses, and new imported clothing in general. Second, it is possible that there was always an abundance of torn and mended clothing in the colonial period, and that the travel literature emphasizes the new and impressive, while turning a blind eye to the old and tattered. It may have simply been a matter of emphasis, given that the travel literature was meant, in great part, to impress the readers. Finally, it could be that the probate inventories simply emphasize the old and tattered because the clothes already belonged to someone, and that there were more new clothes in Mexico City than can be seen in the inventories. However, the fact that people bought so many used and old clothes in the auctions recorded in the probate inventories suggests that torn and mended clothes were a staple of daily life in sixteenth-century Mexico City. Future studies using probate inventories or other sources of data in the seventeenth and eighteenth century may help clarify whether there were historical changes in the quality of the clothes of colonizers in New Spain.

6

How to Build Sociotechnical Systems

Tools, Livestock, and Slaves

Among the belongings of Spanish colonizers, one may find numerous slaves, livestock, and tools. The three could certainly belong in different categories that have little in common with one another. The category of tools includes a wide variety of needles, hammers, shears, sharpening stones, and what seems to be an endless variety of inanimate objects. Livestock consisted mostly of sheep, horses, and cattle. They were used as a source of wool, leather, and food, and as draft animals, although horses certainly served the purposes of display. Slaves were human beings, but they appear in the probate inventories alongside many material belongings. In fact, writing about enslaved people who appear in such dehumanizing ways in the documents caused me much anxiety as I wrote this chapter. My intention is to show the cruel ways in which colonizers treated them and wrote about them, while showing respect for their humanity and their lives as I write. At first glance, very little suggests that a tool, say a shoe tree, could belong together in the same category as a slave, or with livestock, aside from the expectation that they will work and produce for their owner.

In spite of their apparent differences, the categories of slaves, livestock, and tools are worth examining together for two main reasons. The first reason is mostly emic: the Spanish thought of them as belonging together. Spanish colonizers listed them together in the inventories repeatedly, linking them with phrases like "two slaves and their tools," or "some tools and nine mules." The fact that the people compiling the inventories linked them together indicates that colonizers often did not think of these categories as entirely independent of one another, and that examining them in tandem could be productive. A second reason is mostly etic: modern scholars have argued repeatedly that we must think of technology as composed of not only tools and materials, but also embodied skills, knowledge, the coordination of labor, traditions of practice, and other sociocultural factors that form part of creating and using things (Dobres 2000; Lemonnier 1993; Pfaffenberger

How to Make a New Spain. Enrique Rodríguez-Alegría, Oxford University Press. © Enrique Rodríguez-Alegría 2023.
DOI: 10.1093/oso/9780197682296.003.0007

1992). The idea implied in the probate inventories—that tools, slaves, and livestock belong together in a way that is meaningful—presents the opportunity to bring to fruition the links between tools and socioeconomic factors proposed by these authors.

To examine the technologies of colonizers, it is useful to keep in mind the concept of *sociotechnical systems*, defined as "the distinctive technological activity that stems from the linkage of techniques and material culture to the social coordination of labor" (Pfaffenberger 1992:497). Scholars have developed this concept in part to overcome the limitations of thinking about technology only as made up of tools and artifacts, or even only as made up of tools, techniques, and knowledge. By examining sociotechnical systems, scholars have tried to understand how tools, techniques, knowledge, and practices are linked to people, society, political and economic systems, legal systems, and scientific traditions. Sociotechnical systems can also be developed and managed through ritual action (Levine and Carballo 2014; Pfaffenberger 1992; Rodríguez-Alegría et al. 2015). Scholars working on questions related to technology in different time periods have embraced the idea that one must take multiple social and cultural factors into account when studying technological change (e.g., Alexander 2019; Ingold 1997; Navas et al. 2014; Rodríguez-Alegría 2008a, 2008b, 2012b; Scaramelli 2008).

Pfaffenberger (1992:501) argues that sociotechnical systems "can be understood . . . only by acknowledging that they produce power and meaning as well as goods." The idea that sociotechnical systems are related to power is central to this chapter. Still, I maintain focus on the actions of people when relating to different aspects of technology. Notice that many of the sentences in the previous paragraphs could give the impression that I believe that sociotechnical systems are something with volition or something that develops on its own. As with previous chapters, I will stubbornly hold on to the idea that an analytical concept—in this case, a sociotechnical system— will not do the work in this story. I aim to examine how people related to tools, technologies, and labor. Otherwise, I run the risk of arguing that my approach takes the actions of people seriously, but letting technology be the active subject of each sentence, or the analytical concept that does the actions that I believe humans were doing. Technology did not change anything. It is just a concept. People are the active part in this story of technology. They are the ones making decisions, choosing tools, using tools, forcing others to work, and sometimes seeing little choice but to do the work that they are forced to do. Sometimes, they may have felt like they had no choice at all but use the tools and techniques that were available. The conditions in which they related to technology may not have been of their making, but they sometimes had the ability to make at least some decisions regarding how they related to those conditions.

The sociotechnical systems of Spain and central Mexico in the sixteenth century seem so radically different that it is difficult not to think of this case as a meeting between two disparate technological worlds. Europeans at the time used metal tools primarily for cutting, striking, and building. They made weapons and armor of steel and used iron parts in their furniture. They used scissors, and metal knives for cutting, and for all sorts of daily needs. They had herds of large animals that they used for transportation, work, and as a source of food and raw materials, such as leather and wool. They developed a range of sociotechnical systems to support the exploitation of those animals. In contrast, Indigenous peoples in Mesoamerica generally used stone tools, including ground stone and chipped stone tools. Obsidian was a daily necessity in central Mexico, used for making blades, scrapers, projectile points, and symbolic items (Figure 6.1; Clark 2012; Levine and Carballo 2014; Pastrana 1998, 2007; Pastrana and Carballo 2017). Indigenous people in Mesoamerica also used tools made of clay, wood, cloth, and plant fibers

5 cm

Figure 6.1 Assortment of obsidian tools from Xaltocan, Mexico. Photo by John Millhauser. Used by permission.

(Brumfiel 1991; Hernández Álvarez 2019; Hernández Álvarez and Peniche May 2012). Different Indigenous groups in the Americas also used metals, although for the most part, these were used for personal adornment, display, and religious purposes but not for cutting (Hosler 1994, 2003; Maldonado 2012; Pillsbury et al. 2017). To obtain the materials and create the tools, each group had their own systems of apprenticeship, supply, transportation, and coordination of labor.

In this chapter, I focus on some of the technologies of Spanish colonizers that can be addressed with the data provided by the probate inventories. I begin by discussing tools and livestock. They are the material aspects that are mentioned most commonly in the probate inventories. Later, I will focus on slaves, their skills, and the few aspects of their experiences that can be gleaned from the probate inventories. The central question in this chapter echoes questions asked earlier: what tools did colonizers own? Did the Spanish adopt Indigenous technologies? Did they adopt Indigenous tools? Did they only adopt the products of Indigenous technologies? The probate inventories provide partial yet complex answers.

Tools of Metal, Wood, and Stone

Tools are the material aspects of technology that appear most prominently in the probate inventories. They are also the material remains of technology that archaeologists typically work with: pieces of obsidian, nails, fragments of clay and glass, and other artifacts. One could argue that previous chapters have dealt with tools already. Pottery, for example, could be considered an indispensable tool for storing food and water, cooking, and serving food (Braun 1983). In this chapter, I focus on tools that have not been discussed in previous chapters. I divide the discussion of tools into two. First, I discuss tools that can be associated with production, such as hammers, scissors, needles, and other things used to work. Later, I discuss weapons, including swords, lances, daggers, and many different items used to carry, store, or display weapons. Most items in this category can be typically associated with conflict and battles, but could sometimes be used for hunting. I have decided to discuss them along with tools because weapons figure prominently in discussions about technology and technological change. Comparisons of the weapons of Indigenous peoples and Spaniards, and of metal swords (or any kind of metal edge tool) and obsidian, abound in the literature (e.g., Bruhn de

Hoffmeyer 1986; Cervera Obregón 2014). A discussion of the sociotechnical systems of colonizers would be incomplete without addressing swords, daggers, and other weapons.

Tools

The inventories contain over 1,166 items that can be classified as tools, other than weapons (Appendix 6.1). It is difficult to come up with a specific number of tools because of the vague language used in the inventories. Some of the items are boxes of tools, but they do not specify how many tools are in a box, or even the size of the box. The tools include the kinds of artifacts that readily come to mind when thinking about technology in colonial Mexico: over sixty-six scissors, twenty-seven boxes with knives, and thirteen hammers. Only five knives are listed individually in the inventories, while the others are listed in the twenty-seven boxes of knives. The number of knives in each box is usually not specified, but when it is, the boxes contain either two or twelve knives, and only one box is listed as containing one knife. Some of the knives seem specialized, such as the *tranchetes*, a type of curved knife used by shoemakers (Figure 6.2). Scissors and knives are some of the well-known Spanish introductions to Mexico, and they were some of the first metal cutting tools adopted by Indigenous people. But tools that may not immediately come to mind as part of colonial society are much more numerous in these inventories: 400 *tablas de curar* (boards for curing leather), 203 *hormas* or shoe trees, over 30 thimbles, 25 cases full of tools that are not listed individually plus one case full of surgery tools, countless needles, 21 unspecified tools for ironworking, and others.

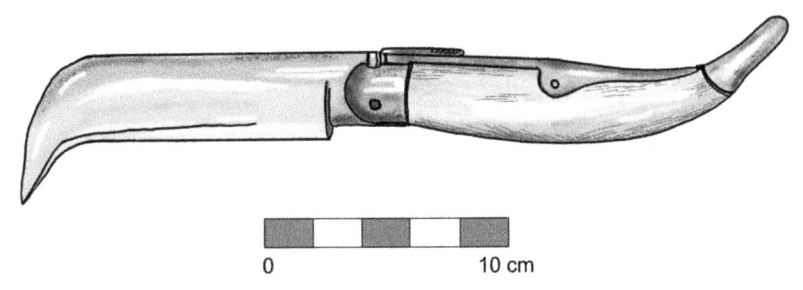

0   10 cm

Figure 6.2 Tranchete. Drawing by Sam Wilson. Used by permission.

It is clear that many of these tools are useful to make things that were traditionally Spanish. The shoe trees were useful for making the leather shoes that the Spanish wore, but not necessary for making the sandals worn by Indigenous people. The boards for curing leather were useful for colonizers, who raised livestock and used a lot of leather, but not as much for Indigenous people, who had their own techniques for preserving animal hides. The tools for ironworking were new in the Americas. One of the striking patterns is simply the wide variety of tools, some for general uses (e.g., knives, scissors, hammers), some for woodworking, others for working iron, for leather, for working with cloth (e.g., scissors, thimbles, needles, awls), for tool maintenance (e.g., files and sharpening stones), for weighing different materials (e.g., scales and weights), for working with horses, for surgery (e.g., syringes and cases of tools for surgery), and a variety of other specialized uses.

The tools with the highest frequencies in the inventories were not equally distributed among colonizers. Some of them were distributed according to occupational specialization. Alonso de Zapardiel, a shoemaker who died in 1562 in Mexico City, owned all of the leather curing boards and all of the shoe trees. He owned three Black slaves, one of them a woman, plus an additional slave who had run away. Clearly, he had plenty of work, as reflected by the number of tools and the slaves that he used for labor. Only four decedents owned hammers, but in this case, the occupations include two expected occupations and two surprises. It is no surprise that Bartolomé Hernández, a carpenter, and Diego Delgado, a blacksmith owned hammers. On the other hand, Antonio Martínez, a presbyter, and Francisco de Sigüenza a tailor, owned hammers even though hammers are not commonly associated with their occupations. The cutting tools that come to mind when thinking about colonial technology, including scissors and knives, were not quite evenly distributed either: 14 individuals owned at least one pair of scissors and nine people owned knives by the boxful. They may have been looking to sell or trade them.

Guillermo Boils Morales (2015) has argued that in New Spain, tools that had different parts and should be considered simple machines, such as pulleys, hoists, and even wheels, were initially made of wood. Only the parts that were subject to frequent friction or repetitive impact were made of iron (2015:76). He adds that metal tools were highly valued, in part because of their scarcity and in part because the wooden components of different tools—handles and other wooden parts—could be replaced easily, whereas the metal parts required a smith. He also claims that the metal tools that were considered of the highest quality were imported. Colonizers, he believes, preferred them over metal tools made in New Spain, but imported tools were scarce. He cites a letter that a colonizer sent to Spain, requesting over 1,000 machetes to sell them, because he would certainly find buyers and make good money. Colonizers also found reason to struggle over the sale of repaired tools. By 1568, an ordinance dictated that no smith could purchase an old tool and repair it to sell it, and that they may only repair tools for their current owner (2015:79). Implicit in the creation of the ordinance are conflicts between colonizers over the resale of poorly repaired tools.

Boils Morales (2015) also claims that in the early decades after the conquest, Indigenous people did not use the hammers, shovels, anvils, and other metal tools of the Spanish not because they wished to reject those tools, but because they were scarce. Based on historical chronicles, especially Sahagún, he claims that the use of European tools by Indigenous people was "quite extensive" by the 1570's (2015:75). Archaeological research provides partial support for his claims, although archaeologists have found compelling evidence of the continuation, and even enhancement, of the use of stone tools and other Indigenous technologies after the conquest. Indigenous people did not adopt Spanish tools everywhere, nor did they do so rapidly. The quick adoption of superior metal tools everywhere in the Americas, and the rapid abandonment of stone tools is a myth that has been perpetuated by modern scholarship but that does not stand up to the material evidence available (Rodríguez-Alegría 2008a, 2008b; Rozat 2004). King and Konwest (2019:91) argue that there is not "one easy story of technological change with the advent of colonialism, whether it is one of replacement, continuity, technological innovation, political resistance, or economic oppression." The patterns of adoption of European technologies is varied in terms of tempo and in terms of its relationship to the abandonment of Indigenous technologies in Mesoamerica and elsewhere (Alexander 2019; Forde 2017; Navas et al. 2014; Rodríguez-Alegría 2008a, 2016a).

Weapons and Defensive Items

The second major category of tools in the documents consists of weapons. This is a complex category, sharing permeable boundaries with other categories, such as clothing and other tools used for storage. It includes edge weapons (swords, daggers, and spears), firearms (arquebuses), projectile weapons (crossbows and bolts), defensive items (helmets, shields, and body armor), and many accessories used to carry, store, or operate the different weapons (sheaths, belts, ramrods, and storage cases; Table 6.1). These weapons could be used to fight, but also for display. The swords, lances, and armor could be particularly striking because of their shine, hardness and size, and because they were the deadly weapons of conquistadors. Indigenous people were prohibited by law to own Spanish weapons, but men in different towns asked for permission to wear swords for display, in clear demonstration of the symbolic power of these weapons (Bauer 2001:54; Haskett 1991:161–162; Rodríguez-Alegría 2010; Wood 2003:53). Some of the many accessories used to carry weapons, as well as the armor and helmet, could arguably belong among clothing. The fact that I have included them here in a discussion of weapons as tools should not obscure the multiple uses of these items, and the varied perception that people may have had of them.

The most common weapon, by far, in the inventories is the sword (Table 6.1). Steel swords came in two main sizes. Broadswords had blades between 115 and 125cm long, and handles between 35 and 40cm long (Figure 6.3). They were designed to be held with two hands (Cervera Obregón 2014:41). Shorter swords had blades that were approximately 70 to 80cm long, and they were designed to be wielded with a single hand (Cervera Obregón 2014; Pohl and Robinson 2005:48). Short swords were the most common in Spain at the time, and Pohl and Robinson (2005:47) indicate that "most swords were sharpened on both edges, but usually blunted at the tip in order to slash at an opponent without it becoming entangled in surcoats and chain mail." Less frequent in the inventories, by far, were daggers and lances. They are not described in any detail in the inventories, although one of the daggers was described as having a protective rim on its handle, a tip, and a silver chain. It may have been a particularly fancy dagger, but the others lack descriptions that would enable comparison. If daggers were the shortest of the edge weapons, lances were, by far, the longest. The wooden body of lances came in different lengths, "but most were probably about 12ft long" (366cm; Pohl and Robinson 2005:48) and conquistadors used them on horseback to break formations of Indigenous warriors. The head of the lances were made of steel. Colonizers used a variety of accessories to carry their edge weapons, mostly sword belts and sheaths made of leather and sometimes velvet. The belts used to carry swords were very long. The person would wrap the belt twice around the waist to distribute the weight of the sword between both hips (Pohl and Robinson 2005:48–49).

Table 6.1 Weapons in the inventories.

Edge and point weapons	espada	sword	35
	daga	dagger	7
	puñal	dagger	2
	lanza	spear	2
	lanzón	spear	1
	alfanje y espada	sable and sword	1
Firearms	arcabuz	arquebus	2
Projectile weapons	ballesta	crossbow	6
	ballesta con once tiros	crossbow	1
	ballesta con un carcaxe con ciertos tiros	crossbow	1
	ballesta con yuntas y bizutes	crossbow	1
	virotes	bolts	18
Accessories	frasquillo de arcabuz		1
	maleta de baqueta	case for ramrods	1
	medias baquetas	ramrod	7
	puño de espada	sword handle	1
	recámara de armas	gun barrel	1
	baqueta	ramrod	16
	bayna	sheath	1
	talabarte	sword belt	23
	talabarte con sus tiros	sword belt with strips of leather	1
	vaina de cuchillos	knife sheath	2
	vaina de espada	sword sheath	3
	vaina de terciopelo	velvet sheath	1
Defensive weapons and armor	rodela	buckler or shield	7
	adarga	oval leather shield	1
	casco	helmet	2
	coraza	armor (probably breast and back plates)	2
Miscellaneous	más armas	more weapons	1
	brocal	could be a knife handle or a piece of a firearm	1

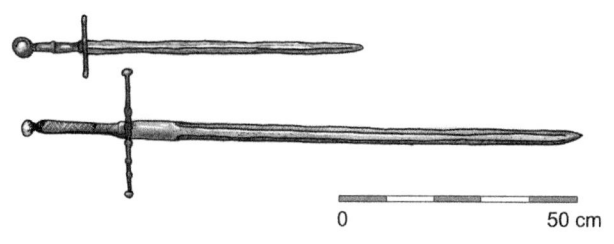

0   50 cm

Figure 6.3 Broadsword and sword. Drawing by Sam Wilson. Used by permission.

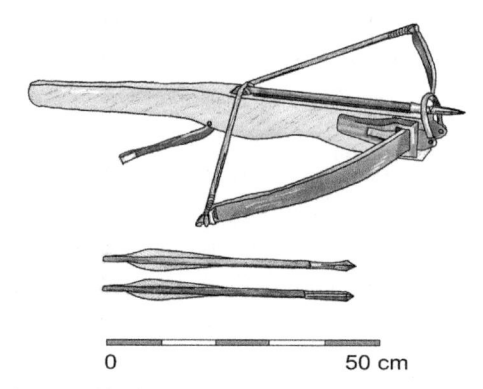

0   50 cm

Figure 6.4 Crossbow and bolts. Drawing by Sam Wilson. Used by permission.

Much less frequent in the inventories were projectile weapons, including only nine crossbows and eighteen bolts (Figure 6.4). There were no bows in the inventories. Crossbows existed since before the fourth century AD, and by the fourteenth century all European armies used them, including the Spanish. They often used bolts that were 30cm long and had steel tips, and they were powerful enough to pierce through armor at close range (Pohl and Robinson 2005:48). Although crossbows were precise and powerful, they took long to load and operate, even longer than firearms like the arquebus. Up to three people were needed to operate a crossbow, given the many mechanical parts and the strength needed to load it. For every 8 to 12 arrows that an Indigenous warrior could shoot with a bow, a Spaniard could shoot one bolt with a crossbow. For those reasons, and perhaps others, they were not as popular as other weapons, and they slowly fell into disuse in the colonial period (Bruhn de Hoffmeyer 1986:25–26; Cervera Obregón 2014:41).

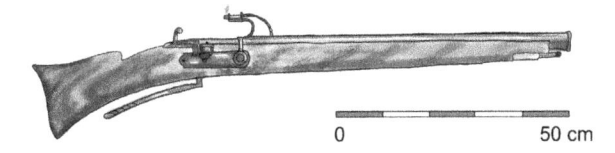

0   50 cm

Figure 6.5 Arquebus. Drawing by Sam Wilson. Used by permission.

Firearms were the least common of all the weapons in the inventories. Bruhn de Hoffmeyer (1986) argues that firearms were still in an experimental stage in the years after the conquest, which can partially explain their rarity. Only two arquebuses (Figure 6.5) appear in the inventories, and they lack any description or commentary about their quality, appearance, or attributes. Arquebuses are a kind of shotgun made of wood and metal. To fire its round bullets or pellets, a soldier needed to clean it, load it with gunpowder, load the projectile, light a wick, and wait for the explosion. Scholars have described arquebuses as slow, difficult to control, unstable, and unreliable, especially in humid climates. They have also commented that the noise made by arquebuses and the damage they could inflict were effective in the battles of the conquest (Bruhn de Hoffmeyer 1986). They could be especially useful if fired in groups to concentrate the fire upon groups of enemies (Cervera Obregón 2014:41–42). Evidently, they were not particularly popular among colonizers.

The decedents left very little in terms of armor and defensive weapons among their belongings. Historical sources about the conquest are contradictory when describing how much armor Spanish conquistadors wore during the conquest. Some sources, including a few Indigenous pictorials, sometimes depict conquistadors wearing armor, but sometimes they wear no body armor at all (Bruhn de Hoffmeyer 1986; Pohl and Robinson 2005:48). Armor, usually made of steel and iron, can get hot in hot climates, and even cause skin burns. Armor was also expensive, and many of the men who participated in the conquest could not afford it. Thus, it is possible that most conquistadors did not wear any armor. They may have even worn the quilted cotton armor vests that Indigenous people wore, which could provide protection against some edge weapons and projectiles (Bruhn de Hoffmeyer 1986:15; Cervera Obregón 2014:41; Urquiola Permisán 2004:207). These quilted cotton vests (Figure 6.6), known as *escaupiles* (from the Nahuatl *ichcaupilli*; Pohl and Robinson 2005:71), appear only once in the probate inventories, in the inventory that belonged

0   50 cm

Figure 6.6 Escaupil. Drawing by Sam Wilson. Used by permission.

to Lope Hernández, who died in 1545. Diego de Morillas, another colonizer, purchased it for 0.75 pesos of gold (Cont. 197 N.21 18), a very low
price. Other sources, especially those written by conquistadors, describe
the soldiers as wearing armor. It is possible that the conquistadors lacked
armor in the earliest battles, but obtained armor later, along with other
supplies that they got from Spain (Pohl and Robinson 2005:48). It is also
possible that the conquistadors who wrote their accounts thought that
their narrative would be more impressive if they described their armies as
wearing armor, and thus embellished their stories. Regardless, it is clear
that most colonizers that form part of this study did not even own armor.
Armor was probably rare during the conquest, and even harder to find
among early colonizers.

Shields were not particularly numerous either in the early colonial period, and they were often round or ovaloid (Figure 6.7). The round shields
were often made of steel or wood, and they were quite heavy, making them
difficult to use in combat (Cervera Obregón 2014:41). Ovaloid shields, also
described as heart-shaped in the literature because of their indentations
on the top and bottom of the shield, were known as *adargas*. They were of
Hispano-Moresque tradition, and they were made of ox hide. Adargas were
lighter than metal or wood shields, but effective in protection against many
projectiles and edge weapons (Bruhn de Hoffmeyer 1986; Cervera Obregón
2014:41; Pohl and Robinson 2005:41).

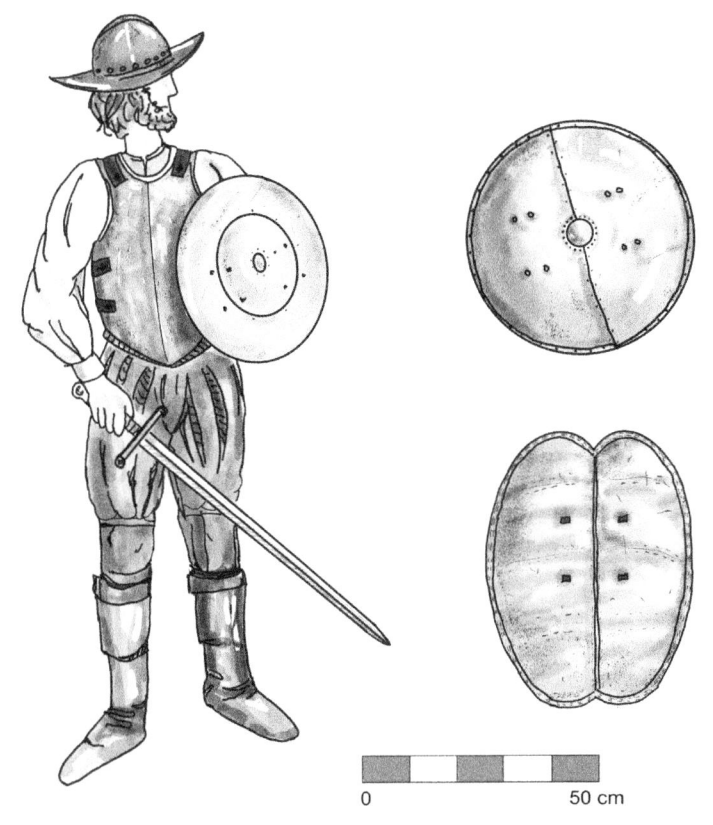

0   50 cm

Figure 6.7 Shields: *rodela* (top) and *adarga* (bottom). Drawing by Sam Wilson. Used by permission.

Although there were clearly more weapons than decedents, only twenty-three of the inventories listed any weapons at all (Table 6.2). An additional five inventories listed accessories related to weapons and defensive items, such as sheaths, belts, and armor, but no weapons. Neither of the women owned weapons or related accessories. Most commonly, colonizers owned an edge weapon or two, and rarely did they own firearms or projectile weapons. In fact, twenty-two out of the twenty-three inventories that contain weapons contained an edge weapon, and of those, twenty contain at least one sword. Only six contain at least one dagger. The colonizer who seems to have the most weapons by count owned sixteen bolts, but there was no crossbow in his probate inventory. If the data are an accurate reflection of the lived experience in colonial Mexico City, approximately every other colonizer owned

Table 6.2 Distribution of weapons between the inventories, by category of weapons.

	Edge weapons	Firearms	Projectile weapons	Total
Alonso de Castro	2	0	0	2
Alonso de Zapardiel	2	0	1	3
Alonso García	1	0	0	1
Andrés de Plasencia	3	0	0	3
Baltasar Godínez	0	0	18	18
Bartolomé González	2	0	0	2
Bartolomé Hernández	2	0	0	2
Cristóbal Rodríguez	1	1	0	2
Diego Delgado	2	0	1	3
Francisco de Sigüenza	4	0	0	4
Hernán Núñez Caballero	1	0	0	1
Juan de Oliva	1	1	1	3
Juan Gómez	7	0	0	7
Juan Gutiérrez de Grado	2	0	0	2
Juan Negrete	2	0	1	3
Lope Hernández	4	0	3	7
Miguel Rodríguez	1	0	2	3
Pedro de Algoibar	1	0	0	1
Pedro de Madrid	1	0	0	1
Pedro Vázquez	1	0	0	1
Rodrigo Ruano	2	0	0	2
Salvador Franco	4	0	0	4
Salvador Márquez	2	0	0	2
Total	48	2	27	77

an edge weapon, and most frequently, it was a sword rather than a dagger. No wonder some Indigenous men wanted to be seen walking around with the weapons that colonizers displayed so frequently!

Indigenous Tools

Historical sources show that colonizers sometimes admired the quality of Indigenous tools, but that does not mean that they necessarily adopted them.

Adopting a tool or any other aspect of a sociotechnical system is a matter of tradeoffs. People weigh a range of social, economic, performance, and other characteristics that are difficult to disentangle as they choose different tools (Lemonnier 1993). The tools that are found in most archaeological excavations in sites that were occupied by Indigenous people, besides pottery, include obsidian blades and projectile points (Figure 6.1), as well as occasional spindle whorls, bone needles, and *manos* and *metates* (Figure 6.8), the typical tools used for grinding maize. Of these, the tools that have interested modern scholars the most are obsidian tools, probably due to their ubiquity in archaeological sites.

Spanish chroniclers sometimes wrote about the sharp edges of obsidian blades. Díaz del Castillo (1966:113) went as far as stating that the obsidian weapons of Indigenous warriors were sharper than Spanish razors. Francisco Hernández (see Ximenez 1615: Book 4, Part 2, Chapter 13) also commented, perhaps with some exaggeration, that obsidian was sharper than anything that could be imagined, and with one blow it could split a man in two, but it broke and dulled easily. He wrote that obsidian could be ground and used to clean off cloudiness in the eyes (probably cataracts), an intriguing procedure that sounds a bit unpleasant. Other chroniclers also observed the brittleness and tendency to dull of obsidian blades (Clark 1989:312). Thus, colonizers saw an important advantage in obsidian tools: sharpness. But they also saw an important disadvantage: brittleness. Spanish colonizers sometimes requested obsidian tools for shaving (Clark 1989; Sahagún 1963:233; Saunders 2001), although Clark (1989) has argued that the request for such blades for shaving seems overstated, and that they probably used obsidian blades for other purposes as well. Such requests are rare in the ethnohistoric literature, and their rarity may be due to one of two factors that point in

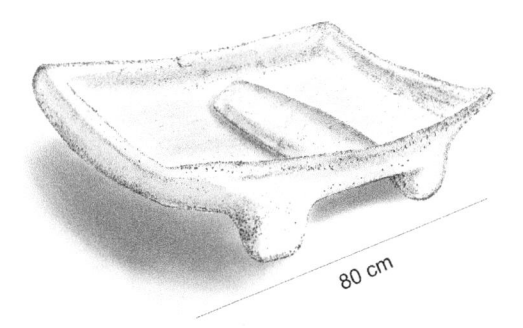

Figure 6.8 Mano and metate. Drawing by Sam Wilson. Used by permission.

different directions. First, the scarcity of stone tools in the ethnohistoric literature may be a simple reflection of a lack of use of obsidian among colonizers. Colonizers may have admired the sharpness of obsidian, but they kept using the metal cutting tools that they were accustomed to. Second, the sources may not be a clear reflection of the material worlds of colonizers. Many ethnohistorical sources contain information on material goods, but they were certainly not written to convey all information about the material world. They were not written to aid in determining how often colonizers used obsidian tools. Perhaps Spanish colonizers used more obsidian and other Indigenous stone tools than the sources indicate.

Regardless of the admiration of obsidian tools that chroniclers sometimes expressed, tools that one may typically associate with Indigenous people from central Mexico are absent from the probate inventories. They were common in Indigenous houses, yet none of them are found in the inventories of colonizers. Manos and metates were associated with Indigenous women (Biskowski 2000; Brumfiel 1991). Given their strong gender and ethnic associations, it would have been surprising to find them in the inventories of colonizers, male or female. Grinding maize, like any other technique, required learning and practice, and most colonizers did not go through the learning process that Indigenous girls went through to learn to use a mano and metate effectively. Manos and metates certainly appear in other documents, such as the Codex Tepetlaoztoc, among the things that were given to the Spanish as tribute (Valle 1994), but they are clearly associated with women. This particular codex contains one example of tribute rendered in food, including ten women to grind it with their manos and metates for the Spanish (Valle 1994: Fol. 11B; Figure 6.9). It is clear that the use of the tools was associated with Indigenous women, although the ones who would benefit from it would be Spanish colonizers.

In fact, it is not only maize grinding tools that are absent from the documents. Out of 1,166 tools and 149 weapons and related items listed, there are only 38 stone tools. Many of them are not described in any detail. Some of them were sharpening stones. They were probably a flat, smooth stone, just rough enough so that one could slide the stone along the edge of a metal tool (a sword, for example) and sharpen it without ruining the blade. In contrast, there are more than three times as many scissors ($n = 66$) in the inventories. There are no obsidian tools in the inventories, unless some of the stones that are not described in any detail were obsidian, which is speculative. The information does not indicate that Spaniards used stone tools for

Figure 6.9 Woman with mano and metate as drawn in the Codex Tepetlaoztoc, Folio 12r. The British Museum, used by permission.

cutting or grinding, at least not with their own hands. Indigenous stone tools may be absent from the inventories simply because colonizers did not own or use them, or because they were not considered important or valuable enough to be included in a probate inventory, in spite of the very many other small and practically worthless items included.

The inventories mention only fourteen tools that were specifically made in Mexico. Of those, twelve were stones that belonged to Rodrigo Ruano. They are only described as "de la tierra" (Cont. 5575, N.37). They could be obsidian, but that is only speculation. Ruano was a merchant, so he was probably not using the stones but rather looking to sell them. The other locally made tools include a stick used in dyeing cloth or perhaps leather (*palo para teñir*) known as *palo de Campeche*, or logwood. It is an item that could be considered a tool or perhaps an ingredient or product, or something other than a tool, but it was used for creating dyes. Another Mexican item was a leather bag, but it is not described further.

Archaeological data could help further clarify questions regarding the use of obsidian tools among colonizers. To my knowledge, obsidian tools are not found frequently in the houses of Spanish colonizers in Mexico City. Archaeologists have reported finding obsidian blades in Hernán Cortes' house, among colonial (glazed pottery), majolica, Aztec III pottery, and Red Ware, but the publication I have seen thus far does not state with clarity whether the obsidian was found in a clearly colonial context (Barrera Rivera and García Guerrero 2017). Future studies should incorporate microartifact analysis, which could either yield microliths (microscopic pieces of obsidian) that would identify the presence and use of obsidian among colonizers, or document their absence with clarity. Based on the infrequent mention of obsidian blades in the ethnohistoric evidence, and on their absence in the probate inventories, I believe that colonizers did not adopt obsidian blades with much frequency, but future studies could help understand this possibility further.

Recent archaeological research in Guerrero, Mexico, brings up an important possibility: Indigenous people probably provided the copper and tin that the Spanish used to make some of their weapons, especially firearms and related items that they used in the conquest and in the years that followed. García Zaldúa and Hosler (2020) used information from historical sources to argue that Spanish colonizers lacked knowledge of mining and smelting copper ores. They used archaeological evidence and materials analysis to show that Indigenous people in El Manchón, Guerrero, had metallurgical traditions that preceded the Spanish arrival by centuries. Conquistadors learned of the Indigenous expertise in these technologies and even wrote in letters to Spain about the good quality of native copper and tin for making weapons. Soon, conquistadors made their own contribution to Indigenous smelting. They introduced the use of bellows and forges, and Indigenous people adopted them to increase their production. Thus, conquistadors relied on Indigenous specialists who used their own technologies and metallurgical expertise to provide copper and tin ores to make weapons, coins, and household objects (García Zaldúa and Hosler 2020). The study by García Zaldúa and Hosler is an important reminder that the people who made Spanish-traditions tools could depend on products made by Indigenous producers with their own technologies of manufacture. Maintaining Spanish technologies could at times depend on Indigenous people and their tools, knowledge, labor, and access to materials. Alejandro

Pastrana (1998:195–198) made precisely that argument in his study of obsidian mining in Postclassic and colonial Mexico. He believes that Spanish colonizers probably encouraged obsidian mining and tool use among Indigenous people as part of the sociotechnical system of silver mining. Indians made obsidian tools, then used those tools to cut and process animal hides and make the ropes, bags, and scaffolds they needed for mining silver. The use of indigenous obsidian in mining is an example of how the use of stone as a material for cutting tools could support mining for a metal that was used for its shine and beauty.

Livestock

Besides tools, the sociotechnical systems of colonizers included living things. So important were horses in the conquest that many conquistadors claimed to owe their success first to God, and then to horses (Bennett and Hoffmann 1991:105). After the conquest, many colonizers owned livestock, including horses, sheep, goats, and cattle. Colonizers used them in productive activities, especially to obtain wool, leather, meat, and dairy, and as draft animals. They used horses for transportation and battle, and for display. The use of horses for display cannot be understated. People in Mexico even include horses as part of one of the emblematic characters in Mexican culture, the charro (Matasanz 1965:544). In fact, Indigenous people were often impressed by colonizers on horseback and requested permission to ride horses in addition to wearing Spanish attire and carrying swords (Bauer 2001:54; Haskett 1991:161–162; King and Konwest 2019:90; Rodríguez-Alegría 2010; Wood 2003:53). Colonial figurines often show people on horseback, a clear indication of how impressive a horseback rider could be. Whether as sources of food or raw materials, as draft animals, or for display, animals were variously related to wealth and power, two aspects of sociotechnical systems.

The total number of animals owned by the decedents is difficult to pin down. The language used to account for animals is vague. For example, one may find "some mares" or "horses" listed, without a specific number attached to them. Also, livestock can be found listed alongside batches of tools, with vague language about numbers or types of tools and animals. While the numbers of items are difficult to verify with precision, there are still useful patterns in the inventories.

One of the clearest patterns is that if there was an animal that colonizers tended to own, it was the horse. There are approximately 183 horses[1] in the inventories. Horses were typically described or sold with different things, including with "a bit in its mouth," with its saddle, its reins, or with its gear, among other descriptions. A more reliable statistic than the total count of horses is the number of decedents who owned horses: out of twenty colonizers who owned any animals, nineteen of them owned at least one horse. This could mean that about half the colonizers owned a horse (nineteen out of thirty-nine in this sample). Lockhart (1999:86) discusses that among the typical comments included in letters from colonizers to their families in Spain, one may find people claiming that they owned horses. Lockhart even states that according to these letters "every Spaniard has a horse to ride." The letters may have only been halfway exaggerated if we notice the high proportion of colonizers that apparently owned horses according to these inventories. Further, it seems that if a colonizer owned only one or two animals, they were usually horses: Alonso de Zapardiel owned one or two horses, Juan de Oliva owned two mules, Martin Carrasco owned two horses and a mule, Maese Gregorio de Heredia owned a horse and a mule, and Baltasar Godinez owned my favorite, a *jaca*, meaning a short horse or a pony. Mateo García was the only exception in this pattern, owning two cows but no horses.

The decedents also owned quite a few equestrian items. A total of 265 items listed in the inventories fall into the category of equestrian items, including spurs, bridles, saddles, horseshoes, whips, bells, and others. An interesting aspect of the equestrian items is that nine decedents did not own horses or any livestock, but owned equestrian items. For example, Alonso de Castro (Cont. 197, N.21) did not list any horses among his belongings, but he listed six spurs, four bits, and two stirrups. Only five inventories contain livestock but do not list any equestrian items. If we add up the people who owned horses and the people who owned equestrian items, the total number of decedents who owned either or both is twenty-eight. In other words, most people owned horses or were ready to ride. Horses emerge as the animal that most people had or were ready to interact with in colonial Mexico City. Matasanz (1965:541) argued, perhaps not too hyperbolically, that by 1550 Mexico City was oversaturated with horses.

---

[1] The vocabulary describing horses also varied, and they are mentioned as horses, mules, colts, and fillies. The language can be confusing, at times listing mares, for example, but also explaining that some of them were male and some female, or including other contradictions that are hard to explain. Therefore, it is better to discuss them as horses in general.

Many people made a living producing equestrian items in Mexico City. By 1549 there was a guild of horse saddle and accessory makers in Mexico City (Recio Mir 2012:14). Other documentary sources point to the presence of carriages and carts as early as the years of the conquest. By 1574, Felipe II wrote in a royal decree that there were plenty of horse-drawn carriages in New Spain, and in the seventeenth century, different authors commented on the proliferation of horse-drawn carriages and ornate saddles and litters in Mexico City (Recio Mir 2012). Still, there are no such carriages in the probate inventories consulted.[2] Perhaps the carriages were impressive, but not many people owned them.

Horses and related items were a major technological change in central Mexico, but their history of adoption is complex. Indigenous people in Mesoamerica did not have draft animals in the pre-Hispanic era, and the largest domestic mammal they had was the xoloitzcuintle, the beautiful native dog. The largest grazing animal they knew was the deer. People carried their own goods on their "backs with the aid of a tumpline and carrying frame or basket" (Berdan 2014:113), and porters, known as *tlamemeh*, carried goods over long distances. After the conquest, Indigenous people adopted the use of horses as draft animals and for long-distance portage, but it would take decades before they could do so in significant numbers. The Codex Tepetlaoztoc mentions that *tlamemeh* were part of the encomienda given to a colonizer in 1527–1528. It depicts them walking with their trumplines (Valle 1994: Fol. 12B). The image is probably an accurate depiction of how these particular *tlamemeh* carried out their tribute work, not just because that is how the image depicts them, but because the number of tlamemeh is quite high: 300 to carry chickens, 60 to carry *pinole* (probably toasted, ground maize), and 1,200 to carry the rest of the tribute goods (Valle 1994, vol. 2: 62). I doubt there were that many horses available to Indigenous porters, especially so soon after the conquest. Gibson (1964:222–223) writes that colonizers relied on Indigenous porters and repeatedly opposed legislation meant to prohibit or regulate the use of human porters, even into the seventeenth century. Thus, horses did not represent an improvement in terms of transportation for Indigenous people, at least not for a long time. In

---

[2] There are plenty of *bigas* in the inventories, a term that today refers to horse-drawn carts, reminiscent of the carts used in gladiatorial combat in Rome. But the bigas in the inventories are most likely an accessory of clothing, although I have been unable to find a source that defines them as such. They are all in the inventory of a tailor, and there is nothing to indicate that they were used for transportation.

fact, it seems like colonizers quickly adopted an Indigenous technology—human porters—but made it difficult for Indigenous people to adopt their horses.

For a long time, the Spanish tried to limit the horses available to Indigenous people. By 1597, colonial authorities decreed that Indigenous folks could keep as many as six horses for transportation and carriage (Gibson 1964:358). King and Konwest (2019:90) have found requests from Indigenous people from three towns in Oaxaca to have horses to carry goods also in 1597. Owning horses or other European animals used for transportation became one of several key characteristics of Indigenous merchants in the colonial period, according to Lockhart (1992:194). Still, adopting horses does not mean that Indigenous people stopped carrying goods on foot with tumplines over long distances. Historical sources indicate that *tlamemeh* and other porters continued walking with merchandise on their backs at least into the twentieth century, although I assume that porters became rarer through time. The loads they carried were impressive, ranging between 23 to 91 kg per person (Hirth 2016:240–241). Thus, eventually, both colonizers and locals used horses for many purposes in the colonial period, in a land where previously everything had been transported by foot or canoe.

But horses were hardly the only animals that colonizers owned. The animals that appear the most in the inventories are caprines, including sheep and goats. Sheep were an important part of the Iberian economy in the sixteenth century. Although the Spanish had merino sheep, this particular variety of sheep was prized for its soft wool and Spanish law forbade exporting merino sheep, given their importance in the economy. Thus, the first sheep in the New World were most likely churros, which have "thick, shaggy underfur which yields a long-staple wool that mats easily" (Bennett and Hoffmann 1991:99). The churros thrived, in part for their ability to obtain nutrition and water from dew and leaves during the dry season in central Mexico. But colonizers brought merino sheep soon enough during the sixteenth century and the sheep reproduced quickly into the hundreds of thousands (Urquiola Permisán 2004:222–224), making fine wool available for local production of cloth.

A total of 372 items in the inventories mention sheep, and 350 of them are in the inventory belonging to Alonso García. Another small herd of appears in Lope Hernández's inventory, including one goat, two billy goats, one ram, twenty-two sheep, and six cows. Thus, even though there were a lot of caprines in the inventories, they were mostly owned by one person,

Alonso García. To make matters more complicated, as these inventories often do, there are over 3,372 caprines in the inventories, although only the 372 mentioned already were owned by decedents. The other 3,000 appear in the inventory that belonged to Juan Díaz Caballero (Cont. 197, N.21, 4: 3 verso), in a complicated passage that reveals that he was taking care of 3,000 sheep and 14 horses that belonged to someone named Francisco Figueroa. Figueroa had returned to Castile and left Caballero in charge of his sheep and horses, and in charge of his house and hacienda in Mexico. When Caballero died, he left his neighbor, Alonso Galante, to take care of all the animals, the house, and the hacienda, but made it clear that they still belonged to Figueroa. I do not count these animals as part of the belongings of Caballero, although they can be a reminder of the numerous sheep and goats that roamed over central Mexico after the conquest. There were a lot of sheep, although in the hands of few people. While there were more sheep than horses, more people interacted with horses on a daily basis than with sheep. As early as 1526, the Cabildo of Mexico City started to grant land for raising sheep in the outskirts of the city (Matasanz 1965:538).

Finally, a third category of animals that appear in the inventories is cattle, including cows, bulls, and oxen. They are less frequent than horses, and certainly much less frequent than caprines: a total of sixty-six items in the inventories mention cattle. Ownership of cattle is also very limited. Only three decedents owned all of the cattle. One of them, Alonso García, owned 60 head of cattle. Bartolomé de Prado owned four oxen, and Mateo García owned the other two cows. But the probate inventories should not give the impression that there were very little cattle in New Spain. On the contrary, in the region of Nueva Vizcaya (north of Mexico City, and roughly in the modern states of Durango and Chihuahua), there were hundreds of thousands of cattle in the late sixteenth century. The price of beef dropped about 75 percent in Mexico City between 1532 and 1538 as a result of such an abundant supply. Mexico became the greatest exporter of cattle in the New World (Bennett and Hoffmann 1991:95–96).

The absence of pigs in the inventories deserves commentary. Pigs are considered by some scholars to be even more important than horses in the conquest of the Americas because of their adaptability, fertility, and their ability to devour native plants and clear land for colonizers. They were a staple of the diet of colonizers (Bennett and Hoffmann 1991:101–102). There were very many pigs in Mexico City since the 1520s. They found plenty of food in the maize tribute provided by Indigenous people, and they multiplied quickly. Given their abundance in Mexico City, by 1531 their price was very low and people lost much interest in raising them (Matasanz 1965:537). Yet, they are entirely absent from the probate inventories.

The first conquistadors brought horses with them, and after the conquest, colonizers brought livestock from the Caribbean islands consistently. Matesanz (1965:536) argues that they brought livestock in such quantities that cattle ranchers in the Caribbean tried to limit trade in 1523 to prevent colonizers in Mexico from depleting all of their livestock. The growth of populations of grazing animals in central Mexico in the early colonial period has been called "extraordinary," and explained by the lack of competition from any native grazing animals, and the abundant vegetation, including in agricultural fields, grasslands, and forests (Melville 1997:6). In addition to bringing livestock to the highlands of central Mexico, colonizers also took plenty of cattle to the lowlands along the Gulf of Mexico and raised it by the hundreds of thousands by the mid-1500s (Sluyter 1996:162). But the growth of grazing animal populations is not an unqualified story of success. Instead, it was the result of inaccurate assessments of the resources available in central Mexico, and a failure to predict the destruction that the animals would wreak upon the fragile resources (Melville 1997). The destruction caused by grazing animals became a major point of contention between Indigenous farmers and Spanish ranchers. Grazing animals often pastured in Indigenous agricultural fields, not by mistake, but because people took them there to graze (Matasanz 1965:538–539). As early as the 1550s, Viceroy Velasco ordered that cattle had to be removed from the central regions of New Spain, to protect the agricultural fields where Indigenous people produced most of the produce that supplied the cities with food (Melville 1997:24).

Ownership of livestock is one of the questions where the probate inventories make an interesting contribution. A total of twenty people are listed as owning livestock of any kind, which is slightly more than the number of people who owned slaves. As discussed previously, when people owned one animal, they tended to own a horse. Even though about half of the decedents owned livestock, just one of them owned the great majority of the animals in the inventories: Alonso García, discussed previously as the owner of many sheep and goats. A total of 444 items in the inventories relates to his ownership of livestock, although as I have warned earlier, this should not be understood as meaning that he owned 444 animals; it is just an approximation of the animals he owned. García may have also owned the greatest variety of animals, including some 350 sheep, 60 head of cattle, and 34 mares or horses. Rodrigo Ruano was another high-frequency owner, with forty-six horses. Livestock was highly desired,[3] especially horses for transportation, but some types of livestock were in the hands of only a few people.

Slaves

The last aspect of the sociotechnical system I discuss here consists of humans that were listed alongside many physical objects in the probate inventories: slaves. Slavery had been a part of pre-Columbian and Iberian societies long before the conquest, although it was quite different in the two places. Owning slaves, or at least having Indigenous or Black servants, was something that many colonizers expected out of life in the colonies. Conquistadors expected to have slaves even during their military expeditions in the Caribbean and elsewhere in the Americas (Restall 2003:50–51). Owning slaves in the colonies was a matter of cultural continuity for Spaniards, although I would not claim that cultural continuity justifies it in any moral way. It was a way to manage labor, and, ironically, it symbolized honor and civilization among Spaniards (Bennett 2003:31). The probate inventories provide glimpses of the lived experience of enslaved people, their occupations, their abuse, and the ways that they were exchanged along batches of tools used in production.

Slavery in Mexica society was different from slavery in any of the Spanish colonies. Berdan (2014:189–191) argues that among the Mexica, slavery was a transitory status that was not inherited. People could become slaves either by being captured in a battlefield, by severe impoverishment due to debt, or by committing some crimes that were punishable by slavery, such as theft.

---

[3] In spite of the desire for horses and of the value of cattle, the inventories reveal at least one occasion in which authorities had a difficult time selling them, although perhaps they were stealing some of the livestock. In 1545, authorities tried to auction Alonso García's cattle, but had a really difficult time doing so. Authorities they tried to sell the cattle at 1 silver real per head. Allegedly, nobody bought the cattle, and thus they sold all of the cattle to a man called Alonso de Moral for an undisclosed price. My guess is that it was difficult to own and take care of cattle, so nobody would buy it, but the undisclosed price of the sale makes me think that authorities also took advantage of the situation and took some of the money for themselves. The difficulties in selling Alonso García's livestock continued, and authorities tried to sell fifteen mares at five pesos six tomines each. Nobody would buy them, so they sold all of the mares to Pedro Muñoz for eighty-six pesos and two tomines, which was the total price that they were selling for to begin with (Cont. 197 N.21 5).

"Slaves were not considered property; rather, they retained rights to marriage and possessions, sometimes acquiring slaves themselves. And they were not neglected ritually" (Berdan 2014:190). She adds that some enslaved people got out of their slave status by working enough to fulfill their obligations, whereas some enslaved people who were particularly rebellious could be fit with collars and sold in marketplaces. Indigenous slavery changed drastically after the Spanish conquest. Since 1542, royal law prohibited Indigenous people from owning slaves, and by the late 1540s, very few Indigenous masters owned any slaves (Gibson 1964:154). Lockhart (1992:111) has argued that by the mid-sixteenth century, neither Spaniards nor Indigenous people owned many Indigenous slaves at all.

Colonizers wanted to profit from forced labor and turned to African slavery. The first Black people, most of them enslaved but some of them conquistadors, had arrived with Cortés during the conquest. Some came from the Caribbean and others directly from Europe and Africa (Aguirre Beltrán 1981:19–20; Restall 2003:52–53; Velázquez Gutiérrez 2018). The estimates of the numbers of enslaved Black folks that were brought to New Spain vary in terms of numbers of people, geographic extension, and chronology (Table 6.3). Some estimates refer to New Spain, Mexico, or Mexico City more narrowly. The chronology varies from the entire colonial period to specific decades or years. In spite of such variation, the estimates are consistently astounding. In spite of the numbers of slaves brought over, Cope

Table 6.3 Estimates of the number of Black people in Mexico and New Spain.

Region	Black population	Period	Source
New Spain	>15,000	Mid-sixteenth century	García-Martínez 2010:201
New Spain	200,000–250,000 African slaves	1576 to 1650	Velázquez and Iturralde Nieto 2012:63
Mexico	200,000 slaves	Entire period of slave trade (1521–1810)	Curtin 1969:46
Mexico	36,500 Black people	1521 to 1594	Cope 1994:13
Mexico City	8,000 enslaved Black folks; 12,000 free Black folks	1521 to 1594	Cope 1994:13
Mexico City	10,595 Africans, free and enslaved	1570	Aguirre Beltrán 1981

(1994:13) argues that "the number of slaves available rarely matched the colonials' demand." Given the number of enslaved people trafficked, Bennett (2003) has labeled New Spain as a "slave society" to highlight the importance of slavery in urban areas in the Spanish colonies.

The number of enslaved people and vague ideas about their ethnicity (or whether the Spanish labeled them as "negros" or "indios") is difficult to calculate with precision based on the information provided in the probate inventories. The inventories sometimes mention "slaves" or "some slaves" but without specifying the number of people in question. Seldom do they mention the names of the enslaved. The way they are treated in the documents represents objectification in its most extreme form: another item in the list of things that belong to a colonizer. Zabala (2010:152) argues that colonizers considered slaves "more a thing than a person," although in certain circumstances, they would be considered persons if it was convenient to their masters. I considered the possibility that the term *esclavos* in the probate inventories referred to some inanimate object also, and not necessarily to living, breathing, humans, but the information always led me to the conclusion that they were indeed enslaved people. A related problem is that the same slave or slaves may appear more than once in an inventory, but given that they are often not mentioned by name or numbered, it was sometimes difficult to tell whether they were mentioned multiple times in the same document or whether there were two different enslaved people with the same name. The lack of precision in the documents may be due to the lack of humanity assigned to some slaves by the people compiling the inventories, and perhaps to how sloppy recordation facilitated theft and fraud involving the belongings of the decedents. In his demographic study of Black slaves in colonial Mexico, Aguirre Beltrán (1981:205) commented that colonizers never counted the number of Black slaves carefully.

In spite of these challenges, I believe there were as few as twenty-nine slaves, and as many as thirty-two (Table 6.4).[4] If there were twenty-nine slaves for thirty-nine decedents, it would be approximately three slaves for every four free colonizers. It is clear that there were a lot of enslaved people in Mexico City in the sixteenth century, almost as many enslaved people as

---

[4] In a previous analysis of the same data, I argued there may have been as few as thirty and as many as forty slaves (Rodríguez-Alegría 2016a:47). The discrepancy between the two calculations highlights the difficulties presented by the language of the probate inventories.

Table 6.4 Slaves in the inventories. The "indeterminate" column refers to slaves whose race or gender was unspecified in the documents. Numbers followed by a question mark refer to slaves that might be counted twice in the documents.

Decedent	Date	Black male	Black female	Indigenous male	Indigenous female	Indeterminate	Total
Salvador Márquez	1541			4, +1 escaped	2, +1?		7 or 8
Rodrigo Ruano	1542	2					2
Alonso Serrano	1545			1			1
Hernando Ladrón	1545	1					1
Lope Hernández	1545	1			4	1 female	6
Martín Carrasco	1545	1					1
Diego Delgado	1551	1					1
Andrés de Plasencia	1560		1				1
Alonso de Zapardiel	1562	3	1				4
Juan Gutiérrez de Grado	1578				1		1
Antonio Martínez	1586		2 escaped, +1?				2 or 3
Hernán Núñez Caballero	1586	1, +1?	1				2 or 3
Total		10 or 11	5 or 6	6	7 or 8	1	29 to 32

there were colonizers,[5] or perhaps even more enslaved people than colonizers if the probate inventories underestimate the number of slaves.

Breaking down the population of enslaved people in these inventories in terms of the racial categories that the Spanish used (often just "negro" or "indio") and gender is informative. I was able to identify between thirteen or fourteen Indigenous slaves. Only one of the Indigenous slaves appears in

---

[5] The number of African slaves in the inventories is perhaps different than what one would expect given the demographic patterns reported by Aguirre Beltrán (1981:205–207). He wrote that the European population in Mexico City in 1570 was 9,495, whereas the Black population was 10,595. The discrepancy could be due to different factors. First, it is possible that the number of African slaves in the probate inventories is underrepresented. Perhaps colonizers did not report all of their slaves, especially those who died without a will. Second, it is possible that the discrepancy is simply due to the fact that my estimates are strictly about slaves, whereas Aguirre Beltrán's estimates are about Black populations, including both slaves and free Black folks. Third, my estimate is for a period of approximately five decades, whereas Aguirre Beltrán provides an estimate for a specific year, 1570. Finally, the discrepancy may be due to a combination of all of these factors. Regardless, all estimates indicate that the slave population of Mexico City was high.

a document from 1578. Four appear in a document of 1545, and the rest of them in documents from 1541, one year before trade in Indigenous slaves was forbidden. I also identified between fifteen and seventeen Black slaves in the inventories. Their numbers increased slightly as the number of Indigenous slaves decreased: only two Black slaves were sold in 1542, whereas four were sold in 1562, and between four and six in 1586. The Indigenous population decreased significantly during the *cocoliztli* (fever and bleeding of unknown pathogenesis) epidemic of 1545–1548. During that decade, colonizers began exploiting the silver mines in Mexico in earnest, and thus increased their demand for Black slaves (Aguirre Beltrán 1981:205; Gerhard 1993:22, 25). This calculation would give us an enslaved population with slightly more Black slaves than Indigenous slaves in Mexico City, with the important caveat that as the Indigenous slave population decreased, the population of Black slaves increased.

Among the Black slaves, mostly labeled as *negro* in the inventories, I could identify ten or eleven males and five or six females. Among the Indigenous slaves, I identified six males and seven or eight females. In addition, there was one female slave whose race or ethnicity could not be identified with the information provided. The number of female slaves in this group, especially Indigenous females, is a reminder that it was not just Indigenous men who provided labor for colonizers. The work of Indigenous men as forced labor in *encomiendas* (grants of Indigenous labor to Spaniards) has been a subject of interest for scholars for some time, especially because it was such an important aspect of labor in colonial Mexico. But female labor was important too, and women probably provided domestic work in the houses of colonizers, cooking, cleaning, and washing for them, perhaps raising children, as well as acting, willingly or unwillingly, as sexual partners, as judged by the many children colonizers bore with their slaves.

Scholars have used both historical records and human remains to determine that many enslaved people in early colonial Mexico City did housework, specialized work in craft production, and sometimes did hard labor. In many regions of New Spain, their work included mining, construction, and plantation work, and many were exploited sexually (Wesp 2020; Zabala 2010:154). Several of the slaves in these documents are simply listed as slaves, and no indication of specialization is offered; however, a few of the probate inventories contain clear clues of specialization among slaves if not outright mentions of their occupations. Three of the slaves were listed as craft specialists. One was an Indigenous tailor named Luis Gómez who was listed among the seven slaves owned by Salvador Márquez in 1541. Another one was a "tailor's official" named Juan, also listed among the slaves owned by Salvador Márquez. In Chapter 5, I discuss that a good number of the clothes owned by the decedents were made by Indigenous people, and here we have one example in which even if the master tailor was a Spaniard, his team was composed of Indigenous people. Thus, clothes that are listed in the inventories as *de la tierra*, but not as being made by Indigenous people specifically, might have been made by Indigenous people after all, even if under the supervision of a Spaniard.

Another example of an enslaved man who was a craft specialist was a Black shoemaker named Juan, who was sometimes described as a "shoemaker's official" (*oficial de zapatero*) and other times as a "tanner" (*curador*), most likely in reference to his work tanning leather for shoes. His master, Alonso de Zapardiel, was a shoemaker who listed three Black slaves in 1562, including a woman and a 15-year-old male among his belongings. Juan is one more example of a slave who was sold in auction with all of his tools, probably for tanning leather and perhaps also for making and repairing shoes (Cont. 203, N4, R8). An additional example makes it clear that the slave was a craft specialist even without listing him as such. In 1551, Diego Delgado, a smith, listed among his belongings a Black slave "with all the tools necessary for the forge." Clearly, the slave worked as a smith or a smith's assistant, even though he is not listed as such. The occupations of the rest of the slaves are difficult to tell, and they probably did all kinds of work, ranging from domestic work to work for craft specialists, and perhaps other work.

The occupation of the owners may not have determined the work that the owners gave to their slaves, but they offer some clues as to the work of enslaved people and they help understand who owned slaves in colonial Mexico City. A total of twelve decedents are listed as owning slaves, so that about one in four colonizers in Mexico City owned at least one slave. Their occupations varied. Five of them do not have an occupation listed in their probate inventory, and I could not figure it out from their belongings with much certainty. Of the people whose occupations were listed, three were craft specialists, two were probably merchants, and two were religious figures. The craft specialists include a shoemaker, a tailor, and a smith. The religious figures include a cleric and a presbyter, and I will add that there were only four religious figures in the entire sample of decedents, making it two out of four who owned slaves. Thus, the enslaved people in these inventories probably did work for specialists, also carried merchandise, did house work, and performed whatever other work the religious figures had them do.

Besides race, gender, and occupation, another category is important in understanding slavery in these inventories: the runaway slaves. Four of the slaves are listed as having run away from their owners, who asked on their deathbed that their slaves be brought back and made to provide more services to their families or other inheritors. Among them, Juan, a Black shoemaker official, had run away (Cont. 203, N4, R8), as had Jorge, an Indigenous slave that belonged to a tailor (Cont. 5575 N.13). Finally, two unnamed Black female slaves that belonged to Antonio Martínez, a presbyter, had run away. All three cases are interesting because the runaway slaves in question included a craft specialist and another enslaved person that worked for a tailor, plus two enslaved females who worked for a religious figure. Clearly, the conditions that made enslaved people run away are not just related to abuse in the context of hard labor. Being enslaved was bad enough, and abuse could be found whether the slave was a craft specialist, and even for enslaved people that worked for religious figures. Abuse of slaves was common, and it comes through in the probate inventories even though they were not designed to document abuse and even though the documents were compiled by owners who would probably claim that they were good owners to their slaves. At least three of the slaves that appear in the documents, two Indigenous females and one Indigenous male, were described as branded with the king's mark (*herrados con el hierro del rey*). I suspect others were branded as well, but the documents do not say so.

As expected, wealth seems to be correlated with ownership of slaves. Slaves were expensive. Toward the end of the sixteenth century, a slave could cost approximately 400 pesos (Wesp 2020:96). Prices for the slaves in the inventories consulted here varied from 35 pesos of an unspecified type of gold for a female Indigenous slave in 1541, to as much as 300.5 pesos of oro de minas for a Black male slave who worked tanning leather for a shoemaker and was sold with all of his tools (Table 6.5). There is much variation in prices over time, although the data are insufficient to discern clear temporal patterns or patterns related to how gender or ethnicity affected prices. Sometimes male slaves owned by one person sold for more than the female slaves, and vice versa.

Owning slaves could represent increased productivity for the master, and increased wealth. Several authors have remarked that owning slaves was a status symbol in colonial Mexico, and perhaps it was associated with wealth

Table 6.5 Prices of slaves sold in auction.

Decedent	Year	Enslaved person	Price	Type of gold	Price in maravedís
Salvador Márquez	1541	Indian slave, female, named Juana, branded with the king's iron	35	na	
Salvador Márquez	1541	Indian slave, female, branded with the king's iron	55	na	
Salvador Márquez	1541	Indian slave, male, called Luis Gómez, tailor	57.5	de minas	25,875
Salvador Márquez	1541	Indian slave, male, called Juan, looks ill, with tailoring tools	58	común	17,400
Salvador Márquez	1541	Indian slave, male, called Francisco, branded with the king's iron	145	de minas	65,250
Alonso Serrano	1545	Indian slave, male	42	de minas	18,900
Lope Hernández	1545	Black slave, male, called Hernando	101	na	
Diego Delgado	1551	Black slave, male, with several blacksmith tools	225	na	
Andrés de Plasencia	1560	Black slave, female, called Inés	156	de minas	70,200
Alonso de Zapardiel	1562	Black slave named Gaspar, 15 years old, male	182	de minas	81,900
Alonso de Zapardiel	1562	Black slave named Juan, male, tanner, with all of his tools	300.5	de minas	135,225
Antonio Martínez	1586	Black slave, female	235	na	
Hernán Núñez Caballero	1586	Black slave, male	315	común	94,500
Hernán Núñez Caballero	1586	Black slave, male, called Antón	392	na	
Hernán Núñez Caballero	1586	Black slave, female, named María	402	común	120,600

(Bennett 2003; Wesp 2020), confirming, to an extent, Lemonnier's broader idea about technology: "the marking of social differences may be one of the basic functions of technical choices" (1993:19). I was unable to calculate the total worth of five of the twelve decedents who owned slaves. Still, the seven decedents whose total worth I calculated and who also owned slaves include some of the wealthiest people in the sample (Table 6.6). The three wealthiest decedents owned slaves, and then the fifth, seventh, eighth, and ninth wealthiest also. Control of labor emerges, not surprisingly, as one of the factors associated with wealth in colonial Mexico.

Besides working for their wealthy masters, enslaved women sometimes had children with them. Those children were considered illegitimate. The inventories contain some examples of decedents who recognized their illegitimate children and left an inheritance for them. My first reaction was one of surprise at how well colonizers took care of the children they had with their slaves, although later I realized that there may have been many children that were not recognized in the probate inventories and thus we have no record of them. Only five of the decedents recognize illegitimate children in their wills, and the low number may be due to several factors. Two important factors are that not all of the decedents knew or recognized any or all of their illegitimate children, and that not all of the inventories contain a will. Some are only inventories and auction lists written after the person died.

Table 6.6 Wealth and slave ownership.

Decedent	Number of slaves owned	Rank by wealth
Hernán Núñez Caballero	2 or 3	1
Antonio Martínez	2 or 3	2
Alonso Serrano	1	3
Martín Carrasco	1	5
Diego Delgado	1	7
Juan Gutiérrez de Grado	1	8
Andrés de Plasencia	1	9
Alonso de Zapardiel	4	na
Hernando Ladrón	1	na
Lope Hernández	6	na
Rodrigo Ruano	2	na
Salvador Márquez	7 or 8	na

The inventories that do not include a will provided no opportunity for the decedent to recognize his children. For these reasons, the evidence cannot reveal how often colonizers recognized their illegitimate children. Instead, the evidence simply reveals how often the illegitimate children received an inheritance from their father. In the sample studied, five out of thirty-nine inventories leave any sort of inheritance for illegitimate children, and in all cases the children's mother was enslaved and the inheritors were almost always boys. In fact, all of the illegitimate children who were recognized by name as inheritors were boys. The only exception is Lope Hernández, who named male inheritors and made room for other illegitimate children that may show up after his death, whether boys or girls.

Receiving an inheritance as an illegitimate child was not necessarily good for everyone involved, especially for the mother. In fact, having a child with a master could even result in more work for the slaves, including for the child's mother, after the master died. Lope Hernández (Cont. 197 N.21 (18)) provides an example of the treatment of enslaved mothers and illegitimate children in his will from 1545. When Hernández wrote up his will, he recognized having two children with two of his slaves, and the treatment that the mothers and the children received was different. One of the slaves was an Indigenous woman named Beatriz, and Hernández set her free when he died. The son he had with Beatriz received 100 pesos in oro de minas, half of the mares he had (there are twelve in his inventory), and his slaves. The other slave who had a child with Hernández was an Indigenous woman named Ana. He left 90 pesos (probably in oro de minas as well) for his child, but instead of freeing Ana, he left her as the child's slave and "for him to do whatever he wants with her for ten years." After the ten-year period, Ana could go free. Finally, he left the other half of his mares, probably six, to his child. As is clearly seen in this example, one of the boys got 100 pesos plus almost all of the slaves, but his mother went free, whereas the other boy got his own mother as a slave. There is nothing in the inventory that explains the different treatment of the slaves and the children in this will. But the will does not stop there. Hernández also declared that if more children between him and Indigenous women turn up after his death, they should divide the mares equally between the children, and they should keep the slaves instead of selling them. The mothers of his children would receive five pesos each for clothing and cacao, or approximately one twentieth of the amount in cash that the children received, and no horses or slaves. In comparison, he left thirty pesos for his niece's wedding in Castile. Alonso Serrano, another decedent, had three children with an Indigenous slave and declared that upon his death she should be set free so she could serve the children until they grew up (Cont. 197 N.21 (15)). The other inventories do not have as many details about what would happen to the slaves or to the children after the master's death.

Of course, many of the enslaved people were sold upon the master's death, and that is why they appear in the auction records. As discussed above, sometimes they were sold with their tools, and sometimes they were sold with their own pillows and blankets. At least one of the decedents, Juan Gutiérrez de Grado, left a female Chichimec slave for a specific person, Francisco Gómez, and asked that Gómez pay 100 pesos for her even though he clarified that she was worth more. On one occasion, a slave was inventoried but he died before being sold in auction (Cont. 197 N.21 (10)).

The probate inventories provide limited information about slavery in early colonial Mexico City. Perhaps the biggest surprise is that the accounting of slaves could at times be a bit sloppy in these documents, confounding the expectation that slaves would be accounted for with precision and in great detail due to their value as labor. Even the number of slaves and their gender and ethnicity or race can be difficult to figure out from the data in the documents. Still, the documents provide evidence that there were between twenty-nine and thirty-two slaves in the documents. The enslaved population was pretty high, and it was approximately half Indigenous and half Black, whether from Africa, Iberia, or the Caribbean. Twelve of the colonizers had slaves, and they had different occupations, including craft production and religious occupations. Some of the slaves were occupational specialists and some were domestic servants. But work in the house or in craft production should not be taken to imply that treatment of enslaved people was good. The documents include examples of enslaved people that had run away, including two slaves that belonged to a cleric. At least five, and probably more, of the decedents had children with their slaves, and they left some inheritance to their illegitimate children and on some occasions made the mother the children's slave. Other times, when the master died, the slaves were simply sold in auction, often with batches of tools.

Conclusion

Very little in the probate inventories indicates that Spanish colonizers adopted Indigenous tools for their own use. The data do not indicate that colonizers used obsidian blades for cutting or any other lithic tools, aside from sharpening stones. Sismondo (2010) has argued that one of the general explanations for why some technologies stay with us for a long time is that we already have those technologies, and they are difficult to get rid of simply because they are what we have. They fulfill certain roles, both social and material. In other words, technologies are difficult to eradicate because people involve them in sociotechnical systems. Part of those systems has to do with practice and skill: the bodily engagement with tools. Dobres (2000) has argued that when studying technology one must keep in mind how human bodies engage with tools and with one another through practice. Tools do not determine how technology works. People determine how technology works in the ways that they use tools, get used to the tools, get used to the movements and different practices with the tools, and go through repeated motions and practices. Sociotechnical systems also include more than the person using the tools. People set up technologies that support other technologies, so that, for example, people who made obsidian tools provided some of the technology needed to cut and process animal hides, which in turn allowed some people to make bags, rope, and scaffolds used in mining. In turn, miners obtained the silver that the Spanish desired (Pastrana 1998). People involved in sociotechnical systems are involved in its reproduction. The many guilds that created systems of apprenticeship and quality control for many different crafts are but one formal example of how people do not just use technologies, but also participate in their continuity. Thus, the fact that colonizers kept their tools may not mean that their tools and technologies were superior or better than Indigenous ones. Instead, it may simply mean that the people were used to their own tools and kept them out of habit and practice. They may have thought their tools were better simply because they had them. For example, tailors, seamstresses, and anyone else who knew how to use their scissors, needles, and thimbles continued to use them, given that they spent much time learning to use them and adapting their bodily practices to them. And perhaps they valued durability more than sharpness when deciding whether to get metal or obsidian cutting tools. They had already gone through a learning process, sometimes involving membership in guilds, and they continued using the tools and technologies they knew to use.

Other scholars have found similar patterns elsewhere in Mesoamerica, especially when studying the earliest colonizers, as is the case in the present study. Card and Fowler (2019) found little technological transfer between Indigenous people and the first one or two generations of Spanish colonizers in Ciudad Vieja, El Salvador. They believe that individuals brought their own "items and skills with them in settling San Salvador" (2019:205) and that people exchanged products, rather than techniques of making those products. Their observation is an important reminder that changes in technological traditions can occur over generations, as people learn to use different tools and adapt their habits and practices to the materials and technological traditions available.

Another important aspect of sociotechnical systems was symbolism. Some tools, especially weapons and armor, were used for display as well as for physical effect. Some of the livestock, especially horses, could be used for transportation and to be seen around town on top of an impressive horse or in a carriage. The desire of Indigenous people to emulate these practices, to ride horses and carry swords, speaks to the symbolic power of these things (Bauer 2001:54; Haskett 1991:161–162; Rodríguez-Alegría 2010; Wood 2003:53). Slaves performed a lot of labor, and they also became status symbols in New Spain (Bennett 2003). No study of technology in colonial Mexico would be complete without considering the relationship of these technologies with power, both in the sense of controlling labor and in the sense of displaying status. Colonizers often felt encouraged to keep their technologies not just because they were useful from a utilitarian point of view, but also because they were symbolically powerful as well.

It is still possible that Spanish colonizers adopted Indigenous tools, especially stone tools, more than the written documents indicate. As discussed previously, written documents paint a limited picture of the material world. In the case of probate inventories, the main motivation was not to describe the material belongings of colonizers thoroughly, but rather to describe enough to explain the total prices of the belongings that were sold. Other motivations that shaped the content and level of detail were theft and fraud, and the knowledge of the scribes and officials compiling the inventories. Therefore, it is possible that there were stone tools in the houses and among the belongings of colonizers, but they were left out of the inventories because they may not have been seen as worthy from a monetary standpoint. Detailed archaeological work, especially focusing on the presence of microliths in well-controlled colonial contexts may yield clues regarding the use of stone tools in the houses of colonizers. Of course, an additional challenge would be to associate such debitage with colonizers, but by finding (or not) such artifacts, archaeologists may develop techniques and questions that may open up new lines of inquiry on this matter.

Aside from tools, two elements of colonial sociotechnical systems that seem ubiquitous were horses and slaves. Many colonizers owned them, enough for me to think that as long as colonizers could afford them, they would have them. Approximately half of the decedents owned horses, and even more than half owned tools associated with horseback riding, including spurs, bridles, and others. Over one-quarter of colonizers owned slaves, often multiple slaves, male and female, Indigenous and Black. Ownership of slaves seems to have been expensive, but expected and highly desired; therefore, we see an association between wealth and ownership of slaves.

Even if colonizers were generally not abandoning their traditional tools and adopting Indigenous ones, the evidence shows that colonizers often borrowed Indigenous technologies or incorporated them into their own. If we think beyond the idea of a Spaniard using an Indigenous tool, and think of sociotechnical systems instead, then there is evidence that the Spanish adopted Indigenous technologies, especially by conscripting labor. In Chapter 1, I discussed how the city and the houses where the Spanish lived were built by Indigenous people using the materials and engineering techniques that they had been using for centuries. In this chapter, the evidence shows the presence of many enslaved Indigenous and Black people in Spanish houses. Many of them were sold with the tools that they used, and they must have worked in ways that they were familiar with. An Indigenous woman who cooked in a Spanish house, for example, must have use her *mano* and *metate* to grind maize, vegetables, and spices. In that way, even if we say that the Spanish did not use Indigenous tools, they adopted both the person and the person's tools, but placed them in a different social arrangement: slavery or forced labor. They enslaved both the individual and his or her technological ability. Conscription of labor could even outlast the life of a colonizer, and we have seen examples in which decedents left their slaves to other colonizers or even to serve their own children. An important part of this process is how power was of prime importance in technological change, as people were enslaved. Technological change and continuity were not a matter of progress, but a matter of changing relations of power in New Spain.

7

How to Link Wealth and Consumption, or Not

The preceding chapters have examined various aspects of the material worlds of colonial Mexico City, often focusing on whether Spanish colonizers in general were using imported or European-tradition goods, or items made by Indigenous producers. Another theme that previous chapters examine is the wealth of colonizers, as reflected in their probate inventories. In this chapter, I bring both themes together, to evaluate the relationship between wealth and the patterns of consumption of colonizers. The relationship between ethnicity, wealth, and patterns of consumption has been of interest to many scholars in the Spanish colonies because of its relevance to issues of power (e.g., Charlton and Founier 2011; Deagan 2001; Fournier 1998; Fournier García 1997; Jamieson 2000a, 2000b; Oland 2014, 2017; Rodríguez-Alegría 2003, 2005b, 2010; Tarble 2008; Van Buren 1999; Voss 2012). I ask two questions that may initially seem simple and easy to answer: were European imports more expensive than locally produced goods, or more expensive than items made by Indigenous people? Did wealthier colonizers consistently use more expensive European imports than poorer colonizers? These two questions converge to bring up a question of greater importance in the study of colonial Latin America: did colonizers in the sixteenth century share ideas about consumption and standards of taste that were then mediated by their wealth? More specifically, was ownership of European goods among colonizers limited mostly by their wealth?

I begin this chapter by examining the arguments that different scholars have presented about consumption, ethnicity, and wealth in the Spanish colonies, and assessing their empirical basis and theoretical implications. Then, I examine the questions above with the data from the probate inventories by studying two main patterns in the data. The first pattern is the relationship between the origin of different objects and their price. In other words, were imported items more expensive than locally produced goods? And were items made by Spaniards more expensive than Indigenous products?

How to Make a New Spain. Enrique Rodríguez-Alegría, Oxford University Press. © Enrique Rodríguez-Alegría 2023.
DOI: 10.1093/oso/9780197682296.003.0008

The second pattern I examine is the net value of each inventory and whether each decedent owned more imported or local goods. The results that emerge from my analysis carry important implications about the material world, consumption, and power in the Spanish colonies.

Studies of Wealth and Consumption in the Spanish Colonies

Scholars who study the Spanish empire have proposed two general opposite ideas about consumption patterns and their link to class, ethnicity, and wealth. The first idea has been proposed by scholars who emphasize that Spanish colonizers used Spanish, European, and to some extent also Asian goods to seek distinction from Indigenous people and to display their wealth and power in the colonies. They used European clothing, furniture, and tableware, most of which was quite different from the items made by Indigenous people. The scholars who have proposed these ideas believe that colonizers shared ideas about distinction and taste, and that they also pursued a unitary strategy for how to relate to Indigenous people, or at least they shared a set of material practices and consumption patterns. They rejected Indigenous material goods as long as they could afford expensive imports. Only poor colonizers would regularly use Indigenous tableware, for example, and if they could have afforded more expensive imports, they would have used them (Benítez 1993; Charlton and Fournier 2011; Deagan 1983, 2001; Kuwayama 1997; Lister and Lister 1982, 1987; McEwan 1991, 1992, 1995).

Kathleen Deagan, in her pioneering efforts to study gender archaeologically, added demographic considerations to her studies of consumption among colonizers in the Caribbean (1983, 1995). She argued that besides a low socioeconomic status, intermarriage between Spanish men and Indigenous women was another factor that could bring Indigenous goods into Spanish houses. According to Deagan, colonizers, who were mostly men, used Spanish material culture in their public presentation as a way of creating and maintaining a unified identity among colonizers. The material things that the Spanish used in public included technologies of house construction and also Spanish clothing and display goods, including pottery. This ideology placed great value upon Spanish things, including language, material culture, and social behaviors. Along with Catholicism, valuing Spanish material culture highly was a way of creating unity among colonizers, who came from a country that had only recently been unified and that still had strong regional identities and cultures, some of which survive until today (Deagan 2001). But given that very few colonizers were female (6.3 percent of all passengers registered as sailing to the Indies; Boyd-Bowman 1968:xvi), many colonizer men married or cohabited with Indigenous women. Those women brought Indigenous material culture into the houses of colonizers, but mostly into private parts of the house, including the kitchen and other areas not associated with display. Thus, in Deagan's model, different people acted as bearers of culture traits and by living together, they created criollo cultures.[1]

Scholars who emphasize that colonizers had a singular strategy of distinction and a monolithic idea of taste in material culture share some general assumptions that are often implicit in their work. They share the idea that society is made up of socioeconomic strata, and in the case of the Spanish empire, strata were strongly tied to ethnicity. By socioeconomic strata I simply refer to people who are in different hierarchically arranged socioeconomic positions. I do not wish to imply that the scholars I have cited have agreed upon a definition of strata, or even used the term at all. People who belonged to different strata shared ideas about consumption and they had similar knowledge of what was desirable, as well as similar goals and strategies for obtaining those goals. Another idea that these scholars share is that wealth was a main cause of variation in consumption patterns. This position has been most clearly expressed by Charlton and Fournier (2011) who argue that variation in pottery use can be explained by simple economic variables (see also Burgos Villanueva 1995).

The position taken by these scholars raises points of broad importance beyond colonial Mexico. Perhaps people's choices are more limited than one would typically think, and they are severely constrained by ethnicity, and mediated by class or wealth. If people share standards of consumption widely, one's ability to choose may be more illusory than many of us like to think, which may explain how social groups can seem to act cohesively and to share material practices and worlds. Most scholars do not explain how different groups and social classes come to agree on standards of consumption and taste. The assumption seems to be born out of theories that defined

---

[1] It is beyond the scope of this chapter to review the various critiques of Deagan's model. On one hand, it has been hailed as the most influential model to come out of historical archaeology (Voss 2008d). It has been cited numerous times within historical archaeology and beyond. On the other hand, archaeologists have called into question its applicability, both in the contexts examined by Deagan and elsewhere, based both on empirical and theoretical grounds (e.g., Jamieson 2000a, 2000b; Rodríguez-Alegría 2005a, 2016a; Voss 2008d).

culture as bundles of static traits, and that viewed people as carriers of those traits (e.g., Foster 1960; discussed in Rodríguez-Alegría 2005a).

These ideas are important beyond colonialism because they may mean that people who belong in different social classes or strata share ideas and knowledge about consumption. In fact, these ideas are in some ways similar to ideas proposed by Bourdieu (1984), in his study of taste and distinction. Bourdieu argued that taste, or a preference for certain material goods or specific aesthetics, is closely related to a person's social class or socioeconomic status. He considers that taste, consumption, negative judgments of taste, and the rejection of some types of material goods are strong barriers between social classes, especially as people with greater educational capital extend negative judgments of taste against others. Wealth may place strong constraints on patterns of consumption and limit the choices that people have, but people use judgments of taste to present their limited choices as a matter of deliberate choice. When someone manages to move up the social hierarchy in terms of economic status, Bourdieu argues, their attempts at display through consumption act as a barrier to social mobility, by revealing the true social origins of the person.

A second idea about the relationship between socioeconomic status and consumption in the Spanish colonies describes a different scenario. Not all scholars working in the Spanish colonies have found a clear link between ethnicity, economic status, and patterns of consumption among colonizers. Their studies have found that there was no monolithic pattern of consumption. It is true that many Spaniards tried to reproduce a way of life that was familiar to them, and an integral part of their way of life was, of course, their material worlds. But there are also observable variations in archaeological frequencies of Indigenous and imported ceramics in Spanish households that cannot be explained by economics alone. Some of the variations in consumption can be explained by the political and social strategies, and they show that not everyone shared ideas of taste or practices of separatism from Indigenous people (Jamieson 2000a, 2000b; Rodríguez-Alegría 2003, 2005b, 2016a; Van Buren 1999; Voss 2008d, 2012). Also, practices and patterns of consumption varied according to people's situation, location, and relations to the people around them. A single person could even have different consumption practices depending on whether they were in a major city or a rural house (Jamieson 2000a). I have argued in the past that some colonizers gave and received gifts from powerful Indians, ate with Indigenous people, used Indigenous pottery sometimes as a sign of hospitality, and adopted other kinds of Indigenous material culture. They did so in part to forge alliances, socialize, make friends, and negotiate their social position in the new colonial world (Rodríguez-Alegría 2005a, 2016a). Colonizers did not share the desire to reject Indigenous material goods. They shaped their consumption patterns according to their own social worlds and intentions.

There are a few broadly relevant assumptions implicit in these findings. Perhaps most important is the idea that even if people fit into different social classes or strata, their position does not entirely determine their taste and their social goals and strategies. Even when there is some level of inter-group unity, solidarity, or common practices, there is also variation. In fact, a main critique of models that emphasize social classes and their role in determining patterns of consumption is the danger of turning people into peons who consume according to their social position without much variation. Tarble (2008:54) argues that "the analysis of material objects offers more than just a distinction between social groups; it can reveal the meaningful contexts of their acquisition and use, not just the structural relationship between their users" (see also Howson 1990). Thus, Tarble's critique leads to a second assumption of these studies, which is that the objects that we find were acquired and used in different ways, and not just to display status. This assumption is hard to deny, but it tends to be forgotten in studies that emphasize identity as a main determinant of consumption patterns.

The studies that have emphasized variation in patterns of consumption echo some of the broad arguments made by Sydney Mintz (1985) in his classic study of sugar. Mintz argued that consumption was related to relationships of power, and not just as a reflection of such relationships. Consumption has a strong potential to be transformative. It could transform social relationships and patterns of production and trade. As people consume some goods, they can also change patterns of consumption of other goods. In *Sweetness and Power*, Mintz focused consistently on social classes rather than individuals, but his work assumed that there was some meaningful historical variation in the patterns of consumption as people within social classes slowly adopted different goods (sugar, coffee, and tea, among others) and altered patterns of production and trade.

Both sides of this debate bring up important issues. Most immediately important to this debate is a general characterization of consumption and material practices in the Spanish colonies. Were Spanish colonizers in the sixteenth century unified by clear and monolithic practices of consumption that emphasized Spanish material culture as a symbol of their unity and power? Or did different individuals pursue their own strategies, sometimes in recognition of Indigenous power and often not in rejection of Indigenous material worlds? This discussion could help understand how much socioeconomic factors can determine the material choices of individuals in a context in which status, power, and classes were in flux, as was the case in sixteenth-century Mexico City.

Probate Data

The data contained in the probate inventories can help contribute to this debate in four main ways. First, many items in the inventories contain information about the prices of items, their origin, and other comments about their quality. Thus, the inventories can help understand whether imported items were more expensive than locally made or Indigenous products, and what other factors affected the price of different items. Second, the probate inventories have allowed me to calculate the net worth of several colonizers. By examining the probate inventories, it will be possible to tell whether wealthier colonizers used more European products than local goods, and whether poorer colonizers used more local products. Third, the probate inventories contain information on items not typically found by archaeologists, such as clothing, cloth, and furniture. Thus, the probate inventories can bring the debate beyond ceramics, the category that has dominated the debate due to its ubiquity in archaeological sites. And finally, the probate inventories draw attention to a context that is normally not taken into consideration, but that was indeed important in exchange in the sixteenth-century: the public auction of the belongings of decedents.

Origin and Price

The data from the probate inventories contain the prices of over 900 items, making them ideal to check whether there was a consistent relationship between the place of manufacture and the prices of items. Were imported items more expensive than locally made items? Were Indigenous products cheaper than European ones? What factors, besides origin, affected the price of items? To study the patterns of prices, I focus on a few items that appear frequently in the probate inventories, making comparisons easier and patterns clearer.

Comparing the prices of items in the inventories may not match exactly how people compared prices in sixteenth-century Mexico. When people compare prices today or in the past, they may consider a range of factors. One factor could be the average price of the item, or rather, what a person might think is the average price of an item based on their experience. Another factor could be the person's knowledge of other available items and whether they are cheaper or more expensive; in other words, one-to-one comparisons that are independent of the average price. Other factors can enter into account as someone considers prices, including convenience, availability, need, a personal connection to the vendor, and others. Some people may try to maximize what they get for their money, while others may try to just satisfy their needs. Thus, comparing prices is only one dimension of how people made decisions in the past, and reporting only average prices is not enough. Any discussion of prices should consider central tendencies as well as dispersion of prices.

The prices of items sold in auction, as recorded in the inventories, may present challenges for interpretation, but they are nevertheless a reliable source of information. In the sixteenth century, Tomás de Mercado was inspired to write a pioneering study of the Andalusian economy. He observed that prices were different in Andalusia and in the different colonies that he visited, including New Spain (Mercado 1985). He commented, for example, that a slave who was priced by the King at 100 ducats in Hispaniola, could be sold for 120 ducats in New Spain, and for 150 in Peru (1985:59). Among the many topics he wrote about, in his combination of moral philosophy, theology, and economics, he tried to explain the differences in prices. He argued that the king imposed prices, which he referred to as the legal way of fixing prices. Then people negotiated and changed prices in auctions and sales, which he called the natural or accidental way of fixing prices (1985:52). He added that people changed prices depending on the quality of products, supply and demand, and the context in which goods were traded (in auctions, in markets, in private sales, and others). He also commented that the prices of items in auctions were often cheap, but not unreasonably so, and that often things sold for a fair price (1985:77, 91–95). His comments gave me confidence that the data from the probate inventories were a useful reflection of the price of items in sixteenth-century New Spain.

In the probate inventories, there are 118 shirts with clear information on prices, making them the best item in the entire data set for a comparison between the prices of locally made and imported items. To my surprise, the

Table 7.1 Price of shirts.
Prices are in maravedís. All cases are included.

Origin	Mean	n	Std. Deviation
Locally made	776.17	12	1235.62
na	417.04	70	387.35
Imported	599.04	36	236.44
Total	509.09	118	513.44

average price of locally made shirts is higher than that of imported shirts, but the average price of imported shirts is comfortably within a standard deviation of the average of imported shirts (Table 7.1). This means that even though the average price of locally made shirts is higher than that of imported shirts in this data set, the prices are not statistically too different. My initial reaction after seeing these results was to declare them unreliable, given Mercado's observation that imported items were more expensive in New Spain than in Andalusia. Other scholars agree that things were more expensive in Mexico City in comparison with Seville (e.g., Vilar 1976:11; Vilches 2010). Upon further reflection, the probate inventories are one source of data, and although they are imperfect, they are reliable. The data deserve further scrutiny rather than a quick dismissal.

A look at the entire data set (Appendix 7.1) could help make sense of these unexpected results. It is clear that some of the cheapest shirts were made locally in Mexico; however, there are two other aspects of the data worth noticing. First, the cheapest shirts were also described as old, torn, or both. Thus, the price was affected by the origin of the shirts and by their condition. Second, the two most expensive shirts in the data set, by far, were also made locally. The most expensive ones are among a group of four outliers, and the other two outliers include a shirt without any information of place of manufacture, and another one made in Europe. The two most expensive shirts belonged to a clergyman, and there is no additional information about their quality, besides that they were white. I speculate that they were special shirts worn in religious ceremonies, and therefore more expensive, but the idea is based only on the very expensive price of these shirts and the fact that they belonged to a cleric. I have no way of knowing whether I am imposing my own bias when speculating this way. The next four most expensive shirts were all described as *labradas*, or fancy.

Table 7.2 Price of shirts (outliers removed).
Prices are in maravedís.

Origin	Mean	n	Std. Deviation
Locally made	251.40	10	173.72
na	386.13	69	290.46
Imported	572.23	35	175.80
Total	431.45	114	269.69

Clearly, the fact that they were fancy factored in their price, whether they were imported or made locally.

These four outliers must be having a strong effect on the average prices. The two most expensive shirts, for example, are over 1,000 maravedís more expensive than the third most expensive shirt. To try to neutralize the effect of outliers, I recalculated the average price of shirts after removing the four outliers (Table 7.2). The revised average and standard deviations show that if we exclude the outliers, imported shirts were more expensive than locally made shirts. There is no overlap between the average prices for locally made and imported shirts within one standard deviation. The outliers had increased the average price of locally made shirts.

Hose (labeled as *medias*) are among the few other items with enough cases to make a similar comparison, although I would avoid making statistical comparisons because the prices of hose may not be reliable in this particular case. The cheapest hose in the data set include several items that do not have a place of manufacture specified, but the cheapest that have a specific origin are imported from Castile. The most expensive item lacks an origin, but the next several items among the most expensive are all locally made. Thus, the prices are the opposite of what one would expect: imports are cheaper than locally made items. It is worth noting that all of the hose with an origin in this data set belonged to the same individual, Juan de Campomanes (Cont. 197 N.21 (13)), and were thus sold in auction on the same day. The price of the locally made hose was apparently driven up by the fact that they were made of wool, making them warmer in the cold climate of central Mexico. There are no comments on the quality of these hose, making it impossible to assess whether any other aspects of quality affected their price.

Although it would seem from this data set that locally made hose were more expensive, or that hose made of wool were more expensive, there are important comments in the document that make me doubt the reliability of the data on prices. The document states that Juan de Campomanes, the decedent, died dragged by a river. The people who found his belongings in a few suitcases tied to a horse commented that the belongings were dirty and ridden by pests. The belongings were put up for auction quickly before they decayed further. There were allegedly three different occasions in which the authorities tried to sell the goods, but nobody would buy them, so the scribe himself ended up buying the clothes and promising to pay for them in two installments. Did the scribe take advantage of the situation and price the items to his own benefit? Or did he pay prices that would be considered reasonable? More information would be required to understand these prices. This document is a reminder that the data used in this chapter should be complimented and evaluated when data from other contexts are available, including market prices, other auctions, and any other documents that may have recorded prices.[2]

The data on prices can support different ideas simultaneously. If one emphasizes central tendencies, the data support the idea that on average, imported shirts were more expensive than locally made shirts. However, if one emphasizes dispersion of the data, locally made shirts could sometimes be cheaper and sometimes be more expensive than imports. The prices of individual shirts were not distributed along a continuum that went perfectly from cheap and locally made on one end to expensive and imported on the other end. The quality of the items made a difference in terms of prices. Mercado knew that, and he wrote that the quality and condition of clothes

---

[2] The point is not that the data from Juan de Campomanes' inventory should be left out of the analysis altogether, but rather, that the data should only be used when there are data from other sources that can help evaluate the data in Campomanes' inventory. For example, the analysis of the prices of shirts that appears earlier in this chapter includes two locally made shirts and seventeen imported shirts from Campomanes' inventory. However, including those shirts in the statistics did not force me to change my interpretation at all. If I eliminated the shirts in Campomanes' inventory from the calculations the results were comparable to the results achieved if I had included them. That simply means that the price Campomanes paid for the shirts was close to average, and it did not affect the inference drawn from the statistical analysis.

If one only takes into consideration the hose labeled as *calzas* in the data set, there is only one example of locally made calzas to discern any trends. The single locally made item is cheaper than any of the imported ones, but more data would be needed to study the pattern further. Juan de Campomanes' inventory presents a similar problem when studying the prices of pillows. The imported pillows sold in his auction are cheaper than locally made pillows sold in other auctions. Different factors may account for this, including that the imported pillows were old and tattered, and that the locally made pillows were described as "fancy" (*labradas*). Fancy pillows were probably more coveted than old and tattered pillows, regardless of where they were made, but given that the only prices of imported pillows come from Campomanes' inventory, the data are not enough to tell with certainty.

made a difference in their pricing, and that the same could be applied to other things, "whether the horse is lame or treacherous, or the slave is sick, thieving, or prone to escaping, or the sword has hairs" (1985:70).[3] In fact, two locally made shirts were the most expensive in the data set. Not many other items of clothing present enough data to make a similar analysis, because there are too few items with prices, or because the items have prices but lack enough (or any) indications of their origin.

An important lesson to learn from this analysis is that even though imported items were, on average, more expensive, in the right context, at the right moment, people in Mexico City could find an imported item at a good price, sometimes even cheaper than some locally made items. The context of exchange or the price history of some items may not usually be available, especially in archaeological contexts, but one should keep in mind that different people could obtain an imported luxury here and there, regardless of their economic standing, if they got lucky at an auction or if they had the right connections. The condition of the items could also help bring the price down. Chipped porcelain, for example, could sometimes be bought for a good price in auction.

The prices of pottery (Table 7.3), whether made of ceramics, glass, or other materials, would be most useful to archaeologists, although the descriptions found in the documents are difficult to match with the typologies used today (Chapter 4). The data make it difficult to identify any patterns correlating prices with origin, type, decoration, or most other attributes of pottery. However, the clearest correlation is between the material of the pottery and its price. Three items made of silver, including a salt shaker listed as being made of gold-plated silver (*plata dorada*), are the most expensive individual items among the pottery. Items made of tin, *peltre*, and glass were much cheaper. The average price of a pot (excluding items made of silver, and considering only individual pots) is comparable to the average price of a shirt, or approximately 482 maravedís. However, the average price of a silver pot, considering the only three silver items in the data set that have prices, is almost nine times as high, or 4,287 maravedís.

One of the owners of the silver pottery items in this data set was Antonio Martínez, who had the inventory with the second highest net worth in this study. He seasoned his food in style with the gold-plated silver salt

---

[3] My translation of the original, which reads: "Otras veces está el defecto en la calidad y condición de la ropa: que o el caballo es manco o es traidor, o el esclavo enfermo, ladrón, huidor, o la espada tiene pelos" (Mercado 1985:70).

Table 7.3 Prices of pottery in the probate inventories.

Date	Item	Price (in maravedís)	Material	Comments	Source
1581	bowl	56.25			Cont. 219, N2, R8
1545	batejuela	112.50		for cleaning gold	Cont. 197, N.21, 2
1545	glass	136.00	glass		Cont. 197 N.21 (22)
1562	jar	150.00			Cont. 200, N.2, R.2, 1
1586	basin	156.25			Cont. 228, N1, R1
1581	bowl	262.50	with ivory	for cleaning·	Cont. 219, N2, R2
1545	lebrillo	374.00			Cont. 197 N.21 (22)
1554	plate and bowl	408.00	tin		
1545	pan	476.00		sold with two broilers	Cont. 197 N21 (10)
1545	barber's basin	544.00	with a tin brim		Cont. 197 N21 (10)
1545	basin	544.00		sold with a spoon	Cont. 197 N.21 (22)
1565	wash basin	544.00			Cont. 210 N1, R87
1545	plate	544.00	tin		Cont. 197 N21 (10)
1565	pan	544.00			Cont. 210 N1, R86
1545	basin	680.00			Cont. 197 N21 (10)
1545	basin	748.00			Cont. 197 N21 (10)
1545	basin	748.00			Cont. 197 N21 (10)
1578	basin	1,050.00	tin		Cont. 229, N1, R5
1565	bowl	1,088.00		sold with a small box	Cont. 210 N1, R56
1560	cup	2,700.00	silver		Cont. 473, N.2, R.1, 1
1586	salt shaker	3,562.50	gold plated silver		Cont. 228, N1, R1
1560	small jar	6,600.00	silver		Cont. 473, N.2, R.1, 1

shaker. The other two silver items, a cup and a small jar, appear in Andrés de Plasencia's inventory, only the ninth most expensive inventory in the list, and worth about one-eighth of the total worth of Antonio Martínez's inventory. It is notable that Antonio Martínez (Cont. 228 N1 R1) also owned two Chinese porcelain pots, which sold for 3 tomines, or the equivalent of 102 maravedís. The price of these imported, fine pots is a lot cheaper than one would expect if imported pottery was consistently more expensive than local pottery. It seems like a low price for porcelain, especially in comparison with the many other pots listed (although not described) in the inventories. The data from the probate inventories show that the material of the pot (whether it was silver or ceramic) could make a very big difference in the price of the pottery, and that other factors could bring the price of pottery down, as was the case with fine pottery brought from across the oceans.

Wealth and Consumption

If it is true that wealth was associated with consumption of imported things in general, then the data in the probate inventories should show that inventories that contain a higher percentage of imported items also have higher net worth than inventories that have a lower percentage of imported items. A linear regression can help understand whether the percentage of imported goods in an inventory can help predict the wealth of a colonizer. The ability of the percentage of imported goods to predict the wealth of a colonizer depends on how strongly both variables are correlated. If they are perfectly correlated, then one variable will predict the other one quite accurately. Of course, it would be unreasonable to predict that the percentage of imports will help predict the net worth of an inventory perfectly, as is the case with most variables used in the social sciences (Ho 2017:163; Whittier et al. 2020:547). An assumption made is that the people compiling the inventories were just as likely to mention imported items as they were to mention locally made items. In other words, I assume that the assessment of origin in the inventories is random, not biased toward imports or toward locally made items, and therefore an accurate reflection of the origin of the items owned by the decedents. This assumption is discussed in more detail in the previous chapters, and it is addressed further below.

Figure 7.1 is a scatterplot of the inventories and a line of best fit, or a line that represents the relationship between the variables in the data set in an idealized, linear manner (Whittier et al. 2020:553). The x axis of the plot represents the percentage of imported items in an inventory, considering only items that are clearly labeled as imported or locally made. The y axis represents the value of the inventory, using only the twenty-three grade A inventories (Chapter 1). The line of best fit in this case is close to horizontal as the x axis increases. One would expect it to go up along the y axis if there

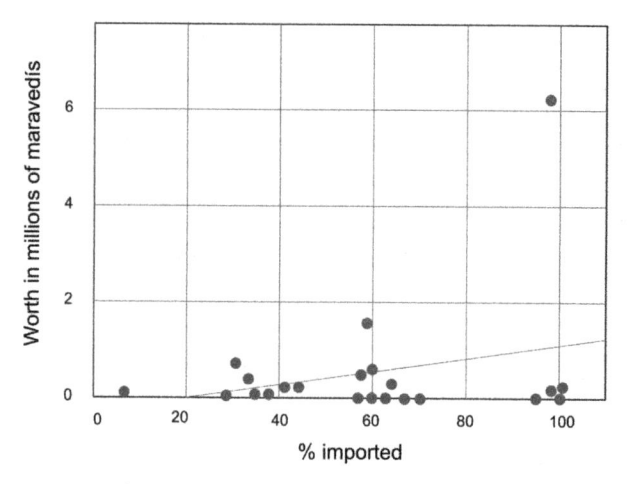

Figure 7.1 Percent of imported items in each inventory compared to the value of the inventory. Each dot represents a probate inventory.

was a strong correlation between an increasing percentage of imported items and an increase in the value of the inventories. Another relevant observation in this plot is that the data points are scattered all over the plot, instead of resembling a roughly elliptical cloud of points along the line of best fit. That is because as the x axis increases, the values of different cases are not increasing steadily along the y axis. The R-square statistic (Table 7.4) represents the proportion of variation in the net worth of an inventory that is explained by the percentage of imports in each inventory (in other words, how much variation in the y axis can be explained by the x axis; Ho 2017:176). In this case, the R-square (0.064) indicates that the percentage of imports in an inventory can only explain 6.4 percent of the variation in the net worth of the inventories. Thus, the percentage of imports is very weakly related to the net worth.

Perhaps there was a true lack of correlation between wealth and consumption of imports among the early colonizers in Mexico City, assuming still that the data used for this statistic are random. It is also possible that the

Table 7.4 R-square statistic of the relationship between the value of an inventory and the percent of imported items in the inventory.

Model	R	R-square	Adjusted R-square	Std. error of the estimate
1	.254[a]	.064	.020	1378746.236

lack of correlation reflects that the decedents were truly part of a social class, in spite of the significant differences in their total worth and their different occupations. Specifically, they could belong to the "popular classes" defined by Rodríguez Vázquez (1995) for Seville and discussed in Chapter 2. These popular classes had inventories worth less than 1 million maravedís, and they were defined by Rodríguez Vázquez solely on their worth. Perhaps people who were much wealthier than these decedents owned more imported things, but the data in this study provide little opportunity to evaluate the possibility.

Examining some individual cases could help understand the pattern better. First, the decedent with the highest net worth, Hernán Núñez Caballero (AGI Cont, 232, N.2, R.3), had one of the highest percentages of imported items in his inventory (97.8 percent; Table 7.5). His total worth of over 6.7 million maravedís places him clearly above the wealth of the rest of the decedents. His worth is so high in part because he declared investments in both Spain and New Spain of over 20,000 pesos (some 6 million maravedís). He would be among the wealthiest men in the data set even without these investments. His inventory declared forty-five imported items to one locally made item, a tablecloth. The imported items include a variety of clothing items, including hats, hose, and shirts, as well as imported boxes and chests. All of them seem to be his personal belongings rather than lots of items for trade. His case seems to support the idea that wealthier colonizers owned more imported things than poorer colonizers, although I would caution against using one example as representative of broad trends, especially because the second richest man in the data set shows a rather different percentage of imports in his inventory.

Antonio Martínez (AGI Cont. 228, N1, R1) is another decedent with a very high net worth. His inventory is worth just under 1.6 million maravedís, placing him well above the line that marks the popular classes defined by Rodríguez Vázquez (1995). Just like Núñez Caballero, Martínez's inventory lists more imported items than locally made goods; however, the percentage of imports is much lower in this case (58.3 percent). His percentage of imports is comparable to that in most of the other inventories in the data set. Taken together, the two most expensive inventories show that a wealthy person could certainly own more imported goods than others, but this was not always the case.

Another interesting point can emerge from discussing Pedro Vázquez (Cont. 197 N.21(16)), whose inventory was worth some 68,901 maravedís.

Table 7.5 Proportion of local and imported items in each inventory.

	Net worth	N local	N imported	% Imported
Hernán Núñez Caballero	6,704,930	1	45	97.8%
Antonio Martínez	1,597,950	5	7	58.3%
Alonso Serrano	716,934	9	4	30.8%
Bartolomé González	516,589	4	6	60.0%
Martin Carrasco	441,258	21	28	57.1%
Maese Gregorio de Heredia	351,352	4	2	33.3%
Diego Delgado	206,144	10	7	41.2%
Juan Gutiérrez de Grado	201,731	55	42	43.3%
Andrés de Plasencia	190,981	22	39	63.9%
Alonso de Castro	178,753	0	3	100.0%
Juan Gomez	115,075	8	18	69.2%
Bartolomé de Prado	107,762	0	5	100.0%
Miguel Rodríguez	105,455	3	4	57.1%
Francisco de Sigüenza	84,238	32	17	34.7%
Juana Bautista	79,762	0	19	100.0%
Pedro Vazquez	68,981	27	2	6.9%
María de Espinosa	65,475	1	2	66.7%
Juan De Campomanes	48,654	33	49	59.8%
Juan Diaz Caballero	38,069	3	5	62.5%
Salvador Franco	36,709	1	19	95.0%
Alonso Garcia	27,114	5	3	37.5%
Pedro de Madrid	14,737	0	3	100.0%
Bartolome Hernandez	6,281	28	11	28.2%

His belongings listed twenty-seven locally made goods and only two imports (Table 7.5). Thus, he had the lowest percentage of imports in the data set. It is important to note that he was not the poorest of all of the decedents. His inventory declares that he was not married but he had a son with an Indigenous woman. He certainly owned both Spanish and locally made clothes, and the number of locally made items in his inventory is inflated by eighteen ribbons that he declared. Even if we eliminated the ribbons, he would still own nine local items to two imports, making it a low percentage of imports. Did he own more locally made goods because he socialized more with Indigenous people than other colonizers in the data set? Or were the people compiling his inventory more likely to find locally made goods than others? Or are there other explanations that can account for this pattern? Regardless, the fact that he owned a much higher quantity of local goods in comparison to imports breaks with the pattern of other decedents, including the poor ones. Juana Bautista, the woman who ranks just one spot higher than him in terms of wealth, had an inventory with 100 percent imported items (Cont. 219, N.2, R.3). And all seven of the inventories with a lower net worth than his had a much higher percentage of imported items.

The point is not that there were no wealthy people that owned mostly imported goods. The point is that there may not be a clear and consistent pattern that shows that. Some wealthy people, like Núñez Caballero, may have strongly preferred imports. Some, like Martínez, may not have cared as much to own imports. Some poorer people, like Pedro Vázquez, may have owned mostly locally made goods. Others may have had more imported goods among their belongings.

The results of both the linear regression and the data used to calculate it must be qualified carefully. They include items in all categories, whether pottery, clothing, furniture, and any other category. Combining all of the categories of material into a single cross tabulation enriches the data by increasing sample size and making the statistical calculations possible, but the results make it difficult to understand whether any of the individual categories show a clear association between wealth and ownership of local or imported goods. Perhaps there is such an association between imported clothing and wealth, for example, or between imported furniture and wealth.

Previous chapters have provided glimpses of the association between wealth and ownership of some items. For example, some of the wealthiest decedents had sillas de caderas, the impressive portable chairs of colonizers. Still, four of the top ten wealthiest colonziers did not own any sillas de caderas. Also, some of the poorest colonizers owned these chairs, perhaps because they made them or because they had access to them for reasons other than wealth (Chapter 3). Most colonizers did not own any Indigenous clothes, but they certainly owned plenty of locally made clothes, whether made by Spaniards, Indians, Africans, or a combination of all of them (Chapter 5). Wealthy colonizers tended to have slaves, although not all of them did. Some colonizers whose net worth was not reliable also owned slaves (Chapter 6). Thus, the association of any category of items and wealth seems inconsistent. It defies any retrospective interest in a neat, clear pattern.

The archaeological literature on the relationship between wealth and consumption is mostly based on ceramics (e.g., Charlton and Founier 2011;

Fournier 1998; Fournier García 1997; Lister and Lister 1982, 1987; Oland 2014, 2017; Rodríguez-Alegría 2003, 2005b, 2010). Ceramics are among the most abundant artifacts found archaeologically, and they can be studied to determine which fragments are locally made or imported, and which can be considered finer or lesser quality, making them ideal for this sort of study (Chapter 4). Archaeologists often also study the historical background of different sites to assess the relationship between consumption and wealth with independent lines of evidence. Unfortunately, there are only two pots in the data set used for the cross tabulation presented earlier, making it impossible to compare directly with archaeological patterns. But the data presented here lend support to my previous study of ceramics and wealth in the historic center of Mexico City.

My study was based on ceramics excavated by the PAU in eight houses in the center of Mexico City, all of them houses of colonizers (Chapters 2, 4; Rodríguez-Alegría 2003, 2005b, 2016a). The archaeologists and historians working for the PAU had provided socioeconomic histories of some of the people who lived in the houses, using independent lines of evidence; that is, the material analysis focused exclusively on the artifacts, and the sociohistorical profiles were reconstructed using historical documents. Several interesting patterns emerged from this study. First, all of the houses contained both European ceramics and local, Indigenous pottery. It was clear that none of the houses, whether wealthy or poor, entirely rejected Indigenous pottery. In fact, the large proportion of Indigenous pottery in the houses was surprising to me when I finished the analysis. Second, the proportion of imported and Indigenous ceramics in the houses varied. Some houses had more imports than Indigenous ceramics, and vice versa. And third, consumption of more imported pottery was not consistently associated with wealth. Some of the wealthiest households used more Indigenous ceramics than the poorest households, and one of the poorest households used more Asian porcelain than the wealthiest households (Chapter 4; Rodríguez-Alegría 2003, 2005b). Based on this study, I argued that there was not a single ideology of consumption, or a single strategy of display that characterized colonizer households, and that wealth alone could not explain the differences in patterns of consumption. Instead, I argued, the social connections and strategies of different colonizers could explain the archaeological patterns better. Some colonizers were indeed invested in preserving a Spanish image and they used fine imported pottery to put their ethnicity on display and keep up appearances, but other colonizers were more interested in their local ties, and in establishing and strengthening relationships with powerful Indigenous people, and they also showed an appreciation for the things produced by local producers. There was no single or monolithic standard for consumption that colonizers agreed upon.

The present study, which focuses on a variety of categories of material culture and as many as twenty-three decedents is largely in agreement with the archaeological study, which focuses on only one category of material (ceramics) and on eight houses excavated by the PAU. The main contribution of the probate inventories is a much larger sample size and a greater variety of categories of material culture. The agreement between the two studies provides independent confirmation of archaeological results of this type of analysis, and makes me feel encouraged that further archaeological research could yield verifiable results.

Changes Over Time

Sources from the seventeenth and eighteenth centuries describe the luxuries, Spanish fashions, and socioeconomic stratification in colonial Mexico. Thomas Gage, for example, wrote about the world of ostentatious clothes in seventeenth-century Mexico City (Thompson 1958:68–70). Although his writings are full of exaggeration, presenting a world of incredible luxury— even enslaved people wore fine jewelry—there may be some truth to Gage's descriptions of luxury in colonial Mexico. Further, casta paintings also depict social stratification, luxury, and differences in consumption among different groups in colonial Mexico. These paintings mostly separate people into racial groups based on the degree of admixture between Spaniards, Black people, and Indigenous people, and they show differences in patterns of consumption and the material worlds of different casta groups. Spaniards are often depicted living in luxury, with fine clothes and imported goods, whereas Indigenous people and other groups are often depicted in rags or with less satisfactory material goods (Carrera 2003; Katzew 2004). These paintings may not be a neutral description of life in New Spain. They certainly deride their subjects with stereotypes and generalizations, but at the same time, they are a source of information about the material world of New Spain, however problematic. There were also palaces in New Spain (*Artes de México* 1991), and even a quick tour of museums like the Franz Mayer Museum offer impressive views of the luxuries of New Spain. Many of these luxuries were imported, and it is hard to believe that they could possibly be shared between people in all socioeconomic positions.

There is a strong possibility that consumption of imported things developed over time. In other words, perhaps there is a correlation between the year of the inventories and the percentage of imported items that people owned. It could be that in the early decades after the conquest, all sorts of colonizers used locally produced items, and whatever imports they could find, but later, in the late sixteenth century, access to imported items had improved and people were more likely to own and use imported things. And maybe they were also more likely to seek distinction from castas and criollos by showing off their imported things.

The data in the probate inventories can help study whether there was a temporal trend in the use and ownership of imports. I began by dividing the inventories into two categories: early, or inventories compiled between 1532 and 1551, and late, or inventories compiled between 1560 and 1586. The division is arbitrary, in the sense that it is not tied to any specific historical event, but it may help suggest a temporal trend even with such few cases in the data set. The average of the percentage of imports in the early group (49 percent) is lower than the average of the percentage of imports in the late group (75.1 percent). Thus, a quick look at the averages supports the idea that the percentage of imports owned by people changed through time. Figure 7.2 is a scatterplot of the inventories and a line of best fit, using the same logic in the linear regression discussed previously (Figure 7.1), except that this time the x axis of the plot represents the year of each inventory, and the y axis represents the percentage of imported items in the inventory. In this case, the line of best fit increases over time, meaning that over time, there were more imported goods in the inventories. The R-square statistic this time is 0.50, meaning that the year of the inventory can explain about 50 percent of the variation in the percentage of imported items. A correlation value of 0.50 is the boundary between what is considered a moderate and a strong correlation (Whittier et al. 2020:544). It is a stronger correlation than the one between percentage of imports and the value of the inventory, although the passage of time is not sufficient to explain the increase in imported items in the inventories. People were not passive in the creation of their material worlds. Their decisions changed over time. The supply of imports probably increased, as did trade between the colonies and Spain, and people took advantage of the greater availability of imported items.

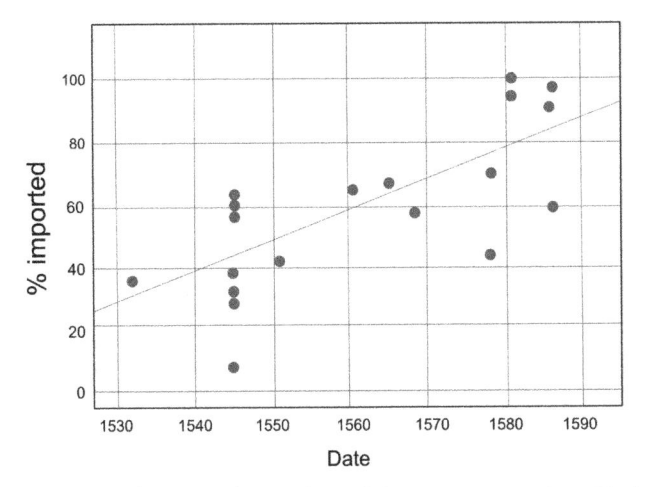

Figure 7.2 Percent of imported items in each inventory over time. Each dot represents a probate inventory.

Conclusion

Together, the study of the probate inventories and the previous ceramics study support four empirical conclusions. First, even the poorest colonizers had access to imported goods. Some of those goods may have come with them as they crossed the ocean, and some of them they may have purchased in Mexico, perhaps even in the auctions that provide the data for this study. Second, even the wealthiest colonizers used locally made products. There was little aversion or rejection of Indigenous goods. Previous chapters have shown that colonizers preferred a lot of their familiar material culture, but when there were locally made products that resembled the imports, they were glad to wear them, use them to serve food, eat them, and otherwise own them. Third, a pattern of association between wealth and consumption of imported or Indigenous goods is not consistent. In fact, the data presented in the first part of the chapter show that imported goods were not always more expensive than local goods. Even if imports could be more expensive than local goods on average, it was also possible to find expensive locally produced items, and cheap imported goods as well. And fourth, over time, as the seventeenth century approached, people consumed a greater percentage of imports than earlier in the colonial effort. The results suggest that the desire for imported things probably increased, or that there was more availability of imported goods over time. In sum, people's wants and desires, their personal connections, patterns of trade, and their social strategies are better explanations of variation in consumption patterns than wealth.

The results from Mexico City are broadly relevant about how we may think of social class and consumption. As discussed previously, Bourdieu (1984) drew attention to the importance of considering class and the education associated with class, in explaining taste. Bourdieu was in part refuting the belief that taste was biological or natural, and emphasizing that society and education play a big role in determining taste and patterns of consumption. The present study partially agrees with Bourdieu's general conclusion because the consumption patterns of colonizers were indeed characterized by the use of European and Asian imports. Those were the things that colonizers had learned to like through a lifetime of exposure to those goods, using them, and desiring them. In that sense, Bourdieu's comments can explain the central tendencies in the data, or the broad pattern of consumption of European goods.

But the archaeological analysis and the probate inventories also show that the material worlds of colonizers were not characterized by a rejection of Indigenous material goods, and that economic variables cannot explain variation fully. Even after a lifetime of learning and shaping taste and consumption patterns, people can obtain and use different kinds of material culture depending on their needs, social connections, goals, and desires. The patterns support the arguments presented by Mintz (1985), who emphasized that consumption is related to relationships of power, and that it can help transform society, and patterns of trade and production. In this case, different colonizers bought goods from Indigenous people and interacted with them in a variety of economic and social contexts. Wealth, social class, and ethnicity were all in flux, as seen in previous chapters, and so were the material worlds of colonizers. Mintz's work is an invitation to put patterns of consumption in a historical sequence, given the transformative capacity of consumption. It is possible that later in the colonial period, perhaps in the seventeenth or eighteenth centuries, the upper classes or peninsular Spaniards rejected many Indigenous goods consistently, but this study cannot offer insights into those time periods other than suggesting that such a pattern began to take shape in the sixteenth century. For most of that initial century of colonization, regardless of wealth and status, colonizers used and consumed plenty of Indigenous and local products.

Conclusion

The Material Worlds of Spanish Colonizers

When Spanish colonizers and their slaves arrived in Mexico City in the sixteenth century—many would say invaded—they entered a world unlike anything they had ever experienced. Many things looked different, ranging from the architecture of the Mexica, to their clothes, their furniture, and their food. But if there was something that some colonizers recognized quickly, it was social rank and economic opportunities. Some Spaniards immediately sought alliances with powerful Indigenous lords. The Spanish knew who was in power and who could benefit them, and many colonizers started seeking power and economic benefits across ethnic lines. Many colonizers, regardless of their interest in power and alliances, wanted to find food, clothes, and material things that they were accustomed to, or that at least resembled their traditional material worlds. They set out to make a new version of Spain in Mexico City.

Making material worlds that seemed familiar would prove to be a challenge. Colonizers in the sixteenth century lived in a city that was mostly Indigenous. In 1519, it was one of the biggest cities in the world. It was an island in a lake system, connected to the mainland by causeways. It had canals that flowed with water and canoes through the city, a large and orderly market, and a religious and administrative center with monumental architecture unlike anything colonizers had ever seen (López Austin and López Luján 2017; Matos Moctezuma 1988; Rojas 2017; Sanders 2008). After the last battles of the conquest of Tenochtitlan came to an end in 1521, and the Spanish declared victory, "Indigenous Tenochtitlan lived on" (Mundy 2015:3). Colonizers lived among the ruins of Mexica temples, and sometimes next to Mexica architecture where people still practiced their pre-Columbian religious rituals (Toussaint 1956:15). By 1538, the Spanish crown decreed that Indigenous temples be torn down and the stone be used to make Catholic churches and monasteries (Tovar de Teresa 1985). But three years later, Indigenous builders were hard at work constructing their own

How to Make a New Spain. Enrique Rodríguez-Alegría, Oxford University Press. © Enrique Rodríguez-Alegría 2023.
DOI: 10.1093/oso/9780197682296.003.0009

tecpan or lordly house a few hundred meters southwest from where their old great pyramid once stood (Mundy 2015:109). A team of two colonizers and two Indigenous men worked together to draw the plan for the colonial city, even though the city was still standing (Mier y Terán Rocha 2005:82; Sodi Miranda 1994:17). Armed with the detailed knowledge of the Indigenous men, they maintained the general organization of the city, and its orientation to the cardinal directions. They laid streets mostly where there were already streets (Tovar de Teresa 1985:10), but they were not passive when confronted with the monumental task of building houses where there was already a city. People may have found obstacles and possibilities in the environment that was already built, but the city did not dictate their actions.

Scholars have argued that the houses of Spanish colonizers looked military, uniform, and simple (Kubler 1948), but the remains of houses excavated at the heart of Mexico City show how much Indigenous people contributed their own aesthetics and techniques to these houses. Teams of Indigenous builders got to work on building houses for colonizers. The Indigenous builders used the engineering techniques, materials, tools, and traditions that they knew. In other words, they used pre-Hispanic technology to build the houses of colonizers. Sometimes they used the layout of the city and the existing architecture to build houses. Sometimes they used Mexica architecture as foundations for the colonial houses (Del Olmo Frese 2003; Hinojosa Hinojosa 2003:23; Terreros Espinosa 2003:248; Viart Muños and Martínez Meza 2003:121). Sometimes they broke through Mexica architecture to build new houses, just like they had done when expanding their pre-Hispanic architecture or erecting new buildings for the empire of the Triple Alliance (Barrera Rodríguez and Martínez Meza 2010; Barrera Rodríguez et al. 2012). They laid out foundations using vertical wooden pylons to manage shifting and subsiding in the soft and humid terrain in Mexico City (Barrera Rodríguez et al. 2003:207; Mundy 2015:194). They used andesite, basalt, and tezontle, often recycled from the monumental architecture of the Mexica (Barrera Rodríguez and Rivas García 2003; Terreros Espinosa 2003:244). They even combined the use of different materials in different rooms of the same house, but we do not know for sure why. It could be that they built the houses piecemeal, or that they simply worked with whatever materials were available to finish a project. They often used white or red plaster, and polished it to a high luster (Terreros Espinosa 2003). Thus, the houses of the Spanish may have looked military and simple on the inside, but inside, they had many of the finishing techniques and aesthetic aspects of the temples of the Mexica. In the process of building the houses of colonizers, Indigenous people also built their place in the world. They created rank within their work units. Some of them obtained distinction and earned respect as masons, carpenters, or engineers, among other occupations, just like they had before the conquest. By creating the material worlds of colonizers, Indigenous people sometimes created aspects of their own social worlds (Chapter 2).

The things found in the houses of colonizers were also important in making the colonial world. Scholars have argued that in the Spanish colonies, everyday material culture was important for display, to seek distinction from Indigenous people, to build unity among colonizers, and to reproduce a Spanish way of life through specific practices and patterns of consumption (Bauer 2001; Benítez 1993; Deagan 1983, 1998, 2001; Lister and Lister 1982; McEwan 1991, 1992, 1995). Whereas colonizers lived in houses made with many technological and aesthetic aspects of Indigenous engineering, their choices in terms of Indigenous furniture were quite limited. In central Mexico, Indigenous furniture was extremely simple, consisting mostly of petates or reed mats for sitting and sleeping, and occasionally reed boxes (Aguilera 1985). Colonizers considered beds essential for civilization (Jamieson 2000b:166), and they probably extended civilizing qualities to other items of furniture as well. Spaniards who wanted their own traditional furniture began importing all kinds of objects from Spain, including boxes, chairs, tables, beds, and items related to bedding, such as cushions, mattresses, sheets, and blankets. These items were often quite complex, fancy, decorated, and bulky, as can be seen in the surviving examples in museum collections. It is quite probable that people simply did not curate much simpler furniture, explaining their absence in museum collections. Bringing all of this furniture underscores how deceptive a phrase like "reconstructing a Spanish lifestyle" could be. Colonizers imported furniture from different cities in Spain, and elsewhere in Europe, especially France, Italy, and Flanders. Occupational specialists of different kinds, often organized in guilds, contributed to making furniture (Aguiló Alonso 1993). They included carpenters, smiths, weavers, and people whose work consisted of putting furniture together. Creating the material worlds of Spanish colonizers was a complicated effort. Soon after the conquest, carpenters, smiths, and other specialists began producing European-style furniture in Mexico. Many of them worked with Indigenous people and Africans, whether free or enslaved (Chapter 3).

The probate inventories show that in addition to importing furniture and making furniture in colonial Mexico, colonizers also incorporated some

Indigenous products into their furniture. Beds and bedding are a good example. Colonizers often slept on European beds, most often with imported mattresses. Sometimes they used pillows made in Mexico, and sometimes pillows brought from Europe. Most often they used sheets that were made in Europe, but they used blankets woven in Mexico. Unless these patterns are simply a product of systematic bias in the probate inventories, it seems like colonizers generally liked the warm blankets that Indigenous people wove. They slept on their European-style beds, so strongly associated with civilization, on European mattresses and with Indigenous blankets. Thus, colonial furniture in Mexico was the product of Europeans, African, and Indigenous people, and making a material world that colonizers considered civilized depended on the work of all groups (Chapter 3).

Aside from using the furniture to rest, sit, sleep, eat, and store things, colonizers took advantage of the symbolic potential of the furniture. They quickly learned, for example, that their silla de caderas, their portable and foldable chairs, were quite impressive to Indigenous people. Sometimes they used the chairs to show off their own status and power or to show the status and power they aspired to. But other times they presented such chairs to powerful Indigenous lords, as a recognition of their power, and as a way to forge alliances (Díaz del Castillo 1942:127; *Lienzo de Tlaxcala*). On one hand, it is difficult to know how often these gifts of sillas de caderas took place. It could be that the few cases mentioned in the chronicles are exceptional. On the other hand, the few examples of Spaniards giving gifts of symbolically charged furniture to Indigenous lords underscores that some Spaniards recognized rank and power among Indigenous people and looked for benefits in alliances. This point is not new, given that scholars who have studied political and military aspects of the conquest have written about alliance-building strategies (e.g., Matthew and Oudijk 2007; Restall 2003). But I extend this point here to broaden the ways in which we can understand furniture and power in the colonial period. Furniture was not just a part of strategies of marking difference between ethnic groups. It was also a part of strategies of forging alliances between powerful people across ethnic lines (Chapter 3).

Food is perhaps the first category of material culture that comes to mind when people think about socialization and sharing. It is also a category of material culture that can bring up the challenges of cross-cultural interaction. Scholars have emphasized that colonizers ate local foods for survival, to socialize with Indigenous people and accept their hospitality, and to enjoy their flavor (Coe 1993; Rodríguez-Alegría 2002, 2005a, 2016a), and they imported their own foods to maintain a familiar diet, and to avoid seeing their bodies become more like the bodies of Indigenous people (Earle 2012). Spanish colonizers in the sixteenth century ate maize, a grain that was then unknown in Europe, as well as the unfamiliar spice and heat of Mexican chilies. They saw innumerable unknown dishes and ingredients, and they probably could not predict how pervasive a few of those would become in cuisines all over the world, including tomatoes, chilies, and cacao, among others (Coe 1993). Colonizers incorporated many of the unfamiliar ingredients into their diets. They ate maize, amaranth, chili, tomatoes, Mexican hawthorn, black cherry, pine nuts, and prickly pear fruit (Montúfar López 2003). They drank so chocolate so frequently that it has gained a somewhat legendary status in the historical literature for its popularity among colonizers (Pierce 2003). Some of the local fauna that colonizers ate was somewhat familiar, given that they had similar species in Europe at the time, including rabbit, different kinds of waterfowl, and fish. They also ate turkey (Valentin Maldonado 2003), although archaeological data indicate that they preferred a more familiar animal that they brought across the ocean: the chicken (Barrera Rodríguez et al. 2008:24).

Even as they enjoyed local dishes and ingredients, colonizers imported all kinds of plants and animals for food. They imported "wheat, olives, onions, garlic, lettuce, radishes, parsley, carrots, eggplant, spinach, chickpeas, lentils, cauliflower, asparagus, melons, cantaloupes, squashes, cucumber, rice, citrus fruits, tea, and spices such as cinnamon, black pepper, and saffron" (Stoopen 1997:28). Faunal remains in archaeological excavations reveal that colonizers brought, raised, and ate many different animals, including goats, sheep, pigs, and cattle. Most of these animals appear frequently in the probate inventories, except for pigs. The historical literature includes comments on the abundance of pigs in early colonial Mexico (Matasanz 1965:537), leading me to believe that their absence in the documents could be due to their abundance and low price (Chapter 6). Analysis of faunal remains in some of the houses of colonizers in Mexico City shows that colonizers generally preferred imported fauna, but they ate plenty of local animals. The animals they ate were often hunted or raised by Indigenous people and sold in the market, showing that the Spanish relied on Indigenous production and market exchange to obtain much of their food (Chapter 4; Guzmán and Polaco 2003; Montúfar López 2000; Montúfar López and Valentín Maldonado 1998; Valentín Maldonado 2003).

To store, cook, and eat those foods, colonizers used a wide variety of pottery, some of it imported across both the Atlantic and Pacific Oceans and some of it made locally by colonizers or by Indigenous potters. Scholars have debated why the patterns of adoption of Indigenous pottery and the use of imported pottery vary between the houses of colonizers all over the Spanish colonies. The explanations focus variably on issues of taste, economics, socialization, the demographic and gendered aspects of colonization, and the politics of display (e.g., Charlton and Fournier 2011; Charlton et al. 1995; Deagan 1983, 1995, 1998, 2001; Fournier 1998; Fournier García 1997; Jamieson 2000a, 2000b, 2004; McEwan 1992, 1995; Rodríguez-Alegría 2005a, 2005b, 2016a; Voss 2005, 2008a). But the thousands of fragments of pottery that archaeologists find every day are a reminder of the fact that pottery was a daily necessity in the sixteenth century, regardless of economic, political, or social interests. The people who compiled the probate inventories classified pottery mostly in terms of form and use, emphasizing the practical uses of pottery. Rarely do the documents mention much about the aesthetic aspects of pottery or even their origin. These documents remind us not to overlook the many uses of pottery, besides symbolic or aesthetic factors (Chapter 4). Sometimes, aesthetics and practical aspect combined, as was the case with chocolate cups, which colonizers began making after adopting the delicious Mesoamerican beverage. Other pottery was adapted to store chocolate securely, and for other purposes related to the new colonial customs in Mexico (Pierce 2003:254).

In spite of the emphasis on the functions of pottery in the documents, and the lack of information on origins and aesthetics, archaeologists have managed to identify the origins of different types of pottery, and study its use as symbolic and aesthetic objects. Colonizers imported some of their pottery from Europe, mostly from Andalusia, and to a lesser extent from Italy (Lister and Lister 1982, 1987). They also imported pottery from Asia, especially China, starting in the late sixteenth century. They considered Chinese porcelain, with its delicate forms and intricately decorated surfaces to be the most elegant and desirable of the ceramic pottery (Kuwayama 1997). And they brought some pottery also from other colonies in the Caribbean (Lister and Lister 1982).

Colonizers also began producing pottery in Mexico soon after they began to settle. They brought glazing technologies, which were not part of potting traditions in pre-Hispanic central Mexico. They glazed their cooking pots with lead, which made the pots shiny and green, amber, or brown. Because of this glaze, it was noticeably different from the cooking pots of the Mexica. Colonizers often enameled their serving vessels with tin and lead, making the pottery shiny and white. Sometimes the enamel could be of different colors, most frequently yellow, different shades of blue, or gunmetal, depending on the effect that different minerals could have on the color of the enamel (Deagan 1987; Fournier 1990, 1998; Lister and Lister 1982, 1987). People in different parts of the world worked making, selling, and transporting pottery to supply the needs and desires of colonizers. To meet the basic needs of a household, for pottery, furniture, and other goods, people got involved in networks of production and exchange that affected local economies as well as economies across the Atlantic and the Pacific (Chapter 4).

In spite of such a variety of imported pottery and locally made pottery, many colonizers also adopted Indigenous pottery in their own houses. Archaeologists have found plenty of Red Ware pottery in the houses of colonizers in the center of Mexico City, and even though some of it has changes in terms of form and decoration that could be considered colonial innovations, for the most part, Indigenous potters did not alter their forms or decoration to please Spanish tastes (Rodríguez-Alegría 2002, 2016a). Sometimes, even elite colonizers commissioned Indigenous pottery for their own feasts and celebrations, as was the case when Martín Cortés, the son of Hernán Cortés, celebrated his son's baptism with Indigenous pottery that he had made to order (Charlton et al. 1995; Suárez de Peralta [1589]1990:185), or when a Spanish official ordered pottery from the Indigenous potters of Cuauhtitlan (Barlow 1951; Hernández Sánchez 2012:96). A combination of historical documents and archaeological evidence suggests that colonizers sometimes used Indigenous pottery and ate Indigenous foods. The use of Indigenous pottery was not, I argue, just a matter of necessity or of making do with low quality pottery. Instead, it was part of commensal practices in which colonizers would share with powerful Indigenous people, forge alliances, cozy up to Indigenous power, and obtain material and immaterial benefits (Rodríguez-Alegría 2005a, 2016a). Regardless of their specific motivations, it is remarkable that colonizers imported food and pottery, engaged in local production of both, and consumed the products of Indigenous producers as well. A rejection of Indigenous products and technologies is simply not evident in the historical or archaeological data (Chapter 4).

Clothing is one category of material culture that one would assume shows a clear rejection of Indigenous products from the part of colonizers. There is plenty of literature on the association of clothing with ethnicity, social class, and other factors of personhood and identity (Gallardo 2014; Joyce 2000, 2005; Loren 2010, 2015; McKim-Smith 2006; Roach and Eicher 1973; Sousa Congosto 2007; Wobst 1977). The probate inventories initially give the impression that colonizers rejected Indigenous clothing entirely, although patterns in the probate inventories reveal that the use of Indigenous products for dress was quite common in the sixteenth century. The clothes that colonizers wore are clearly Spanish fashions. They began covering their body with a shirt—often quite billowy—and hose, attached to a doublet. On top of those, they typically wore a smock, and on top of that, a cape or a coat. To cover their legs and feet they often wore socks of different kinds, and on top of that maybe a soft leather shoe. On top of that still, they wore either boots, or hard leather shoes, or any other variety of shoes, boots, or sandals. Women wore a similar range of clothes, beginning with a billowy shirt, on top of which they would wear a doublet, and then a smock or a tunic. And of top of that, they wore a dress, and perhaps a loose dress on top of the dress (Bernis 1962). It is thus no surprise that they owned a lot of clothing items: around 42 percent of their belongings by count were clothes and items used to repair and mend clothing. However, they owned very few Indigenous garments, and when they did, I believe that they were trying to sell them. The items appear only in a handful of inventories, and they were most described as new (Chapter 5).

The fact that there were such few Indigenous clothes in the inventories, and that the overwhelming majority of clothes were Spanish fashions should not obscure an important pattern: 42.6 percent of the items with a clear indication of their origin in the probate inventories were made locally in the Americas, whether by Indigenous producers or by Spanish colonizers who quite often worked with Indigenous producers. Colonizers often used cloth made by Indigenous people or clothes made in part or fully by Indigenous weavers and tailors. And of course, a little over half the time they wore clothes imported from Europe, whether they were clothes that they themselves brought or clothes they bought after living in Mexico. Most of the time, they described clothes and textiles made by Indigenous people in overwhelmingly favorable terms. Whenever they described European clothes negatively, they were commenting not on the initial quality of the clothes, but on wear and tear on them. In fact, given the descriptions in the probate inventories, colonizers in the sixteenth century wore old, torn, or mended clothing more often than they wore new clothes (Chapter 5). Observers in the seventeenth century may have described Mexico City as a world of fine fashions

(Thompson 1958:68), but the probate inventories show that in the sixteenth century, people wore old, tattered, and mended clothing. These descriptions of clothing show that Indigenous people quickly learned to make Spanish-style clothing and they tapped into the colonial market for Spanish clothing, and that colonizers depended on both local production and on transoceanic trade to get their clothes. More important is the fact that if colonizers were using their clothes to mark distinction from Indigenous people, or to display their status, or to dress in a moral and hygienic way (unlike Indigenous people, who looked naked to colonizers), they often depended on Indigenous people to do so. Strategies to seek distinction and to impose colonial ideas of morality depended on the work of Indigenous people and Africans, who also worked as tailors (Chapter 5).

The things that Spanish colonizers brought impacted not only local patterns of consumption, but patterns of production as well. The conquest and colonization of the Americas could be seen as a clash between people who used a variety of steel tools, and people who used stone tools. But the process was more complex than just steel and stone. To make clothes, furniture, and many other things, colonizers brought their own tools, livestock, and slavery. The probate inventories give the impression that colonizers brought an endless variety of tools of iron, steel, and wood, including scissors, knives, nails, hammers, shoe trees, tanning boards, and many others. Although firearms were rare, many colonizers carried swords with them, to use as weapons and for display. They also brought animals for food, labor, and raw materials (especially wool and leather), into a world where Indigenous people did not have any large domestic mammals. The numbers of sheep and goats were high enough to cause environmental damage in the sixteenth century. Cattle also thrived, and the government of Mexico City even prohibited it from the lands adjacent to the city due to the damage it was causing in agricultural fields (Matasanz 1965; Melville 1997). Still, the animal that most people were prepared to interact with was the horse. It was a useful animal for transportation, and certainly an impressive animal for display. To complete the suite of technological changes of the colonization process, colonizers enslaved Indigenous people and brought black enslaved people from Africa and the Caribbean to exploit them for work in rural areas, cities, houses, and specialized production. Thus, tools, livestock, and slaves were three important parts of the complex sociotechnical systems of colonial Mexico City. There is little indication in the probate inventories that colonizers adopted the stone tools of Indigenous people for their own use (Chapter 6).

Given modern ideas of progress from stone tools to bronze and iron, it could initially seem like the technological changes that the Spanish brought were an improvement upon Indigenous stone tools and their lack of draft animals. However, the story of technological change is more complex than that. Closer scrutiny reveals that whereas colonizers kept their own traditional tools, they also benefited from Indigenous technologies. Pastrana (1998:195–198) has argued that colonizers encouraged the continuation of obsidian tool use among Indigenous people because they used obsidian to cut leather for bags and scaffolds and for other purposes necessary for silver mining. Any colonizer who ate a tortilla, a tamal, or any food made with ground maize or ground chilies benefited from Indigenous technologies, such as the mano and metate, and the skilled women who used those tools on a daily basis, which were necessary for grinding maize. Indigenous people also built the houses of Spaniards with Indigenous technologies and built the dams and aqueducts that protected Mexico City from flooding and supplied it with fresh water (Chapter 2). They supplied the city with plenty of food that they grew, hunted, or fished using their own technologies, including agricultural technologies, stone tools, and nets, among others. Spanish colonizers often adopted Indigenous pottery for their own use, and all of it was made with Indigenous technologies (Chapter 4). The conquistadors who battled against Indigenous troops probably used copper smelted with Indigenous traditions, perhaps with the addition of Spanish bellows, to make some of their weapons for the conquest (García Zaldúa and Hosler 2020). Thus, the fact that Indigenous tools are so rare in the probate inventories does not mean that colonizers rejected Indigenous technologies as inferior. It simply means that colonizers were accustomed to their own tools, which they had grown up with and had learned to use throughout their lives. Tool use requires expertise and knowledge, and this first generation of colonizers had the expertise and knowledge to use their own traditional Spanish tools. The results echo those found in El Salvador by Card and Fowler (2019), who found little adoption of Indigenous technologies by the first generations of Spanish colonizers.

Another important facet of technological change in colonial Mexico City is that the technologies that colonizers brought presented advantages and disadvantages when compared to Indigenous technologies. They required trade-offs, as technologies always do (Lemonnier 1993). They were not a simple matter of progress. A good example of the negotiation between different strengths and drawbacks of technology is the use of steel instead of obsidian. Whereas obsidian was extremely sharp, even sharper than any steel blade, it was quite brittle. Steel swords, for example, were durable and easy to sharpen, whereas Indigenous weapons made of obsidian could shatter and needed to be replaced or repaired more frequently (Clark 1989; Ximenez 1615: Book 4, Part 2, Chapter 13). Perhaps colonizers continued using their traditional steel tools, favoring their durability over the sharpness of Indigenous tools. The use of livestock is another example that illustrates that the technologies of colonizers had both positive and negative aspects. Livestock, especially cattle and sheep, presented a source of food, labor, and raw materials (leather and wool, among others) for colonizers. But the large populations of grazing animals caused environmental degradation, and they often destroyed agricultural fields, causing conflicts between Indigenous farmers and colonial ranchers (Matasanz 1965; Melville 1997).

Of the different aspects of the technosocial systems of colonizers, slavery cannot be ignored for its overwhelmingly negative effects. Whereas it bolstered the social position of slave owners and helped them accumulate wealth and do all sorts of tasks that colonizers did not want to do, it was abusive and destructive of the lives of many Indigenous and Black people. They did all kinds of work in the house and in specialized production, such as leather tanning, shoe making, and others. Many of the enslaved people were abused, and many ran away, which shows that abuse did not just happen in rural plantations. Colonial slavery, with its aspects of ownership over enslaved humans, often across generations, cannot be considered a techno-logical advance in Mesoamerica (Chapter 6).

If colonizers had to figure out how to make or bring many of their material belongings, they also had to figure out how to make money, and I mean that literally: how to make coins of gold and silver. In Mexico, and in many of their colonies, they found less gold than they had dreamed of, even though they got plenty of gold from Indigenous people as tribute (e.g., Valle 1994). They quickly began to dilute the gold with copper to make coins. They thus created at least four different alloys of gold, each one with a lower content of gold per weight than the previous one. The peso de oro was the standard, worth the most. The peso de minas was worth less than the peso de oro because it was 22.5 karats of gold. The peso de oro común was worth even less, given that it was 15 karats, and finally, the peso de tepuzque was 13.6 karats, and named as such after the Nahuatl word for copper (Céspedes de Castillo 1994, Luengo Muñoz 1950:364; Riva Palacio 1977). Colonizers soon came into conflict with one another and with Indigenous people regarding the value of coins and which coins were acceptable for exchange. They adopted the use of cacao beans as media of exchange in transactions with Indigenous people (Caplan 2013:337; Seeger 1978:170), but for the most part, they used gold when dealing with other colonizers. Toward the end of the sixteenth century, they started using more silver than gold. Colonizers also loaned money to one another frequently, and sometimes to Indigenous people. Although a good portion of their wealth was held up in debt, they apparently owned very little in terms of cash (Chapter 1).

Thus, colonizers made some of their money, in the sense that they created new coins to put in circulation in the colonies, but some colonizers made a fortune while others barely made a living. The wealth of the decedents in this study, calculated as the value of their belongings at the time of death, varied quite widely (Chapter 1). At one end of the spectrum, some people barely had any belongings or cash. Most of the decedents were poor, but not destitute. At the other end of the spectrum, some colonizers had immense fortunes and they would be considered quite wealthy even in contemporary Seville. Such a variety of fortunes serves as a reminder of the varied experience of colonizers. At the same time, some Indigenous people maintained power, some became wealthy in the colonial period, and many were poor and enslaved. In sixteenth-century Mexico City, status was in flux for both colonizers and Indigenous people, and there was not a single economic scale that placed colonizers on top and Indigenous people at the bottom. Political and economic maneuvering from both Indigenous people and colonizers were common (Chance 2008; Cline 1986; Haskett 1991; Hernández-Durán 2017; Lockhart 1992; Olko and Szemiński 2018; Ruiz Medrano and Kellogg 2010; Spores 1997; Chapter 1).

The relationship between wealth, power, and patterns of consumption is a question that archaeologists and other scholars have examined (e.g., Charlton and Otis Charlton 1994:248; Gibson 1964:156; Haskett 1991:161–163; Rodríguez-Alegría 2010, 2012b, 2016a:154–183; Terraciano 2001; Von Winning 1988; Wood 2003; Yannakakis 2008). The probate inventories and the archaeological data in this study provide an opportunity to examine whether wealthier colonizers used primarily imported products and poorer colonizers had to settle for locally produced goods. This is a question of both, whether wealth dictated consumption patterns, and whether people shared the idea that imported goods were better and more desirable than locally produced goods. The information in the probate inventories reveals an interesting pattern: wealthier colonizers did not consistently own a lower proportion of locally made things compared to imported things. Most, if not all colonizers valued imported things, but most of them also owned locally made items. The wealthier did not reject locally made things. The poor did not own a greater proportion of locally made things compared to imports. Thus, the data do not support the idea that wealth made some colonizers reject local products and poverty forced them to consume only local products. I believe that people simply consumed locally made items or imported items depending on their ideas about the material world, their personal connections with suppliers, whether vendors or producers, and their needs, and even depending on the connections they wanted to make with Indigenous people. Of course, there is a possibility that the probate inventories do not reflect the ratio of locally made to imported items accurately. Those compiling the inventories did not have in mind a study like the one I am doing, and they may not have recorded the origin of different things carefully or systematically. There must be errors in the data set simply because the goals of the people compiling the documents did not share my goals when making this study. Future research may help clarify this question further (Chapter 7).

Archaeological has provided results that support this conclusion. My previous work indicates that there is little association between greater wealth and ownership of imported pottery, or between poverty and the use of Indigenous ceramics in houses of Spanish colonizers (Rodríguez-Alegría 2003, 2005b, 2016a). Thus, the results are in line with the analysis of the probate inventories, in the sense that they do not show that wealth was the main factor determining consumption. People decided what to use depending on other factors, whether they were personal preference, personal connections, ideas about what was acceptable material culture to own and use, and others. To me, these results are empowering, in the sense that even if people do not know all the choices available to them, and even if people sometimes can have constrained choices, they can nevertheless have an active role in shaping and changing their material worlds.

I began this book with a brief summary of how scholars have changed their perception of Indigenous power in colonial central Mexico in the past few decades. Indigenous people have gone from being perceived as powerless, or as people who were equally under the overwhelming power of Spaniards, to a group in which some members had political authority in the colonial period (e.g., Chance 2008; Cline 1986; Haskett 1991; Lockhart 1992; Spores 1997). It is correct to say that many Indigenous people were poor and oppressed, including among them the enslaved men and women who appear in the probate inventories. But there were also Indigenous leaders, elites, lords, and kings in the colonial period, and they wielded power that Spanish colonizers had to reckon with (Lockhart 1992; Mundy 2015; Ruiz Medrano 2010; Ruiz Medrano and Kellogg 2010; Schroeder 1991; Spores 1997). Indigenous power and social stratification are important factors that shaped the material worlds of colonizers in different ways. In turn, as Indigenous people created some of the material goods that Spanish colonizers used, they actively shaped their own social worlds and lives.

Conquistadors recognized Indigenous lords and forged alliances with them as they moved across the landscape and into Tenochtitlan. Part of their negotiations involved gift exchange, and chairs like the ones found in the probate inventories are but one example of the things given as presents. They also exchanged food, and later on in the sixteenth century, I have argued, colonizers still recognized the power of Indigenous lords and sometimes invited them to eat and drink as they negotiated alliances, friendship, commercial transactions, and other social relations (Chapter 4). But the relationship of the material world and power among Indigenous people was not limited to gift exchanges between elites. Even commoner Indigenous people sometimes found incentives to produce goods for colonizers in the midst of colonial exploitation and oppression. Sometimes, Indigenous people created their own place in the world by making things for the Spanish. Folks who worked in constructing houses for colonizers often did very hard work and were exploited. Some of them moved up in their social hierarchies as they earned respect for their work in construction. Some used their position to control labor. Some learned how to make the kinds of goods that colonizers wanted, including clothes, shoes, furniture, and others, and sold those goods in markets. Others were exploited and abused as the enslaved people of the Spanish. Thus, the material world was related to power in different ways, in terms of consumption and production of things, and as people created their place in the world in part by creating material things.

These interactions are a reminder that we need to see the process of colonization not just as a clash between two ethnic groups, but also as a matter of alliance-building across ethnic lines. Whereas ethnic differences were important in shaping people's lived experiences, legal status, and in other ways, people were also attentive to class and status. They sometimes sought alliances that look less like ethnic solidarity and more like efforts at moving up in the social scale. My intention is to draw attention to the importance of class and social stratification in shaping colonialism and often in breaking down ethnic solidarity and cohesion. And of course, my main intention has been to show how people used, manipulated, and transformed the material world as part of their strategies to build and transform their social worlds.

Appendix 5.1

Appendix 5.1 Items of clothing in the probate inventories.

Item of clothing	Name in the documents	Additional comments	Frequency	%
clothes				
doublet				
	almilla		1	0.04
	corpezuelo	woman's doublet, although it does not appear in a woman's inventory	9	0.40
	corpezuelo de mujer	woman's doublet, although it does not appear in a woman's inventory	1	0.04
	cota		1	0.04
	cotaras		5	0.22
	jubón		77	3.43
	jubón de mujer	women's doublet	2	0.09
shirt				
	camisas		279	12.42
	camisas de hombre	men's shirt	2	0.09
	camisas de mujer	women's shirt	9	0.40
	camisilla	probably an undergarment with no sleeves	1	0.04
	cosete	perhaps a shirt with puffy sleeves	5	0.22
	cosete de frisa	perhaps a shirt with puffy sleeves	1	0.04
hose				
	calcetas		5	0.22
	calzas		109	4.85
	calzones		14	0.62
	calzones de calzas		1	0.04
	medias		150	6.68
	medias calzas		44	1.96

(*continued*)

Appendix 5.1 Continued

Item of clothing	Name in the documents	Additional comments	Frequency	%
	medias frisadas		6	0.27
	medias baquetas		7	0.31
	pierna	probable hose	4	0.18
	piernas	probable hose	24	1.07
	piernas de sábana	probable hose	1	0.04
	zaragüelles		38	1.69
	zaragüelles (carahueles)		1	0.04
	zaragüelles (carapueles)		1	0.04
smock				
	borriquete		2	0.09
	escaupil		1	0.04
	saya	appearing mostly in men's inventories, although Bernis (1962:18) describes it as women's clothes	17	0.76
	sayo		63	2.80
	sayo frailesco	friar's smock	1	0.04
	sayo y capa		5	0.22
	sayuela	appearing only in women's inventories, could refer to tunics or skirts	3	0.13
	sayuelo	short smock (waist or knee-length)	4	0.18
coat				
	ropa		10	0.45
cape				
	capa		45	2.00
	capa de luto	cape for mourning	1	0.04
	capa y sayo		3	0.13
	caparazon		1	0.04
	capeo		6	0.27
	caperuza	hood	8	0.36

Appendix 5.1 Continued

Item of clothing	Name in the documents	Additional comments	Frequency	%
	capeta		2	0.09
	capetillo		1	0.04
	capirote		2	0.09
	capirote con el hábito	cape with habit	1	0.04
	capirote de clérigo	cleric's cape	1	0.04
	capote		7	0.31
	capote con faja de terciopelo	with a velvet girdle	1	0.04
	capote con su hábito	cape with its habit	1	0.04
	capotillo		2	0.09
	capucha		1	0.04
	herreruelo	short cape	28	1.25
	herreruelo del oficio de carpintero	short cape for carpenters	1	0.04
	loba y capirote		1	0.04
jackets				
	chamarra	perhaps a rustic leather jacket	3	0.13
	chamarreta		1	0.04
	chamarrilla		3	0.13
	chaqueta		2	0.09
	turca		9	0.40
	turca (también llamada chamarra)		1	0.04
	turca con faja	jacket with girdle	1	0.04
	turco		6	0.27
footwear				
	alpargatas	rope-soled cloth shoes	22	0.98
	borceguíes	worn between the hose and the shoes, covering the foot and leg up to the knee	26	1.16
	borceguíes de mujer		10	0.45
boots	bota		2	0.09
	botas		62	2.76

(*continued*)

Appendix 5.1 Continued

Item of clothing	Name in the documents	Additional comments	Frequency	%
	botas de baqueta	soft leather boots	1	0.04
	botas de baqueta, par de	pair of soft leather boots	2	0.09
ankle boots	botines		71	3.16
leather sandals	cacles		1	0.04
	chapines	cork-soled leather sandals	49	2.18
	chapines, pares de	pairs of cork-soled leather sandals	60	2.67
slippers	pantufos		11	0.49
	servillas	worn between the hose and the shoes and covering only the foot	28	1.25
	xervillas de mujer		1	0.04
shoes	zapatos		124	5.52
	zapatos de baqueta	soft leather shoes	50	2.23
	zapatos y botines	shoes and low boots listed together	100	4.45
headwear				
caps				
	bonete	cap	25	1.11
	bonete de clérigo	cleric's cap	6	0.27
	bonete de orejas	cap with ear flaps	3	0.13
	bonete y paño de tocar	cap and handkerchief	1	0.04
	gorra		40	1.78
	toca		1	0.04
	toquilla de gorra		1	0.04
hats				0.00
	sombrero		45	2.00
	sombrericos		4	0.18
	sombrerillo		2	0.09
	sombrero y bonete	hat and bonnet	1	0.04
	sombrero y calzas viejas	hat and hose listed together	1	0.04

Appendix 5.1 Continued

Item of clothing	Name in the documents	Additional comments	Frequency	%
head covering				
	almaizal	gauze head covering associated with Moors	2	0.09
	paño de cabeza	head covering	8	0.36
indigenous clothing				
women's shirt	camisas de yndia		1	0.04
	huipil de india	indigenous blouse	1	0.04
	huipiles	indigenous blouse	6	0.27
loincloth	mastiles	from the Nahuatl *maxtle*	3	0.13
	naguas	skirts, slips, or perhaps other undergarments	40	1.78
miscellaneous				
some clothes	algo de ropa		1	0.04
could be soft leather shoes or socks	baquetas		15	0.67
skirt	basquiña		4	0.18
verdugado, garment worn under the skirt	berdugado		1	0.04
vest	coleto		5	0.22
codpieces	coquillas		6	0.27
bodice?	cuerpo		5	0.22
stole	estola		1	0.04
indeterminate	estopa		1	0.04
skirts	faldellín		45	2.00
gloves	guantes		128	5.70
gloves	guantes de aguja		1	0.04
sleeves	mangas		32	1.42
sleeves, puffy	mangas de cosete		1	0.04
sleeves and bodice	mangas y cuerpo		3	0.13
short sleeves	manguillas		3	0.13
veil or shawl	mantilla		12	0.53

(*continued*)

Appendix 5.1 Continued

Item of clothing	Name in the documents	Additional comments	Frequency	%
mantle	manto		26	1.16
mantle with cape	manto con capirote		1	0.04
mantle with cape and bodice	manto con su capirote y jubón		1	0.04
mantle with sleves and bodice	manto con sus mangas y capirote		1	0.04
women's mantle	manto de mujer		1	0.04
shawl	mantón		1	0.04
half sleeves	medias mangas		1	0.04
indeterminate leather item	medios cueros		9	0.40
dress	monjil		1	0.04
thigh covering	muslos		4	0.18
indeterminate leather items	pellejos		17	0.76
cases with clothing	petacas de ropa		2	0.09
belt	pretina		1	0.04
loose dress for women	ropa con hábito		1	0.04
rags	ropilla		28	1.25
rag	ropilla de mujer		1	0.04
rag and hose	ropilla e zaragüelles		1	0.04
rags	ropitas		18	0.80
robe	sotana		2	0.09
underskirt	vasquiña		9	0.40
dress	vestido		1	0.04
clothing	vestimento		1	0.04
Total			2246	100.00

Appendix 6.1

Appendix 6.1 Tools listed in the documents.

	Name in the documents	Number	%
anvil	vigornia	1	0.09
awl	punzón	4	0.34
awl	punzones	3	0.26
awl	punzabante	1	0.09
awl and pliers and hammer	punzabante y tenazas y martillo	1	0.09
awl for working leather	alesnas	2	0.17
awl for working leather	alezna	1	0.09
ax	hacha	10	0.86
bag	bolsa	4	0.34
bag, small	bolsilla	1	0.09
bars and hinges for door	barras y clavazón de puertas	1	0.09
bellows	fuelles	1	0.09
blacksmith horse	caballos de herrería	21	1.80
board	tablero	2	0.17
board for tailor	tablero para sastre	6	0.51
boards for curing leather	tablas de curar	400	34.31
boards for cutting boots	tablas para picar botas	3	0.26
box for raising dough	artesa	2	0.17
burnishing tool	bruñidor	1	0.09
chain for dog with a collar	cadena de perro con una collera	1	0.09
chain for horse	cadena de cavallo	1	0.09
chain for table	cadena de mesa	1	0.09
chisel and sticks that were in the case	escoplo y palos que estaban en la petaca	1	0.09
chisels	escoplos	10	0.86
compass	compás	5	0.43
compass	compases	1	0.09
copper measurements	medidas de cobre	2	0.17

(*continued*)

Appendix 6.1 Continued

	Name in the documents	Number	%
drill	barrena	30	2.57
drill and other small things	barrena y guarniciones viejas y menudencias	1	0.09
drills: small drills	barrenitas	5	0.43
dyeing stick	palo para teñir	1	0.09
file	lima	19	1.63
fish hooks	anzuelos de pescar	20	1.72
forge: parts for a forge	aderezo para fragua de herrero	1	0.09
gadget for distilling alcohol	alquitara	1	0.09
hacksaw	escofina	1	0.09
hacksaw	sierra	8	0.69
hacksaw for sandalmaker	escofinas de chapinero	8	0.69
hammer	martillo	8	0.69
hammer for locksmith	martillo de cerrajero	1	0.09
hammer for stone	martillo de peña	3	0.26
hammer for undetermined function	martillo destalador	1	0.09
handcuffs and hoop	esposas y argolla	1	0.09
handcuffs or manacles	esposas	1	0.09
hatchet	hachuela	6	0.51
hatchet for carpenter	azuela	2	0.17
hatchet: handheld hatchet	hachuela de mano	1	0.09
hoe	azadón	1	0.09
hoop	argolla	1	0.09
hoop for manger	argollas de pesebre	2	0.17
hoop with a nail	armellas	4	0.34
hoop, small	argollilla	2	0.17
iron	hierro	1	0.09
iron bars for construction	viguetas	9	0.77
iron for branding cattle	hierro de herrar ganado	1	0.09
iron for making buttonholes	hierro para hacer ojales	1	0.09
iron hoops	hierro en aros	1	0.09
iron in a sheet and unidentified item	hierro en plancha y bergajon	1	0.09
iron molds: bag of iron molds	bolsa con moldes de hierro	1	0.09
iron plow	reja de arado	1	0.09

Appendix 6.1 Continued

	Name in the documents	Number	%
iron things	cosas de fierro	1	0.09
iron, lead iron	planchuela de plomo	1	0.09
iron: small iron items	hierresillos	1	0.09
irons?	plachas	4	0.34
irons for cutting	hierros de picar	11	0.94
irons for cutting and chiseling	hierros de picar y cincelar	1	0.09
irons for sharpening	hierros para afilar	4	0.34
knife used by shoemakers	tranchetes	3	0.26
knives: box with 12 knives	caja de cuchillos con 12 piezas	1	0.09
knives: box with 2 knives	caja de cuchillos con 2 cuchillos	15	1.29
knives: box with 2 knives and a fork	caja de dos cuchillos y un tenedor	1	0.09
knives: box with a knife	caja con un cuchillo	2	0.17
knives: box with ink well and knives and scissors	caja con su tintero y tijeras y cuchillos	1	0.09
knives: box with knives	caja de cuchillos	6	0.51
knives: box with knives and scissors	caja con cuchillos y tijeras	1	0.09
knives: hiking knive with its sheath	cuchillo de monte en su vaina	1	0.09
knives: scribe's knife	cuchillo de escribanía	1	0.09
lead weight	plomada	1	0.09
lock for box	cerradura de caja	1	0.09
machete	machete	3	0.26
machete and box with 3 knives	machete y cajuela de 3 cuchillos	1	0.09
machetes with their sheaths	machetes con sus vainas	6	0.51
measuring stick	bara de medir	1	0.09
measuring stick	vara de medir	3	0.26
metal lighter?	pedernal de metal	2	0.17
mortar	almirez	3	0.26
mortar made of tin "with its tongue?"	almirez de acofar con su lengua	1	0.09
nails for horseshoes	clavos de herrar	1	0.09
nails: bag of nails	bolsilla con clavos	1	0.09

(*continued*)

Appendix 6.1 Continued

	Name in the documents	Number	%
needle for sewing sandals	almarada	2	0.17
needle: large needle	aguja grande	1	0.09
needle: small needle	aguja pequeña	1	0.09
needles	agujas	2	0.17
needles for shoemaker	agujas de zapatero	13	1.11
needles, bundle with 500 sewing needles	paño con 500 agujas de coser	1	0.09
needles, bundle with needles	paño con agujas	2	0.17
needles: bundles	envueltos de agujas	2	0.17
needles: small bundle	envueltillo con agujas	2	0.17
pewter	peltre	2	0.17
piece of mace reed	pedazo de caña maza	1	0.09
pin, large pin made of iron	perno de hierro	1	0.09
pin, paper with pins	papel con alfileres	1	0.09
pin, paper with pins	papel de alfileres	1	0.09
pincers	tenazas	10	0.86
pincers: pincers and box	tenacilla y caja	1	0.09
pincers: pointed pincers	tenacilla de punta	1	0.09
pliers	alicates	4	0.34
probe	tenta	1	0.09
protective tip for a cane or sword	contera	1	0.09
roaster	asador	5	0.43
roaster or grill, small	braserillo	1	0.09
ruler	regla	4	0.34
scale for weighting gold with a weight of 200	peso para pesar oro con un marco para pesar docientos	1	0.09
scale for weighting silver	peso de pesar plata	1	0.09
scale with its scales and eight weights	peso con su balanza y 8 marcos	1	0.09
scale with its weights	peso con sus balanzas	1	0.09
scale with several weights and missing one weight	peso con ciertas pesas y marco falto	1	0.09
scale with two weights	peso con dos marcos	1	0.09
scissors	tijeras	37	3.17
scissors for trimming candles	tijeras despabiladeras	1	0.09

Appendix 6.1 Continued

	Name in the documents	Number	%
scissors: barber's scissors	tijeras de barbero	11	0.94
scissors: tailor's scissors	tijeras de sastre	17	1.46
screw	tornillo	1	0.09
shoe tree	horna	203	17.41
shoehorn	calzador	3	0.26
small case with a knife and pliers and other cheap stuff	petaquilla de herramental en que ay un chichillo y unas tenazas y otras baratijas	1	0.09
small case with some nails and horseshoes and 4 chain links	petaquilla con ciertos clavos y herraduras y cuatro eslabones de cadenas	1	0.09
stone	piedra	18	1.54
stone "for something"	piedra de algo	2	0.17
stone: bags with pebbles	bolsitas con pedrezuelas	7	0.60
stone: block of rock	brazas de piedra	4	0.34
stone: block of rock, half	media braza de piedra	1	0.09
stone: block of rock, half	medias brazas	4	0.34
stone: sharpening stone	piedra amoladera	1	0.09
stone: slab and stone for sharpening	losa y piedra de amolar	1	0.09
surgery tools: bundle of surgeon's tools	atado de hierros de cirujano	1	0.09
surgery tools: case for surgeon	estuche de cirujano	1	0.09
syringe	jeringa	4	0.34
syringe	jeringuilla	4	0.34
table for carpenter	banco de carpintero	1	0.09
thimble	dedal	7	0.60
thimble: tailor's thimble	dedales de sastre	16	1.37
thimbles and buttons	dedales y botones	1	0.09
thimbles: small case with 7 thimbles and some ribbons	petaquita con 7 dedales y unas cintas de hiladillo	1	0.09
tin in a bundle, for applying tin	envoltorio de estaño para estañar	1	0.09
tool for separating threads	debanadera	1	0.09

(*continued*)

Appendix 6.1 Continued

	Name in the documents	Number	%
tool for shaping nails	clavera	1	0.09
tooling with 2 hammers and pliers and an awl and a small anvil	herramental con 2 martillo y unas tenazas y un punzabante y una vizornia chica	1	0.09
tooling with a hammer for anvil	herramental entero con su martillo de aterragar vigornia	1	0.09
tools "that I do not know what they are"	herramientas que no sé qué son	1	0.09
tools: case with tools	estuche con herramientas	25	2.14
triangular ruler	cartabon	1	0.09
two-handed hacksaw	sierra de dos manos	1	0.09
unknown, possibly a key	clave	1	0.09
weight for scale	peso de balanza	1	0.09
weight for scale and a weight	peso de balanzas con un marco para pesar	1	0.09
weight for scales and a weight of 4 pounds	peso de balanzas y marco de 4 lbs	1	0.09
weight for weighting gold with its weights and a small weight of 50 ps	peso de pesar oro con sus pesas y un marco pequeño de 50 ps	1	0.09
weight for weighting gold with missing weights and with three weights, one of 10, one of 5, and another of 2 pesos	peso de pesar oro con un marco de cien ps que le faltan pesas e con tres pesas una de a diez e otra de cinco e otra de dos pesos	1	0.09
weight, two pounds	marco de dos libras	1	0.09
wooden mallet	copador	1	0.09
Total		1166	100.00

Appendix 7.1

Appendix 7.1 Prices of shirts with an indicated origin.

Decedent	Date	Price in maravedís	Material	Origin	Quality	Source
Juan de Campomanes	1545	68.00		de la tierra	viejas	Cont. 197 N21(13)
Juan de Campomanes	1545	68.00		de la tierra	viejas	Cont. 197 N21(13)
Salvador Franco	1581	75.00	anglo		vieja desbaratada	Cont. 219, N2, R2
Salvador Franco	1581	112.50			vieja y rota	Cont. 219, N2, R2
María de Espinosa	1565	136.00			hechas pedazos	Cont. 210 N.1, R.68
Alonso García	1545	136			viejo	Cont. 197 N.21 5
Juan Díaz Caballero	1545	136.00		de la tierra	viejo	Cont. 197, N.21, 4
María de Espinosa	1565	136.00			hechas pedazos	Cont. 210 N.1, R.68
Alonso García	1545	136			viejo	Cont. 197 N.21 5
Juan Díaz Caballero	1545	136.00		de la tierra	viejo	Cont. 197, N.21, 4
Alonso García	1545	136			viejo	Cont. 197 N.21 5
Juan Díaz Caballero	1545	136.00		de la tierra	viejo	Cont. 197, N.21, 4
Salvador Franco	1581	150.00			vieja	Cont. 219, N.2, R.2
Pedro Vázquez	1545	170.00		de la tierra	cortada por coser con su hilo	Cont. 197 N.21(16)
Pedro de Madrid	1581	187.50			rotas	Cont. 219, N.2, R.8
Pedro de Madrid	1581	187.50			rotas	Cont. 219, N.2, R.8
Hernán Núñez Caballero	1586	187.50	ruán		cuellos de olanda	Cont. 232, N.2, R.3
Hernán Núñez Caballero	1586	187.50	ruán		cuellos de olanda	Cont. 232, N.2, R.3
Hernán Núñez Caballero	1586	187.50	ruán		cuellos de olanda	Cont. 232, N.2, R.3
Hernán Núñez Caballero	1586	187.50	ruán		cuellos de olanda	Cont. 232, N.2, R.3

(continued)

Appendix 7.1 Continued

Decedent	Date	Price in maravedís	Material	Origin	Quality	Source
Hernán Núñez Caballero	1586	187.50	ruán		cuellos de olanda	Cont. 232, N.2, R.3
Hernán Núñez Caballero	1586	187.50	ruán		cuellos de olanda	Cont. 232, N.2, R.3
Hernán Núñez Caballero	1586	187.50	ruán		cuellos de olanda	Cont. 232, N.2, R.3
Hernán Núñez Caballero	1586	187.50	ruán		cuellos de olanda	Cont. 232, N.2, R.3
Hernán Núñez Caballero	1586	187.50	ruán		cuellos de olanda	Cont. 232, N.2, R.3
Hernán Núñez Caballero	1586	187.50	ruán		cuellos de olanda	Cont. 232, N.2, R.3
Hernán Núñez Caballero	1586	187.50	ruán		cuellos de olanda	Cont. 232, N.2, R.3
Hernán Núñez Caballero	1586	187.50	ruán		cuellos de olanda	Cont. 232, N.2, R.3
Hernán Núñez Caballero	1586	187.50	ruán		cuellos de olanda	Cont. 232, N.2, R.3
Hernán Núñez Caballero	1586	187.50	ruán		cuellos de olanda	Cont. 232, N.2, R.3
Hernán Núñez Caballero	1586	187.50	ruán		cuellos de olanda	Cont. 232, N.2, R.3
Hernán Núñez Caballero	1586	187.50	ruán		cuellos de olanda	Cont. 232, N.2, R.3
Hernán Núñez Caballero	1586	187.50	ruán		cuellos de olanda	Cont. 232, N.2, R.3
Hernán Núñez Caballero	1586	187.50	ruán		cuellos de olanda	Cont. 232, N.2, R.3
Hernán Núñez Caballero	1586	187.50	ruán		cuellos de olanda	Cont. 232, N.2, R.3
Hernán Núñez Caballero	1586	187.50	ruán		cuellos de olanda	Cont. 232, N.2, R.3
Hernán Núñez Caballero	1586	187.50	ruán		cuellos de olanda	Cont. 232, N.2, R.3
Hernán Núñez Caballero	1586	187.50	ruán		cuellos de olanda	Cont. 232, N.2, R.3
Hernán Núñez Caballero	1586	187.50	ruán		cuellos de olanda	Cont. 232, N.2, R.3
Hernán Núñez Caballero	1586	187.50	ruán		cuellos de olanda	Cont. 232, N.2, R.3
Hernán Núñez Caballero	1586	187.50	ruán		cuellos de olanda	Cont. 232, N.2, R.3

Appendix 7.1 Continued

Decedent	Date	Price in maravedís	Material	Origin	Quality	Source
Hernán Núñez Caballero	1586	187.50	ruán		cuellos de olanda	Cont. 232, N.2, R.3
Hernán Núñez Caballero	1586	187.50	ruán		cuellos de olanda	Cont. 232, N.2, R.3
Hernán Núñez Caballero	1586	187.50	ruán		cuellos de olanda	Cont. 232, N.2, R.3
Hernán Núñez Caballero	1586	187.50	ruán		cuellos de olanda	Cont. 232, N.2, R.3
Hernán Núñez Caballero	1586	187.50	ruán		cuellos de olanda	Cont. 232, N.2, R.3
Bartolomé Hernández	1545	204.00	ruán	traído		Cont. 197 N.21 (22)
Bartolomé González	1545	239.00				Cont. 197, N.21, 2
Bartolomé González	1545	239.00				Cont. 197, N.21, 2
Juan de Campomanes	1545	272.00		Castilla	viejas	Cont. 197 N.21(13)
Juan de Campomanes	1545	272.00		Castilla	viejas	Cont. 197 N.21(13)
Juan Gómez	1578	337.50			vieja, remendada	Cont. 229, N.1, R.5
Bartolomé Hernández	1545	340.00	ruán	traído	viejas y la una rota	Cont. 197 N.21 (22)
Bartolomé Hernández	1545	340.00	ruán	traído	viejas y la una rota	Cont. 197 N.21 (22)
Bartolomé Hernández	1545	340.00	ruán	traído	viejas y la una rota	Cont. 197 N.21 (22)
Francisco de Sigüenza	1532	450.00		de la tierra		Cont. 197, N.6
Francisco de Sigüenza	1532	450.00		de la tierra		Cont. 197, N.6
Francisco de Sigüenza	1532	450.00		de la tierra		Cont. 197, N.6
Francisco de Sigüenza	1532	450.00		de la tierra		Cont. 197, N.6
Martín Carrasco	1545	453.33	ruán	Castilla	nuevas y viejas	Cont. 197 N.21 (10)
Martín Carrasco	1545	453.33	ruán	Castilla	nuevas y viejas	Cont. 197 N.21 (10)

(*continued*)

Appendix 7.1 Continued

Decedent	Date	Price in maravedís	Material	Origin	Quality	Source
Martín Carrasco	1545	453.33	ruán	Castilla	nuevas y viejas	Cont. 197 N.21 (10)
Martín Carrasco	1545	453.33	ruán	Castilla	nuevas y viejas	Cont. 197 N.21 (10)
Martín Carrasco	1545	453.33	ruán	Castilla	nuevas y viejas	Cont. 197 N.21 (10)
Martín Carrasco	1545	453.33	ruán	Castilla	nuevas y viejas	Cont. 197 N.21 (10)
Miguel Rodríguez	1568	475.00				Cont. 208A, N.2, R.1
Miguel Rodríguez	1568	475.00				Cont. 208A, N.2, R.1
Miguel Rodríguez	1568	475.00				Cont. 208A, N.2, R.1
Pedro de Madrid	1581	487.50	traído			Cont. 219, N.2, R.8
Salvador Franco	1581	525.00	traído			Cont. 219, N.2, R.2
Hernán Núñez Caballero	1586	615.00			cuellos de ruán	Cont. 232, N.2, R.3
Hernán Núñez Caballero	1586	615.00			cuellos de ruán	Cont. 232, N.2, R.3
Hernán Núñez Caballero	1586	615.00			cuellos de ruán	Cont. 232, N.2, R.3
Hernán Núñez Caballero	1586	615.00			cuellos de ruán	Cont. 232, N.2, R.3
Juan Gómez	1578	637.50			vieja	Cont. 229, N.1, R.5
Juan Gómez	1578	637.50	traído			Cont. 229, N.1, R.5
Salvador Franco	1581	637.50				Cont. 219, N.2, R.2
Juan de Campomanes	1545	646.00	9 de ruan basto (2 de ellas labradas de negro) y las otras 6 de presila	Castilla	nuevas	Cont. 197 N.21(13)
Juan de Campomanes	1545	646.00	9 de ruan basto (2 de ellas labradas de negro) y las otras 6 de presila	Castilla	nuevas	Cont. 197 N.21(13)

Appendix 7.1 Continued

Decedent	Date	Price in maravedís	Material	Origin	Quality	Source
Juan de Campomanes	1545	646.00	9 de ruan basto (2 de ellas labradas de negro) y las otras 6 de presila	Castilla	nuevas	Cont. 197 N.21(13)
Juan de Campomanes	1545	646.00	9 de ruan basto (2 de ellas labradas de negro) y las otras 6 de presila	Castilla	nuevas	Cont. 197 N.21(13)
Juan de Campomanes	1545	646.00	9 de ruan basto (2 de ellas labradas de negro) y las otras 6 de presila	Castilla	nuevas	Cont. 197 N.21(13)
Juan de Campomanes	1545	646.00	9 de ruan basto (2 de ellas labradas de negro) y las otras 6 de presila	Castilla	nuevas	Cont. 197 N.21(13)
Juan de Campomanes	1545	646.00	9 de ruan basto (2 de ellas labradas de negro) y las otras 6 de presila	Castilla	nuevas	Cont. 197 N.21(13)
Juan de Campomanes	1545	646.00	9 de ruan basto (2 de ellas labradas de negro) y las otras 6 de presila	Castilla	nuevas	Cont. 197 N.21(13)
Juan de Campomanes	1545	646.00	9 de ruan basto (2 de ellas labradas de negro) y las otras 6 de presila	Castilla	nuevas	Cont. 197 N.21(13)

(*continued*)

Appendix 7.1 Continued

Decedent	Date	Price in maravedís	Material	Origin	Quality	Source
Juan de Campomanes	1545	646.00	9 de ruan basto (2 de ellas labradas de negro) y las otras 6 de presila	Castilla	nuevas	Cont. 197 N.21(13)
Juan de Campomanes	1545	646.00	9 de ruan basto (2 de ellas labradas de negro) y las otras 6 de presila	Castilla	nuevas	Cont. 197 N.21(13)
Juan de Campomanes	1545	646.00	9 de ruan basto (2 de ellas labradas de negro) y las otras 6 de presila	Castilla	nuevas	Cont. 197 N.21(13)
Juan de Campomanes	1545	646.00	9 de ruan basto (2 de ellas labradas de negro) y las otras 6 de presila	Castilla	nuevas	Cont. 197 N.21(13)
Juan de Campomanes	1545	646.00	9 de ruan basto (2 de ellas labradas de negro) y las otras 6 de presila	Castilla	nuevas	Cont. 197 N.21(13)
Juan de Campomanes	1545	646.00	9 de ruan basto (2 de ellas labradas de negro) y las otras 6 de presila	Castilla	nuevas	Cont. 197 N.21(13)
Andrés de Plasencia	1560	675.00	ruán	traída		Cont. 473, N.2, R.1, 1
Bartolomé González	1545	695.45	ruán			Cont. 197, N.21, 2
Bartolomé González	1545	695.45	ruán			Cont. 197, N.21, 2

Appendix 7.1 Continued

Decedent	Date	Price in maravedís	Material	Origin	Quality	Source
Bartolomé González	1545	695.45	ruán			Cont. 197, N.21, 2
Bartolomé González	1545	695.45	ruán			Cont. 197, N.21, 2
Bartolomé González	1545	695.45	ruán			Cont. 197, N.21, 2
Bartolomé González	1545	695.45	ruán			Cont. 197, N.21, 2
Bartolomé González	1545	695.45	ruán			Cont. 197, N.21, 2
Bartolomé González	1545	695.45	ruán			Cont. 197, N.21, 2
Bartolomé González	1545	695.45	ruán			Cont. 197, N.21, 2
Bartolomé González	1545	695.45	ruán			Cont. 197, N.21, 2
Bartolomé González	1545	695.45	ruán			Cont. 197, N.21, 2
Andrés de Plasencia	1560	787.50			vieja	Cont. 473, N.2, R.1, 1
Andrés de Plasencia	1560	787.50			vieja	Cont. 473, N.2, R.1, 1
Juana Bautista	1581	875.00		traído		Cont. 219, N.2, R.3
Juana Bautista	1581	875.00		traído		Cont. 219, N.2, R.3
Juana Bautista	1581	875.00		traído		Cont. 219, N.2, R.3
Andrés de Plasencia	1560	900.00			vieja	Cont. 473, N.2, R.1, 1
Juan Gómez	1578	900.00	lienzo	de Olanda	casero	Cont. 229, N.1, R.5
Salvador Franco	1581	1050.00				Cont. 219, N.2, R.2
Francisco de Sigüenza	1532	1,237.50			labradas	Cont. 197, N.6
Francisco de Sigüenza	1532	1,237.50			labradas	Cont. 197, N.6
Andrés de Plasencia	1560	1,537.50	ruán	traída	labrada	Cont. 473, N.2, R.1, 1
Andrés de Plasencia	1560	2,550.00	seda		labrada nueva	Cont. 473, N.2, R.1, 1
Martín Carrasco	1545	3,400.00		de la tierra		Cont. 197 N.21 (10)
Martín Carrasco	1545	3,400.00		de la tierra		Cont. 197 N.21 (10)

References

All probate inventories consulted are at the Archivo General de Indias in the Contratación branch. The Actas de Cabildo are at the Archivo Histórico del Ayuntamiento in Mexico City.

Acuto, Félix A. 2005 The Materiality of Inka Domination: Landscape, Spectacle, Memory, and Ancestors. In *Global Archaeological Theory: Contextual Voices and Contemporary Thoughts*, edited by Pedro Paulo Funari, Andrés Zarankin, and Emily Stovel, pp. 211–236. Kluwer Academic/Plenum, New York.

Aguilera, Carmen 1985 Mueble Prehispánico. In *El mueble mexicano. Historia, evolución e influencias*, edited by Aguilera, Carmen, Elisa Vargas Lugo, Marita Martínez del Río de Redo, Jorge Loyzaga, Luis Ortiz Macedo, Teresa Castelló Iturbide, Manuel Carballo, Ma. Cecilia Martínez López, and Fernando Sánchez Martínez, pp. 13–24. Fondo Cultural Banamex, Mexico City.

Aguiló Alonso, María Paz 1993 *El Mueble en España, Siglos XVI-XVII*. Consejo Superior de Investigaciones Científicas. Ediciones Antiqvaria S.A., Madrid.

Aguirre Beltrán, Gonzalo 1981 *La población negra de México: estudio etnohistórico*. Centro de Estudios Históricos del Agrarismo en México, Mexico.

Alexander, Rani T. (editor) 2019 *Technology and Tradition in Mesoamerica after the Spanish Invasion: Archaeological Perspectives*. University of New Mexico Press, Tucson.

Amaral, Adela 2017 Social Geographies, the Practice of Marronage, and the Archaeology of Absence in Colonial Mexico. *Archaeological Dialogues* 24(2):207–223.

Anawalt, Patricia R. 1981 *Indian Clothing before Cortés: Mesoamerican Costumes from the Codices*. University of Oklahoma Press, Norman.

Appadurai, Arjun (editor) 1986 *The Social Life of Things: Commodities in Cultural Perspective*. Cambridge University Press, Cambridge.

Artes de México, #12. Palacios de la Nueva España: sus tesoros interiores. n.a. 1991 Stable URL: https://www.jstor.org/stable/24326889.

Barlow, Robert H. 1951 E1 Códice de los alfareros de Cuauhtitlan. *Revista Mexicana de Estudios Antropológicos* XII:5–13.

Barrera Rivera, José Álvaro 1999 El rescate arqueológico en la Catedral y el Sagrario Metropolitanos de la Ciudad de México (1991–1996). In *Excavaciones en la Catedral y el Sagrario Metropolitanos. Programa de Arqueología Urbana,* edited by Eduardo Matos Moctezuma, pp. 21–30. Instituto Nacional de Antropología e Historia, Mexico City.

Barrera Rivera, José Álvaro, and Alicia Islas Domínguez 2018 *Arqueología urbana en la reconstrucción arquitectónica del Recinto Sagrado de Tenochtitlan.* Instituto Nacional de Antropología e Historia, Mexico City.

Barrera Rodríguez, Raúl 2002 El antiguo Palacio de Odontología de la UNAM a través de su espacio y tiempo arqueológicos. B.A. Thesis, Escuela Nacional de Antropología e Historia, Mexico City.

Barrera Rodríguez, Raúl 2003 Antiguo palacio de odontología de la UNAM: crónica de un rescate arqueológico. In *Excavaciones del Programa de Arqueología Urbana.* Colección

Científica 452, edited by Eduardo Matos Moctezuma, pp. 173–190. Instituto Nacional de Antropología e Historia, Mexico City.

Barrera Rodríguez, Raúl 2006 Excavaciones recientes en el recinto sagrado de Tenochtitlan. In *Arqueología e historia del Centro de México. Homenaje a Eduardo Matos Moctezuma*, edited by Leonardo López Luján, David Carrasco, and Lourdes Cué, pp. 273–289. Instituto Nacional de Antropología e Historia, Mexico City.

Barrera Rodríguez, Raúl and José María García Guerrero 2017 Hallazgos recientes en el Nacional Monte de Piedad, Centro Histórico de la Ciudad de México. *Arqueología Mexicana* 28(163):34–41.

Barrera Rodríguez, Raúl, and Gabino López Arenas 2008 Hallazgos en el recinto ceremonial de Tenochtitlan. *Arqueología Mexicana* 93:18–25.

Barrera Rodríguez, Raúl, Gabino López Arenas, Cristina Cuevas Carpintero, Rocío Morales Sánchez, Ulises Lina Sánchez, and Alejandro Funes Salazar 2008 *Informe final del salvamento arqueológico en el predio de Donceles No. 97, Centro Histórico de la Ciudad de México (Centro Cultural de España en México). Volumen I.* Programa de Arqueología Urbana, Templo Mayor, Instituto Nacional de Antropología e Historia, Mexico City.

Barrera Rodríguez, Raúl, and Roberto Martínez Meza 2010 Informe final del proyecto "Programa de Investigación Frente Principal del Templo Mayor de Tenochtitlán (Plaza Manuel Gamio)." Report submitted to the Instituto Nacional de Antropología e Historia, Mexico City.

Barrera Rodríguez, Raúl, Roberto Martínez Meza, Rocío Morales Sánches, and Lorena Vázquez Vallin 2012 Espacios rituales frente al Templo Mayor de Tenochtitlan. *Arqueología Mexicana* 116:18–23.

Barrera Rodríguez, Raúl, Lorena Medina Martínez, and Ricardo Rivera García 1999 *Excavaciones en el patio posterior del exconvento de Santa Teresa La Antigua.* Archaeological report presented to the Programa de Arqueología Urbana, Museo del Templo Mayor, Instituto Nacional de Antropología e Historia, Mexico City.

Barrera Rodríguez, Raúl, and Flor Ma. Rivas García 2003 Rescate arqueológico en el inmueble de la Librería Porrúa, Argentina y Justo Sierra. In *Excavaciones del Programa de Arqueología Urbana*, Colección Científica No. 452, edited by Eduardo Matos Moctezuma, pp. 155–170. Instituto Nacional de Antropología e Historia, Mexico City.

Barrera Rodríguez, Raúl, Ricardo Rivera García, and Lorena Medina Martínez 2003 Excavaciones en el patio posterior del convento de Santa Teresa la Antigua. In *Excavaciones del Programa de Arqueología Urbana*, Colección Científica 452, edited by Eduardo Matos Moctezuma, pp. 197–211. Instituto Nacional de Antropología e Historia, Mexico City.

Bauer, Arnold J. 2001 *Goods, Power, History: Latin America's Material Culture.* Cambridge University Press, Cambridge.

Beaule, Christine 2015 Andean clothing, gender and indigeneity in Colonial Period Latin America. *Critical Studies in Men's Fashion* 2(1):55–73.

Benavente, Fray Toribio de 1985 *Historia de los indios de la Nueva España*, edited by Claudio Esteva. Información y Revistas, SA, Madrid.

Benítez, Fernando 1993 La vida palaciega. *Artes de Mexico: Centro Historico de la Ciudad de México* 1:31–34.

Benítez, José R. 1933 *Alonso García Bravo. Planeador de la Ciudad De México y su Primer Director de Obras Públicas.* Compañía de Fomento y Urbanización, Mexico City.

Bennett, Deb and Robert S. Hoffmann 1991 Ranching in the New World. In *Seeds of Change: Five Hundred Years since Columbus*, edited by Herman J. Viola and Carolyn Margolis, pp. 90–111. Smithsonian, Washington.

Bennett, Herman L. 2003 *Africans in Colonial Mexico: Absolutism, Christianity, and Afro-Creole Consciousness, 1570–1640*. Indiana University Press, Bloomington.

Bérchez, Joaquín 1999a Pinturas del gobernador, alcalde y regidores de México ("Códice Osuna"). In *Los Siglos de Oro en los Virreinatos de América 1550–1700*, edited by Sociedad Estatal para la Conmemoración de los Centenarios de Felipe II y Carlos V, pp. 243–245. Ediciones el Viso, Madrid.

Bérchez, Joaquín 1999b Maqueta de la catedral de México. In *Los Siglos de Oro en los Virreinatos de América 1550–1700*, edited by Sociedad Estatal para la Conmemoración de los Centenarios de Felipe II y Carlos V, pp. 226–233. Ediciones el Viso, Madrid.

Berdan, Frances F. 2014 *Aztec Archaeology and Ethnohistory*. Cambridge University Press, Cambridge.

Berdan, Frances F. 2017 Structure of the Triple Alliance. In *The Oxford Handbook of the Aztecs*, edited by Deborah L. Nichols and Enrique Rodríguez-Alegría, pp. 439–450. Oxford University Press, Oxford.

Berdan, Frances F. and Patricia Rieff Anawalt (editors) 1992 *The Essential Codex Mendoza*. University of California, Berkeley.

Bernis, Carmen 1962 *La Indumentaria Española en Tiempos de Carlos V*. Instituto Diego Velázquez, Madrid.

Biskowski, Martin 2000 Maize Preparation and the Aztec Subsistence Economy. *Ancient Mesoamerica* 11:293–306.

Blum, Dilys E. 2006 Textiles in Colonial Latin America. In *The Arts in Latin America 1492–1820*, organized by Joseph J. Rishel with Suzanne Stratton-Pruitt, pp. 146–154. Yale, New Haven.

Boils Morales, Guillermo 2015 El hierro al inicio de la Nueva España. *Boletín de Monumentos Históricos* 35:70–99.

Boone, Elizabeth Hill 2000 *Stories in Red and Black: Pictorial Histories of the Aztecs and Mixtecs*. University of Texas, Austin.

Boone, Elizabeth Hill 2017 Seeking Indianness: Christoph Weiditz, the Aztecs, and feathered Amerindians. *Colonial Latin American Review*, 26(1):39–61, DOI: 10.1080/ 10609164.2017.1287323

Bourdieu, Pierre 1977 *Outline of a Theory of Practice*. University Press, Cambridge.

Bourdieu, Pierre 1984 *Distinction: A Social Critique of the Judgement of Taste*. Harvard, Cambridge.

Boyd-Bowman, Peter 1968 *Indice geobiográfico de cuarentamil pobladores españoles de América en el siglo XVI*. Editorial Jus, Mexico City.

Braun, David P. 1983 Pots as Tools. In *Archaeological Hammers and Theories*, edited by James A. Moore and Arthur S. Keene, pp. 107–134. Academic Press, New York.

Bray, Warwick 1997 Metallurgy and Anthropology: Two Studies from Prehispanic America. *Boletín Museo del Oro* 42:37–55.

Bruhn de Hoffmeyer, Ada 1986 Las Armas de los conquistadores. Las armas de los Aztecas. *Gladius* XVII:5–56.

Brumfiel, Elizabeth M. 1991 Weaving and Cooking: Women's Production in Aztec Mexico. In *Engendering Archaeology: Women and Prehistory*, edited by Joan M. Gero and Margaret W. Conkey, pp. 224–251. Basil Blackwell, Cambridge.

Brumfiel, Elizabeth M. 1992 Distinguished Lecture in Archeology: Breaking and Entering the Ecosystem - Gender, Class, and Faction Steal the Show. *American Anthropologist* 94(3):551–567. Stable URL: http://www.jstor.org/stable/680562

Brumfiel, Elizabeth M. 1996 The Quality of Tribute Cloth: The Place of Evidence in Archaeological Argument. *American Antiquity* 61(3):456–462.

Brumfiel, Elizabeth M. (editor) 2005 *Production and Power at Postclassic Xaltocan*. University of Pittsburgh, Pittsburgh.

Burgos Villanueva, Francisco Rafael 1995 *El Olimpo: Un Predio Colonial en el Lado Poniente de la Plaza Mayor de Mérida, Yucatán, y Análisis Cerámico Comparativo*. Instituto Nacional de Antropología e Historia, Mexico City.

Burzio, Humberto F. 1958 *Diccionario de la Moneda Hispanoamericana*, 3 vols. Fondo Histórico y Bibliográfico José Toribio Medina, Santiago de Chile.

Calnek, Edward E. 1974 Conjunto urbano y modelo residencial en Tenochtitlan. In *Ensayos sobre el desarrollo urbano de México*, edited by Woodrow Borah, pp. 11–65. Secretaría de Educación Pública, Mexico City.

Calnek, Edward E. 2003 Tenochtitlan/Tlatelolco: The Natural History of a City. In *Urbanism in Mesoamerica*, Vol. 1, edited by William T. Sanders, Ana G. Mastache, and Robert H. Cobean, pp. 149–202. Instituto Nacional de Antropología e Historia and Pennsylvania State University, Mexico City and University Park.

Canterla, Francisco y Martin de Tovar 1984 Autos de bienes de onubenses fallecidos en la empresa de América en el siglo XVI. In *Actas de las II Jornadas de Andalucía y América*, pp. 227–248. Escuela de Estudios Hispano-Americanos, Seville.

Cañeque, Alejandro 2004 De sillas y almohadones o de la naturaleza ritual del poder en la Nueva España de los siglos xvi y xvii. *Revista de Indias* LXIV(232):609–634.

Caplan, Allison 2013 "Cada uno en su bolsa llevar lo que cien indios no llevarían": Mexica Resistance and the Shape of Currency in New Spain, 1542–1552. *American Journal of Numismatics* 25:333–356. Stable URL: http://www.jstor.org/stable/43580634

Carballo, David 2011 Advances in the Household Archaeology of Highland Mesoamerica. *Journal of Archaeological Research* 19(2):133–189.

Card, Jeb J. and William R. Fowler Jr. 2019 Technological and Cultural Change during the Conquest Period at Ciudad Vieja, El Salvador. In *Technology and Tradition in Mesoamerica after the Spanish Invasion: Archaeological Perspectives*, edited by Rani T. Alexander, pp. 189–206. University of New Mexico, Tucson.

Carrera, Magali 2003 *Imagining Identity in New Spain: Race, Lineage, and the Colonial Body in Portraiture and Casta Paintings*. University of Texas, Austin.

Carrillo, Abelardo and Abelardo Gariel 1969 Notas sobre el mueble precortesiano. *Artes de México: El Mueble Mexicano* 118:6–7.

Cervera Obregón, Marco Antonio 2014 El armamento hispano-mexica. *Desperta Ferro* 12:38–42.

Céspedes del Castillo, G. 1994 La implantación en Indias del sistema monetario castellano. In *Factores de diferenciación e instancias integradoras en la experiencia del mundo iberoamericano: actas: Madrid, 8 al 14 de noviembre de 1992*, pp.151–174. Real Academia de la Historia, Madrid.

Chance, John K. 2008 Indigenous Ethnicity in Colonial Central Mexico. In *Ethnic Identity in Nahua Mesoamerica*, by Frances F. Berdan, John K. Chance, Alan R. Sandstrom, Barbara L. Stark, James Taggart, and Emily Umberger, pp. 133–149. University of Utah, Salt Lake City.

Chapa, Arturo (editor) 2015 *La Acuñación en México: 1535–2015*. Secretaría de Hacienda y Crédito Público, and Casa de Moneda de México, Mexico City.

Charlton, Thomas H. 1968 Post-Conquest Aztec Ceramics: Implications for Archaeological Interpretation. *The Florida Anthropologist* 21:96–101.

Charlton, Thomas H. 1970 El Valle de Teotihuacan: cerámica y patrones de asentamiento, 1520–1969. *Boletín del Instituto Nacional de Antropología e Historia* 41:15–23.

Charlton, Thomas H. 1976 Contemporary Mexican Ceramics: A View from the Past. *Man* 11(4):517–525.

Charlton, Thomas H. 1979 The Aztec-Early Colonial Transition in the Teotihuacan Valley. *Acts of the XLIV International Congress of Americanists, Paris, 1976* IXb:203–208.

Charlton, Thomas H. 1996 Early Colonial Period Ceramics: Decorated Red Ware and Orange Ware Types of the Rural Otumba Aztec Ceramic Complex. In *Arqueología Mesoamericana: homenaje a William Sanders*, edited by Guadalupe Mastache, Jeff Parsons, M. Serra and Robert Santley, pp. 461–479. Instituto Nacional de Antropología e Historia, Mexico City.

Charlton, Thomas H., and Patricia Fournier 2011 Pots and Plots: The Multiple Roles of Early Colonial Red Wares in the Basin of Mexico (Identity, Resistance, Negotiation, Accommodation, Aesthetic Creativity, or Just Plain Economics?) In *Rethinking the Archaeology of Resistance to Spanish Colonialism in the Americas*, edited by Matthew Liebmann and Melissa S. Murphy, pp. 127–148. SAR, Santa Fe.

Charlton, Thomas H., Patricia Fournier, and J. Cervantes 1995 La cerámica del periodo Colonial Temprano en Tlatelolco: el caso de la Loza Roja Bruñida. In *Presencias y Encuentros, Investigaciones Arqueológicas de Salvamento*, pp. 135–155. Dirección de Salvamento Arqueológico, Instituto Nacional de Antropología e Historia, Mexico City.

Charlton, Thomas H., and Cynthia L. Otis Charlton 1994 Aztec Craft Production in Otumba, 1470–1570: Reflections of a Changing World. In *Chipping Away on Earth: Studies in Prehispanic and Colonial Mexico in Honor of Arthur J. O. Anderson and Charles E. Dibble*, edited by Eloise Quinones Keber, with the assistance of Susan Schroeder and Frederic Hicks, pp. 241–251. Labyrinthos, Lancaster.

Charlton, Thomas H., Cynthia Otis Charlton, Deborah L. Nichols, and Hector Neff 2008 Aztec Otumba, AD 1200–1600: Patterns of the Production, Distribution, and Consumption of Ceramic Products. In *Pottery Economics in Mesoamerica*, edited by Christopher A. Pool and George J. Bey III, pp. 237–270. University of Arizona, Tucson.

Chaussard, E., E. Havazli, H. Fattahi, E. Cabral-Cano, D. Solano-Rojas 2021 Over a Century of Sinking in Mexico City: No Hope for Significant Elevation and Storage Capacity Recovery. *Journal of Geophysical Research: Solid Earth* 126(4). https://doi.org/10.1029/2020JB020648

Chávez, Ximena, Alejandra Aguirre, Ana Miramontes, and Erika Robles 2010 Los cuchillos ataviados de la ofrenda 125. Templo Mayor de Tenochtitlan. *Arqueología Mexicana* XVII(103):70–75.

Clark, John 1989 Obsidian: The Primary Mesoamerican Sources. In *La Obsidiana en Mesoamerica*, edited by Margarita Gaxiola and John E. Clark, pp. 299–319. Instituto Nacional de Antropología e Historia, Mexico City.

Clark, John 2012 The Domestication of Stone in Mesoamerica. In *The Oxford Handbook of Mesoamerican Archaeology*, edited by Deborah L. Nichols and Christopher A. Pool, pp. 599–606. Oxford.

Cline, S. L. 1986 *Colonial Culhuacan, 1580–1600: A Social History of an Aztec Town.* University of New Mexico, Albuquerque.

Cochran, Matthew D. and Mary C. Beaudry 2006 Material culture studies and historical archaeology. In *The Cambridge Companion to Historical Archaeology,* edited by Dan Hicks and Mary C. Beaudry, pp. 191–204. Cambridge University Press, Cambridge.

Códice Yanhuitlán 1550 http://bdmx.mx/documento/codice-yanhuitlan

Coe, Sophie D. 1993 *America's First Cuisines.* University of Texas, Austin.

Cope, R. Douglas 1994 *The Limits of Racial Domination: Plebeian Society in Colonial Mexico City, 1660–1720.* University of Wisconsin, Madison.

Corcoran-Tadd, Noa 2016 "Is this the Gold that You Eat?" Coins, Entanglement, and Early Colonial Orderings in the Andes (AD 1532–ca. 1650). In *Archaeology of Entanglement*, edited by Lindsay Der and Francesca Fernandini, pp. 49–76. Left Coast Press, Walnut Creek.

Cortés, Hernán 2003 *Cartas de Relación,* edited by Mario Hernández Sánchez-Barba. S.L. Dastin, Madrid.

Curtin, Philip 1969 *The Atlantic Slave Trade: A Census.* University of Wisconsin, Madison.

Dávila Corona, Rosa María, Montserrat Durán Pujol, and Máximo García Fernández 2004 *Diccionario Histórico de Telas y Tejidos Castellano-Catalán.* Junta de Castilla y León, Varona.

de Gante, Pablo C. 1954 *La Arquitectura de México en el siglo XVI.* Editorial Porrúa, Mexico City.

De Lucia, Kristin 2013 Domestic Economies and Regional Transition: Household Multicrafting and Lake Exploitation in Pre-Aztec Central Mexico. *Journal of Anthropological Archaeology* 32:353–367.

De Lucia, Kristin 2017 Households in the Aztec Empire. In *The Oxford Handbook of the Aztecs*, edited by Deborah L. Nichols and Enrique Rodríguez-Alegría, pp. 247–260. Oxford.

De Lucia, Kristin 2018 Style, Memory, and the Production of History: Aztec Pottery and the Materialization of a Toltec Legacy. *Current Anthropology* 59:741–764.

De Lucia, Kristin, Matthew T. Boulanger, and Michael D. Glascock 2020 Small-scale Household Ceramic Production: Neutron Activation Analysis of Plain and Decorated Ceramics from Pre-Aztec Xaltocan, Mexico. *Ancient Mesoamerica* 1–19. DOI: https://doi.org/10.1017/S0956536120000036.

Deagan, Kathleen 1983 *Spanish St. Augustine: The Archaeology of a Colonial Creole Community.* Academic Press, New York.

Deagan, Kathleen 1987 *Artifacts of the Spanish Colonies of Florida and the Caribbean 1500–1800, Vol. I: Ceramics, Glassware, and Beads.* Smithsonian, Washington.

Deagan, Kathleen 1995 *Puerto Real: The Archaeology of a Sixteenth-Century Spanish Town in Hispaniola.* University Press of Florida, Tallahassee.

Deagan, Kathleen 1998 Transculturation and Spanish American Ethnogenesis: The Archaeological Legacy of the Quincentenary, In *Studies in Culture Contact: Interaction, Culture Change, and Archaeology,* Occasional Paper 25, edited by James G. Cusick, pp. 126–145. Center for Archaeological Investigations, Southern Illinois University, Carbondale.

Deagan, Kathleen 2001 Dynamics of imperial adjustment in Spanish America: ideology and social integration. In *Empires: Perspectives from Archaeology and History*, edited by Susan E. Alcock, Terence N. D'Altroy, Kathleen D. Morrison, and Carla M. Sinopoli, pp. 179–194. Cambridge.

Dean, Carolyn and Dana Leibsohn 2003 Hybridity and its Discontents: Considering Visual Culture in Colonial Spanish America. *Colonial Latin American Review* 12(1):5–35.

Del Olmo Frese, Laura 2003 Conservación arqueológica en el edificio del Antiguo Arzobispado. In *Excavaciones del Programa de Arqueología Urbana*. Colección Científica 452, edited by Eduardo Matos Moctezuma, pp. 215–226. Instituto Nacional de Antropología e Historia, Mexico City.

Del Valle, Ivonne 2009 On Shaky Ground: Hydraulics, State Formation, and Colonialism in Sixteenth-Century Mexico. *Hispanic Review* 77(2):197–220. Stable URL: http://www.jstor.org/stable/40541356

DeMarrais, Elizabeth, Luis Jaime Castillo, and Timothy Earle 1996 Ideology, Materialization, and Power Strategies. *Current Anthropology* 37(1):15–31. Stable URL: http://www.jstor.org/stable/2744153

Díaz del Castillo, Bernal 1942 *Historia verdadera de la conquista de la Nueva España*. Espasa-Calpe, Madrid.

Díaz del Castillo, Bernal 1966 *The True History of the Conquest of Mexico*. March of America facsimile series, no. 7. Translated from the original Spanish by Maurice Keatinge, Esq. University Microfilms, Ann Arbor.

Diel, Lori Boornazian 2018 *The Codex Mexicanus: A Guide to Life in Late Sixteenth-Century New Spain*. University of Texas, Austin.

Dobres, Marcia-Anne 2000 *Technology and Social Agency: Outlining a Practice Framework for Archaeology*. Wiley-Blackwell, Malden.

Dobres, Marcia-Anne and John E. Robb 2000 Agency in archaeology: Paradigm or platitude? In *Agency in Archaeology*, edited by Marcia-Anne Dobres and John E. Robb, pp. 3–17. Routledge, London.

Durán, Fray Diego 1994 *The History of the Indies of New Spain*. Translated by Doris Heyden. University of Oklahoma, Norman.

Earle, Rebecca 2012 *The Body of the Conquistador*. Cambridge.

Edgerton, Samuel Y. 2001 *Theaters of Conversion: Religious Architecture and Indian Artisans in Colonial Mexico*. University of New Mexico, Albuquerque.

Enriquez, María Dolores 1951 *El mueble español en los siglos XV, XVI, Y XVII*. Afrodisio Aguado, Madrid.

Evans, Susan Toby 2005 The Aztec Palace under Spanish Rule: Disk Motifs in the Mapa de México de 1550 (Uppsala Map or Mapa de Santa Cruz). In *The Postclassic to Spanish-Era Transition in Mesoamerica*, edited by Susan Kepecs and Rani T. Alexander, pp. 13–34. University of New Mexico, Albuquerque.

Evans, Susan Toby 2017 Aztec Palaces and Gardens, Intertwined Evolution. In *The Oxford Handbook of the Aztecs*, edited by Deborah L. Nichols and Enrique Rodríguez-Alegría, pp. 229–245. Oxford.

Feduchi, Luis M. 1957 *Antología de la silla española*. Afrodisio Aguado, Madrid.

Flannery, Kent V. (editor) 1976 *The Early Mesoamerican Village*. Academic Press, New York.

Flewellen, Ayana A. 2018 The Clothes on Her Back: Interpreting Sartorial Practices of Self-Making at the Levi Jordan Plantation. PhD Dissertation, Department of Anthropology, University of Texas at Austin.

Forde, Jamie 2017 Volcanic Glass and Iron Nails: Networks of Exchange and Material Entanglements at Late Prehispanic and Early Colonial Achiutla, Oaxaca, Mexico. *International Journal of Historical Archaeology* 21:485–511.

Foster, George 1960 *Culture and Conquest: America's Spanish Heritage*. Viking Fund Publications in Anthropology 27, Wenner Gren Foundation, New York.

Fournier, Patricia 1990 *Evidencias arqueológicas de la importación de cerámica en México, con base en los materiales del ex-convento de San Jerónimo.* Instituto Nacional de Antropología e Historia, Mexico City.

Fournier, Patricia 1998a La ceramica colonial del Tempo Mayor. *Arqueología Mexicana* 31:52–59.

Fournier, Patricia 1998b El Complejo nixtamal/comal/tortilla en Mesoamérica. *Boletín de Antropología Americana* 32:13–40.

Fournier García, Patricia 1997 Tendencias de consumo en México durante los Periodos Colonial e Independiente. In *Approaches to the Historical Archaeology of Mexico, Central, and South America,* edited by Janine Gasco, Greg Charles Smith, and Patricia Fournier-García, pp. 49–58. UCLA Institute of Archaeology, Los Angeles.

Fournier, Patricia and Roberto Junco Sánchez 2019 Archaeological Distribution of Chinese Porcelain in Mexico. In *Archaeology of Manila Galleon Seaports and Early Maritime Globalization,* The Archaeology of Asia-Pacific Navigation 2, edited by Chunming Wu, Roberto Junco Sanchez, and Miao Liu, pp. 215–237. Springer, Singapore. https://doi.org/10.1007/978-981-32-9248-2_13

Fournier García, Patricia and Cynthia L. Otis Charlton 2019 Postconquest Technological Innovation and Effect on Ceramic Traditions in Central Mexico. In *Technology and Tradition in Mesoamerica after the Spanish Invasion: Archaeological Perspectives*, edited by Rani T. Alexander, pp. 35–51. University of New Mexico, Tucson.

Fowler, William 1993 The Living Pay for the Dead: Trade, Exploitation and Social Change in Early Colonial Izalco, El Salvador. In *Ethnohistory and Archaeology*, edited by Samuel Wilson and J. D. Rogers, pp. 181–199. Plenum, New York.

Franklin, Maria 2020 Gender, Clothing Fasteners, and Dress Practices in Houston's Freedmen's Town, ca. 1880–1904. *Historical Archaeology* 54:556–580. DOI: s41636-020-00250-8.

Gallardo Parrodi, María de Lourdes 2011 Conservación del material orgánico de la ofrenda 102 del Templo Mayor de Tenochtitlan. *Arqueología Mexicana* 108:61–65.

Gallardo Parrodi, María de Lourdes 2014 *Las prendas de concha nacarada del templo Mayor de Tenochtitan.* PhD dissertation. Facultad de Filosofía y Letras, Universidad Nacional Autónoma de México, Mexico City.

Gallardo Parrodi, María de Lourdes 2017 Museum and the Conservation of Mexica Cultural Heritage. In *The Oxford Handbook of the Aztecs*, edited by Deborah L. Nichols and Enrique Rodríguez-Alegría, pp. 41–49. Oxford.

Gámez Martínez, Ana Paulina 2003 The Forgotten Potters of Mexico City. In *Cerámica y Cultura: The Story of Spanish and Mexican Mayólica,* edited by Robin Farwell Gavin, Donna Pierce, and Alfonso Pleguezuelo, pp. 227–241. University of New Mexico, Albuquerque.

Garbana, Antonio Francisco 1969 El mueble del siglo XVI y su origen español. *Artes de México, No. 118. El Mueble Mexicano.* Pp. 8–14. Stable URL: https://www.jstor.org/stable/24315659

García Moll, Roberto, y Marcela Salas Cuesta 2011 Arqueología histórica, historia y antropología física. La catedral vieja de México. *Arqueología Mexicana* 108:18–23.

García-Martínez, Bernardo 2010 Los años de la conquista. In *Nueva Historia General de México,* pp. 169–215. El Colegio de México, Mexico City.

García Zaldúa, Johan, and Dorothy Hosler 2020 Copper Smelting at the Archaeological Site of El Manchón, Guerrero: From Indigenous Practice to Colonial-Scale Production. *Latin American Antiquity* 31(3):558–575. doi:10.1017/laq.2019.105

Gasco, Janine 1987 Cacao and the Economic Integration of Native Society in Colonial Soconusco, New Spain. PhD dissertation, Department of Anthropology, University of California, Santa Barbara. University Microfilms, Ann Arbor.

Gasco, Janine 1992 Material Culture and Colonial Indian Society in southern Mesoamerica: The View from Coastal Chiapas, Mexico. *Historical Archaeology* 26:67–74.

Gasco, Janine 2018 Anthropogenic Landscapes of Soconusco, Past and Present. In *Colonial and Postcolonial Change in Mesoamerica: Archaeology as Historical Anthropology*, edited by Rani T. Alexander and Susan Kepecs, pp. 205–226. University of New Mexico, Albuquerque.

Gavin, Robin Farwell, Donna Pierce, and Alfonso Pleguezuelo (editors) 2003 *Cerámica y Cultura: The Story of Spanish and Mexican Mayólica*. University of New Mexico, Albuquerque.

Gell, Alfred 1998 *Art and Agency: An Anthropological Theory*. Clarendon, Oxford.

Gerhard, Peter 1993 *A Guide to the Historical Geography of New Spain*. University of Oklahoma Press, Norman.

Gero, Joan and Margaret Conkey (editors) 1991 *Engendering Archaeology: Women and Prehistory*. Blackwell, Oxford.

Gibson, Charles 1964 *The Aztecs Under Spanish Rule: A History of the Indians of the Valley of Mexico, 1519–1810*. Stanford.

Goggin, John M. 1960 *The Spanish Olive Jar: An Introductory Study*. Yale University Publications in Anthropology, no. 62. Department of Anthropology, Yale University, New Haven.

Goggin, John M. 1968 *Spanish Majolica in the New World: Types of the Sixteenth to Eighteenth Centuries*. Department of Anthropology, Yale, New Haven.

Gosden, Chris 2005 What do Objects Want? *Journal of Archaeological Method and Theory*. 12(3):193–211.

Graeber, David 2011 *Debt: the First 5,000 Years*. Melville House, New York.

Guerrero-Rivero, Saúl, Dolores Tenorio, Melania Jiménez-Reyes, R. Junco-Sánchez, and M. López-Reyes 2020 Commercial Interaction at the Port of Acapulco, Mexico, during the Viceregal Period: A Provenance Study of Ceramic Containers and Regional Wares. *Journal of Archaeological Science: Reports*. 29. 10.1016/j.jasrep.2019.102163.

Guzmán, Ana Fabiola, and Oscar J. Polaco 2003 El consumo de peces en una casa del siglo XVI en la ciudad de México. In *Excavaciones del Programa de Arqueología Urbana*, edited by Eduardo Matos Moctezuma, pp. 39–73. Instituto Nacional de Antropología e Historia, Mexico City.

Haraway, Donna J. 1991 *Simians, Cyborgs, and Women: The Reinvention of Nature*. Routledge, New York.

Hartsock, Nancy 1987 Rethinking Modernism: Minority vs. Majority Theories. *Cultural Critique* 7:187–206.

Haskett, Robert 1991 *Indigenous Rulers: An Ethnohistory of Town Government in Colonial Cuernavaca*. University of New Mexico, Albuquerque.

Hendon, Julia A. 1996 Archaeological Approaches to the Organization of Domestic Labor: Household Practice and Domestic Relations. *Annual Review of Anthropology* 25:45–61. https://doi.org/10.1146/annurev.anthro.25.1.45

Hendon, Julia A. 2004 Living and Working at Home: The Social Archaeology of Household Production and Social Relations. In *A Companion to Social Archaeology*, edited by Lynn Meskell and Robert W. Preucel, pp. 272–286. Blackwell, Malden.

Hendon, Julia A. and Rosemary Joyce (editors) 2004 *Mesoamerican Archaeology: Theory and Practice.* Wiley-Blackwell, Malden.

Henry, Susan L. 1996 Factors Influencing consumer Behavior in Turn-of-the-century Phoenix, Arizona. In *Images of the Recent Past*, edited by Charles E. Orser, pp. 235–259. Altamira Press, Walnut Creek.

Hermann Lejarazu, Manuel A. 2017 El Tributo en oro en la época colonial: el caso del Códice de Tepetlaóztoc. *Arqueología Mexicana* XXIV(144):72–75.

Hernández Álvarez, Héctor 2019 Technological Change of Henequen Decorticating Machines during Yucatán's Gilded Age. In *Technology and Tradition in Mesoamerica after the Spanish Invasion,* edited by Rani T. Alexander, pp. 125–146. University of New Mexico, Albuquerque.

Hernández Álvarez, Héctor, and Nancy Peniche May 2012 Malacates arqueológicos de la península de Yucatán. *Ancient Mesoamerica* 23:441–459.

Hernández Durán, Ray 2017a *The Academy of San Carlos and Mexican Art History: Politics, History, and Art in Nineteenth-Century Mexico.* Routledge, New York.

Hernández Durán, Ray 2017b Aztec Art After the Conquest and in Museums Abroad. In *The Oxford Handbook of the Aztecs*, edited by Deborah L. Nichols and Enrique Rodríguez-Alegría, pp. 689–705. Oxford.

Hernández Sánchez, Gilda 2012 *Ceramics and the Spanish Conquest: Response and Continuity of Indigenous Pottery Technology in Central Mexico.* Brill, Leiden.

Hernández Sánchez, Gilda 2019 Indigenous Pottery Technology of Central Mexico during Early Colonial Times. In *Material Encounters and Indigenous Transformations in the Early Colonial Americas*, edited by Corinne L. Hofman and Floris W.M. Keehnen, pp. 284–307. Brill, Leiden.

Herrera Meza, María del Carmen and Ruiz Medrano, Ethelia 1997 *El Códice de Tepeucila: el entintado mundo de la fijeza imaginaria.* Instituto Nacional de Antropología e Historia, Mexico City.

Herrero García, Miguel 2014 *Los Tejidos en la España de los Austrias.* Centro de Estudios Europa Hipánica, Madrid.

Hicks, Dan 2012 The Material-Cultural Turn: Event and Effect. In *The Oxford Handbook of Material Culture Studies*, edited by Dan Hicks and Mary C. Beaudry, pp. 25–98. Oxford.

Hinojosa Hinojosa, José Francisco 2003 Rescate arqueológico. In *Excavaciones del Programa de Arqueología Urbana.* Colección Científica 452, edited by Eduardo Matos Moctezuma, pp. 15–26. Instituto Nacional de Antropología e Historia, Mexico City.

Hinojosa Hinojosa, José Francisco and Raúl Barrera Rodríguez 2003 El basamento prehispánico de las calles de Luis González Obregón y Argentina. In *Excavaciones del Programa de Arqueología Urbana.* Colección Científica 452, edited by Eduardo Matos Moctezuma, pp. 143–154. Instituto Nacional de Antropología e Historia, Mexico City.

Hirth, Kenneth G. 2016 *The Aztec Economic World: Merchants and Markets in Ancient Mesoamerica.* Cambridge.

Ho, Robert 2017 *Understanding Statistics for the Social Sciences with IBM SPSS.* CRC Press, Boca Raton.

Hodder, Ian 1992 *Theory and Practice in Archaeology.* Routledge, London.

Hodder, Ian 2012 *Entangled: An Archaeology of the Relationships between Humans and Things.* Wiley-Blackwell, Malden.

Hodge, Mary G and Hector Neff 2005 Xaltocan in the Economy of the Basin of Mexico: A View from Ceramic Tradewares. In *Production and Power at Postclassic Xaltocan*, edited by Elizabeth M. Brumfiel, pp. 319–348. University of Pittsburgh and Instituto Nacional de Antropología e Historia, Pittsburgh and Mexico City.

Hodge, Mary G., Hector Neff, M. James Blackman, and Leah D. Minc 1992 A Compositional Perspective on Ceramic Production in the Aztec Empire. In *Chemical Characterization of Ceramic Pastes in Archaeology*, Monographs in World Archaeology No. 7, edited by Hector Neff, pp. 203–220. Prehistory Press, Madison.

Hodge, Mary G., Hector Neff, M. James Blackman, and Leah D. Minc 1993 The Regional Structure of Black-on-Orange Ceramic Production in the Aztec Empire's Heartland. *Latin American Antiquity* 4(2):130–157.

Hosler, Dorothy 1994 *The Sounds and Colors of Power*. MIT, Cambridge.

Hosler, Dorothy 2003 Metal Production. In *The Postclassic Mesoamerican World*, edited by Michael E. Smith and Frances F. Berdan, pp. 159–171. University of Utah, Salt Lake City.

Howson, Jean E. 1990 Social Relations and Material Culture: A Critique of the Archaeology of Plantation Slavery. *Historical Archaeology* 24:78–91.

Ingold, Tim 1997 Eight Themes in the Anthropology of Technology. *Social Analysis: The International Journal of Social and Cultural Practice* 41(1):106–138.

Ingold, Tim 2013 *Making*. Routledge, New York.

Iñañez, Javier G, J.J. Bellucci, Enrique Rodríguez-Alegría, R. Ash, W. McDonough, Robert J. Speakman 2010 Romita Pottery Revisited: A Reassessment of the Provenance of Ceramics from Colonial Mexico by LA-MC-ICP-MS. *Journal of Archaeological Science* 37:2698–2704.

Islas Dominguez, Alicia 1999 El Templo del Sol en el centro ceremonial mexica. In *Excavaciones en la Catedral y el Sagrario Metropolitanos. Programa de Arqueología Urbana*, edited by Eduardo Matos Moctezuma, pp. 51–62. Instituto Nacional de Antropología e Historia, Mexico City.

Jamieson, Ross W. 2000a Doña Luisa and Her Two Houses. In *Lines that Divide: Historical Archaeologies of Race, Class, and Gender*, edited by Stephen A. Mrozowki, and Robert Paynter, pp. 142–167. University of Tennessee, Knoxville.

Jamieson, Ross W. 2000b *Domestic Architecture and Power: The Historical Archaeology of Colonial Ecuador*. Kluwer Academic Publishers, New York.

Jamieson, Ross W. 2004 Bolts of Cloth and Sherds of Pottery: Impressions of Caste in the Material Culture of the Seventeenth Century Audiencia of Quito. *The Americas* 60(3):431–446.

Jevons, W. Stanley 1896 *Money and the Mechanism of Exchange*. Kegan Paul, Trench, Trübner, and Company, London.

Jiménez Badillo, Diego 2003 El rescate arqueológico. In *Excavaciones del Porgrama de Arqueología Urbana*. Colección Científica #452, edited by Eduardo Matos Moctezuma, pp. 87–107. Instituto Nacional de Antropología e Historia, Mexico City.

Johannsen, Niels 2012 Archaeology and the Inanimate Agency Proposition: A Critique and a Suggestion. In *Excavating the Mind: Cross-sections Through Culture, Cognition and Materiality*, edited by Niels Johannsen, Mads Jessen, and Helle Juel Jensen, pp. 305–347. Aarhus University, Aarhus.

Johnson, Matthew 2010 *Archaeological Theory. An Introduction*. Wiley-Blackwell, Oxford.

Johnson, Matthew 2000 Self-Made Men and the Staging of Agency. In *Agency in Archaeology*, edited by Marcia-Anne Dobres and John E. Robb, pp. 213–231. Routledge, London.

Joyce, Rosemary 2000 *Gender and Power in Prehispanic Mesoamerica*. University of Texas Press, Austin.

Joyce, Rosemary 2005 Archaeology of the Body. *Annual Review of Anthropology* 34:139–158. https://doi.org/10.1146/annurev.anthro.33.070203.143729

Kaiser, Susan 1990 *The Social Psychology of Clothing: Symbolic Appearances in Context*. Macmillan, New York.

Katz, S. H., M. L. Hediger, and L.A. Valleroy 1974 Traditional Maize Processing Techniques in the New World. *Science* 184(4138):765–773.

Katzew, Ilona 2004 *Casta Painting: Images of Race in Eighteenth-Century Mexico*. Yale, New Haven.

King, Stacie M. and Elizabeth Konwest 2019 New Materials—New Technologies? Postclassic and Early Colonial Technological Transitions in the Nejapa Region of Oaxaca, Mexico. In *Technology and Tradition in Mesoamerica after the Spanish Invasion: Archaeological Perspectives*, edited by Rani T. Alexander, pp. 73–92. University of New Mexico, Albuquerque.

Kubler, George 1948 *Mexican Architecture of the Sixteenth Century*, Vol. I. Yale, New Haven.

Kuleff, Ivelin and Rumania Djingova 2001 Archaeometric Investigation of Sgraffito Ceramics from Medieval Bulgaria. *Archaeologia Bulgarica* V(3):71–82.

Kuwayama, George 1997 *Chinese Ceramics in Colonial Mexico*. University of Hawaii, Honolulu.

Latour, Bruno 1993 Ethnography of a 'High-Tech' Case. In *Technological Choices: Transformation in Material Cultures since the Neolithic*, edited by Pierre Lemonnier, pp. 372–398. Routledge, London.

Latour, Bruno 1996 *Aramis or the Love of Technology*. Translated by Catherine Porter. Harvard, Cambridge.

Lemonnier, Pierre (editor) 1993 *Technological Choices: Transformation in Material Cultures Since the Neolithic*. Routledge, New York.

Levine, Marc N. and David M. Carballo (editors) 2014 *Obsidian Reflections: Symbolic Dimensions of Obsidian in Mesoamerica*. University Press of Colorado, Boulder.

Lienzo de Tlaxcala Ex-Stendahl Collection, Benson Latin American Collection, University of Texas Libraries, University of Texas at Austin.

Lister, Florence C, and Robert H. Lister 1982 *Sixteenth Century Maiolica Pottery in the Valley of Mexico*. University of Arizona, Tucson.

Lister, Florence C, and Robert H. Lister 1987 *Andalusian Ceramics in Spain and New Spain*. University of Arizona, Tucson.

Lockhart, James 1991 *Nahuas and Spaniards: Postconquest Central Mexican History and Philology*. Stanford.

Lockhart, James 1992 *The Nahuas After the Conquest*. Stanford.

Lockhart, James 1999 *Of Things of the Indies: Essays Old and New in Early Latin American History*. Stanford.

López Arenas, Gabino 2003 Rescate arqueológico en el predio de Correo Mayor 11. In *Excavaciones del Programa de Arqueología Urbana*. Colección Científica #452, edited by Eduardo Matos Moctezuma, pp. 227–234. Instituto Nacional de Antropología e Historia, Mexico City.

López Austin, Alfredo and Leonardo López Luján 2017 State Ritual and Religion in the Sacred Precinct of Tenochtitlan. In *The Oxford Handbook of the Aztecs*, edited by Deborah L. Nichols and Enrique Rodríguez-Alegría, pp. 605–622. Oxford.

López Cervantes, Gonzalo 1974 Porcelana Europea en México. *Boletín I.N.A.H.* 9, Epoca II:49–52.

López Cervantes, Gonzalo 1976 *Cerámica colonial en la Ciudad de México*. Instituto Nacional de Antropología e Historia, Mexico City.

López Luján, Leonardo 2009 La Tlaltecuhtli. In *Escultura Monumental Mexica*, by Eduardo Matos Moctezuma and Leonardo López Luján, pp. 381–447. Fundación Conmemoración, Mexico City.

López Luján, Leonardo, and Gabriela Sánchez Reyes 2012 El jaguar mexica de la calle Emiliano Zapata en la ciudad de México. *Arqueología Mexicana* 115:78–81.

Loren, Diana DiPaolo 2010 *The Archaeology of Clothing and Bodily Adornment in Colonial America*. University Press of Florida, Gainesville.

Loren, Diana DiPaolo 2015 Dress, Faith, and Medicine: Caring for the Body in Eighteenth-Century Spanish Texas. In *Archaeology of Cutlure Contact and Colonialism in Spanish and Portuguese America*, edited by Pedro Paulo A. Funari and Maria Ximena Senatore, pp. 143–154. Springer, New York.

Low, Setha 1995 Indigenous Architecture and the Spanish American Plaza in Mesoamerica and the Caribbean. *American Anthropologist* 97(4):748–762.

Luengo Muñoz, Manuel 1951 Sumaria noción del poder adquisitivo de la moneda en Indias durante el siglo XVI. *Anuario de Estudios Americanos* VIII:35–57.

Malafouris, Lambros 2013 *How Things Shape the Mind: A Theory of Material Engagement*. MIT, Cambridge.

Maldonado, Blanca 2012 Mesoamerican Metallurgical Technology and Production. In *The Oxford Handbook of Mesoamerican Archaeology*, edited by Deborah L. Nichols and Christopher A. Pool, pp. 616–628. Oxford.

Malinowski, Bronislaw 1922 *Argonauts of the Western Pacific*. Routledge, London.

Mantecón Navasal, José Ignacio (editor) 1956 *Información de Méritos y Servicios de Alonso García Bravo, Alarife que Trazó la Ciudad de México*. Estudios y Fuentes del Arte en México III. Instituto de Investigaciones Estéticas, Universidad Nacional Autónoma de México, Mexico City.

Manzanilla, Linda (editor) 1986 *Unidades Habitacionales Mesoamericanas y sus Áreas de Actividad*. Universidad Nacional Autónoma de México, Mexico City.

Marías, Fernando 1999 Planta de la Catedral de México. In *Los Siglos de Oro en los Virreinatos de América 1550–1700*, edited by Sociedad Estatal para la Conmemoración de los Centenarios de Felipe II y Carlos V, pp. 246–247. Ediciones El Viso, S.A., Madrid.

Marichal, Carlos 2015 El Peso de plata o *Real de a ocho* en España y América: Moneda universal del Antiguo Régimen. In *La Acuñación en México: 1535–2015*, edited by Arturo Chapa, pp. 19–59. Secretaría de Hacienda y Crédito Público, and Casa de Moneda de México, Mexico City.

Mariscal, Ivonne Pablo 1998 *Investigación Histórica del Predio Justo Sierra #33*. Report on file at the Consejo de Arqueología, Instituto Nacional de Antropología e Historia, Mexico City.

Márquez Morfín, Lourdes 1993 La evolución cuantitativa de la población novohispana: siglos XVI, XVII, y XVIII. In *El Poblamiento de México: una visión histórico-demográfica. Tomo II: el México Colonial*, edited by Ana Arenzana, pp. 36–63. Secretaría de la Gobernación, Consejo Nacional de Población, Mexico City.

Márquez Morfín, Lourdes and Rebecca Storey 2017 Population History in Precolumbian and Colonial Times. In *The Oxford Handbook of the Aztecs*, edited by Deborah L. Nichols and Enrique Rodríguez-Alegría, pp. 189–200. Oxford.

Marroqui, José María 1969 *La Ciudad de México*. Jesús Medina, Mexico City.

Martín Morales, Francisco Manuel 2016 *Glosario de Ajuar Doméstico en la Sevilla de Velázquez: Una aproximación a través de los Inventarios Notariales*. https://www.academia.edu/26962588/Glosario_del_Ajuar_Domestico_en_la_Sevilla_de_Vel%C3%A1zquez.

Martínez, José Luis 1988 Construcción de la nueva ciudad. *El Centro Histórico de la Ciudad de México. Artes de México* 1:22–29.

Martínez del Río de Redo, Marita 1985 Mueble Civil. In *El mueble mexicano. Historia, evolución e influencias*. Aguilera, Carmen, Elisa Vargas Lugo, Marita Martínez del Río de Redo, Jorge Loyzaga, Luis Ortiz Macedo, Teresa Castelló Iturbide, Manuel Carballo, Ma. Cecilia Martínez López, and Fernando Sánchez Martínez, pp. 47–70. Fondo Cultural Banamex, Mexico City.

Martínez López-Cano, María del Pilar 1995 *El Crédito a largo plazo en el siglo XVI. Ciudad de México (1550–1620)*. Universidad Nacional Autónoma de México, Mexico City.

Mastache, Alba Guadalupe 2005 El tejido en el México antiguo. *Arqueología Mexicana. Edición especial 19: Textiles del México de ayer y hoy*, pp. 20–28.

Matasanz, José 1965 Introducción de la ganadería en Nueva España 1521–1535. *Historia Mexicana* 14(4):533–566.

Matos Moctezuma, Eduardo 1988 *The Great Temple of the Aztecs*. Thames and Hudson, London.

Matos Moctezuma, Eduardo (coordinator) 1999 *Excavaciones en la Catedral y el Sagrario Metropolitanos: Programa de Arqueología Urbana*. Instituto Nacional de Antropología e Historia, Mexico City.

Matos Moctezuma, Eduardo (editor) 2003 *Excavaciones del Programa de Arqueología Urbana*. Colección Científica 452. Instituto Nacional de Antropología e Historia, Mexico City.

Matos Moctezuma, Eduardo 2012 La Plaza Mayor o Zócalo en tiempos de Tenochtitlan. *Arqueología Mexicana* 116:24–37.

Matos Moctezuma, Eduardo 2017 Ancient Stone Sculptures: In Search of the Mexica Past. In *The Oxford Handbook of the Aztecs*, edited by Deborah L. Nichols and Enrique Rodríguez-Alegría, pp. 21–28. Oxford.

Matos Moctezuma, Eduardo, Raúl Barrera Rodríguez, and Lorena Vázquez Vallin 2017 El Huei Tzompantli de Tenochtitlan. *Arqueología Mexicana* 25(148):52–57.

Matthew, Laura, and Michel Oudijk (editors) 2007 *Indian Conquistadors: Indigenous Allies in the Conquest of Mesoamerica*. University of Oklahoma, Norman.

Maurer, Bill, Taylor C. Nelms, and Lana Swartz 2013 "When Perhaps the Real Problem Is Money Itself!": The Practical Materiality of Bitcoin. *Social Semiotics* 23(2):261–277. https://doi.org/10.1080/10350330.2013.777594

Mauss, Marcel 1924/1954 *The Gift*. Cohen & West, London.

McClung de Tapia, Emily and Diana Martínez Yrizar 2017 Aztec Agricultural Production in a Historical Ecological Perspective. In *The Oxford Handbook of the Aztecs*, edited by Deborah Nichols and Enrique Rodríguez-Alegría, pp. 175–188. Oxford.

McEwan, Bonnie G. 1991 The Archaeology of Women in the Spanish New World. *Historical Archaeology* 25:33–41.

McEwan, Bonnie G. 1992 The Role of Ceramics in Spain and Spanish America During the 16th Century. *Historical Archaeology* 26:92–108.

McEwan, Bonnie G. 1995 Spanish Precedents and Domestic Life at Puerto Real: The Archaeology of Two Spanish Homesites. In *Puerto Real: The Archaeology of a Sixteenth-Century Spanish town in Hispaniola*, edited by Kathleen Deagan, pp. 197–229. University Press of Florida, Tallahassee.

McKim-Smith, Gridley 2006 Dressing Colonial, Dressing Diaspora. In *The Arts in Latin America, 1492–1820*, edited by Joseph J. Rishel with Suzanne Stratton-Pruitt, pp. 155–169. Yale, New Haven.

Melville, Elinor G. K. 1997 *A Plague of Sheep: Environmental Consequences of the Conquest of Mexico*. Cambridge, London.

Mercado, Tomás de 1985 *La Economía en la Andalucía del Descubrimiento*. Biblioteca de la Cultura Andaluza. Editoriales Andaluzas Unidas, S.A., Seville.

Meza, Abigail 2013 Presencia africana en el cementerio del Hospital Real de San José de los Naturales. *Arqueología Mexicana* 119:40–44.

Mier y Terán Rocha, Lucía 2005 *La primera traza de la ciudad de México, 1524–1535*. 2 vols. Universidad Autónoma Metropolitana y Fondo de Cultura Económica, Mexico City.

Miller, Daniel 1987 *Material Culture and Mass Consumption*. Blackwell, Oxford.

Miller, Daniel 2005 Materiality: An Introduction. In *Materiality*, edited by Daniel Miller, pp. 1–50. Duke University Press, Durham.

Millhauser, John K. 2017a Aztec Use of Lake Resources in the Basin of Mexico. In *The Oxford Handbook of the Aztecs*, edited by Deborah Nichols and Enrique Rodríguez-Alegría, pp. 301–318. Oxford.

Millhauser, John K. 2017b Debt as a Double-Edged Risk: A Historical Case from Nahua (Aztec) Mexico. *Economic Anthropology* 4(2):263–275.

Minc, Leah D. 2017 Pottery and the Potter's Craft in the Aztec Heartland. In *The Oxford Handbook of the Aztecs*, edited by Deborah L. Nichols and Enrique Rodríguez-Alegría, pp. 355–374. Oxford.

Mintz, Sydney W. 1985 *Sweetness and Power: The Place of Sugar in Modern History*. Penguin Books, New York.

Montúfar López, Aurora 2000 Arqueobotánica del centro ceremonial de Tenochtitlan. *Arqueología Mexicana* VI(31):34–41.

Montúfar López, Aurora 2003 Arqueobotánica de un basurero colonial. In *Excavaciones del Programa de Arqueología Urbana*, edited by Eduardo Matos Moctezuma, pp. 75–84. Instituto Nacional de Antropología e Historia, Mexico City.

Montúfar López, Aurora, and Norma Valentín Maldonado 1998 Estudio arqueobiológico de los sedimentos del subsuelo en el edificio Real Seminario de Minas, 1772, México, D.F. *Arqueología* 20:97–113.

Morehart, Christopher 2017 Aztec Agricultural Strategies: Intensification, Landesque Capital, and the Sociopolitics of Production. In *The Oxford Handbook of the Aztecs*, edited by Deborah Nichols and Enrique Rodríguez-Alegría, pp. 263–280. Oxford.

Mundy, Barbara 2015 *The Death of Aztec Tenochtitlan, the Life of Mexico City*. University of Texas, Austin.

Navas, Ana María, Franz Scaramelli, Anna Di Prinzio, and Kay Scaramelli 2014 Tecnologías de colonización: metalurgia en las misiones religiosas del Orinoco, siglo XVIII. *Revista de Arqueología Americana* 32:129–150.

Neale, Walter C. 1976 *Monies in Societies*. Chandler and Sharp, San Francisco.

Neff, Hector, and Mary G. Hodge 2008 Serving Vessel Production at Chalco: Evidence from Neutron Activation Analysis. In *Place of Jade: Society and Economy in Ancient Chalco*, edited by Mary G. Hodge, pp. 187–226. Department of Anthropology, University of Pittsburgh, and Instituto Nacional de Antropología e Historia, Pittsburgh and Mexico City.

Nemser, Daniel 2017 *Infrastructures of Race: Concentration and Biopolitics in Colonial Mexico.* University of Texas, Austin.

Nichols, Deborah L., Elizabeth M. Brumfiel, Hector Neff, Mary Hodge, Thomas H. Charlton, and Michael D. Glascock 2002 Neutrons, Markets, Cities, and Empires: A 1000-Year Perspective on Ceramic Production and Distribution in the Postclassic Basin of Mexico. *Journal of Anthropological Archaeology* 21:25–82.

Nichols, Deborah L., Christina Elson, Leslie G. Cecil, Nina Neivens De Estrada, Michael D. Glascock, and Paula Mikkelsen 2009 Chiconautla, Mexico: A Crossroads of Aztec Trade and Politics. *Latin American Antiquity* 20(3):443–472.

Nichols, Deborah L. and Enrique Rodríguez-Alegría 2017 Introduction: Aztec Studies: Trends and Themes. In *The Oxford Handbook of the Aztecs,* edited by Deborah L. Nichols and Enrique Rodríguez-Alegría, pp. 1–17. Oxford.

Oland, Maxine 2014 "With the Gifts and Good Treatment That He Gave Them": Elite Maya Adoption of Spanish Material Culture at Progresso Lagoon, Belize. *International Journal of Historical Archaeology* 18:643–667.

Oland, Maxine 2017 The Olive Jar in the Shrine: Situating Spanish Objects within a 15th-17th Century Maya Worldview. In *Foreign Objects: Rethinking Indigenous Consumption in American Archaeology,* edited by Craig N. Cipolla, pp. 128–142. University of Arizona, Tucson.

Olko, Justyna 2014 *Insignia of Rank in the Nahua World: From the Fifteenth to the Seventeenth Century.* University Press of Colorado, Louisville.

Olko, Justyna and Jan Szemiński 2018 Nahua and Quechua Elites of the Colonial Period: Continuity and Change in a Cross-Cultural Context. In *Dialogue with Europe, Colonial Nahua and Quechua Elites in their own Words,* edited by Justyna Oko, John Sullivan, and Jan Szemiński, pp. 9–61. University Press of Colorado, Louisville.

Orozco y Berra, Manuel 1853 *Noticia histórica de la conjuración del Marqués del Valle. Años de 1565–1568. Formada en vista de nuevos documentos originales, y seguida de un extracto de los mismos documentos.* Tipografía de R. Rafael Cadena, Mexico.

Ortiz Crespo, Alfonso 2006 The Spanish American Colonial City: Its Origins, Development, and Functions. In *The Arts in Latin America 1492–1820*, organized by Joseph J. Rishel with Suzanne Stratton-Pruitt, pp. 23–37. Yale, New Haven.

Oudijk, Michel R. 2012 The Conquest of Mexico. In *The Oxford Handbook of Mesoamerican Archaeology,* edited by Deborah L. Nichols and Christopher A. Pool, pp. 459–470. Oxford.

Papadopoulos, John K. 2012 Money, Art, and the Construction of Value in the Ancient Mediterranean. In *The Construction of Value in the Ancient World*, edited by John K. Papadopoulos and Gary Urton, pp. 261–287. Cotsen Institute of Archaeology, Los Angeles.

Parsons, Jeffrey R. 1966 The Aztec Ceramic Sequence in the Teotihuacan Valley, Mexico. Ph.D. dissertation, University of Michigan. University Microfilms, Ann Arbor.

Pastrana, Alejandro 1998 *La explotación Azteca de la obsidiana en La Sierra de Las Navajas.* Colección Científica 383. Instituto Nacional de Antropología e Historia, Mexico City.

Pastrana, Alejandro 2007 *La distribución de obsidiana de la Triple Alianza en la Cuenca de México.* Colección Científica 519. Instituto Nacional de Antropología e Historia, Mexico City.

Pastrana, Alejandro, and David Carballo 2017 Aztec Obsidian Industries. In *The Oxford Handbook of the Aztecs,* edited by Deborah L. Nichols and Enrique Rodríguez-Alegría, pp. 329–342. Oxford.

Pasztory, Esther 2005 *Thinking with Things: Toward a New Vision of Art*. University of Texas, Austin.

Peebles, Gustav 2010 The Anthropology of Credit and Debt. *Annual Review of Anthropology* 39:225–240.

Pérez Mora, Braulio and Georgina Ibarra Arzave 2014 Evidencias arqueológicas de la primera Casa de Moneda en la Nueva España. In *Las Contribuciones Arqueológicas de la Formación de la Historia Colonial: Memoria del Primer Coloquio de Arqueología Histórica*, edited by María de Lourdes López Camacho, pp. 335–357. Instituto Nacional de Antropología e Historia, Mexico City.

Pfaffenberger, Bryan 1992 Social Anthropology of Technology. *Annual Review of Anthropology* 21:491–516. Stable URL: http://www.jstor.org/stable/2155997.

Pierce, Donna 2003 Mayólica in the Daily Life of Colonial Mexico. In *Cerámica y Cultura: The Story of Spanish and Mexican Mayólica*, edited by Robin Farwell Gavin, Donna Pierce, and Alfonso Pleguezuelo, pp. 245–269. University of New Mexico, Albuquerque.

Pillsbury, Joanne, Timothy Potts, and Kim N. Richter (editors) 2017 *Golden Kingdoms: Luxury Arts in the Ancient Americas*. J. Paul Getty Museum and the Getty Research Institute, Los Angeles.

Pitt-Rivers, A.H.L.F. 1875 The Evolution of Culture. In *The Evolution of Culture and Other Essays*, edited by J. Meyer, pp. 20–44. Clarendon Press, Oxford.

Pohl, John and Charles M. Robinson III 2005 *Aztecs and Conquistadores: The Spanish Invasion and the Collapse of the Aztec Empire*. Osprey, Oxford.

Recio Mir, Alvaro 2012 Un nuevo arte en movimiento para la ostentación social: los primeros coches novohispanos y las ordenanzas del gremio de carroceros de la ciudad de México de 1706. *Anales del Instituto de Investigaciones Estéticas* 34(101):13–38.

Renfrew, Colin 2004 Towards a Theory of Material Engagement. In *Rethinking Materiality: The Engagement of Mind with the Material World*, edited by Elizabeth DeMarrais, Chris Gosden, and Colin Renfrew, pp. 23–31. Cambridge.

Restall, Matthew 2003 *Seven Myths of the Spanish Conquest*. Oxford.

Riva Palacio, Vicente 1977 *México a través de los siglos. Tomo II: El Virreynato*. Editorial Cumbre, Mexico City.

Rivas García, Flor, and Raúl Barrera Rodríguez 1997 Informe Preliminar del rescate arqueológico Argentina #15 Librería Porrúa. Report on file at the Programa de Arqueología Urbana, Museo del Templo Mayor, Instituto Nacional de Antropología e Historia, Mexico City.

Rivas P., Jorge F. 2006 Observations on the Origin, Development, and Manufacture of Latin American Furniture. *The Arts in Latin America, 1492/1820,* edited by Joseph J. Rishel with Suzanne Stratton-Pruitt, pp. 476–480. Yale, New Haven.

Roach, Mary Ellen and Joanne B. Eicher 1973 *The Visible Self: Perspectives on Dress*. Prentice-Hall, Englewood Cliffs.

Robb, John 2004 The Extended Artefact and the Monumental Economy: A Methodology for Material Agency. In *Rethinking Materiality: The Engagement of Mind with the Material World*, edited by Elizabeth DeMarrais, Chris Gosden, and Colin Renfrew, pp. 131–139. McDonald Institute for Archaeological Research, Cambridge.

Robb, John 2010 Beyond Agency. *World Archaeology* 42(4):493–520. http://dx.doi.org/10.1080/00438243.2010.520856

Robin, Cynthia 2014 *Everyday Life Matters: Maya Farmers at Chan*. University Press of Florida, Tallahassee.

Robin, Cynthia, and Elizabeth Brumfiel (editors) 2010 *Gender, Households, and Society: Unraveling the Threads of the Past and the Present.* Archaeological Papers of the American Anthropological Association #18.

Robinson, Jancis 2006 *The Oxford Companion to Wine*, Third Edition. Oxford.

Rodríguez-Alegría, Enrique 2002 *Food, Eating, and Objects of Power: Class Stratification and Ceramic Production and Consumption in Colonial Mexico.* PhD dissertation, Department of Anthropology, University of Chicago.

Rodríguez-Alegría, Enrique 2003 Ideologías coloniales y cerámica indígena en la traza mexicana. In *Excavaciones del Programa de Arqueología Urbana,* Colección Científica #452, edited by Eduardo Matos Moctezuma, pp. 309–326. Instituto Nacional de Antropología e Historia, Mexico City.

Rodríguez-Alegría, Enrique 2005a Eating Like an Indian: Negotiating Social Relations in the Spanish Colonies. *Current Anthropology* 46(4):551–573.

Rodríguez-Alegría, Enrique 2005b Consumption and the Varied Ideologies of Domination in Colonial Mexico City. In *The Late Postclassic to Spanish-era Transition in Mesoamerica: Archaeological Perspectives,* edited by Rani Alexander and Susan Kepecs, pp. 35–48. University of New Mexico Press.

Rodríguez-Alegría, Enrique 2008a Narratives of Conquest, Colonialism, and Cutting-Edge Technology. *American Anthropologist* 110(1):33–41.

Rodríguez-Alegría, Enrique 2008b De la Edad de Piedra a la Edad de más Piedra. *Cuadernos de Arqueología Mediterránea* 17:15–30.

Rodríguez-Alegría, Enrique 2010 Incumbents and Challengers: Indigenous Politics and the Adoption of Spanish Material Culture in Colonial Xaltocan, Mexico. *Historical Archaeology* 44(2):51–71.

Rodríguez-Alegría, Enrique 2012a The Discovery and Decolonization of Xaltocan, Mexico. In *Lost in Transition: Decolonizing Indigenous Histories at the "Prehistoric/ Colonial" Intersection in Archaeology,* edited by Maxine Oland, Siobhan Hart, and Liam Frink, pp. 45–65. University of Arizona Press, Tucson.

Rodríguez-Alegría, Enrique 2012b Grinding Corn to Dishing Out Money: A Long-Term History of Cooking in Xaltocan, Mexico. In *The Menial Art of Cooking: Archaeological Studies of Cooking and Food Preparation,* edited by Sarah R. Graff and Enrique Rodríguez-Alegría, pp. 99–118. University Press of Colorado, Boulder.

Rodríguez-Alegría, Enrique 2016a *The Archaeology and History of Colonial Central Mexico: Mixing Epistemologies.* Cambridge.

Rodríguez-Alegría, Enrique 2016b The Material Worlds of Colonizers in New Spain. In *Archaeologies of Early Modern Spanish Colonialism,* edited by Sandra Montón-Subias, María Cruz Berrocal, and Apen Ruiz, pp. 39–59. Springer, New York.

Rodríguez-Alegría, Enrique 2017 A City Transformed: From Tenochtitlan to Mexico City in the 16th Century. In *The Oxford Handbook of the Aztecs,* edited by Deborah Nichols and Enrique Rodríguez-Alegría, pp. 661–674. Oxford.

Rodríguez-Alegría, Enrique, John Millhauser, and Wesley Stoner 2013 Trade, Tribute, and Neutron Activation: the Colonial Political Economy of Xaltocan, Mexico. *Journal of Anthropological Archaeology* 32:397–414.

Rodríguez-Alegría, Enrique, Franz Scaramelli, and Ana María Navas 2015 Technological Transformations: Adaptationist, Relativist, and Economic Models in Mexico and Venezuela. In *Archaeology of Culture Contact and Colonialism in Spanish and Portuguese America,* edited by Pedro Paulo A Funari and María Ximena Senatore, pp. 53–77. Springer, New York.

Rodríguez-Alegría, Enrique and Wesley Stoner 2016 The Trade in Cooking Pots under the Aztec and Spanish Empires. *Ancient Mesoamerica* 27(1):197–207.

Rodríguez Vázquez, Antonio L. 1995 *Ricos y Pobres: Propiedad y vida privada en la Sevilla del siglo XVI.* Servicio de Publicaciones, Ayuntamiento de Sevilla, Seville.

Rojas, José Luis de 2017 Tenochtitlan. In *The Oxford Handbook of the Aztecs*, edited by Deborah Nichols and Enrique Rodríguez-Alegría, pp. 219–228. Oxford.

Rozat, Guy 2004 El redentor occidental y sus fantasías técnicas. In *Mestizajes tecnológicos y cambios culturales en México*, edited by Enrique Florescano and Virginia García Acosta, pp. 263–310. Centro de Investigaciones y Estudios Superiores en Antropología Social, Mexico City.

Rubial García, Antonio 2012 La Plaza Mayor de la ciudad de México en los siglos XVI y XVII. *Arqueología Mexicana* 116:36–43.

Ruiz Medrano, Ethelia 2010 Fighting Destiny: Nahua Nobles and Friars in the Sixteenth-Century Revolt of the Encomenderos against the King. In *Negotiation within Domination: New Spain's Indian Pueblos Confront the Spanish State*, edited by Ethelia Ruiz Medrano and Susan Kellogg, pp. 45–78. University Press of Colorado, Boulder.

Ruiz Medrano, Ethelia, and Susan Kellogg (editors) 2010 *Negotiation within Domination: New Spain's Indian Pueblos Confront the Spanish State.* University Press of Colorado, Boulder.

Sahagún, Bernardino de 1950–1982 *General History of the Things of New Spain: Florentine Codex.* 13 volumes. Translated by Arthur J. O. Anderson and Charles E Dibble. School of American Research and University of Utah, Santa Fe and Salt Lake City.

Sánchez Vázquez, María de Jesús, and Alberto Mena Cruz 2004 Monedas del Siglo XVI en la Ciudad de México. *Arqueología Mexicana* XVI(65):72–75.

Sanders, William T. 2008 Tenochtitlan in 1519: A Pre-industrial Megalopolis. In *The Aztec World*, edited by Elizabeth M. Brumfiel and Gary M. Feinman, pp. 67–86. Abrams, New York.

Sanoja, Mario, and Vargas-Arenas, I. 2002 *El agua y el poder: Caracas y la formación del Estado colonial caraqueño: 1567–1700.* Banco Central de Venezuela, Caracas.

Sanz Camañes, Porfirio 2004 *Las Ciudades en la América Hispana: Siglos XV al XVIII.* Sílex, Madrid.

Saunders, Nicholas J. 2001 A Dark Light: Reflections on Obsidian in Mesoamerica. *World Archaeology* 33(2):220–236.

Scaramelli, Franz 2008 Encounter, Exchange and Technological Innovation in the Tropical Lowlands of the Orinoco, Venezuela. *Desencuentros Culturales: Una Mirada desde la cultura material de las Américas. Cuadernos de Arqueología Mediterránea* 17:73–82.

Scaramelli, Franz, and Kay Tarble de Scaramelli 2005 The Roles of Material Culture in the Colonization of the Orinoco, Venezuela. *Journal of Social Archaeology* 5(1):135–168.

Schroeder, Susan 1991 *Chimalpahin and the Kingdoms of Chalco.* University of Arizona, Tucson.

Schroeder, Susan 2007 Introduction: The Genre of Conquest Studies. In *Indian Conquistadors: Indigenous Allies in the Conquest of Mesoamerica*, edited by Laura E. Matthew and Michel R. Oudijk, pp. 5–27. University of Oklahoma, Norman.

Seeger, Martin L. 1978 Media of Exchange in 16th Century New Spain and the Spanish Response. *The Americas* 35(2):168–184.

Senatore, Maria Ximena, and Pedro Paulo A. Funari 2015 Introduction: Disrupting the Grand Narrative of Spanish and Portuguese Colonialism. In *Archaeology of Culture*

Contact and Colonialism in Spanish and Portuguese America, edited by Pedro Paulo A. Funari and Maria Ximena Senatore, pp. 1–15. Springer, New York.

Shanks, Michael and Ian Hodder 1995 Processual, Postprocessual and Interpretive Archaeologies. In Interpreting Archaeology: Finding Meaning in the Past, edited by Ian Hodder, Michael Shanks, Alexandra Alexandri, Victor Buchli, John Carman, Jonathan Last, and Gavin Lucas, pp. 3–29. Routledge, London.

Silliman, Stephen 2004 Lost Laborers in Colonial California: Native Americans and the Archaeology of Rancho Petaluma. University of Arizona, Tucson.

Sismondo, Sergio 2010 An Introduction to Science and Technology Studies. Second edition. Wiley-Blackwell, Malden.

Sluyter, Andrew 1996 The Ecological Origins and Consequences of Cattle Ranching in Sixteenth-Century New Spain. Geographical Review 86(2):161–177.

Sodi Miranda, Federica 1994 La cerámica novohispana vidriada y con decoración sellada del siglo XVI. Instituto Nacional de Antropología e Historia, Mexico City.

Sousa Congosto, Francisco de 2007 Introducción a la historia de la indumentaria en España. Istmo, Madrid.

Spores, Ronald 1997 Mixteca Cacicas: Status, Wealth, and the Political Accommodation of Native Elite Women in Early Colonial Oaxaca. In Indian Women of Early Mexico, edited by Stephanie Wood, Susan Schroeder, and Robert Haskett, pp. 185–198. University of Oklahoma, Norman.

Stoopen, María 1997 Las Simientes del Mestizaje en el Siglo XVI. Artes de México 36:20–29.

Suárez de Peralta, Juan 1990 (1589) Tratado del Descubrimiento de las Indias. Consejo Nacional para la Cultura y las Artes, Mexico City.

Tarble, Kay 2008 Coffee, Tea, or Chicha? Commensality and Culinary Practice in the Middle Orinoco Following Colonial Contact. In Desencuentros Culturales: Una Mirada Desde la Cultura Material de las Américas. Cuadernos de Arqueología Mediterránea 17, edited by Apen Ruiz, pp. 53–72. Laboratorio de Arqueología de la Universidad Pompeu Fabra, Barcelona.

Terraciano, Kevin 2001 The Mixtecs of Colonial Oaxaca. Stanford.

Terreros Espinosa, Eladio 2003 Excavaciones en el predio de Donceles 97 del centro histórico de la ciudad de México. In Excavaciones del Programa de Arqueología Urbana. Colección Científica 452, edited by Eduardo Matos Moctezuma, pp. 239–255. Instituto Nacional de Antropología e Historia, Mexico City.

Tezozomoc, Alvarado 2012 Crónica Mexicana. Biblioteca Antológica, Mexico.

Therrien, Monika 2016 Displacing Dominant Meanings in the Archaeology of Urban Policies and Emergence of Santafé de Bogotá (Colombia). In Archaeologies of Early Modern Spanish Colonialism, edited by Sandra Montón-Subias, María Cruz Berrocal, and Apen Ruiz, pp. 11–38. Springer, New York.

Thompson, J. Eric S. (editor) 1958 Thomas Gage's Travels in the New World. University of Oklahoma, Norman.

Torquemada, F. Juan de 1975–1983 Monarquía indiana: de los veinte y un libros rituales y Monarquía indiana, con el origen y guerras de los indios occidentales, de sus poblazones, descubrimiento, conquista, conversión y otras cosas maravillosas de la mesma tierra. Vol. 2, Book 5. Universidad Nacional Autónoma de México, Mexico City.

Toussaint, Manuel 1956 Introducción. In Información de Méritos y Servicios de Alonso García Bravo, Alarife que Trazó la Ciudad de México. Estudios y Fuentes del Arte en México III, edited by José Ignacio Mantecón Navasal, pp. 7–23. Instituto de Investigaciones Estéticas, Universidad Nacional Autónoma de México, Mexico City.

Tovar de Teresa, Guillermo 1985 Antonio de Mendoza y el urbanismo. *Cuadernos de Arquitectura Virreinal* 2:3–19.

Tucker, Robert C. (editor) 1978 *The Marx-Engels Reader*. Second edition. Norton, New York.

Turner, Terrence 2012 (1980) The Social Skin. *HAU: Journal of Ethnographic Theory* 2(2):486–504.

Urquiola Permisán, José Ignacio 2004 Los textiles bajo el mestizaje tecnológico. In *Mestizajes tecnológicos y cambios culturales en México,* edited by Enrique Florescano and Virginia García Acosta, pp. 201–259. Porrúa, Mexico City.

Valentín Maldonado, Norma 2003 Análisis del material zoológico. In *Excavaciones del Programa de Arqueología Urbana.* Colección Científica 452, edited by Eduardo Matos Moctezuma, pp. 27–37. Instituto Nacional de Antropología e Historia, Mexico City.

Valero de García Lascuráin, Ana Rita 1991 *Solares y conquistadores: Orígenes de la propiedad en la Ciudad de México.* Instituto Nacional de Antropología e Historia, Mexico City.

Valle P., Perla 1995 *Códice de Tepetlaóztoc (códice Kingsborough), Estado de México.* El Colegio Mexiquense, Toluca.

Van Buren, Mary 1999 Tarapaya: An Elite Spanish Residence Near Colonial Potosi in Comparative Perspective. *Historical Archaeology* 33(2):101–115.

Van Valkenburgh, Parker, Sarah Kelloway, Daniela Zevallos Castañeda, and Diego Bedoya Vida 2018 Caracterización química de cerámica colonial temprana en el sitio de Carrizales, Lambayeque, Perú. *Actas CNA, III Congreso Nacional de Arqueología. Vol. II.* Ministerio de Cultura, Lima.

Vela, Enrique 2015 La Joyería en el México Antiguo. Catálogo Visual. *Arqueología Mexicana* Edición Especial 63.

Velázquez Gutiérrez, María Elisa 2018 Calidades, castas y razas en el México virreinal: el uso de categorías y clasificaciones de las poblaciones de origen africano. *Estudios Ibero-Americanos* 44 (3):435–446.

Velázquez, María Elisa and Gabriela Iturralde Nieto 2012 *Afrodescendientes en México: una historia de silencio y discriminación.* Consejo Nacional Para Prevenir la Discriminación and Instituto Nacional de Antropología e Historia, Mexico City.

Viart Muñoz, Ma. Antonieta and Roberto Martínez Meza 2003 Rescate arqueológico. Tercera temporada 1999. In *Excavaciones del Programa de Arqueología Urbana.* Colección Científica 452, edited by Eduardo Matos Moctezuma, pp. 117–124. Instituto Nacional de Antropología e Historia, Mexico City.

Vila Vilar, Enriqueta 1983 La documentación de "Bienes de difuntos" como fuente para la historia social hispanoamericana: Panamá a fines del siglo XVI. In *América y la España del Siglo XVI,* Torno 11, pp. 259–273. Escuela de Estudios Hispano-Americanos, Madrid.

Vilar, Pierre 1976 *A History of Gold and Money, 1450 to 1920.* Verso, New York.

Vilches, Elvira 2010 *New World Gold: Cultural Anxiety and Monetary Disorder in Early Modern Spain.* University of Chicago.

Villella, Peter B. 2016 *Indigenous Elites and Creole Identity in Colonial Mexico, 1500–1800.* Cambridge Latin American Studies Series Number 101. Cambridge.

Virchez, Rosa Guadalupe de la Peña 2003 La Primera Catedral de México. *Arqueología Mexicana* 60:64–67.

Von Winning, Hasso 1988 Aztec Traits in Early Post-Conquest Ceramic Figurines. In *Smoke and Mist,* edited by J. Kathryn Josserand and Karen Dakin, pp. 711–745. BAR International Series.

Voss, Barbara L. 2005 From *Casta* to *Californio*: Social Identity and the Archaeology of Culture Contact. *American Anthropologist* 107(3):461–474.

Voss, Barbara L. 2008a *The Archaeology of Ethnogenesis: Race and Sexuality in Colonial San Francisco.* University of California, Berkeley.

Voss, Barbara L. 2008b Between the Household and the World System: Social Collectivity and Community Agency in Overseas Chinese Archaeology. *Historical Archaeology* 42(3):37–52.

Voss, Barbara L. 2008c Domesticating Imperialism: Sexual Politics and the Archaeology of Empire. *American Anthropologist* 110(2):191–203.

Voss, Barbara L. 2008d Gender, Race, and Labor in the Archaeology of the Spanish-Colonial Americas. *Current Anthropology* 49(5):861–897.

Voss, Barbara L. 2012 Status and Ceramics in Spanish Colonial Archaeology. *Historical Archaeology* 46(2):39–54.

Voss, Varbara L., and Eleanor Conlin Casella (editors) 2012 *The Archaeology of Colonialism: Intimate Encounters and Sexual Effects.* Cambridge.

Wagner, Logan, Hal Box, and Susan Kline Morehead 2013 *Ancient Origins of the Mexican Plaza: From Primordial Sea to Public Space.* University of Texas, Austin.

Wallace, Robert W. 1987 The Origin of Electrum Coinage. *American Journal of Archaeology* 91:385–397.

Weber, Max 1978(1922) *Economy and Society*, edited by Guenther Roth and Claus Wittich. University of California, Berkeley.

Weiditz, Christoph 1994 *Authentic Everyday Dress of the Renaissance: All 154 Plates from the "Trachtenbuch."* Dover, New York.

Wernke, Steven A. 2012 Andean Households in Transition: The Politics of Domestic Space at an Early Colonial *Doctrina* in the Peruvian Highlands. In *Decolonizing Indigenous Histories: Exploring Prehistoric/Colonial Transitions in Archaeology*, edited by Maxine Oland, Siobhan M. Hart, and Liam Frink, pp. 201–229. University of Arizona, Tucson.

Wesp, Julie K. 2020 Working in the City: An Historical Bioarchaeology of Activity in Urban New Spain. *Historical Archaeology* 54:92–109.

White Carolyn L. and Mary C. Beaudry 2009 Artifacts and Personal Identity. In *International Handbook of Historical Archaeology*, edited by Teresita Majewski and David Gaimster, pp. 209–225. Springer, New York.

Whittier, Nancy, Tina Wildhagen, and Howard J. Gold 2020 *Statistics for Social Understanding: with Stata and SPSS.* Rowman & Littlefield, Lanham.

Wobst, H. Martin 1977 Stylistic Behavior and Information Exchange. In *For the Director: Research Essays in Honor of James B. Griffin*, edited by Charles E. Cleland, pp. 317–332. Anthropological Papers No. 61, Museum of Anthropology, University of Michigan, Ann Arbor.

Wood, Stephanie 2003 *Transcending Conquest: Nahua Views of Spanish Colonial Mexico.* University of Oklahoma, Norman.

Ximenez, Francisco 1615 *Qvatro libros de la natvraleza, y virtvdes de las plantas, y animales que estan receuidos en el vso de Medicina en la Nueua España, y la Methodo, y correccion, y preparacion, que para administrallas se requiere con lo que el Doctor Francisco Hernandez escriuio en lengua Latina.* Mexico City. Accessed online on 5-29-2020. https://bibdigital.rjb.csic.es/records/item/13778-quatro-libros-de-la-naturaleza-y-virtudes-de-las-plantas-y-animales

Yannakakis, Yanna 2008 *The Art of Being In-Between: Native Intermediaries, Indian Identity, and Local Rule in Colonial Oaxaca.* Duke University, Durham.

Zabala, Pilar 2010 The African Presence in Yucatan: Sixteenth and Seventeenth Centuries. In *Natives, Europeans, and Africans in Colonial Campeche: History and Archaeology,* edited by Vera Tiesler, Pilar Zabala, and Andrea Cucina, pp. 152–174. University Press of Florida, Gainesville.

Zarankin, Andrés and Pedro Paulo A. Funari 2020 Arqueología de la Arquitectura, una mirada desde América del Sur. *Arqueología de la Arquitectura* 17:1–13. https://doi.org/10.3989/arq.arqt.2020.011.

Index

For the benefit of digital users, indexed terms that span two pages (e.g., 52–53) may, on occasion, appear on only one of those pages.

Tables and figures are indicated by *t* and *f* following the page number